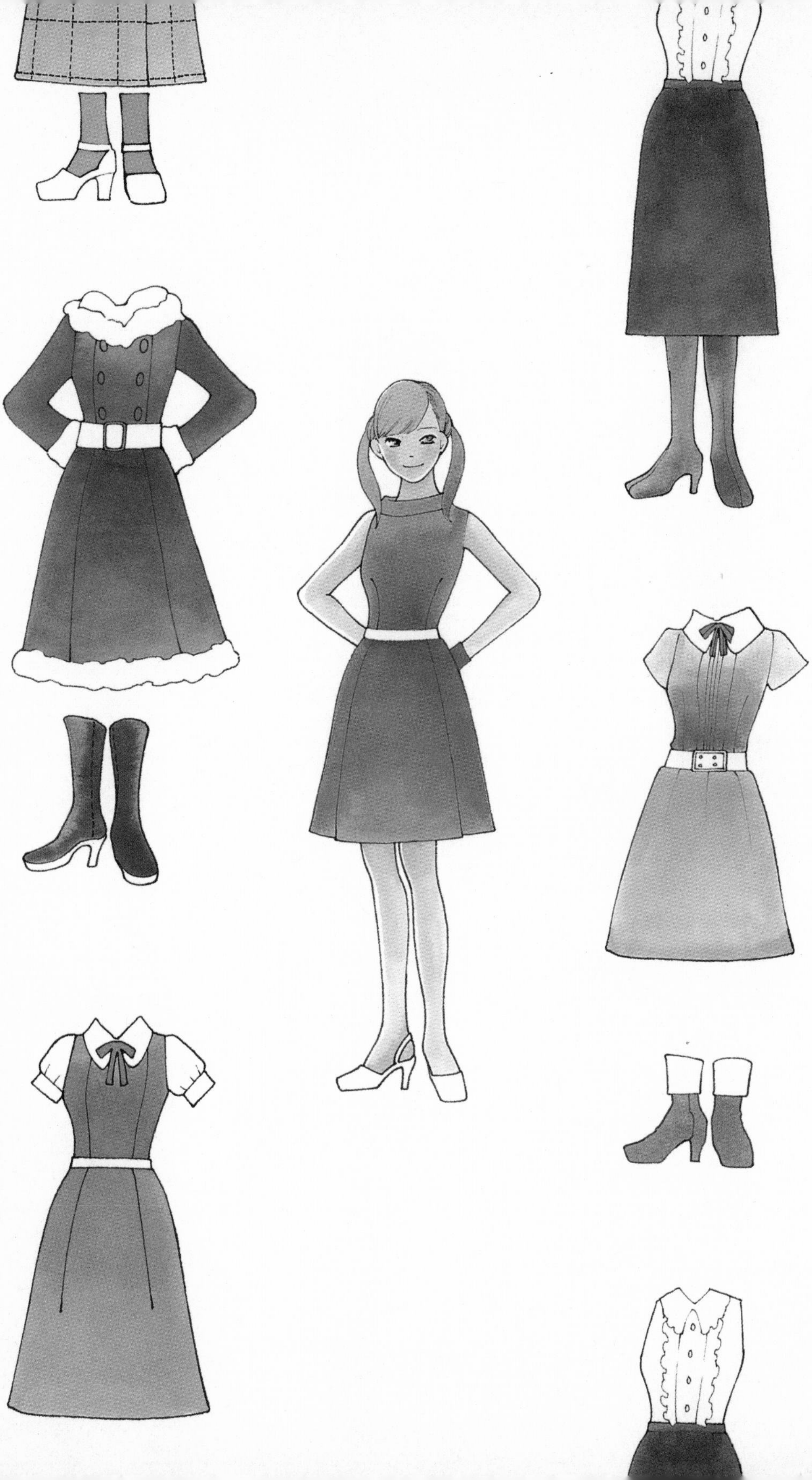

Fantagraphics Books, 7563 Lake City Way NE Seattle, Washington 98115 | Publishers: Gary Groth & Kim Thompson; Translation: Matt Thorn; Editorial Liaison: Gary Groth; Design: Alexa Koenings; Lettering: Paul Baresh, Ian Burns & Priscilla Miller; Production: Paul Baresh; Associate Publisher: Eric Reynolds | *Wandering Son Volume 1* copyright © 2003 Takako Shimura. All rights reserved. First published in Japan by ENTERBRAIN, INC., Tokyo. English translation rights arranged with ENTERBRAIN, INC. No part of this book (except small excerpts for review purposes) may be reproduced in any form or by any electronic or mechanical means without the written permission of the publisher. | To receive a free full-color catalog of comics, graphic novels, prose novels, and other fine works of artistry, call 1-800-657-1100, or visit www.fantagraphics.com. You may order books at our web site or by phone. | Distributed in the U.S. by W.W. Norton and Company, Inc. (800-233-4830); Distributed in Canada by the Canadian Manda Group (800-452-6642 x862); Distributed in the UK by Turnaround Distribution (44 (0)20 8829-3002); Distributed to comics stores by Diamond Comics Distributors (800-452-6642 x215) | ISBN: 978-1-60699-416-0 | Second Fantagraphics printing: August, 2012 | Printed in China

WANDERING SON

Volume One

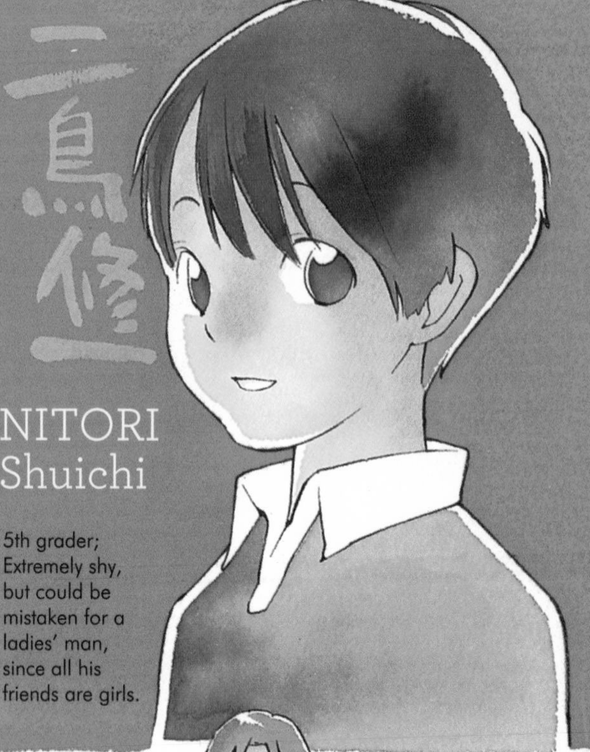
二鳥修一

NITORI Shuichi

5th grader; Extremely shy, but could be mistaken for a ladies' man, since all his friends are girls.

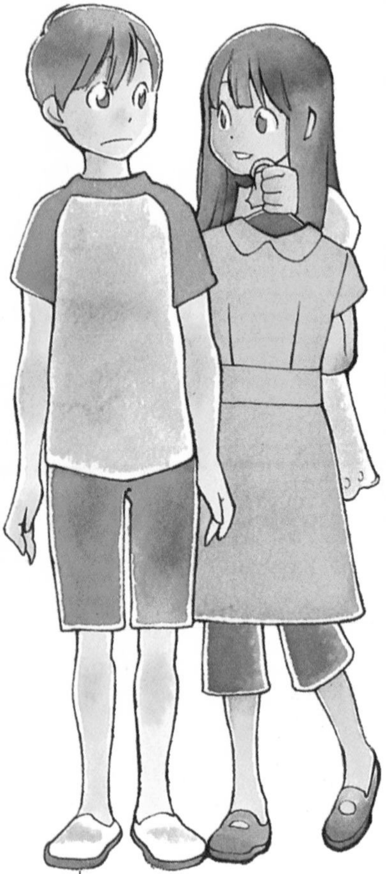

Nitori-kun's* Dad and Mom

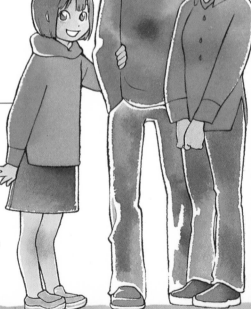

The happy family.

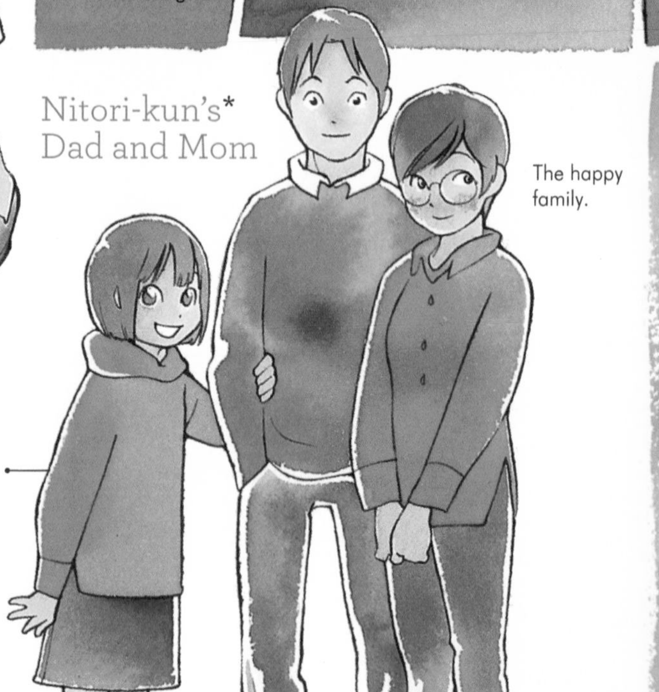

NITORI Maho

Nitori-kun's big sister. A 6th grader. She can be a bit bossy.

CHIBA Saori

Nitori-kun's classmate. Slightly self-centered, emotionally unstable, and a source of annoyance to some of the other girls. A wannabe Christian.

*See the afterword "Sugar and Spice" for details about the translation of Japanese honorifics in Wandering Son.

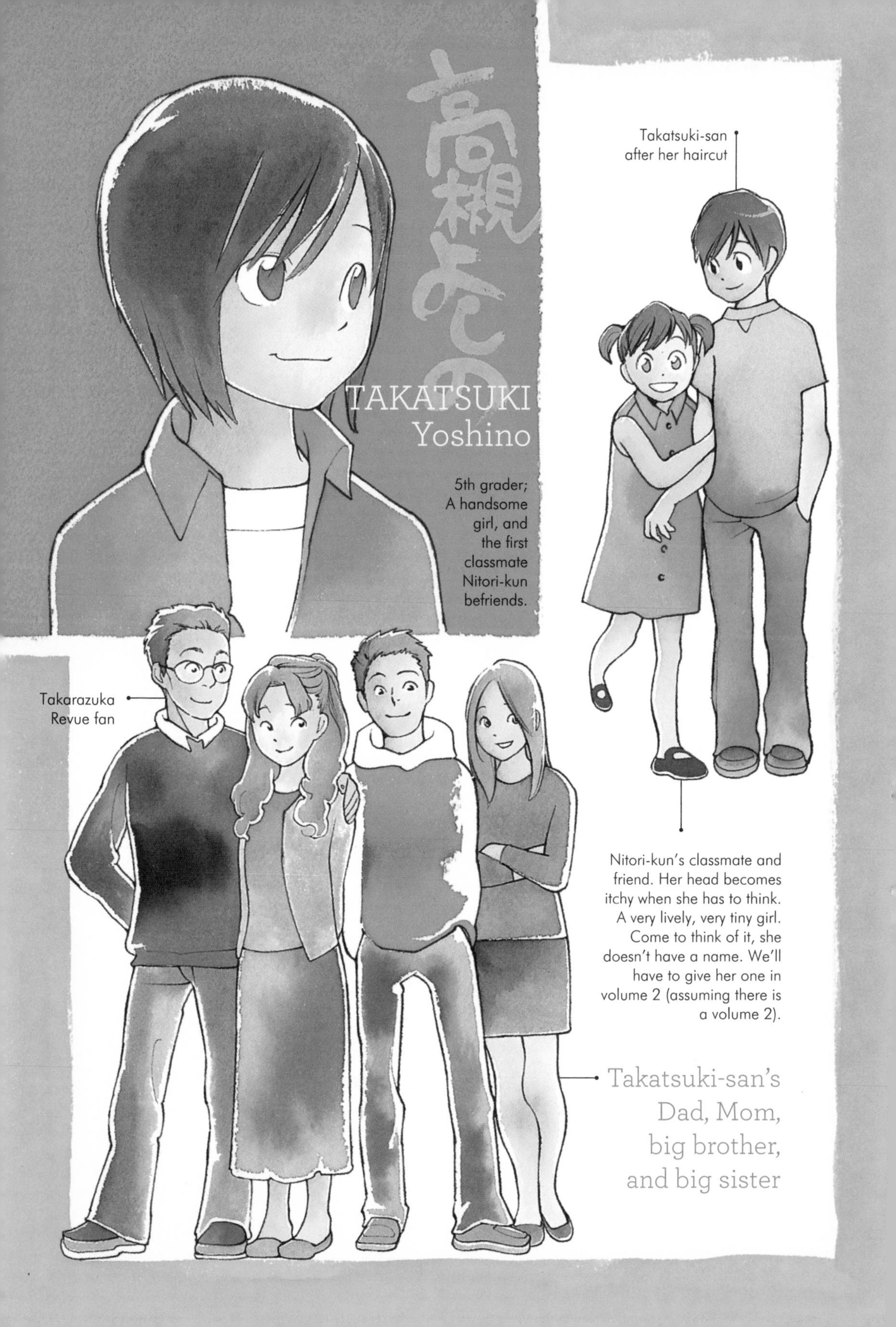
高槻よしの
TAKATSUKI Yoshino
5th grader; A handsome girl, and the first classmate Nitori-kun befriends.
Takatsuki-san after her haircut
Nitori-kun's classmate and friend. Her head becomes itchy when she has to think. A very lively, very tiny girl. Come to think of it, she doesn't have a name. We'll have to give her one in volume 2 (assuming there is a volume 2).
Takarazuka Revue fan
Takatsuki-san's Dad, Mom, big brother, and big sister

JAPANESE PRONUNCIATION GUIDE

VOWELS

a   as in "f<u>a</u>ther"

i   as in "spaghett<u>i</u>"

u   as in "p<u>u</u>t"

e   as in "th<u>e</u>m"

o   as in "p<u>o</u>le"

"Long" vowels are usually indicated by a macron ("ō"), circumflex ("ô") or diaeresis ("ö"), although sometimes the vowel is simply repeated. In personal names, a long "o" is sometimes represented as "oh". In cases where one vowel is followed immediately by a different vowel, but is not in the same syllable, they are often separated by a dash or apostrophe to indicate the end of one syllable and beginning of another. Here are common pairs of vowels that sound to the English-speaker's ear like one syllable (and thus are not separated):

ai   as in "m<u>y</u>"

ei   as in "r<u>ay</u>"

oi   as in "t<u>oy</u>"

ao   as in "c<u>ow</u>"

CONSONANTS *that require clarification*

g   as in "get" (never as in "age")

s   as in "soft" (never like "rise")

t   as in "tale" (never like "d")

ch   as in "church"

Tricky consonants that you don't really have to worry about:

ts   English speakers make this sound all the time ("bats" "nuts"), but have trouble putting it at the beginning of a word. In Japanese, it is always followed by a "u", as in "tsunami".

r   Neither an "r" nor an "l", but literally in between.

ACCENTS

Most English words have "accented" and "un-accented" syllables. This is generally not the case in Japanese, which is more "flat." When English speakers encounter a new word, they tend to accent the first syllable if it has two syllables, the second if it has three, and after that they wing it. If you can't resist accenting a syllable in a Japanese word, accent the first and you'll be fine.

CONTENTS

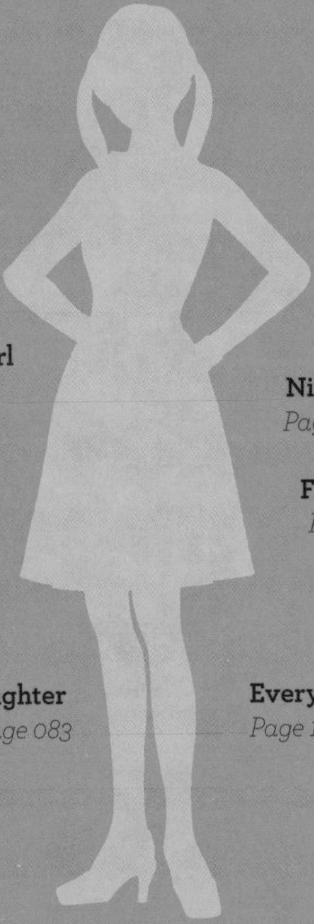

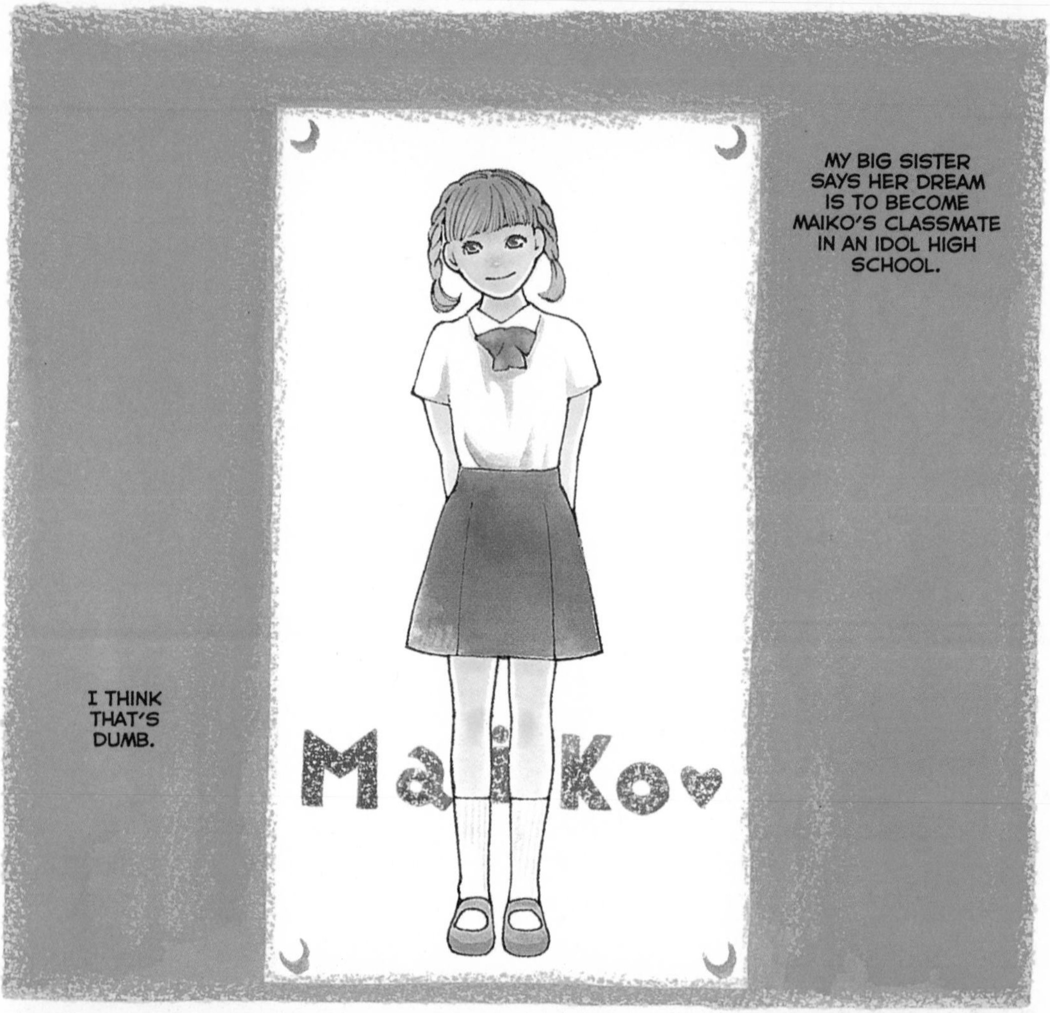
MY BIG SISTER SAYS HER DREAM IS TO BECOME MAIKO'S CLASSMATE IN AN IDOL HIGH SCHOOL.
I THINK THAT'S DUMB.
MaiKo♥

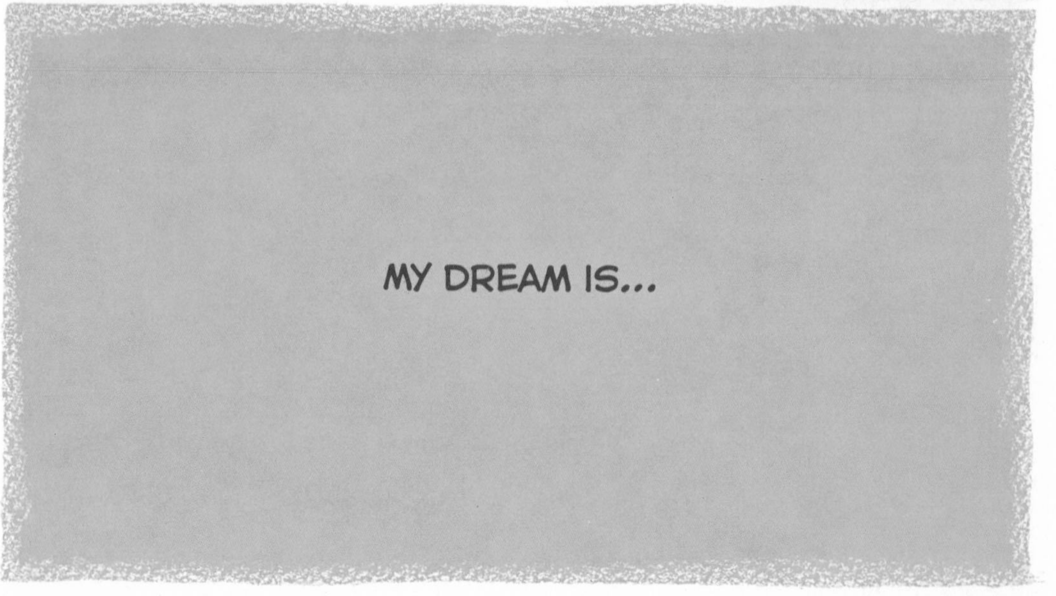
MY DREAM IS...

1

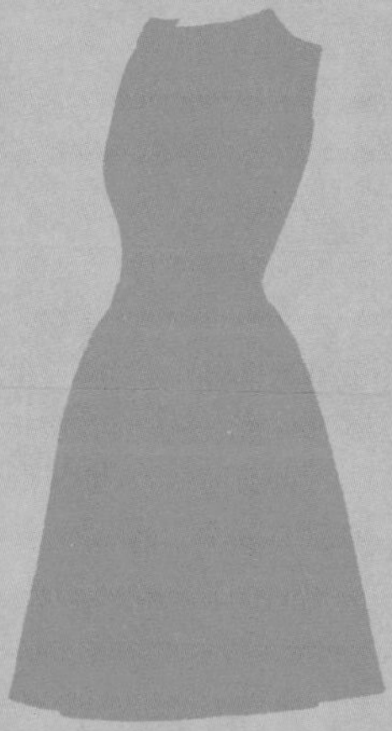

The Boy Who's a Girl

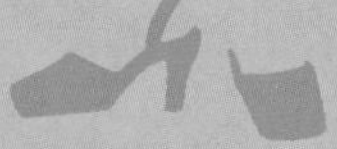

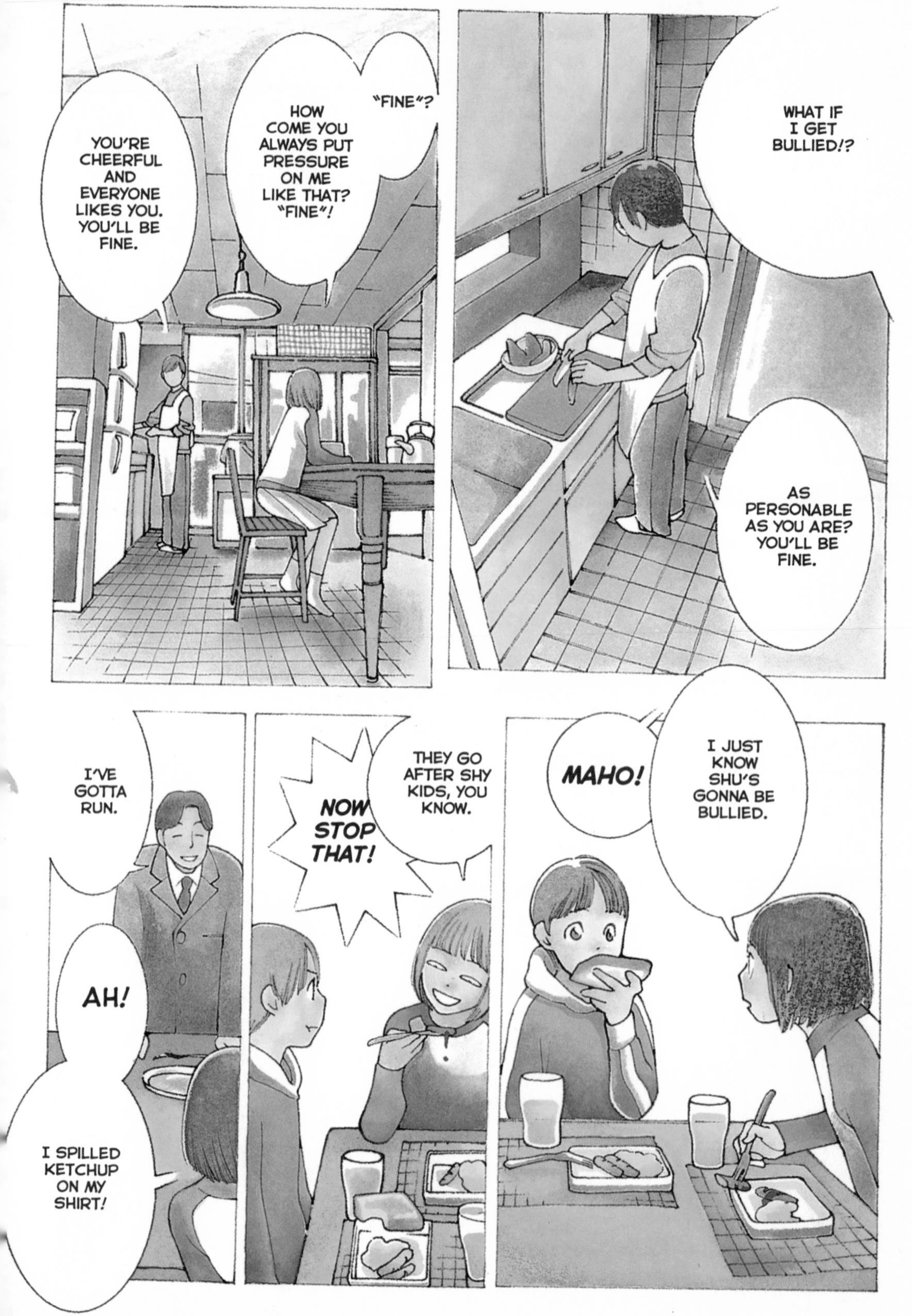
WHAT IF I GET BULLIED!?
AS PERSONABLE AS YOU ARE? YOU'LL BE FINE.
"FINE"?
HOW COME YOU ALWAYS PUT PRESSURE ON ME LIKE THAT? "FINE"!
YOU'RE CHEERFUL AND EVERYONE LIKES YOU. YOU'LL BE FINE.
I JUST KNOW SHU'S GONNA BE BULLIED.
MAHO!
THEY GO AFTER SHY KIDS, YOU KNOW.
NOW STOP THAT!
I'VE GOTTA RUN.
AH!
I SPILLED KETCHUP ON MY SHIRT!

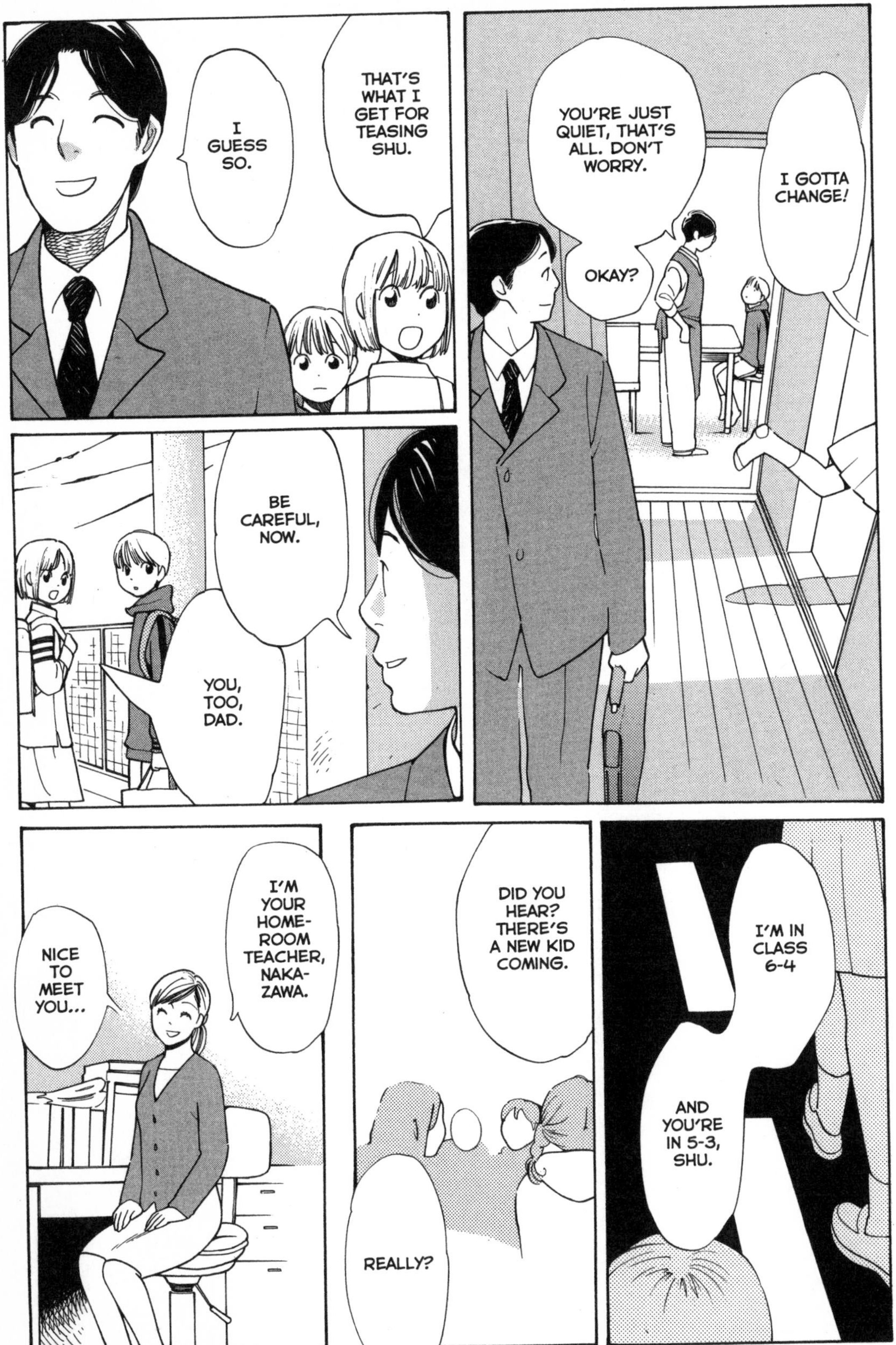
I GOTTA CHANGE!
YOU'RE JUST QUIET, THAT'S ALL. DON'T WORRY.
OKAY?
THAT'S WHAT I GET FOR TEASING SHU.
I GUESS SO.
BE CAREFUL, NOW.
YOU, TOO, DAD.
I'M IN CLASS 6-4
AND YOU'RE IN 5-3, SHU.
DID YOU HEAR? THERE'S A NEW KID COMING.
REALLY?
I'M YOUR HOMEROOM TEACHER, NAKAZAWA.
NICE TO MEET YOU...

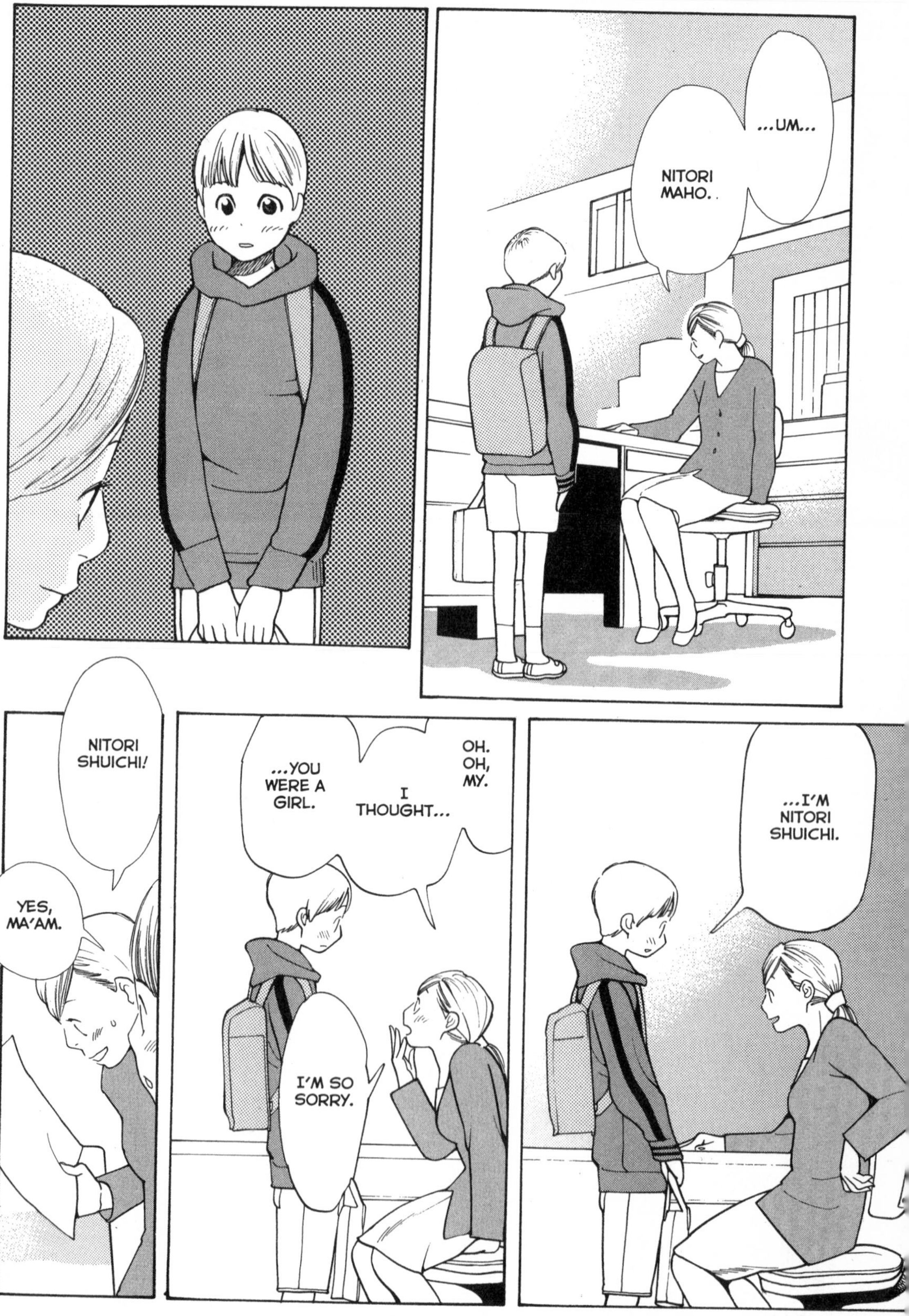
...UM...
NITORI MAHO..
...I'M NITORI SHUICHI.
OH. OH, MY.
I THOUGHT...
...YOU WERE A GIRL.
I'M SO SORRY.
NITORI SHUICHI!
YES, MA'AM.

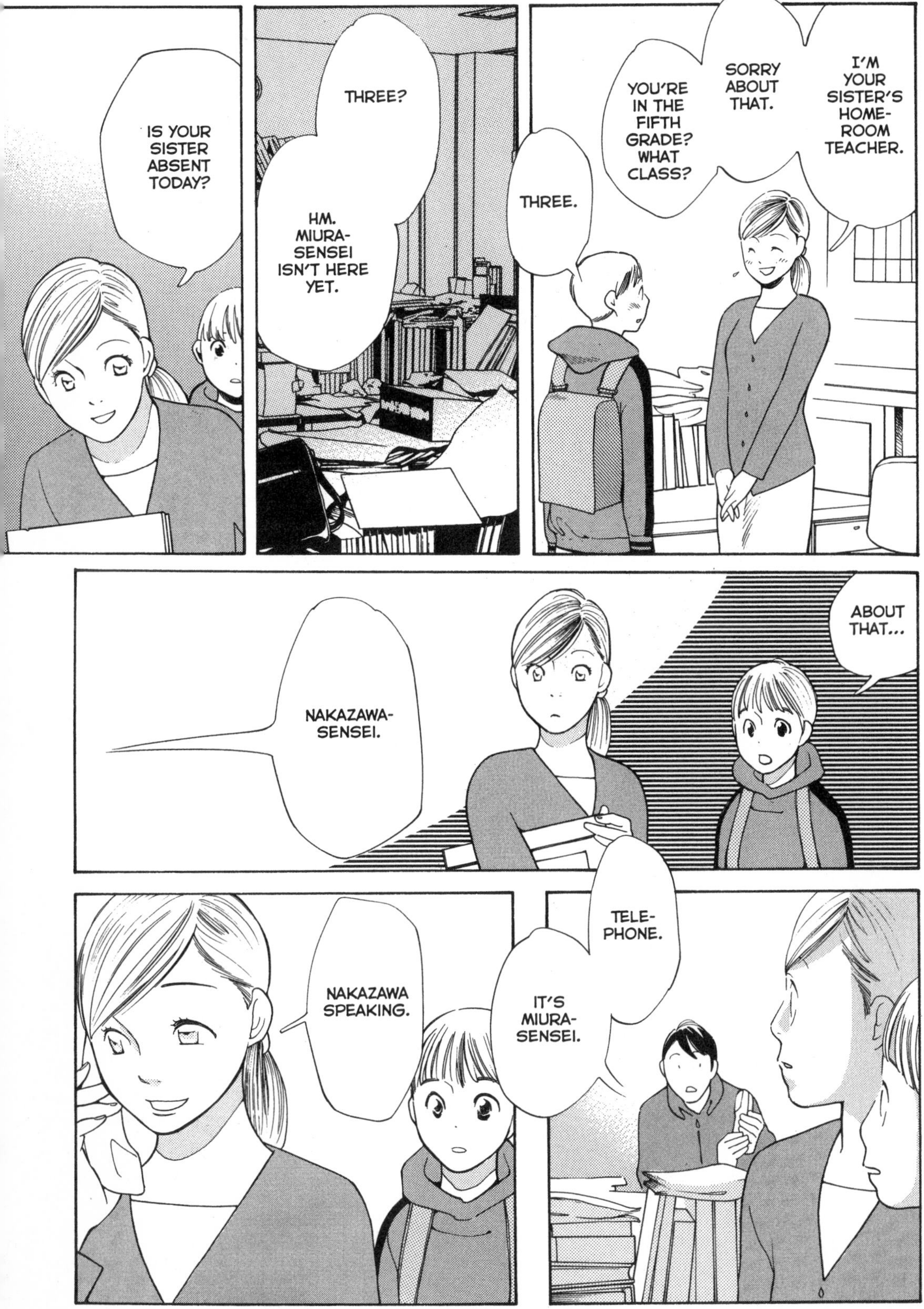
I'M YOUR SISTER'S HOME-ROOM TEACHER.
SORRY ABOUT THAT.
YOU'RE IN THE FIFTH GRADE? WHAT CLASS?
THREE.
THREE?
HM. MIURA-SENSEI ISN'T HERE YET.
IS YOUR SISTER ABSENT TODAY?
ABOUT THAT...
NAKAZAWA-SENSEI.
TELE-PHONE.
IT'S MIURA-SENSEI.
NAKAZAWA SPEAKING.

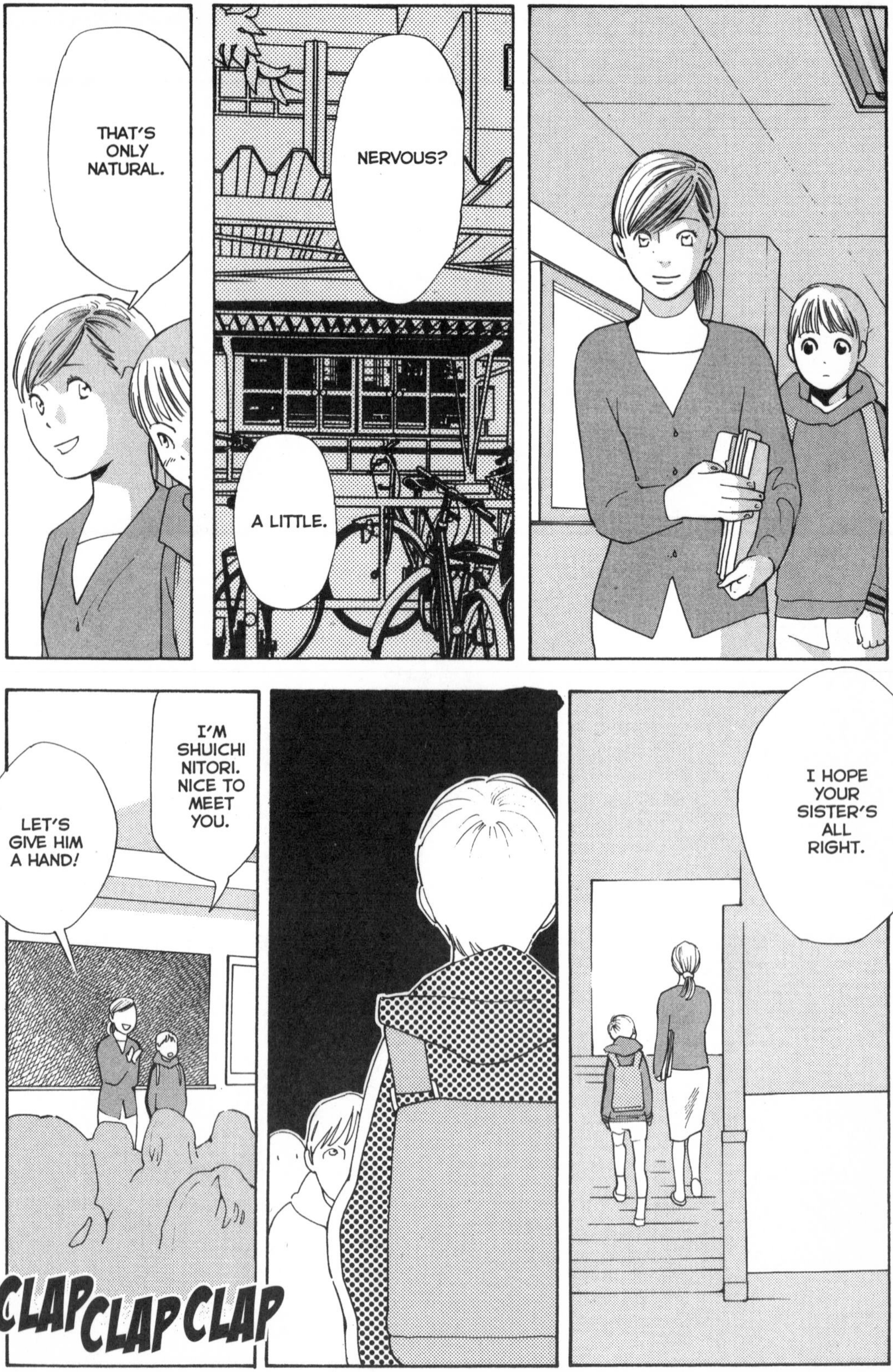
NERVOUS?
A LITTLE.
THAT'S ONLY NATURAL.
I HOPE YOUR SISTER'S ALL RIGHT.
I'M SHUICHI NITORI. NICE TO MEET YOU.
LET'S GIVE HIM A HAND!
CLAP CLAP CLAP

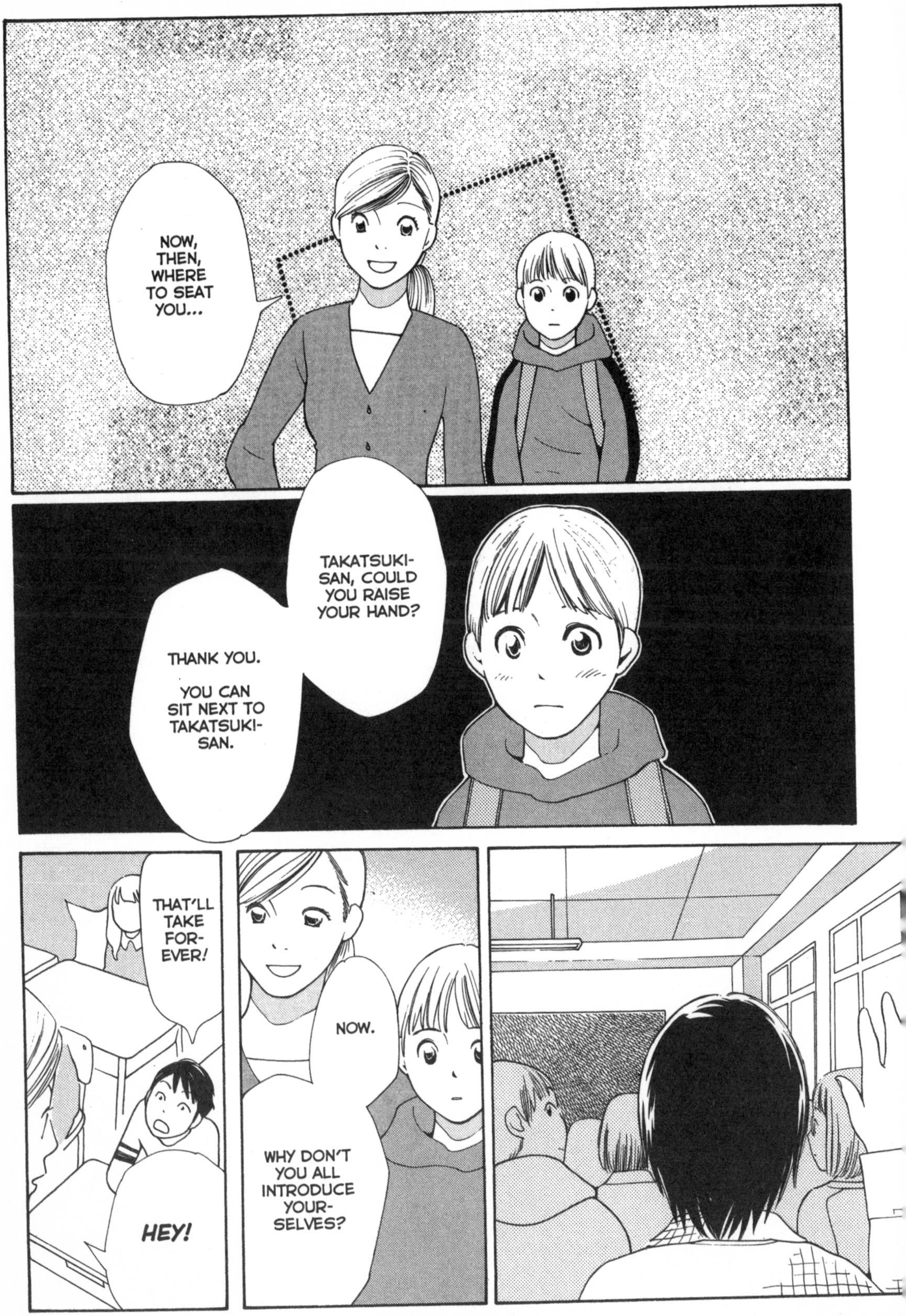
NOW, THEN, WHERE TO SEAT YOU...
TAKATSUKI-SAN, COULD YOU RAISE YOUR HAND?
THANK YOU.
YOU CAN SIT NEXT TO TAKATSUKI-SAN.
NOW.
WHY DON'T YOU ALL INTRODUCE YOUR-SELVES?
THAT'LL TAKE FOR-EVER!
HEY!

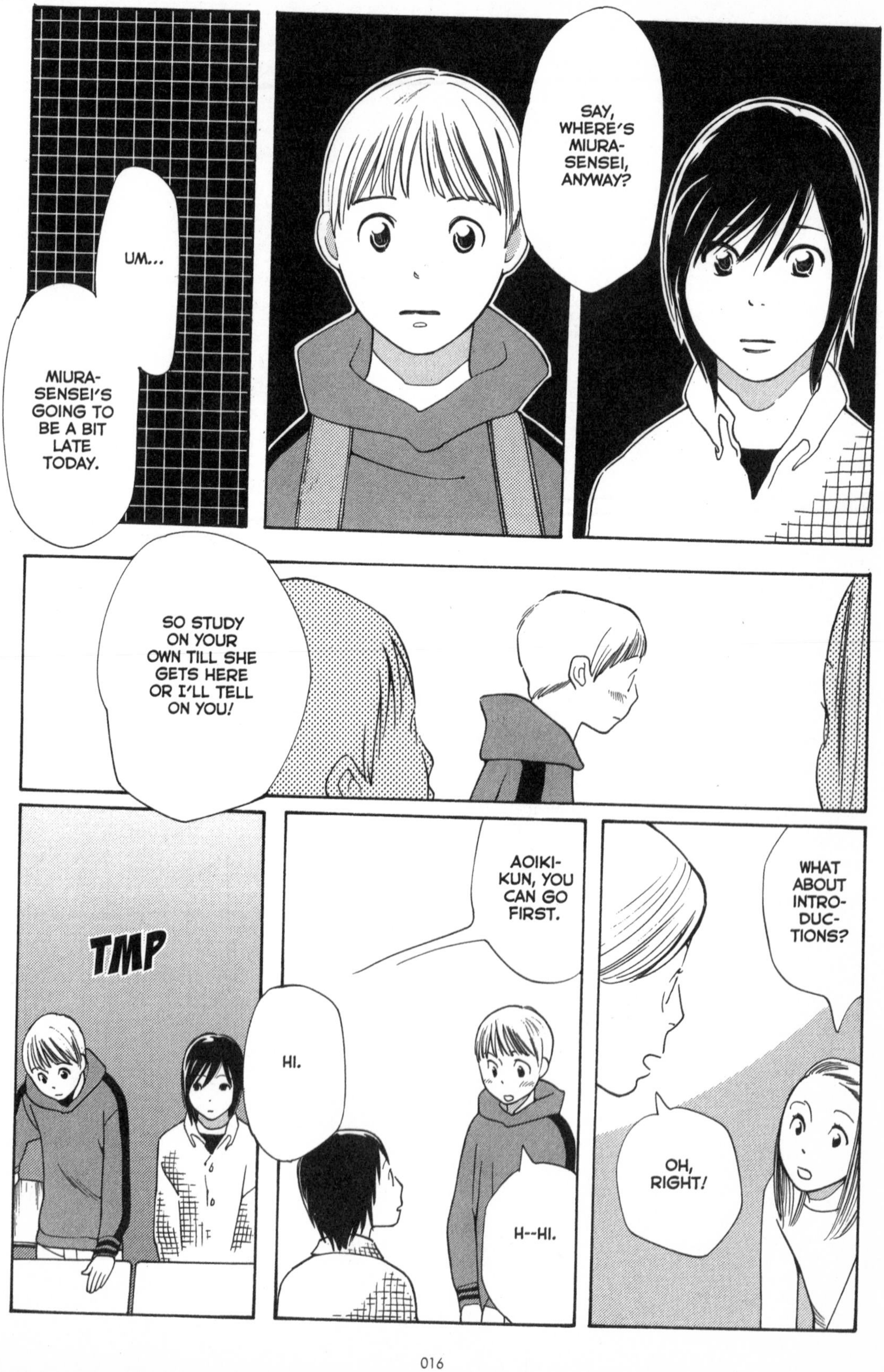
SAY, WHERE'S MIURA-SENSEI, ANYWAY?
UM...
MIURA-SENSEI'S GOING TO BE A BIT LATE TODAY.
SO STUDY ON YOUR OWN TILL SHE GETS HERE OR I'LL TELL ON YOU!
WHAT ABOUT INTRO-DUC-TIONS?
OH, RIGHT!
AOIKI-KUN, YOU CAN GO FIRST.
HI.
H--HI.
TMP

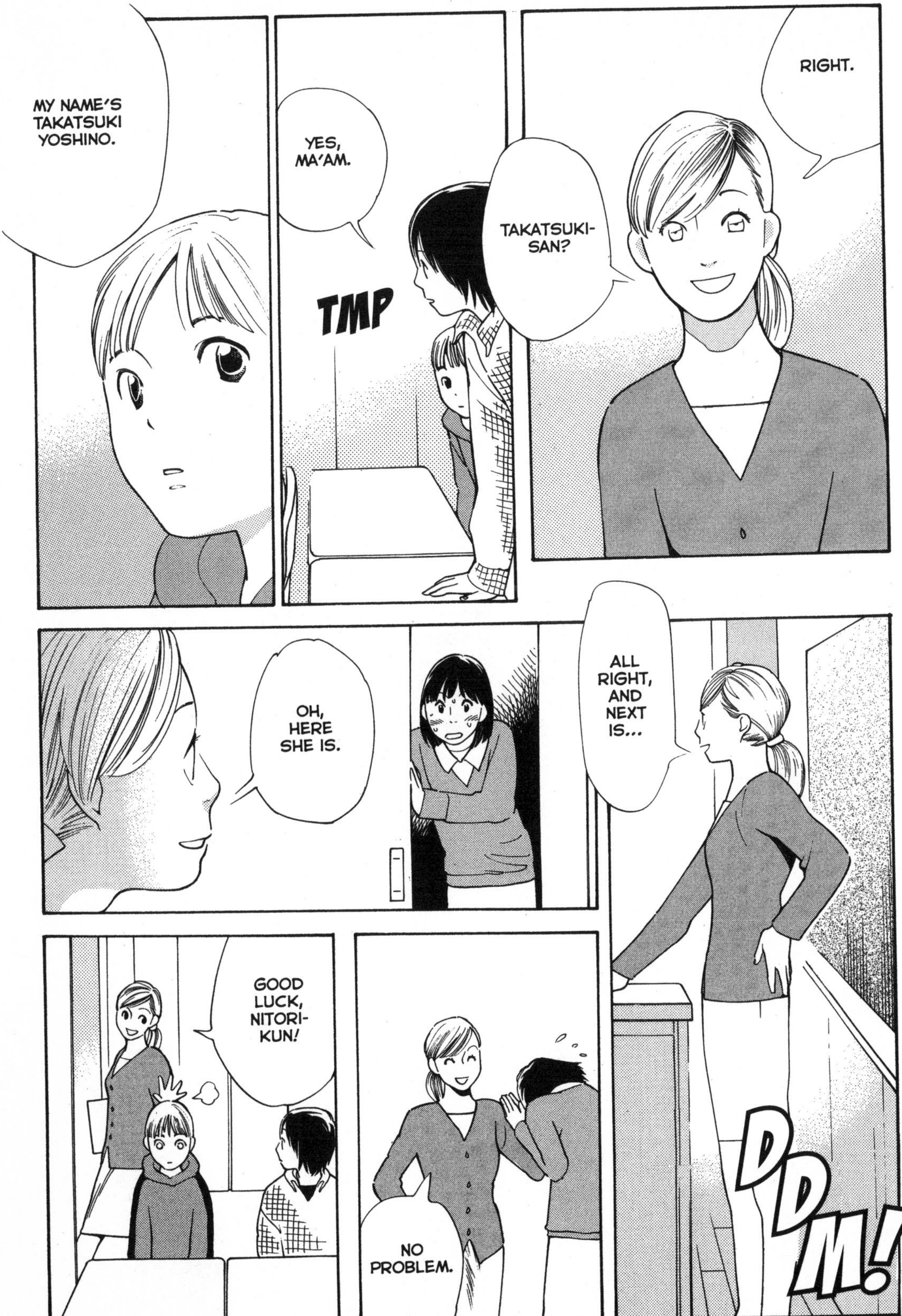
RIGHT.
TAKATSUKI-SAN?
YES, MA'AM.
TMP
MY NAME'S TAKATSUKI YOSHINO.
ALL RIGHT, AND NEXT IS...
DDM!
OH, HERE SHE IS.
NO PROBLEM.
GOOD LUCK, NITORI-KUN!

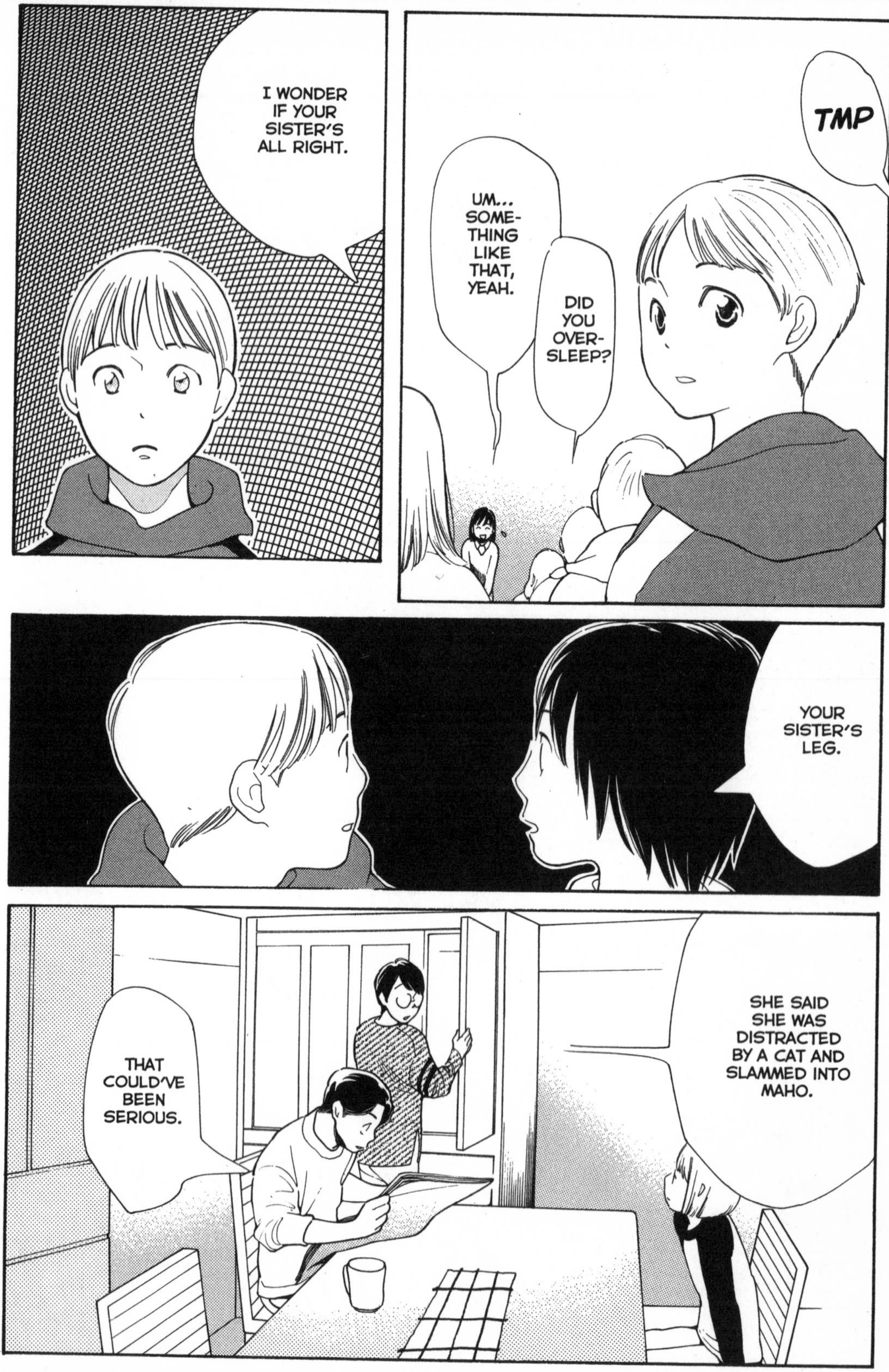
TMP
DID YOU OVER-SLEEP?
UM... SOME-THING LIKE THAT, YEAH.
I WONDER IF YOUR SISTER'S ALL RIGHT.
YOUR SISTER'S LEG.
SHE SAID SHE WAS DISTRACTED BY A CAT AND SLAMMED INTO MAHO.
THAT COULD'VE BEEN SERIOUS.

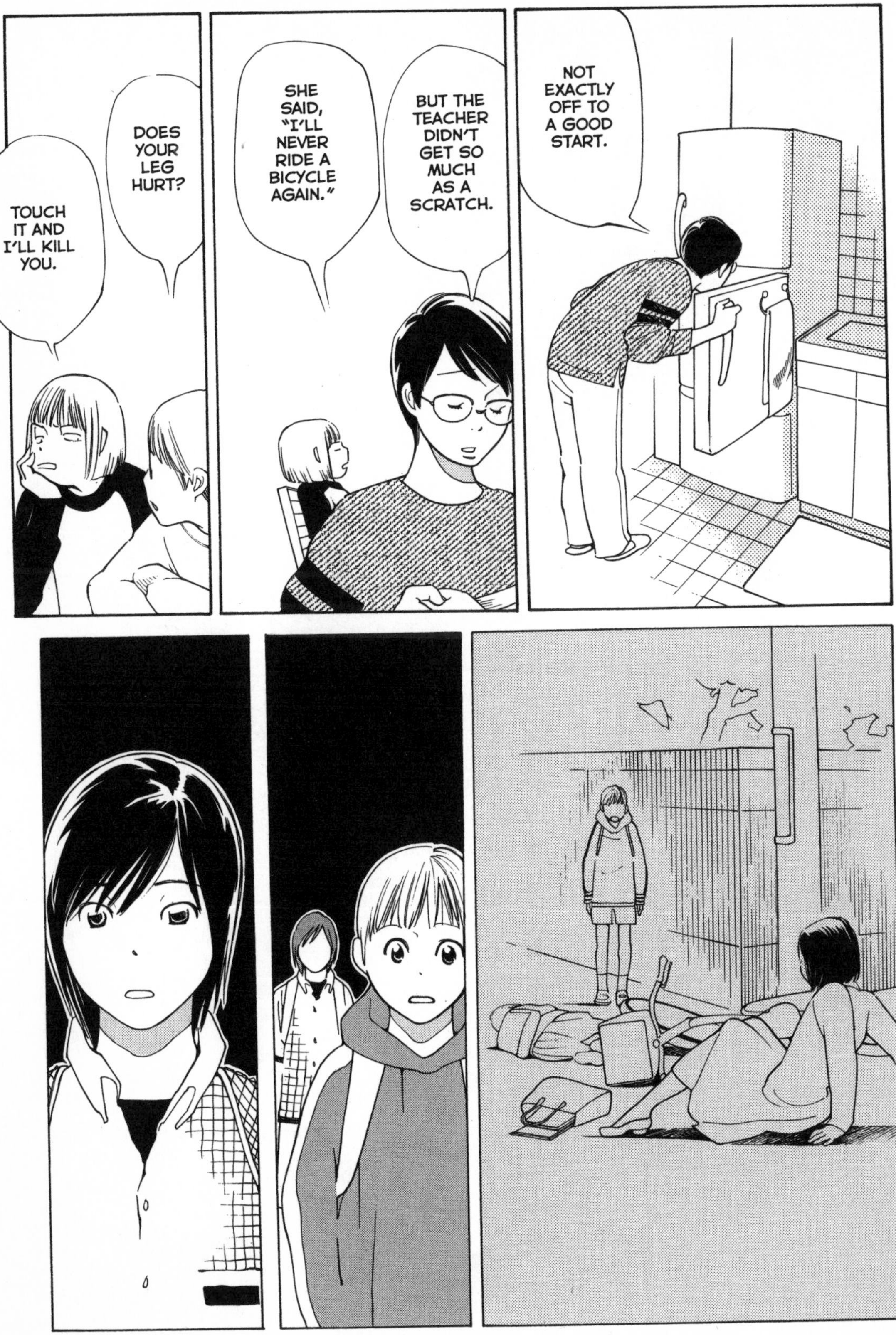
NOT EXACTLY OFF TO A GOOD START.
BUT THE TEACHER DIDN'T GET SO MUCH AS A SCRATCH.
SHE SAID, "I'LL NEVER RIDE A BICYCLE AGAIN."
DOES YOUR LEG HURT?
TOUCH IT AND I'LL KILL YOU.

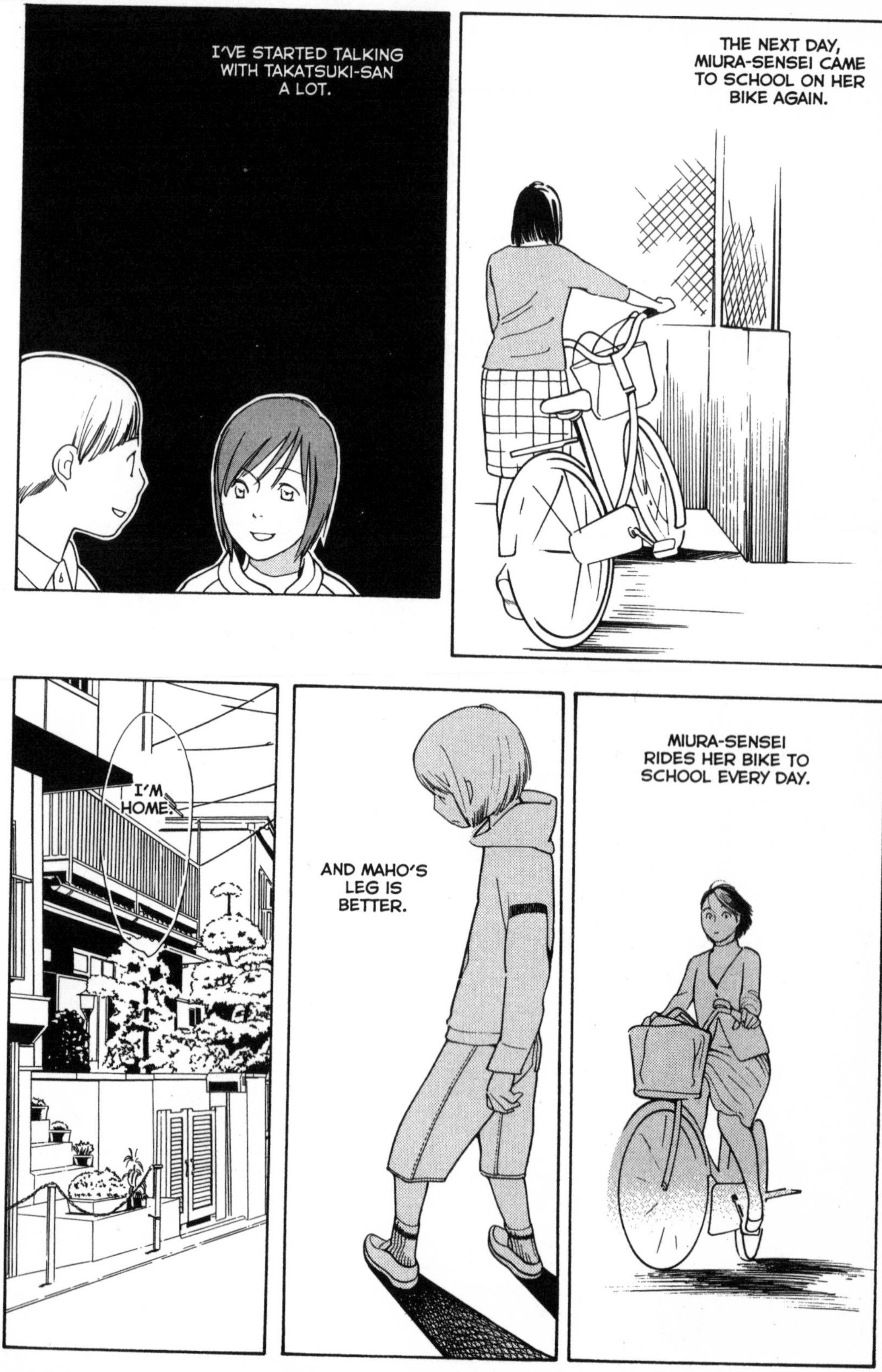
THE NEXT DAY, MIURA-SENSEI CAME TO SCHOOL ON HER BIKE AGAIN.
I'VE STARTED TALKING WITH TAKATSUKI-SAN A LOT.
MIURA-SENSEI RIDES HER BIKE TO SCHOOL EVERY DAY.
AND MAHO'S LEG IS BETTER.
I'M HOME.

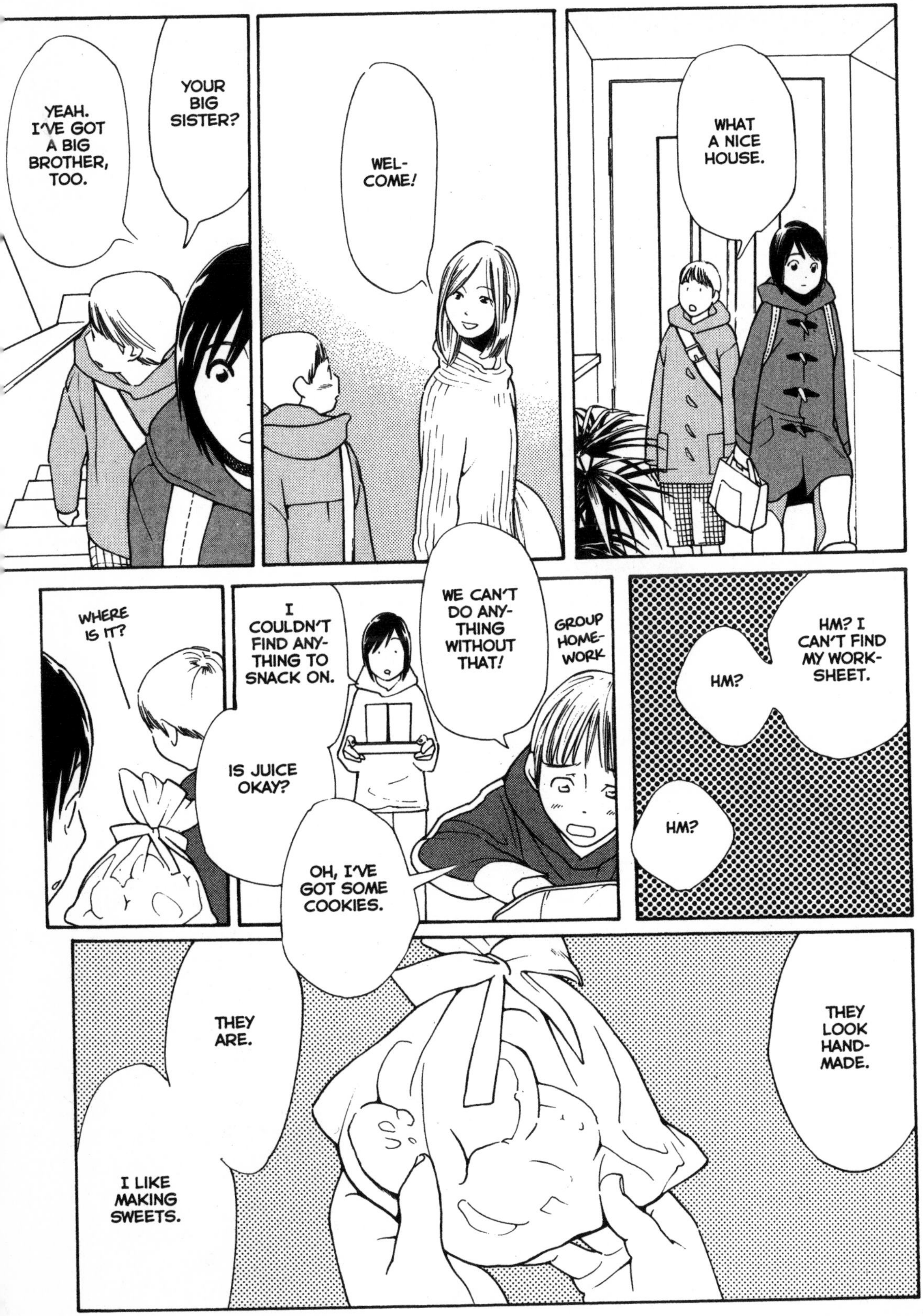
WHAT A NICE HOUSE.
WEL-COME!
YOUR BIG SISTER?
YEAH. I'VE GOT A BIG BROTHER, TOO.
HM? I CAN'T FIND MY WORK-SHEET.
HM?
HM?
GROUP HOME-WORK
WE CAN'T DO ANY-THING WITHOUT THAT!
I COULDN'T FIND ANY-THING TO SNACK ON.
WHERE IS IT?
IS JUICE OKAY?
OH, I'VE GOT SOME COOKIES.
THEY LOOK HAND-MADE.
THEY ARE.
I LIKE MAKING SWEETS.

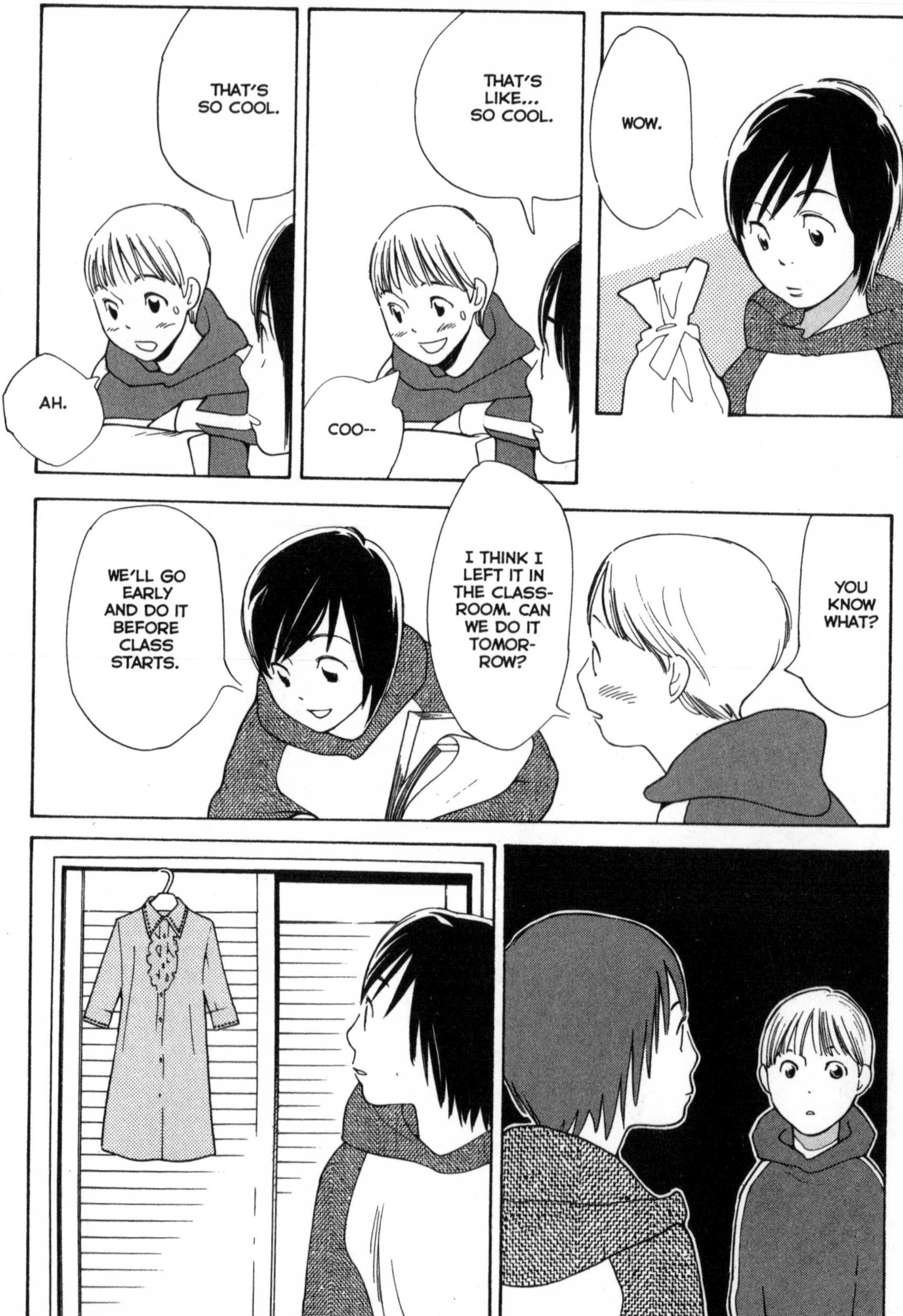
WOW.
THAT'S LIKE... SO COOL.
COO--
THAT'S SO COOL.
AH.
YOU KNOW WHAT?
I THINK I LEFT IT IN THE CLASS-ROOM. CAN WE DO IT TOMORROW?
WE'LL GO EARLY AND DO IT BEFORE CLASS STARTS.

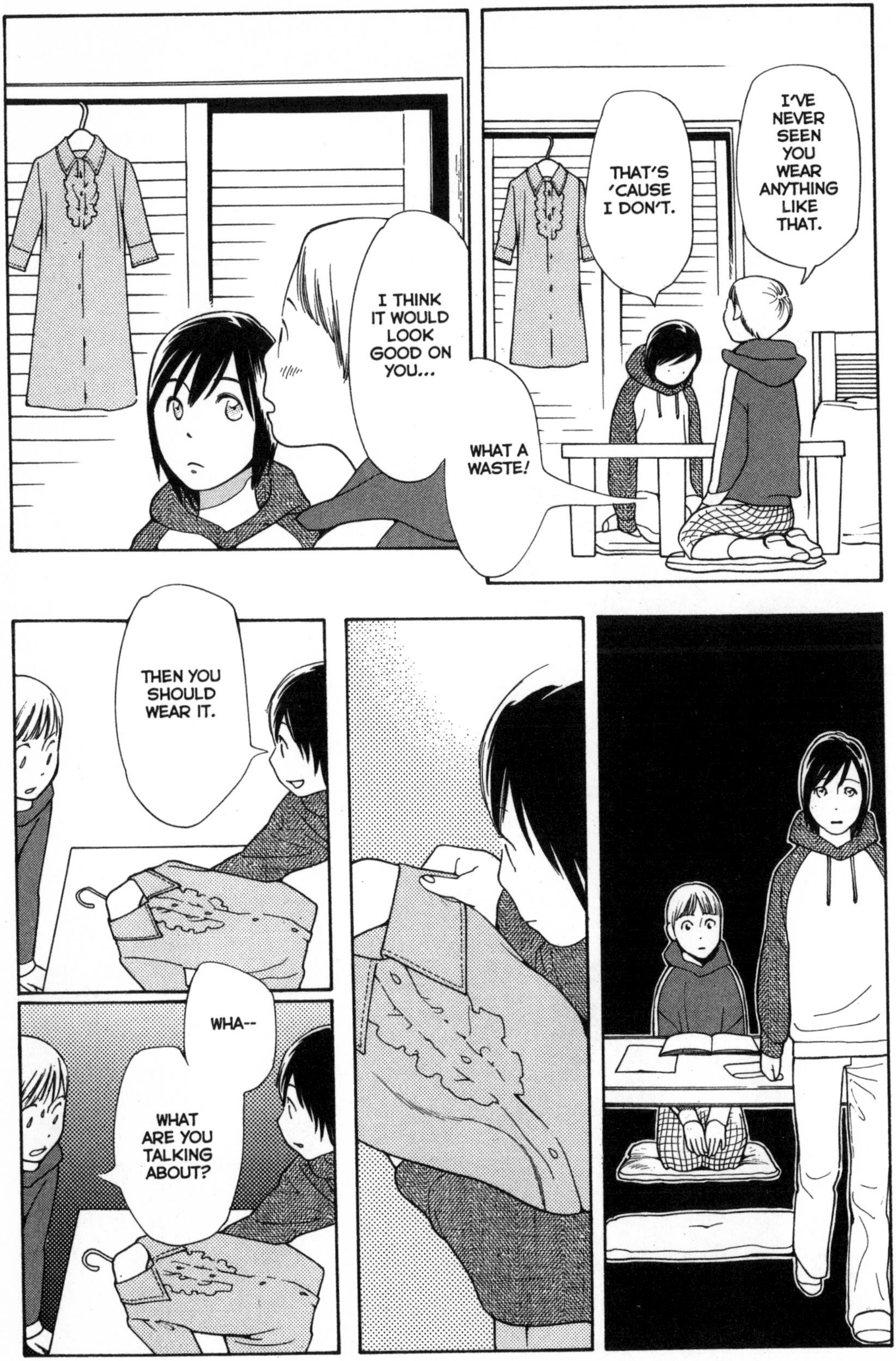
I'VE NEVER SEEN YOU WEAR ANYTHING LIKE THAT.
THAT'S 'CAUSE I DON'T.
I THINK IT WOULD LOOK GOOD ON YOU...
WHAT A WASTE!
THEN YOU SHOULD WEAR IT.
WHA--
WHAT ARE YOU TALKING ABOUT?

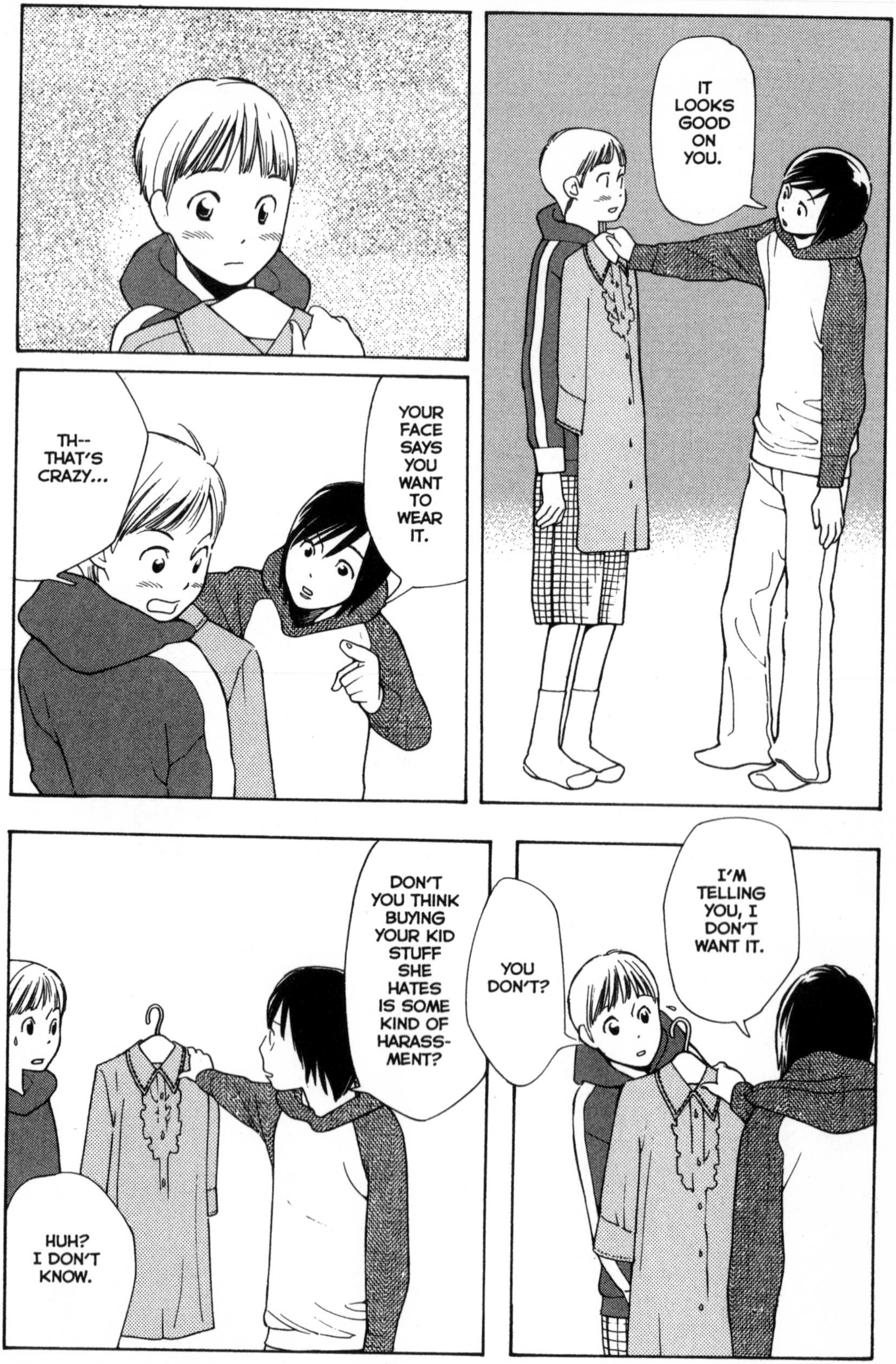
IT LOOKS GOOD ON YOU.
YOUR FACE SAYS YOU WANT TO WEAR IT.
TH-- THAT'S CRAZY...
I'M TELLING YOU, I DON'T WANT IT.
YOU DON'T?
DON'T YOU THINK BUYING YOUR KID STUFF SHE HATES IS SOME KIND OF HARASS-MENT?
HUH? I DON'T KNOW.

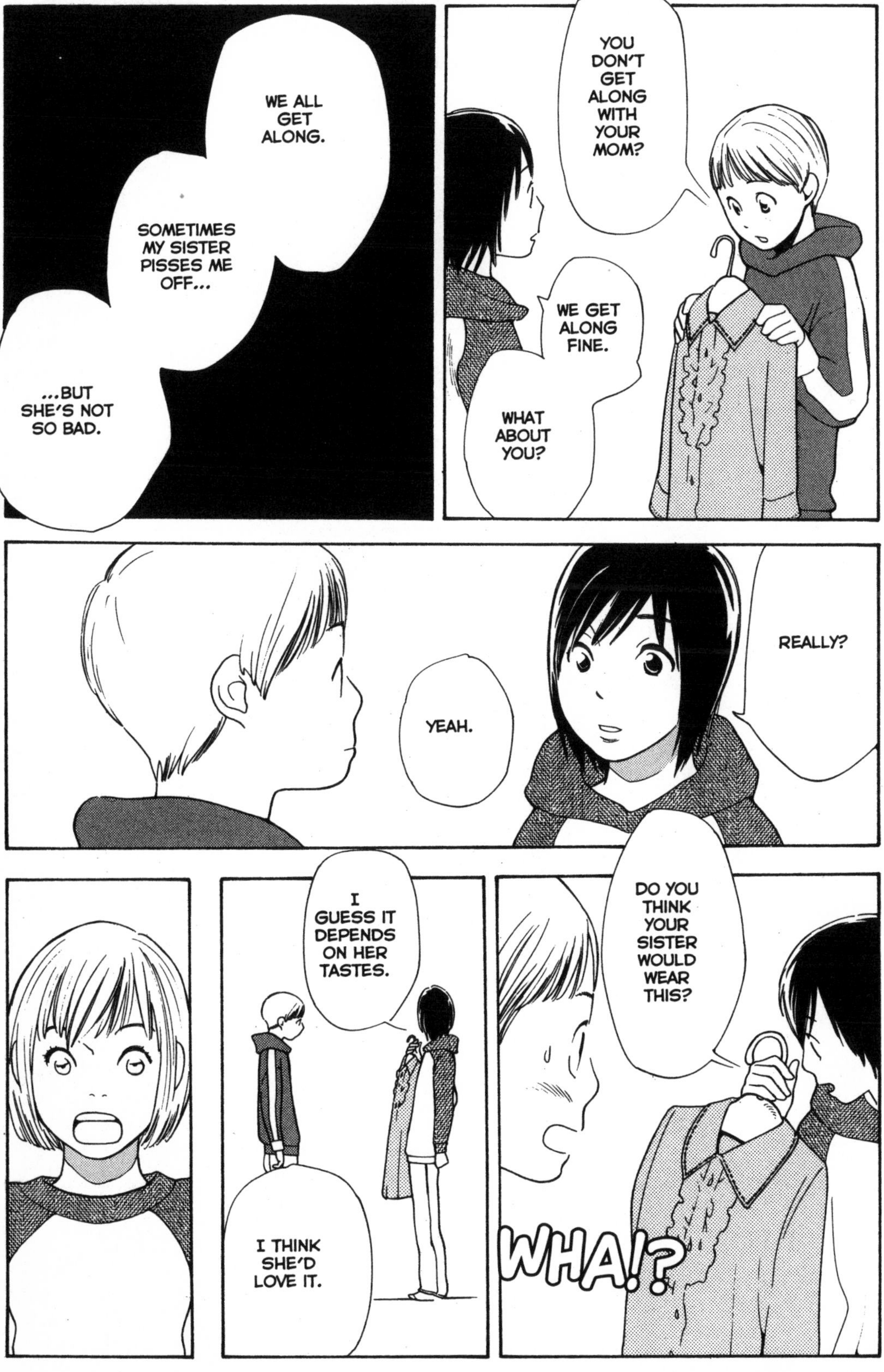
YOU DON'T GET ALONG WITH YOUR MOM?
WE GET ALONG FINE.
WHAT ABOUT YOU?
WE ALL GET ALONG.
SOMETIMES MY SISTER PISSES ME OFF...
...BUT SHE'S NOT SO BAD.
REALLY?
YEAH.
DO YOU THINK YOUR SISTER WOULD WEAR THIS?
I GUESS IT DEPENDS ON HER TASTES.
I THINK SHE'D LOVE IT.
WHA!?

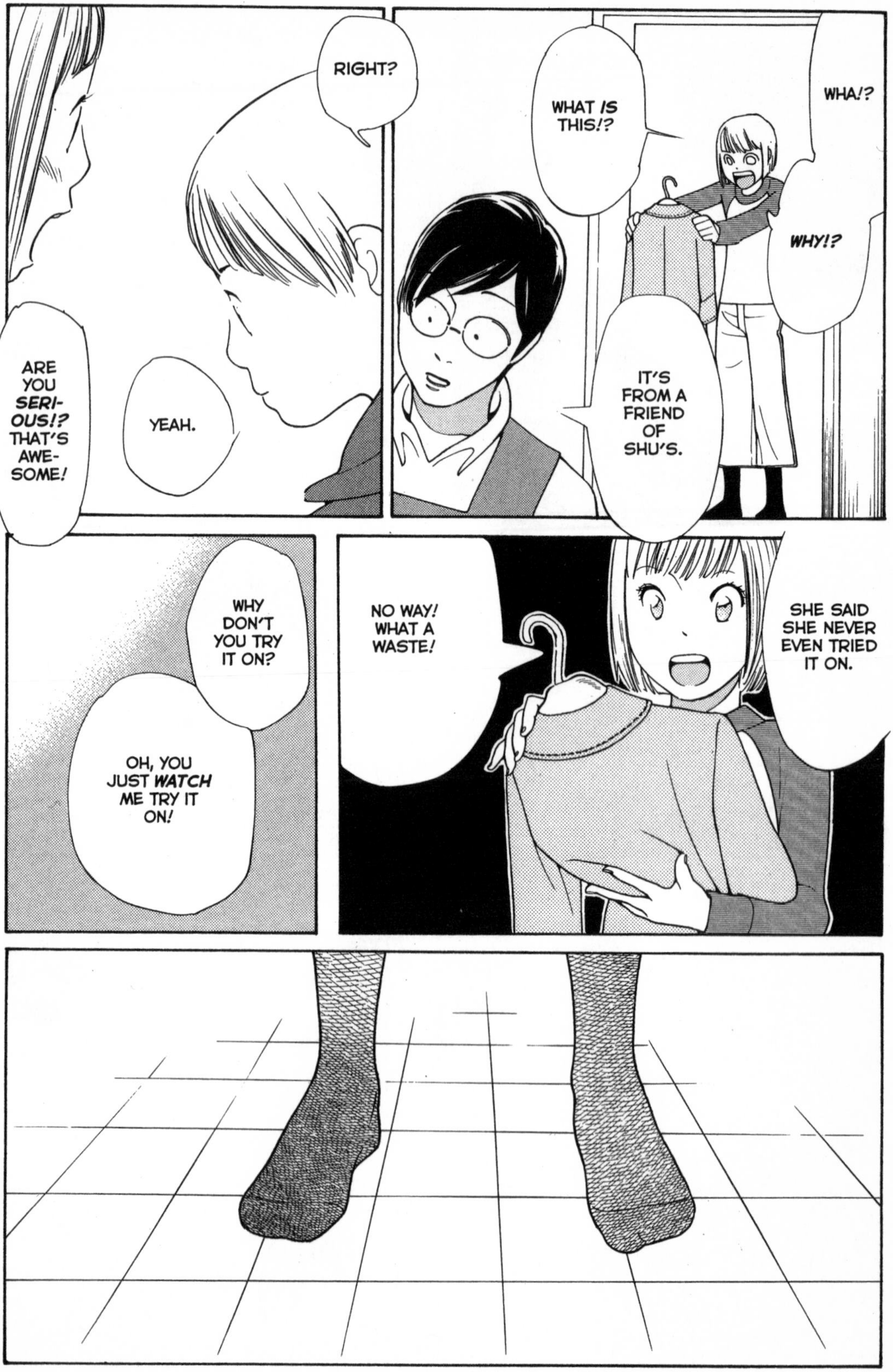
WHA!?
WHY!?
WHAT *IS* THIS!?
IT'S FROM A FRIEND OF SHU'S.
RIGHT?
YEAH.
ARE YOU ***SERI-OUS!?*** THAT'S AWE-SOME!
SHE SAID SHE NEVER EVEN TRIED IT ON.
NO WAY! WHAT A WASTE!
WHY DON'T YOU TRY IT ON?
OH, YOU JUST ***WATCH*** ME TRY IT ON!

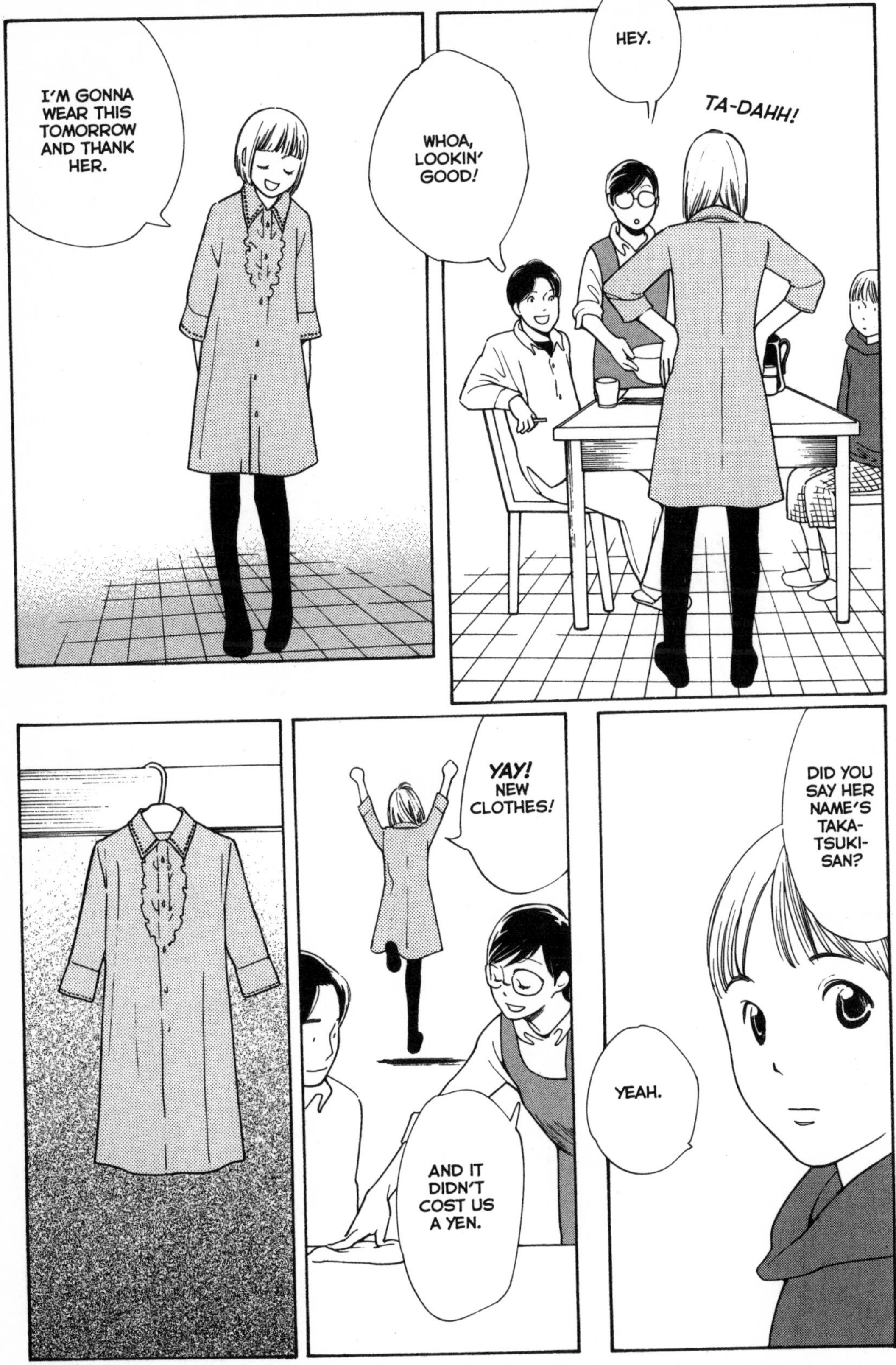
HEY.
TA-DAHH!
WHOA, LOOKIN' GOOD!
I'M GONNA WEAR THIS TOMORROW AND THANK HER.
DID YOU SAY HER NAME'S TAKA-TSUKI-SAN?
YEAH.
YAY! NEW CLOTHES!
AND IT DIDN'T COST US A YEN.

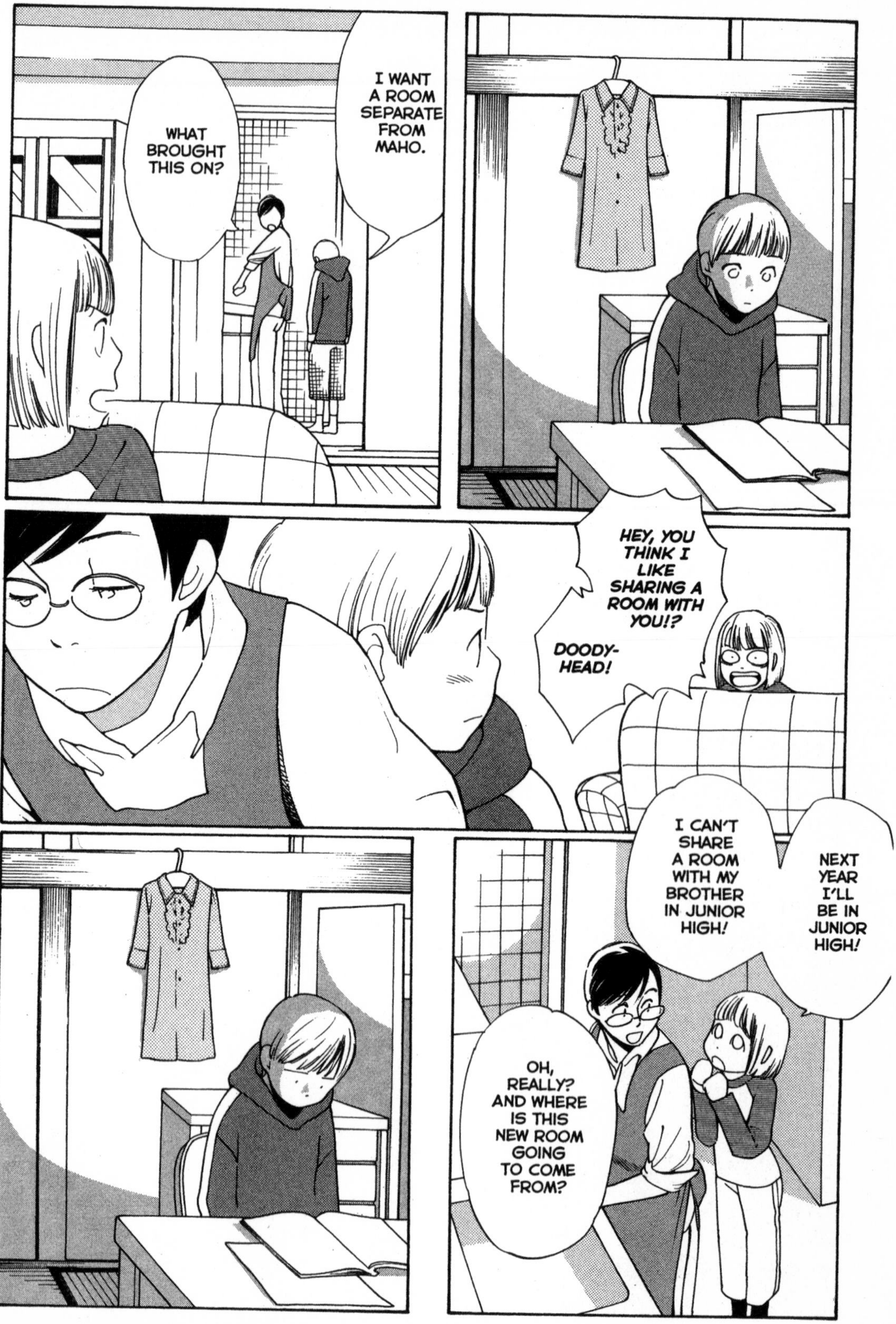
I WANT A ROOM SEPARATE FROM MAHO.
WHAT BROUGHT THIS ON?
HEY, YOU THINK I LIKE SHARING A ROOM WITH YOU!?
DOODY-HEAD!
NEXT YEAR I'LL BE IN JUNIOR HIGH!
I CAN'T SHARE A ROOM WITH MY BROTHER IN JUNIOR HIGH!
OH, REALLY? AND WHERE IS THIS NEW ROOM GOING TO COME FROM?

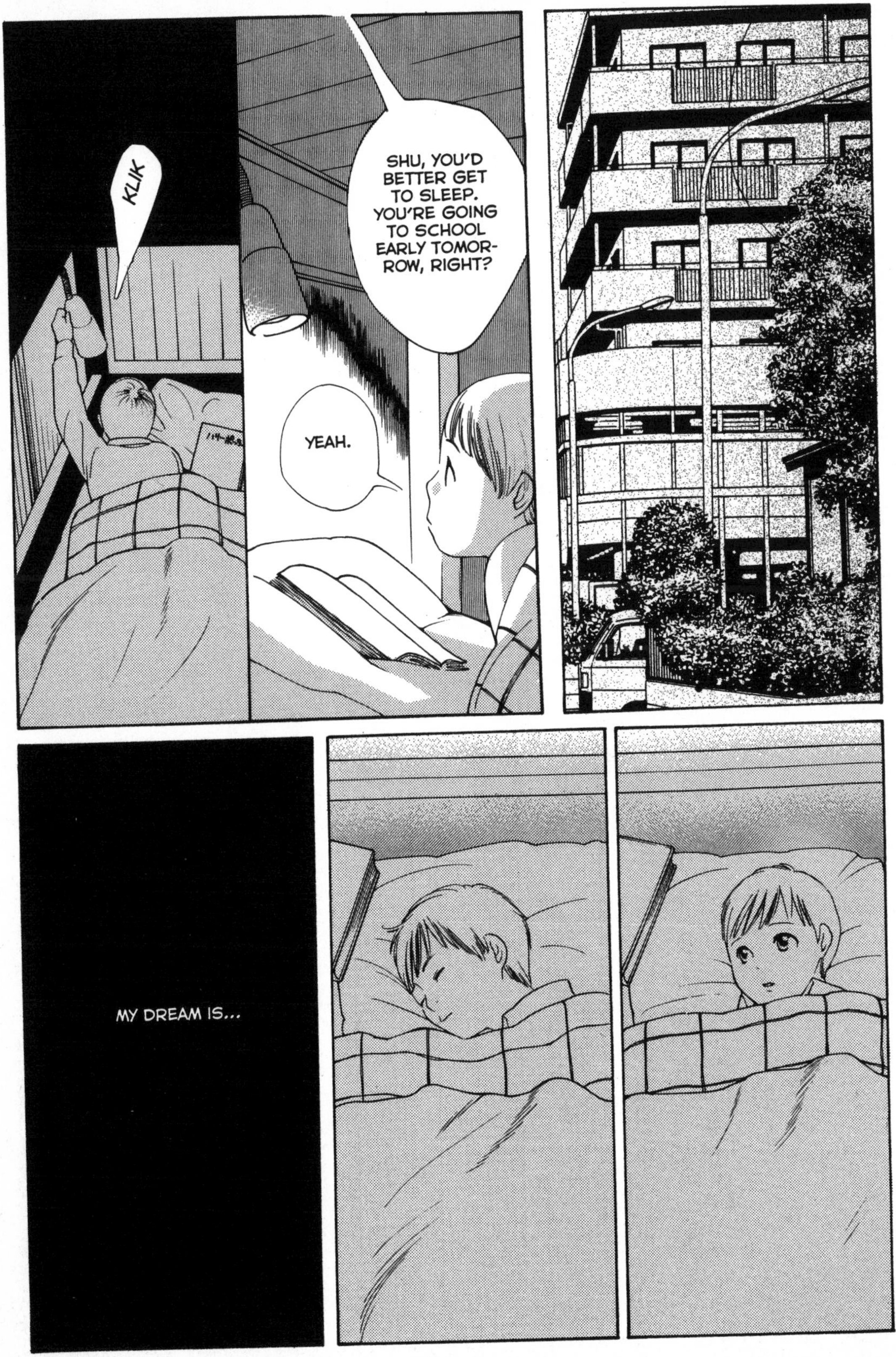
SHU, YOU'D BETTER GET TO SLEEP. YOU'RE GOING TO SCHOOL EARLY TOMORROW, RIGHT?
YEAH.
KLIK
MY DREAM IS...

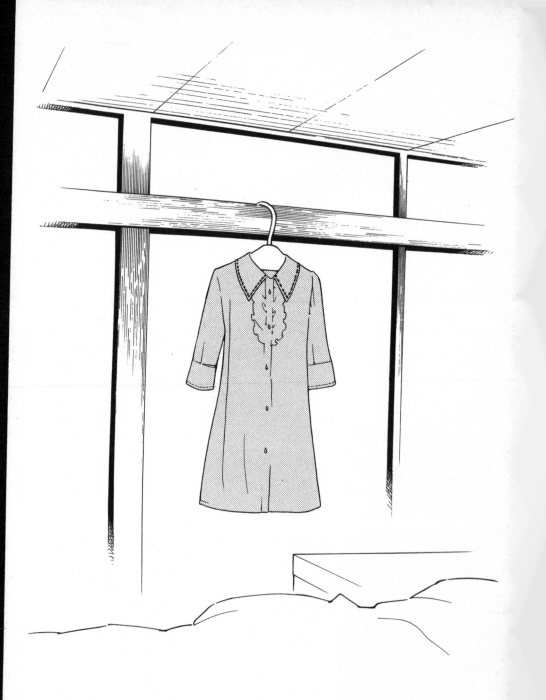

2

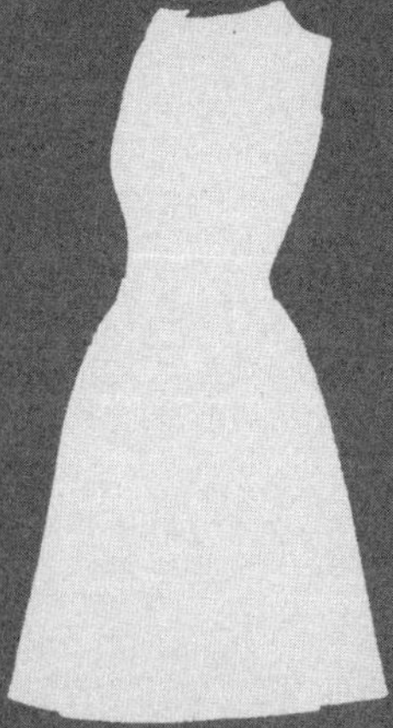

The Wandering Son Wanders On

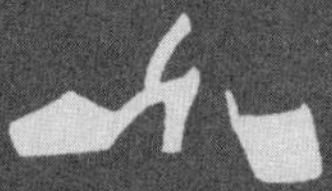

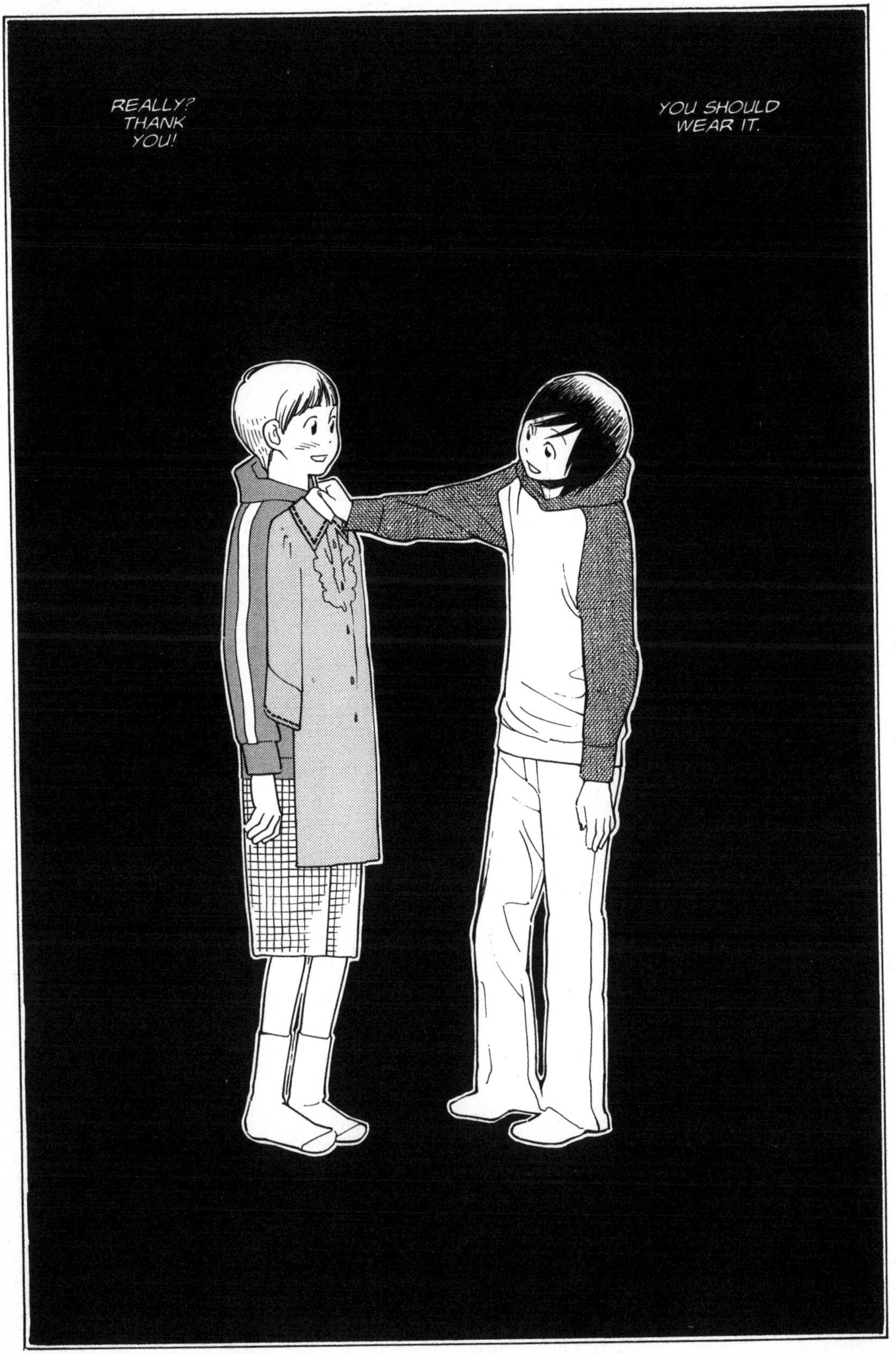
YOU SHOULD WEAR IT.
REALLY? THANK YOU!

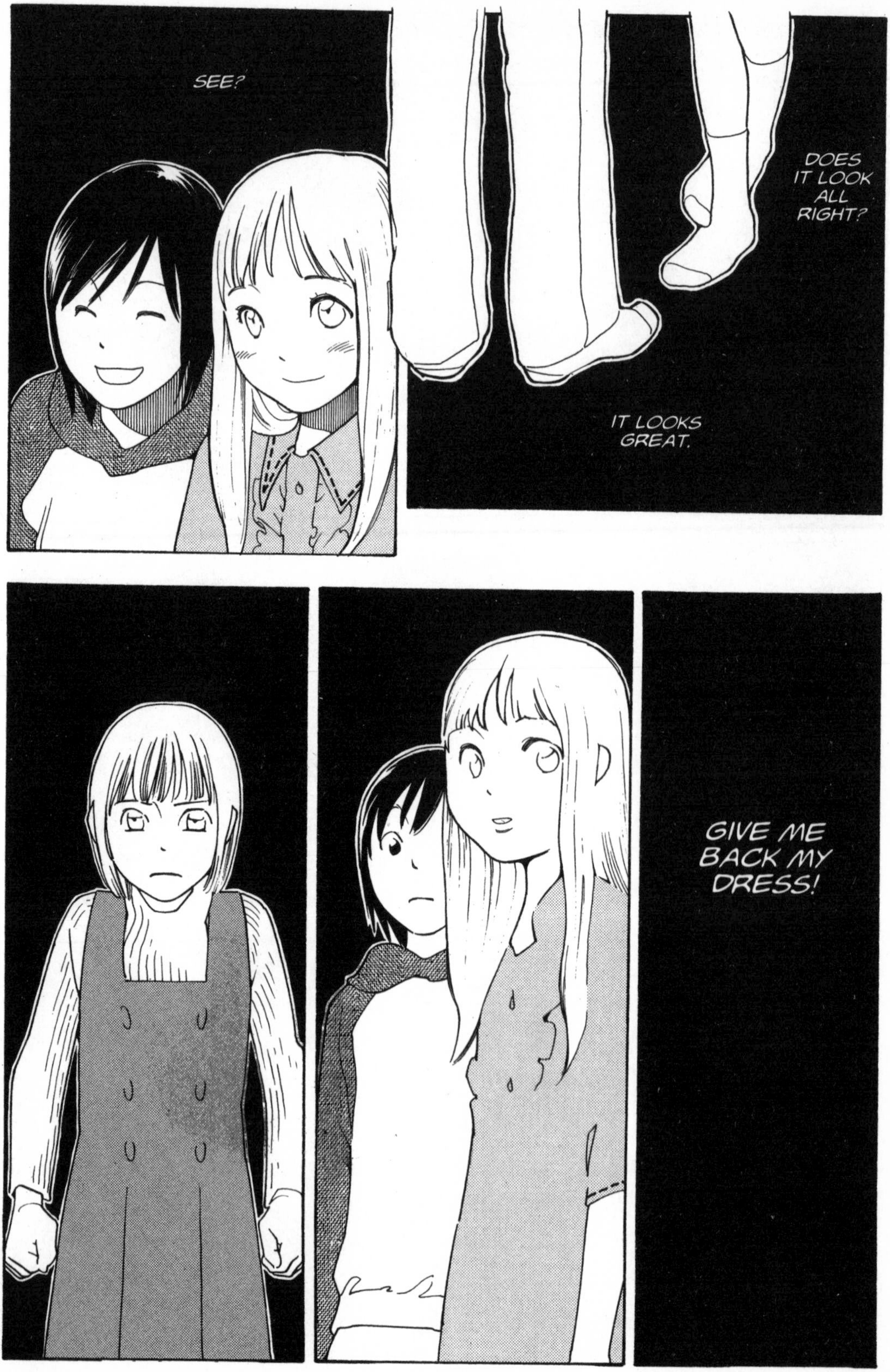
DOES IT LOOK ALL RIGHT?
IT LOOKS GREAT.
SEE?
GIVE ME BACK MY DRESS!

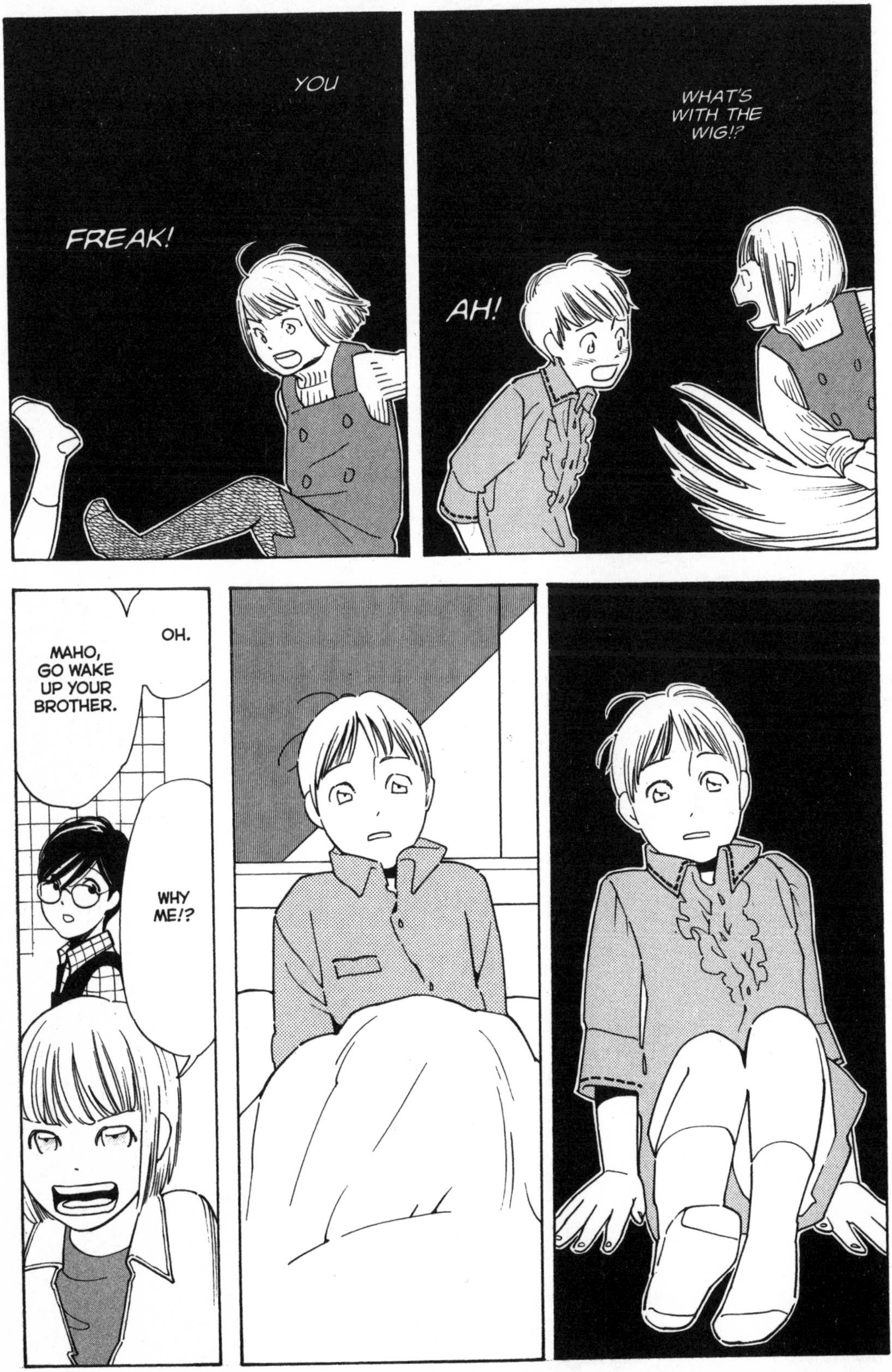
WHAT'S WITH THE WIG!?
AH!
YOU
FREAK!
OH.
MAHO, GO WAKE UP YOUR BROTHER.
WHY ME!?

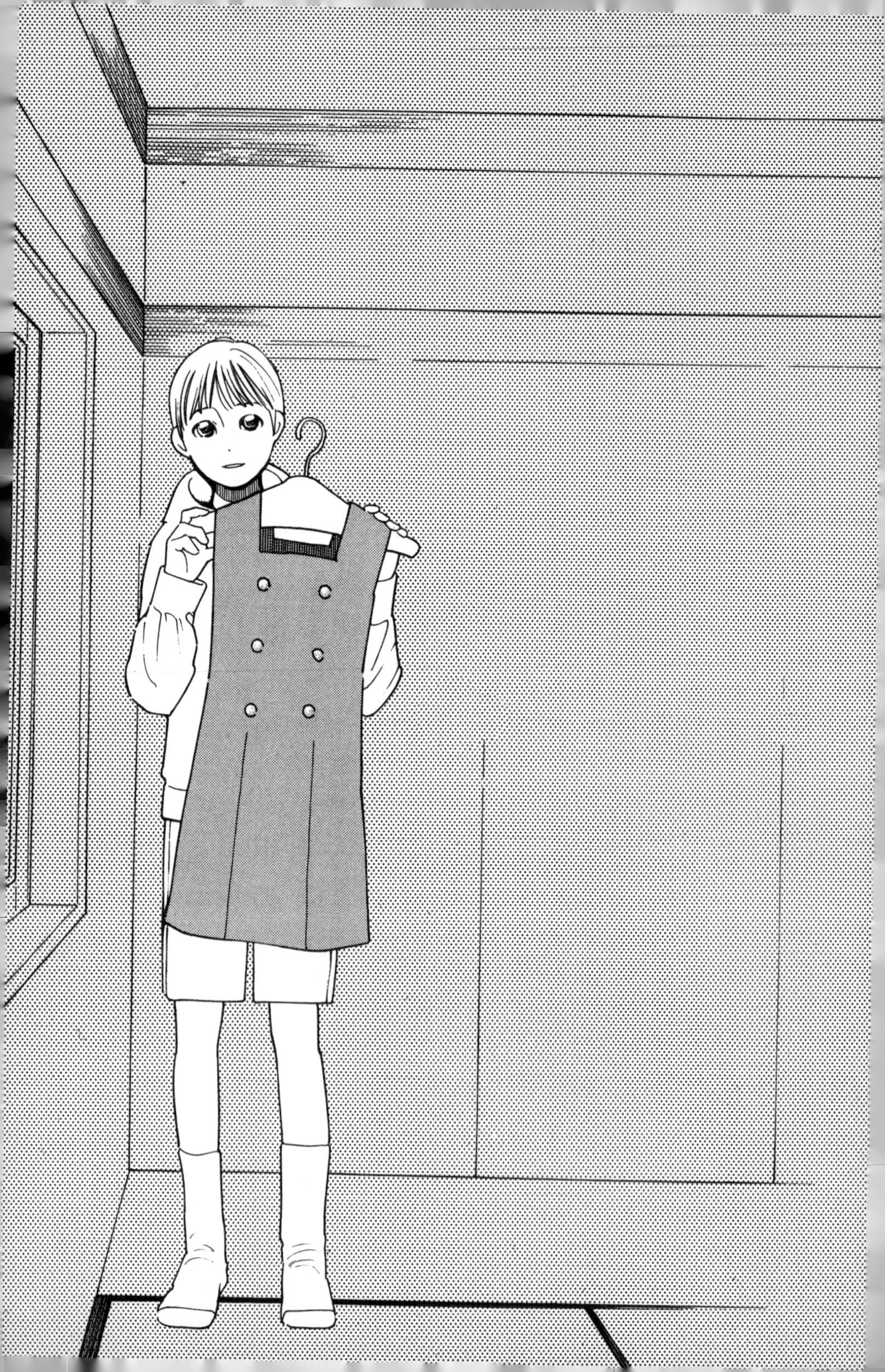

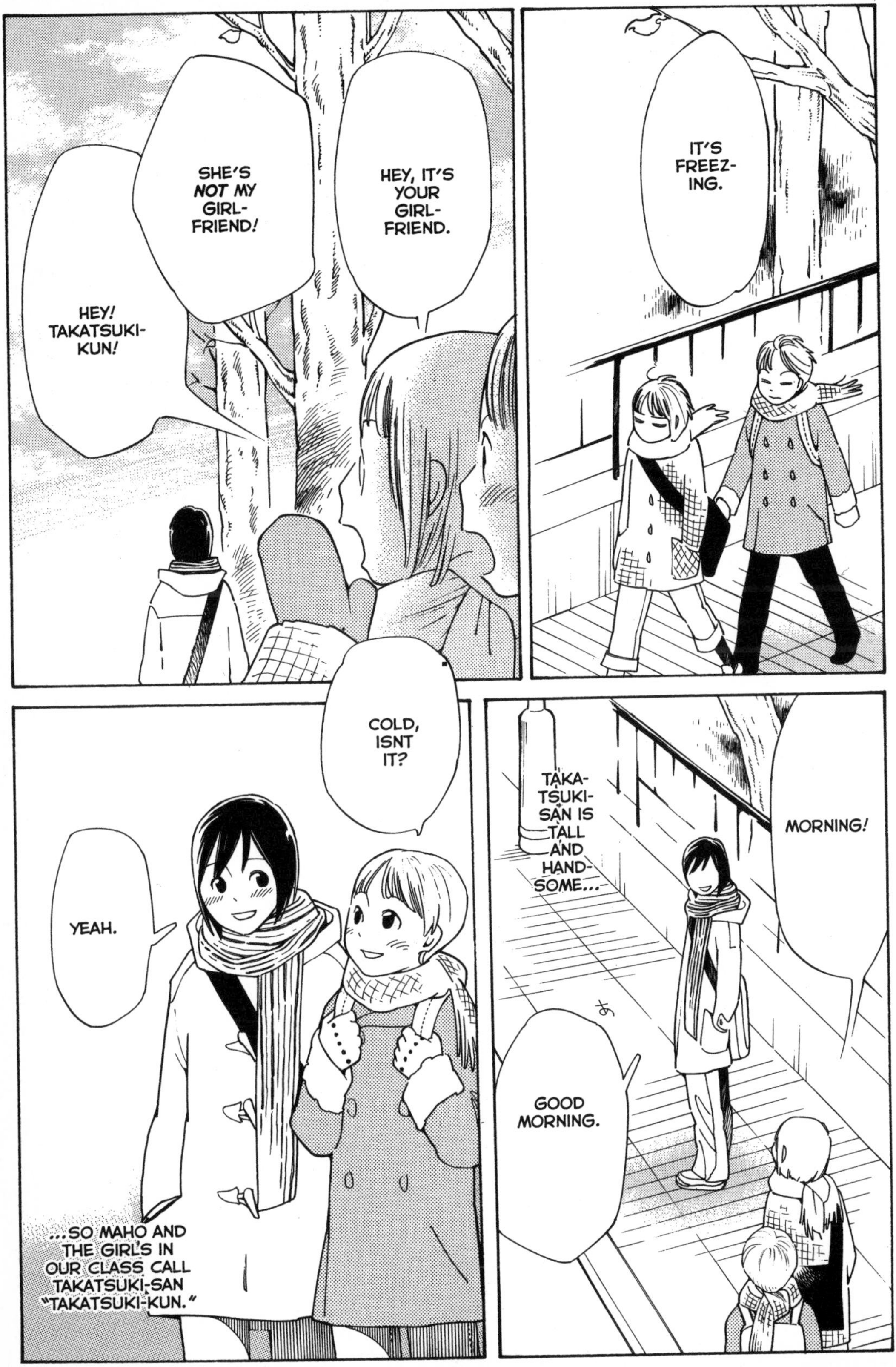
IT'S FREEZ-ING.
HEY, IT'S YOUR GIRL-FRIEND.
SHE'S *NOT* MY GIRL-FRIEND!
HEY! TAKATSUKI-KUN!
MORNING!
TAKA-TSUKI-SAN IS TALL AND HAND-SOME...
あ
GOOD MORNING.
COLD, ISNT IT?
YEAH.
...SO MAHO AND THE GIRLS IN OUR CLASS CALL TAKATSUKI-SAN "TAKATSUKI-KUN."

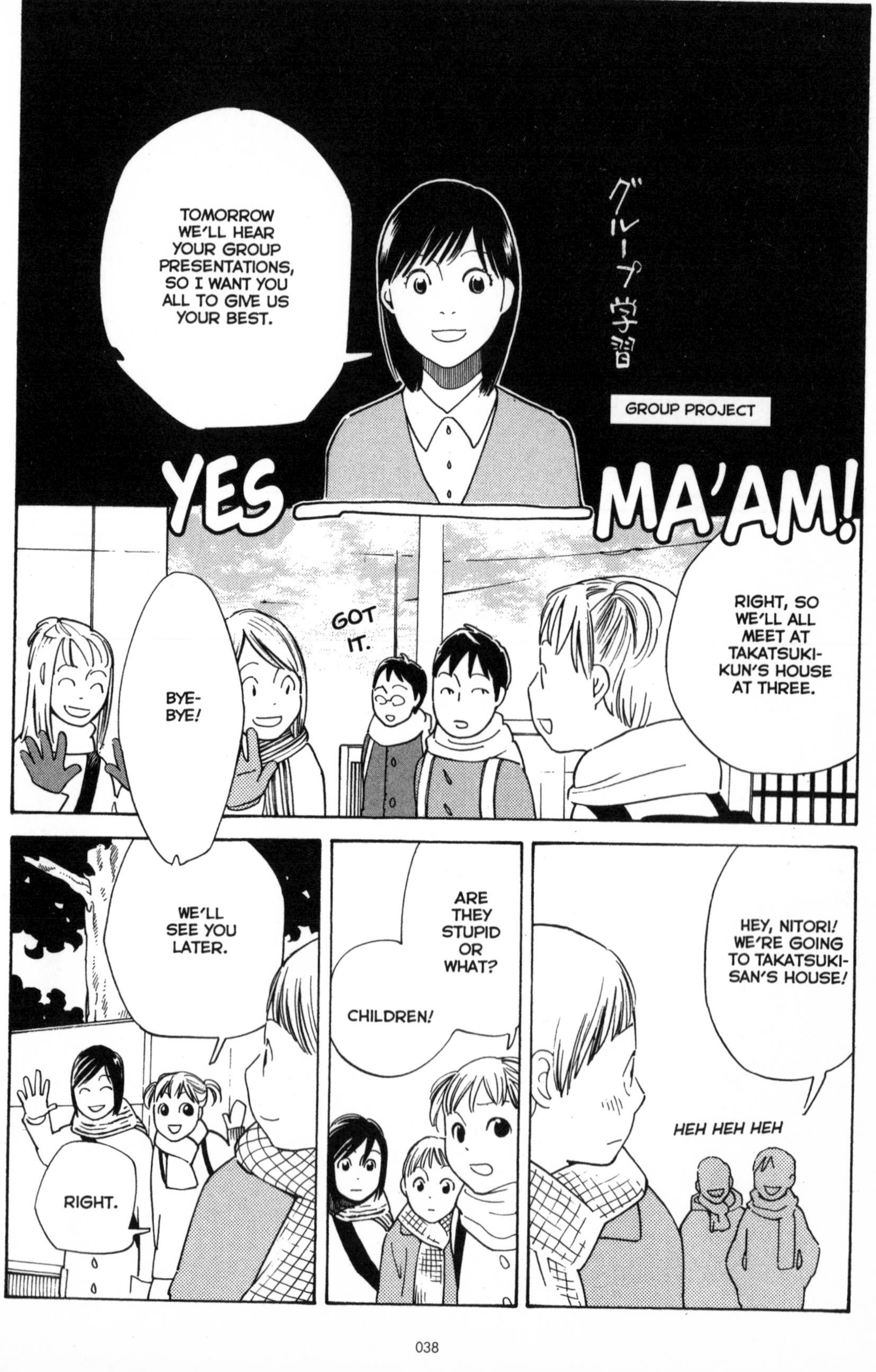
グループ学習
GROUP PROJECT
TOMORROW WE'LL HEAR YOUR GROUP PRESENTATIONS, SO I WANT YOU ALL TO GIVE US YOUR BEST.
YES MA'AM!
RIGHT, SO WE'LL ALL MEET AT TAKATSUKI-KUN'S HOUSE AT THREE.
GOT IT.
BYE-BYE!
HEY, NITORI! WE'RE GOING TO TAKATSUKI-SAN'S HOUSE!
HEH HEH HEH
ARE THEY STUPID OR WHAT?
CHILDREN!
WE'LL SEE YOU LATER.
RIGHT.

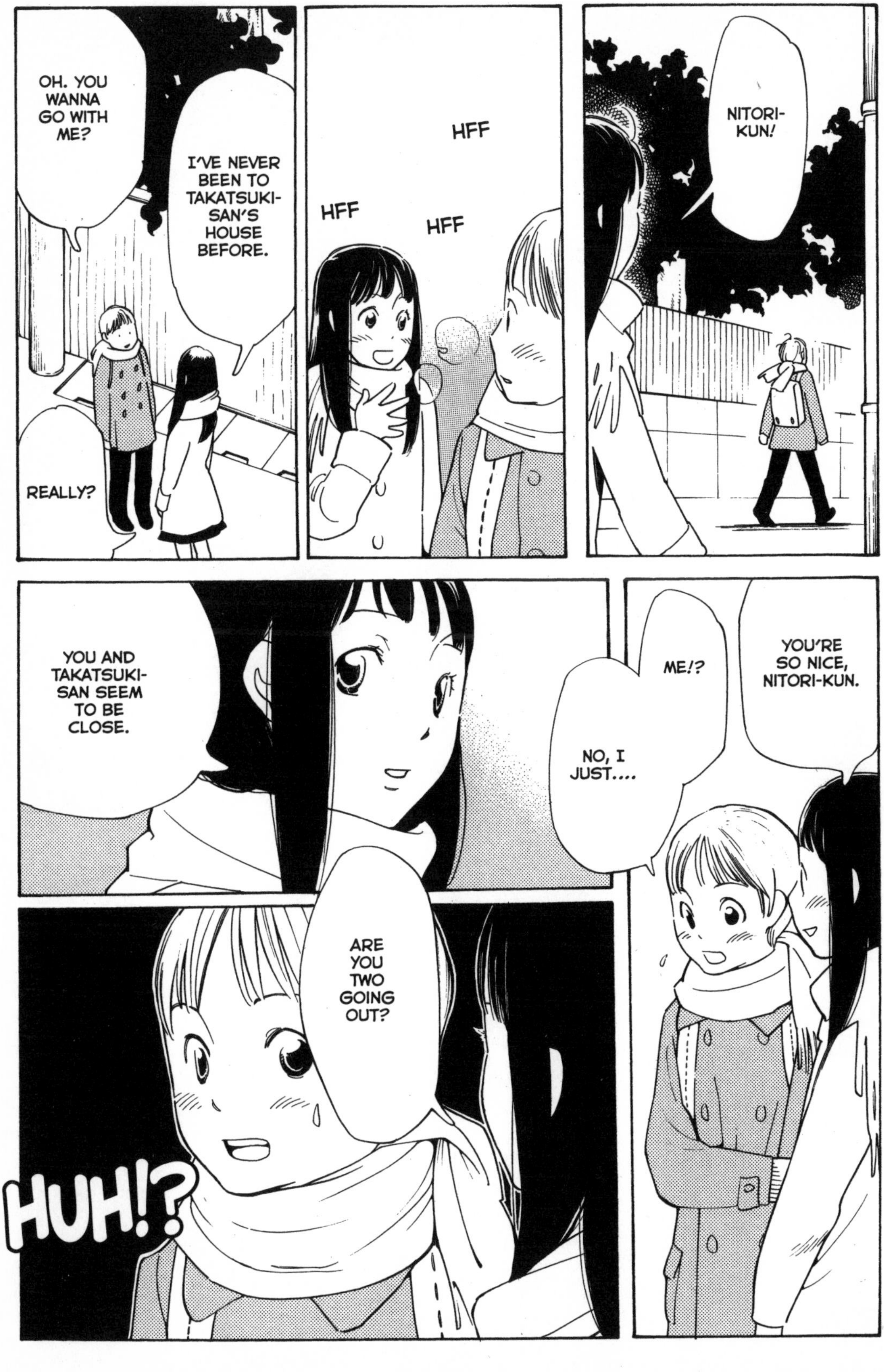
NITORI-KUN!
HFF
HFF
HFF
I'VE NEVER BEEN TO TAKATSUKI-SAN'S HOUSE BEFORE.
OH. YOU WANNA GO WITH ME?
REALLY?
YOU'RE SO NICE, NITORI-KUN.
ME!?
NO, I JUST....
YOU AND TAKATSUKI-SAN SEEM TO BE CLOSE.
ARE YOU TWO GOING OUT?
HUH!?

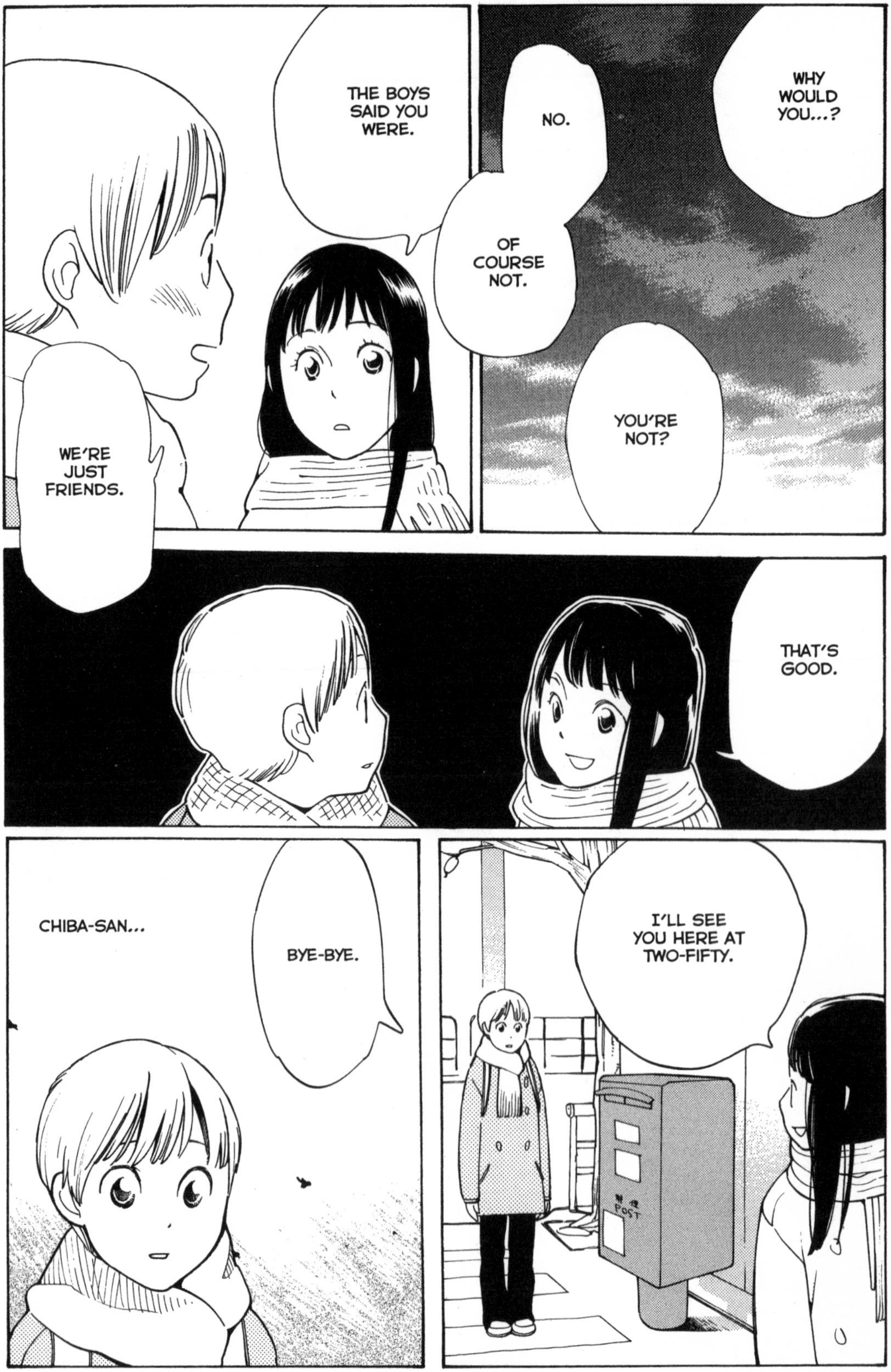
WHY WOULD YOU...?
NO.
OF COURSE NOT.
YOU'RE NOT?
THE BOYS SAID YOU WERE.
WE'RE JUST FRIENDS.
THAT'S GOOD.
I'LL SEE YOU HERE AT TWO-FIFTY.
POST
BYE-BYE.
CHIBA-SAN...

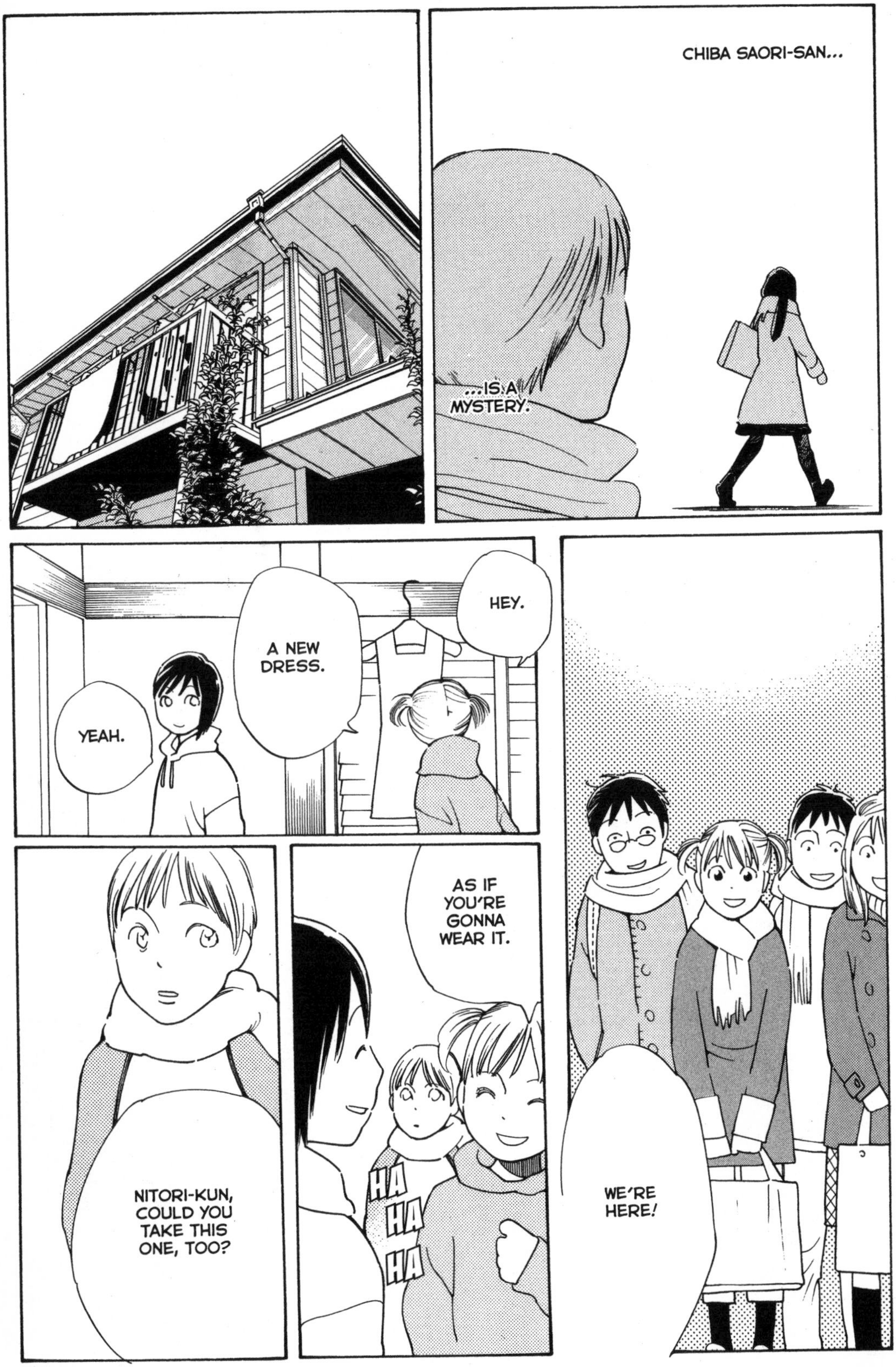
CHIBA SAORI-SAN...
...IS A MYSTERY.
WE'RE HERE!
HEY.
A NEW DRESS.
YEAH.
AS IF YOU'RE GONNA WEAR IT.
HA HA HA
NITORI-KUN, COULD YOU TAKE THIS ONE, TOO?

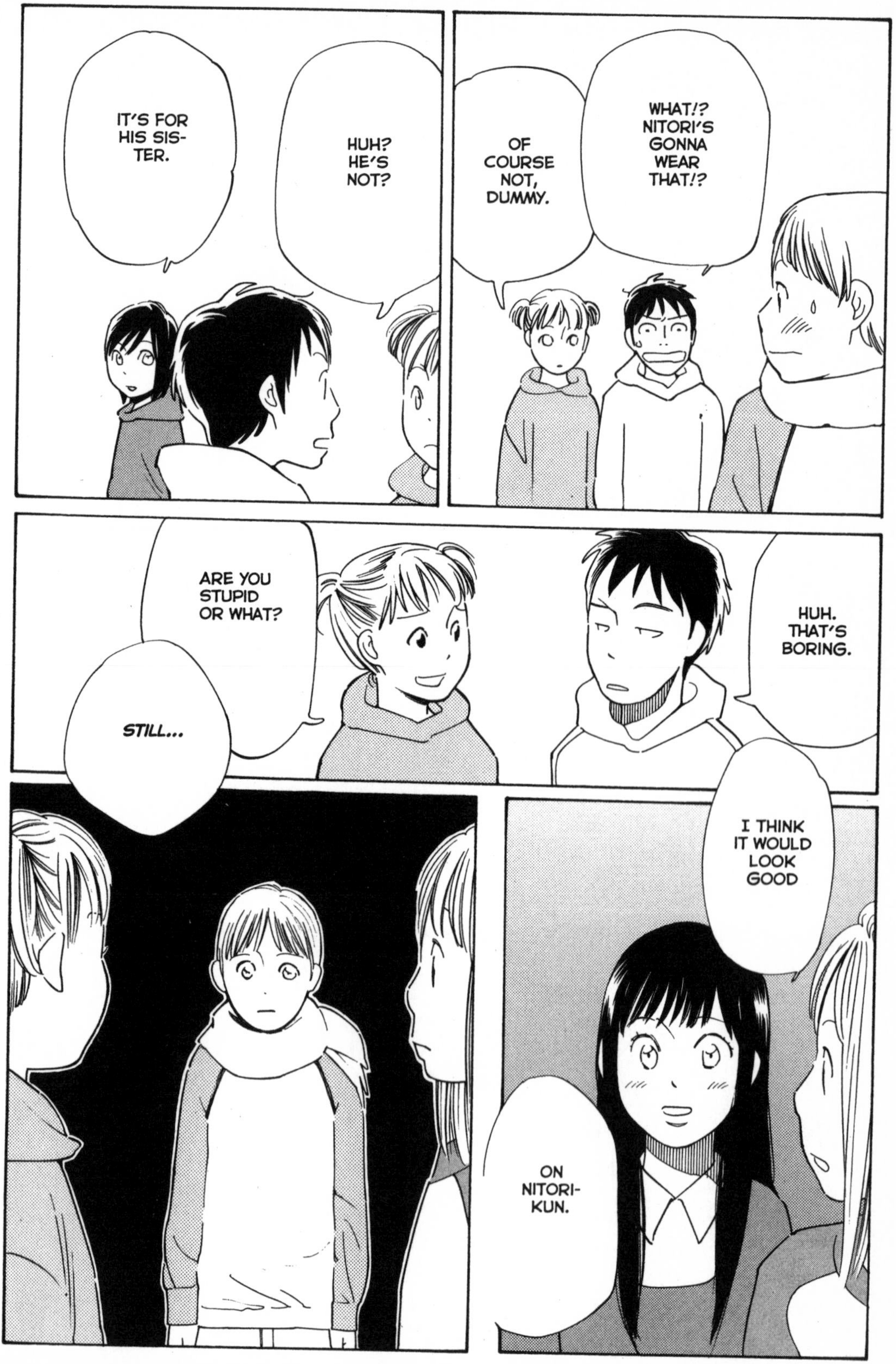
WHAT!? NITORI'S GONNA WEAR THAT!?
OF COURSE NOT, DUMMY.
HUH? HE'S NOT?
IT'S FOR HIS SIS- TER.
HUH. THAT'S BORING.
ARE YOU STUPID OR WHAT?
STILL...
I THINK IT WOULD LOOK GOOD
ON NITORI- KUN.

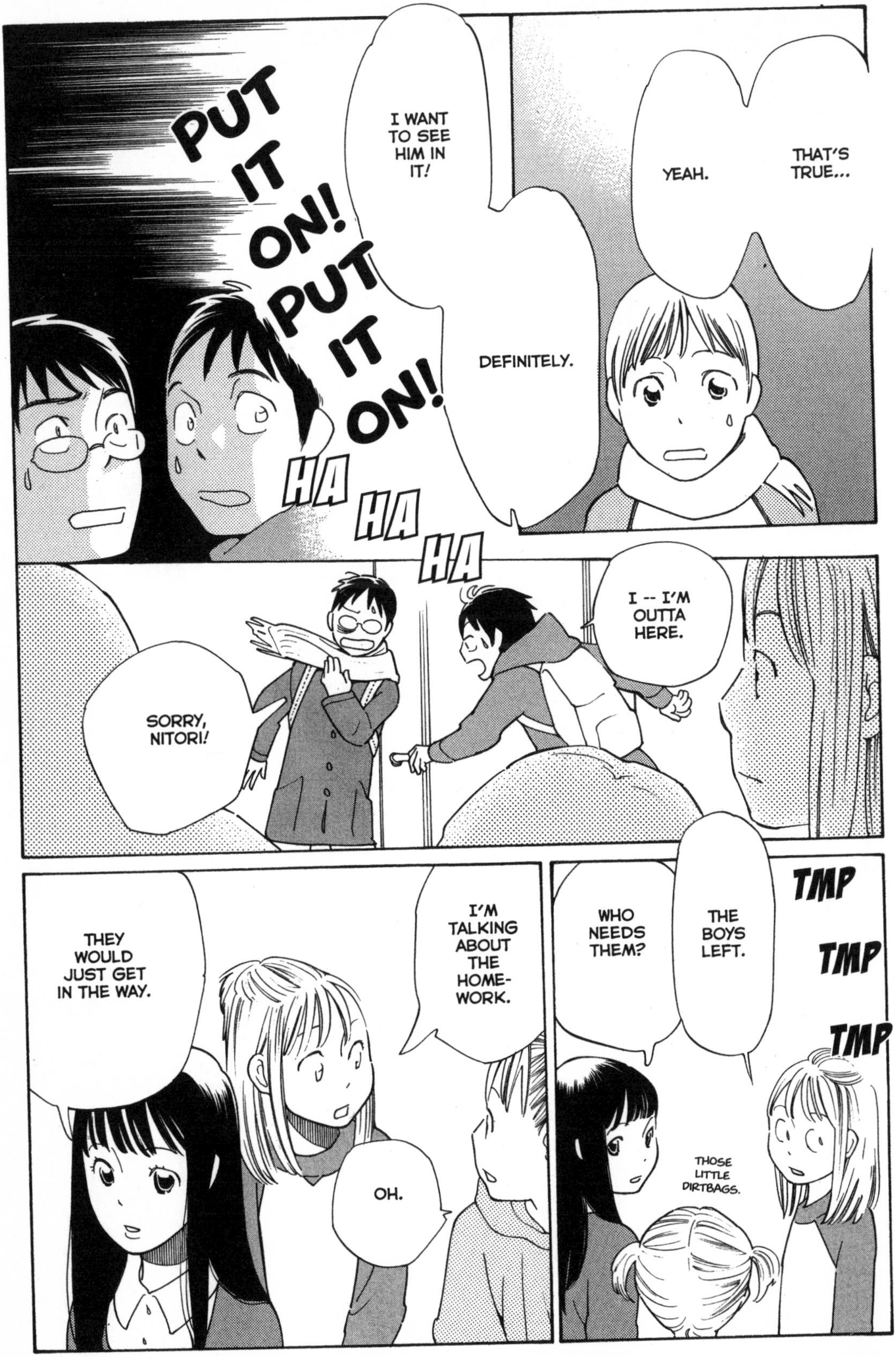
THAT'S TRUE...
YEAH.
I WANT TO SEE HIM IN IT!
DEFINITELY.
PUT IT ON! PUT IT ON!
HA HA HA
I -- I'M OUTTA HERE.
SORRY, NITORI!
TMP TMP TMP
THE BOYS LEFT.
WHO NEEDS THEM?
THOSE LITTLE DIRTBAGS.
I'M TALKING ABOUT THE HOME-WORK.
THEY WOULD JUST GET IN THE WAY.
OH.

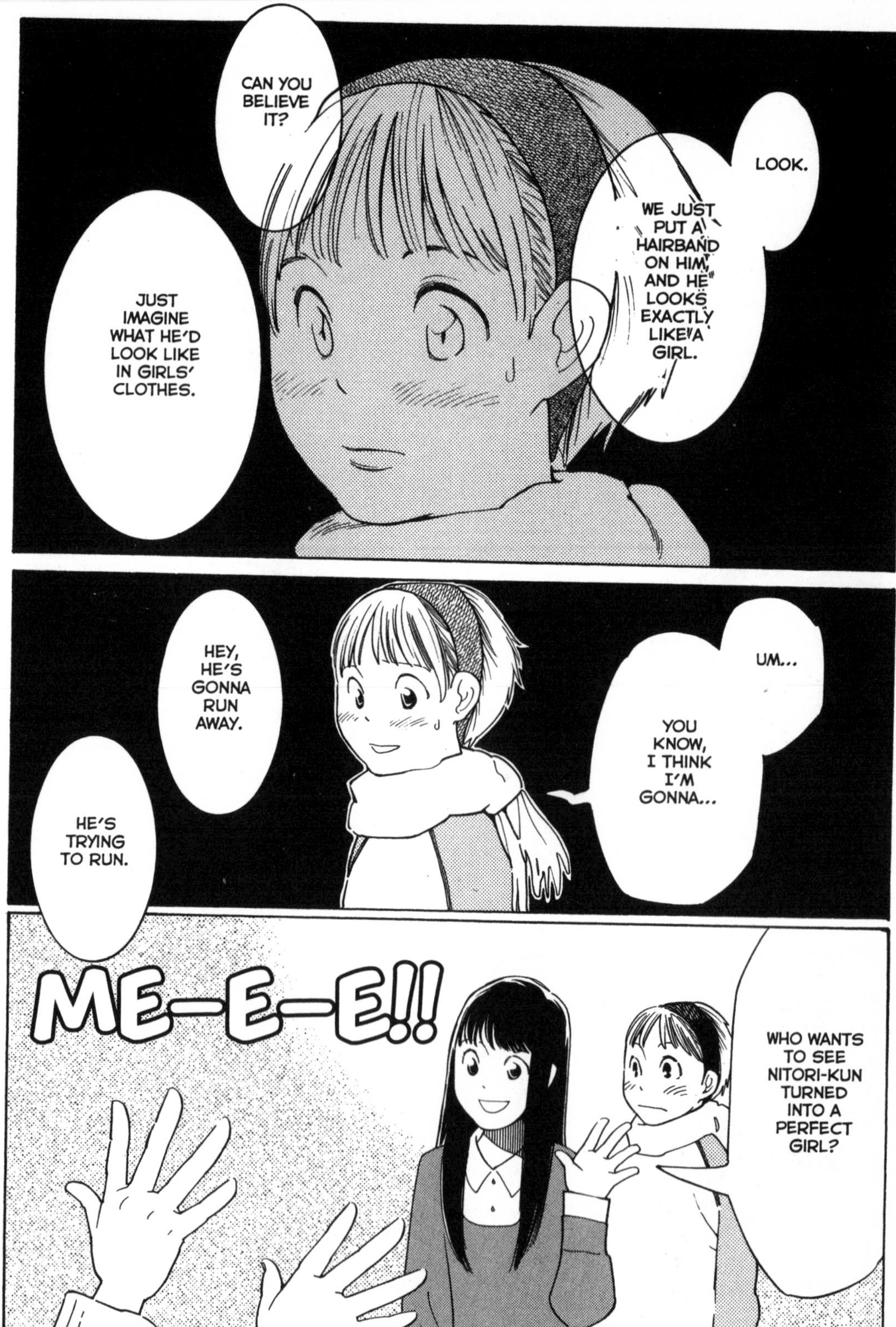
LOOK.
WE JUST PUT A HAIRBAND ON HIM, AND HE LOOKS EXACTLY LIKE A GIRL.
CAN YOU BELIEVE IT?
JUST IMAGINE WHAT HE'D LOOK LIKE IN GIRLS' CLOTHES.
UM...
YOU KNOW, I THINK I'M GONNA...
HEY, HE'S GONNA RUN AWAY.
HE'S TRYING TO RUN.
WHO WANTS TO SEE NITORI-KUN TURNED INTO A PERFECT GIRL?
ME-E-E!!

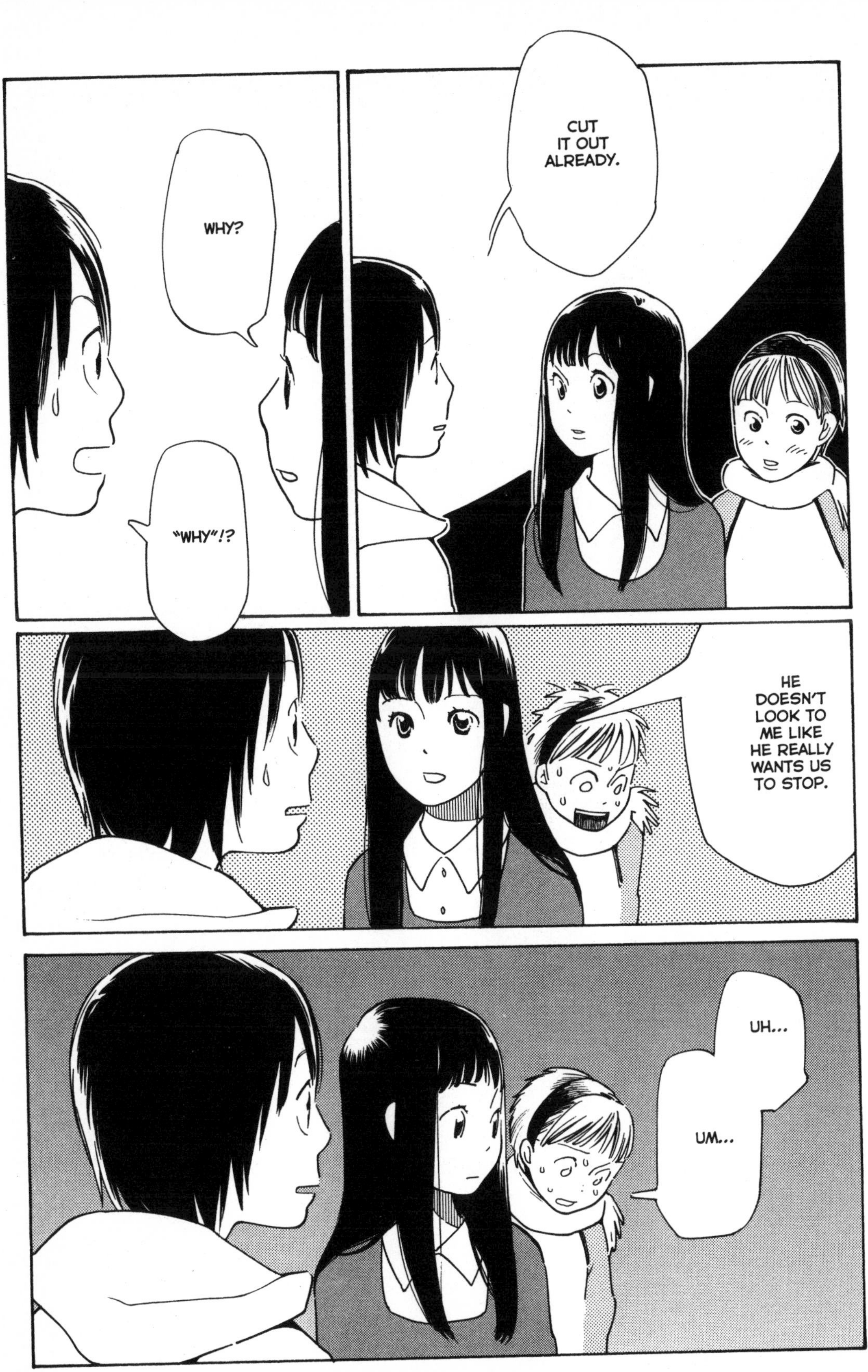
CUT IT OUT ALREADY.
WHY?
"WHY"!?
HE DOESN'T LOOK TO ME LIKE HE REALLY WANTS US TO STOP.
UH...
UM...

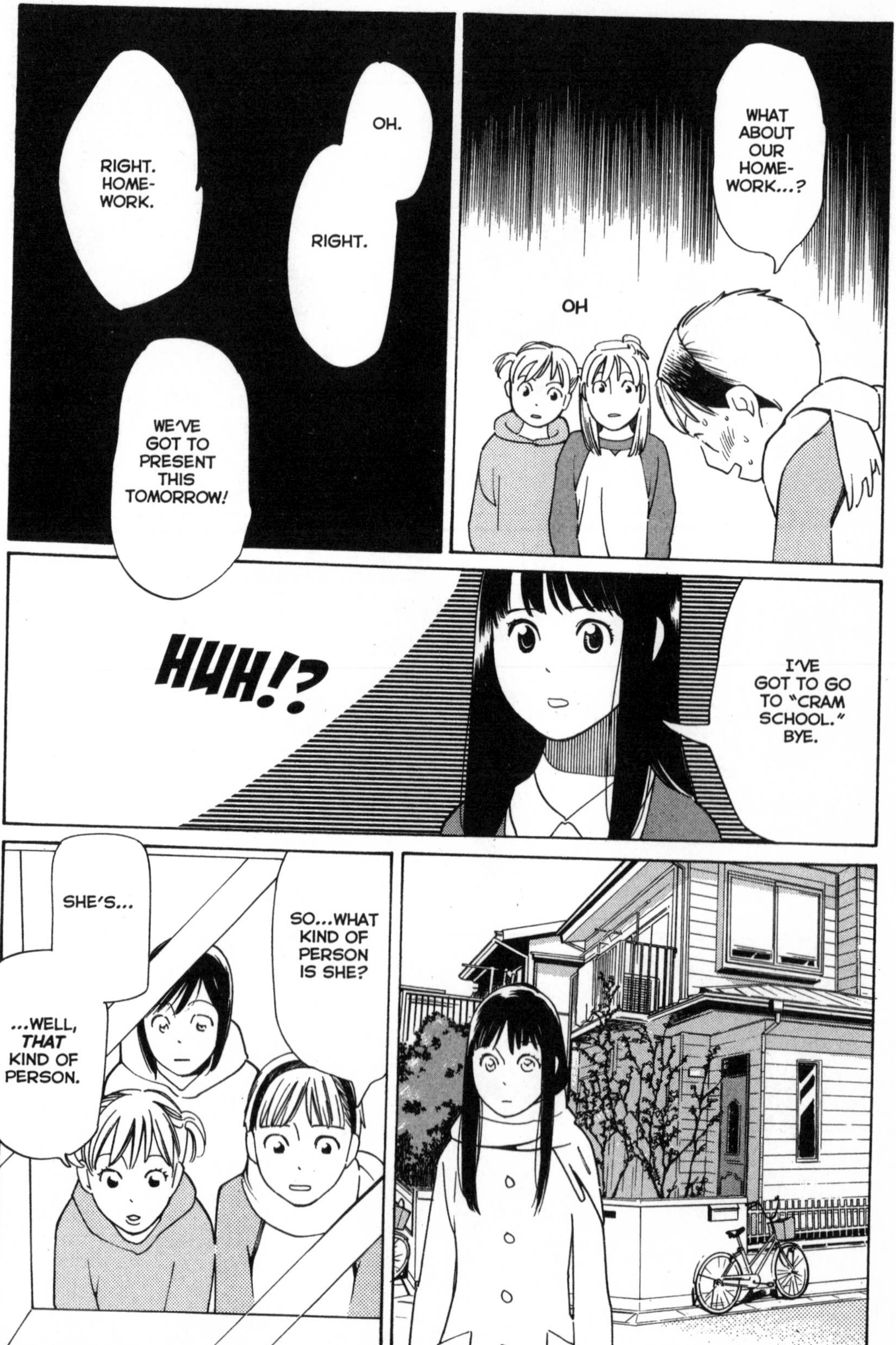
WHAT ABOUT OUR HOME-WORK...?
OH
OH.
RIGHT.
RIGHT. HOME-WORK.
WE'VE GOT TO PRESENT THIS TOMORROW!
I'VE GOT TO GO TO "CRAM SCHOOL." BYE.
HUH!?
SO...WHAT KIND OF PERSON IS SHE?
SHE'S...
...WELL, *THAT* KIND OF PERSON.

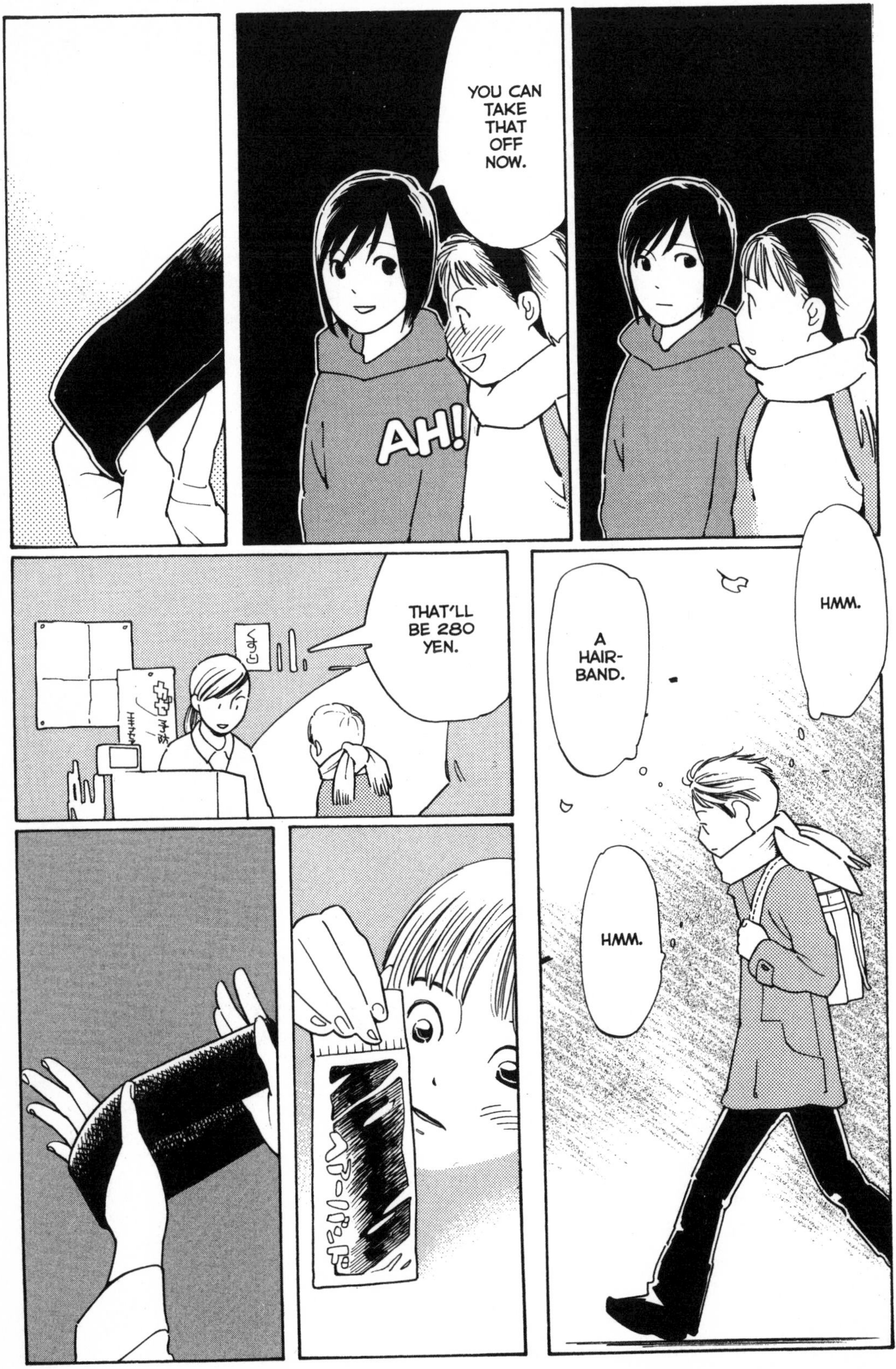
YOU CAN TAKE THAT OFF NOW.
AH!
HMM.
A HAIR-BAND.
HMM.
THAT'LL BE 280 YEN.

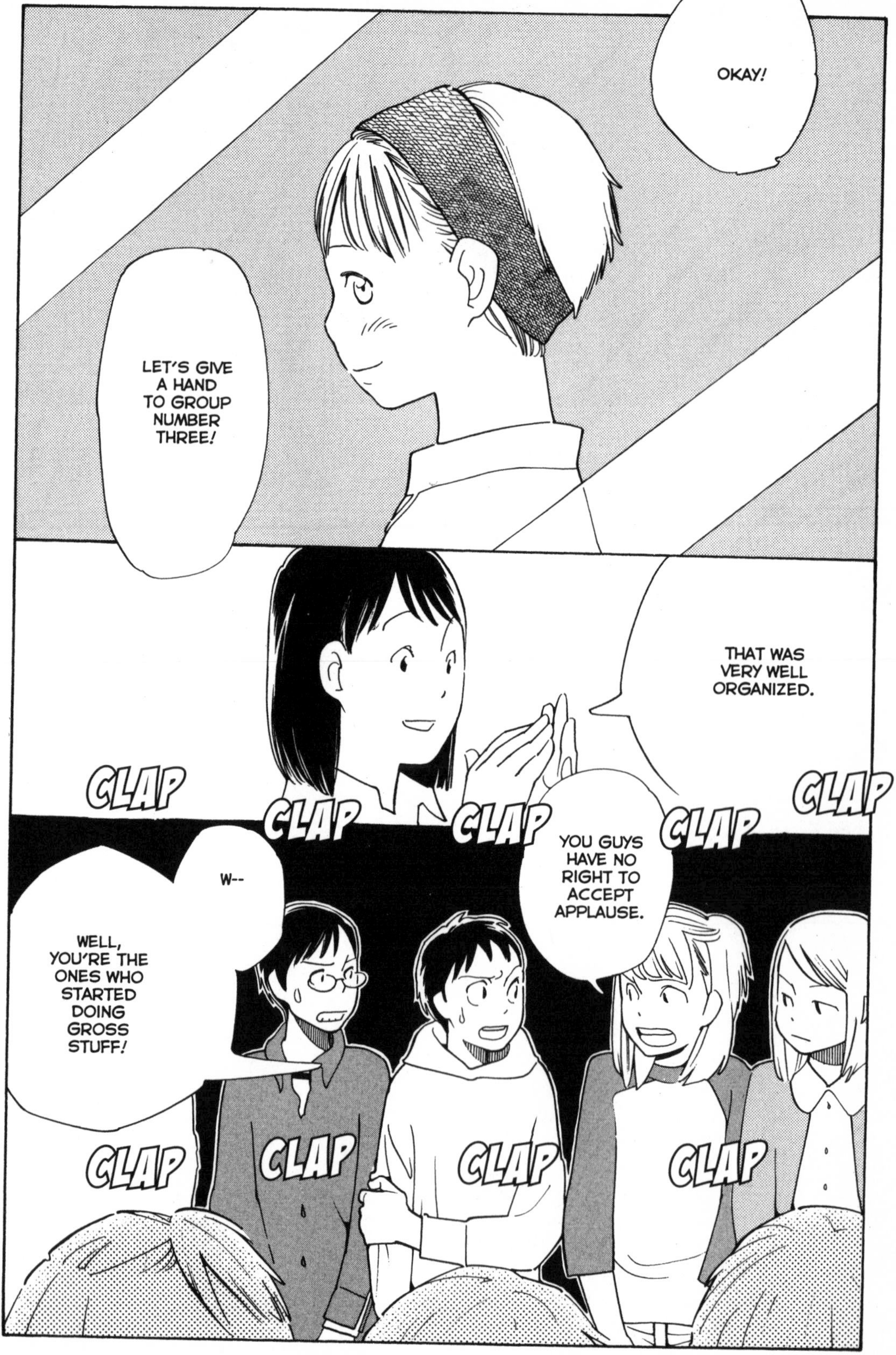
OKAY!
LET'S GIVE A HAND TO GROUP NUMBER THREE!
THAT WAS VERY WELL ORGANIZED.
CLAP
CLAP
CLAP
CLAP
CLAP
YOU GUYS HAVE NO RIGHT TO ACCEPT APPLAUSE.
W--
WELL, YOU'RE THE ONES WHO STARTED DOING GROSS STUFF!
CLAP
CLAP
CLAP
CLAP

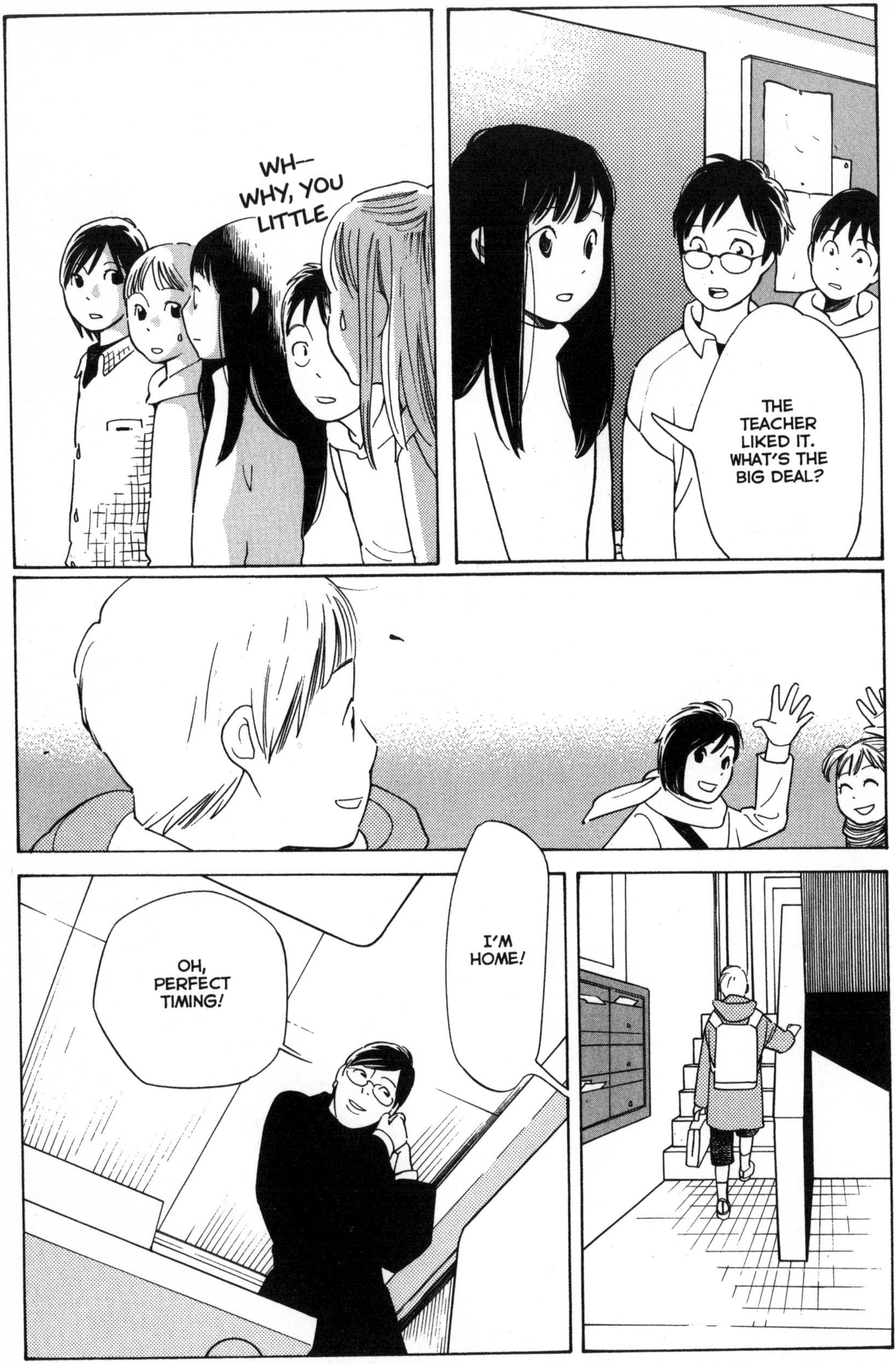
THE TEACHER LIKED IT. WHAT'S THE BIG DEAL?
WH-- WHY, YOU LITTLE
I'M HOME!
OH, PERFECT TIMING!

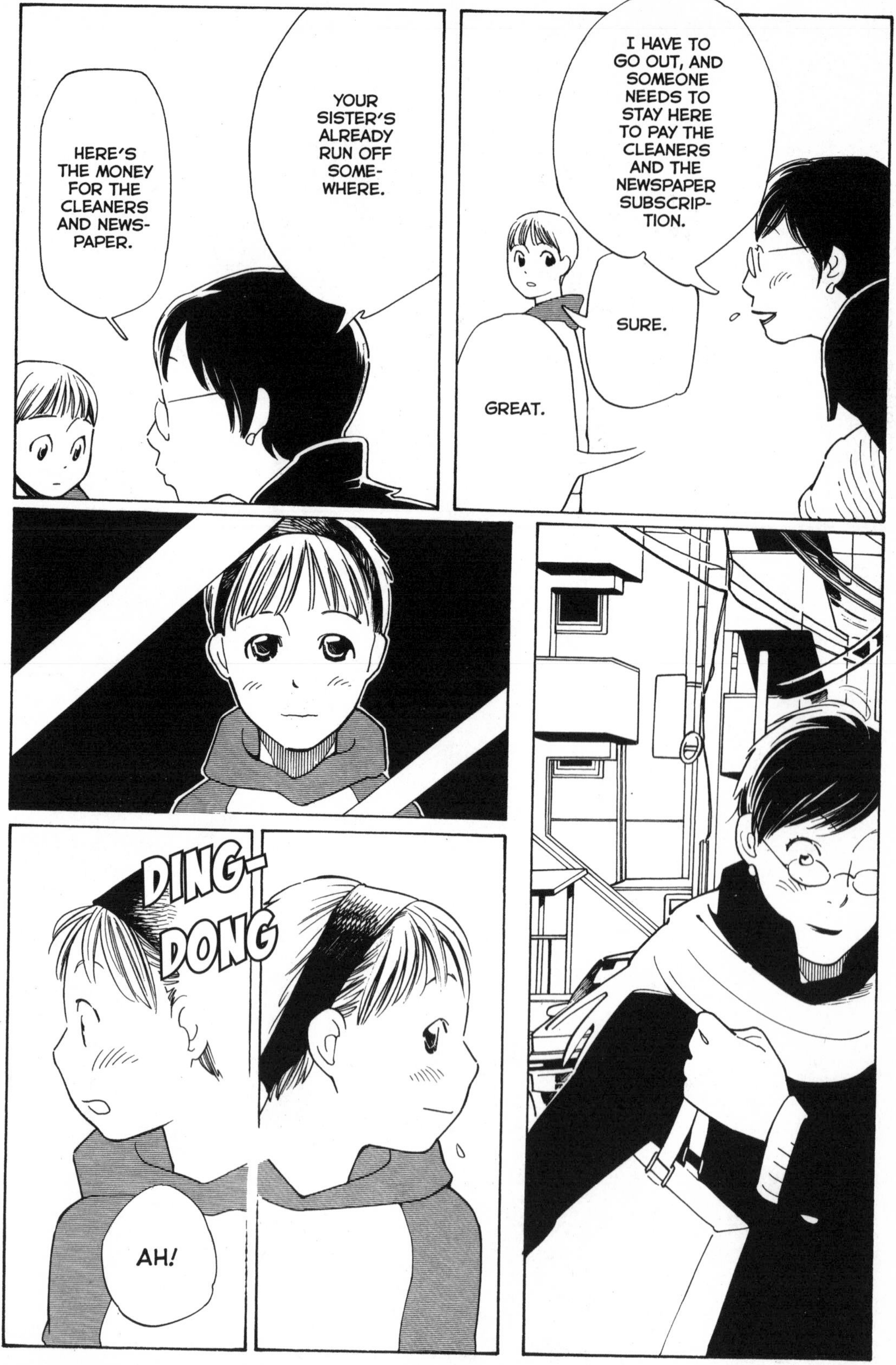
I HAVE TO GO OUT, AND SOMEONE NEEDS TO STAY HERE TO PAY THE CLEANERS AND THE NEWSPAPER SUBSCRIPTION.
SURE.
GREAT.
YOUR SISTER'S ALREADY RUN OFF SOMEWHERE.
HERE'S THE MONEY FOR THE CLEANERS AND NEWSPAPER.
DING-DONG
AH!

OH.

MONEY.

JUST A MOMENT!

HMM. OH, WELL.

ARE YOU HOME ALONE, LITTLE GIRL?

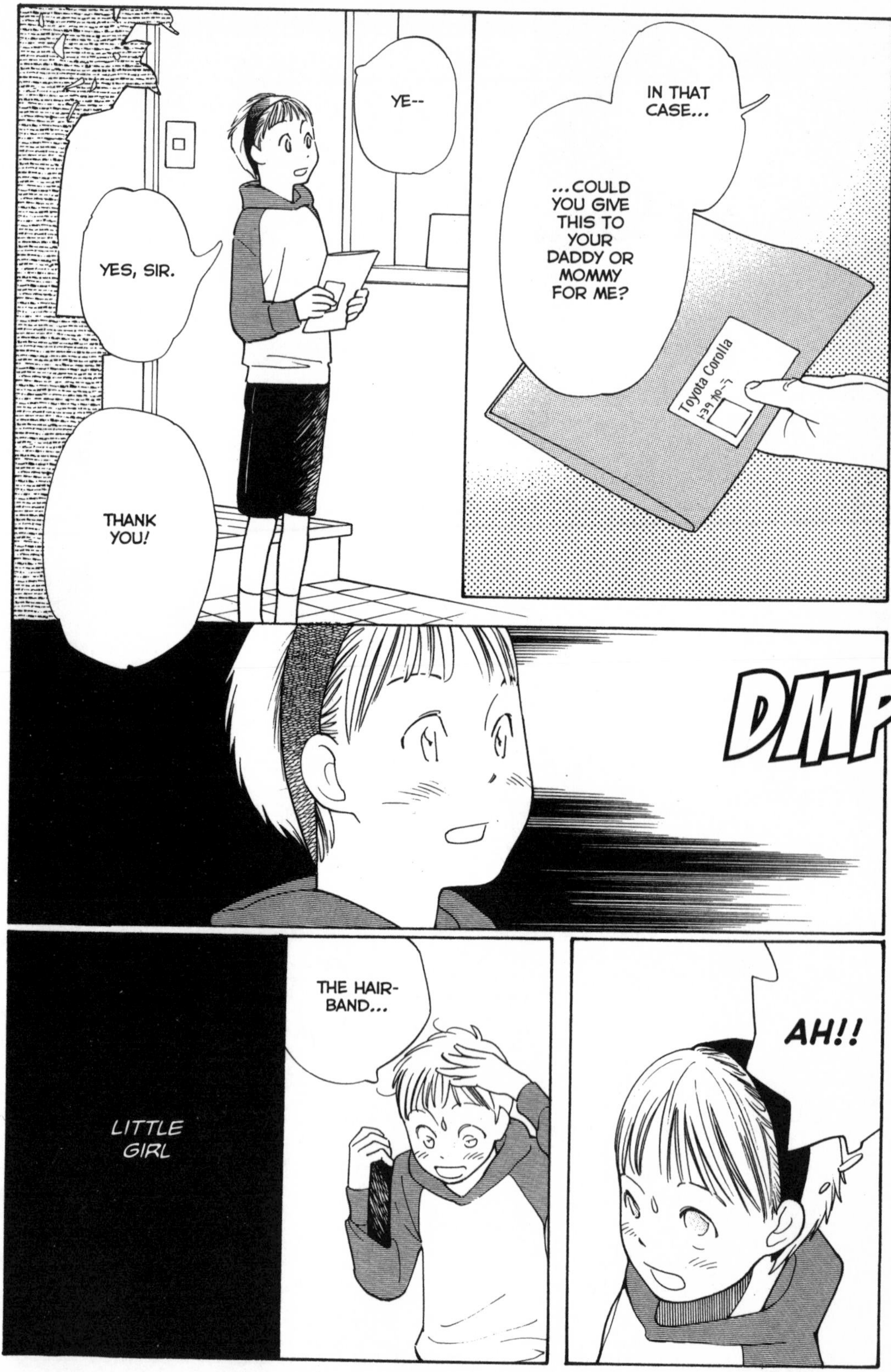
IN THAT CASE...
...COULD YOU GIVE THIS TO YOUR DADDY OR MOMMY FOR ME?
Toyota Corolla
YE--
YES, SIR.
THANK YOU!
DMP
AH!!
THE HAIR-BAND...
LITTLE GIRL

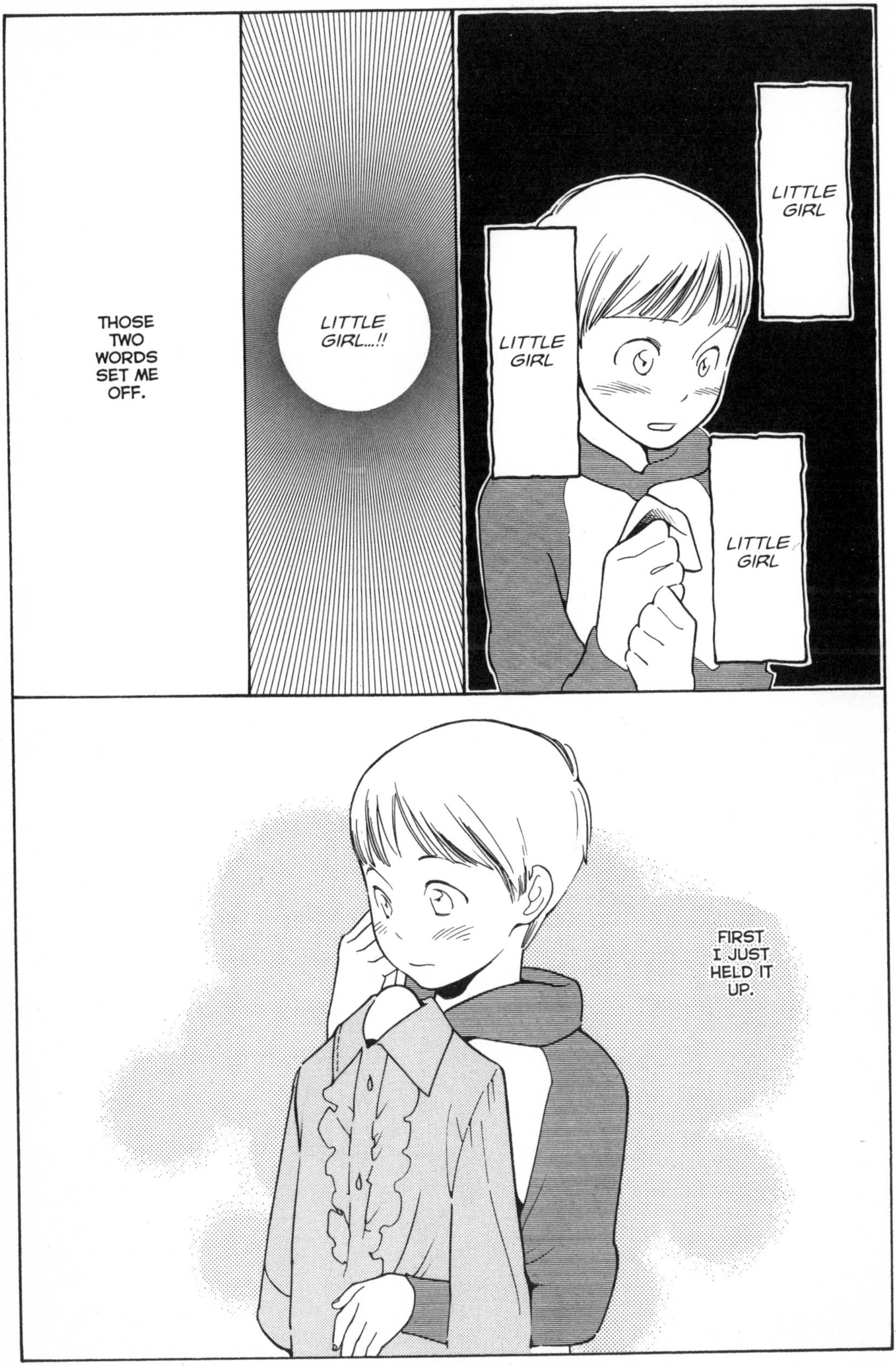
LITTLE GIRL
LITTLE GIRL
LITTLE GIRL
LITTLE GIRL...!!
THOSE TWO WORDS SET ME OFF.
FIRST I JUST HELD IT UP.

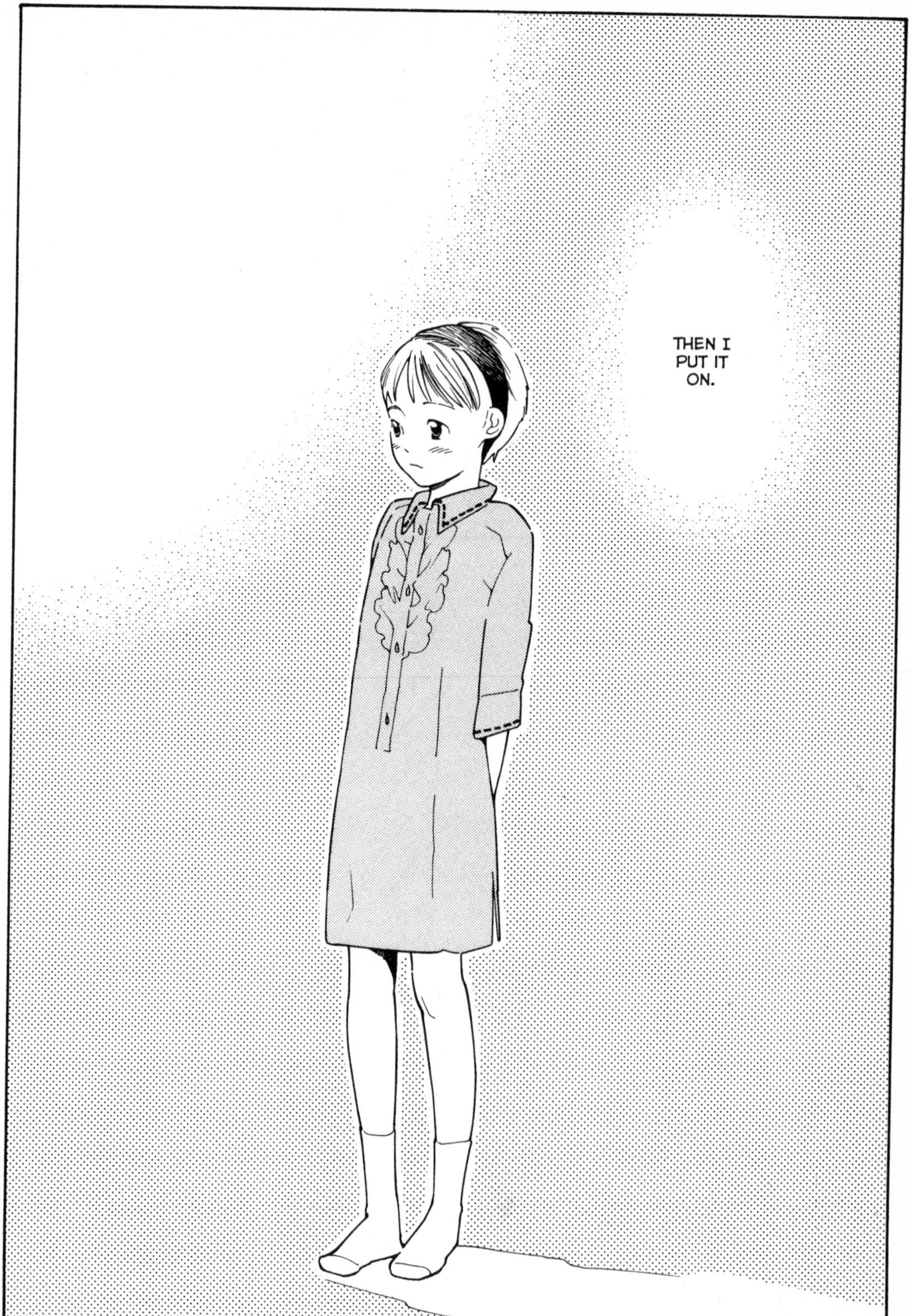
THEN I PUT IT ON.

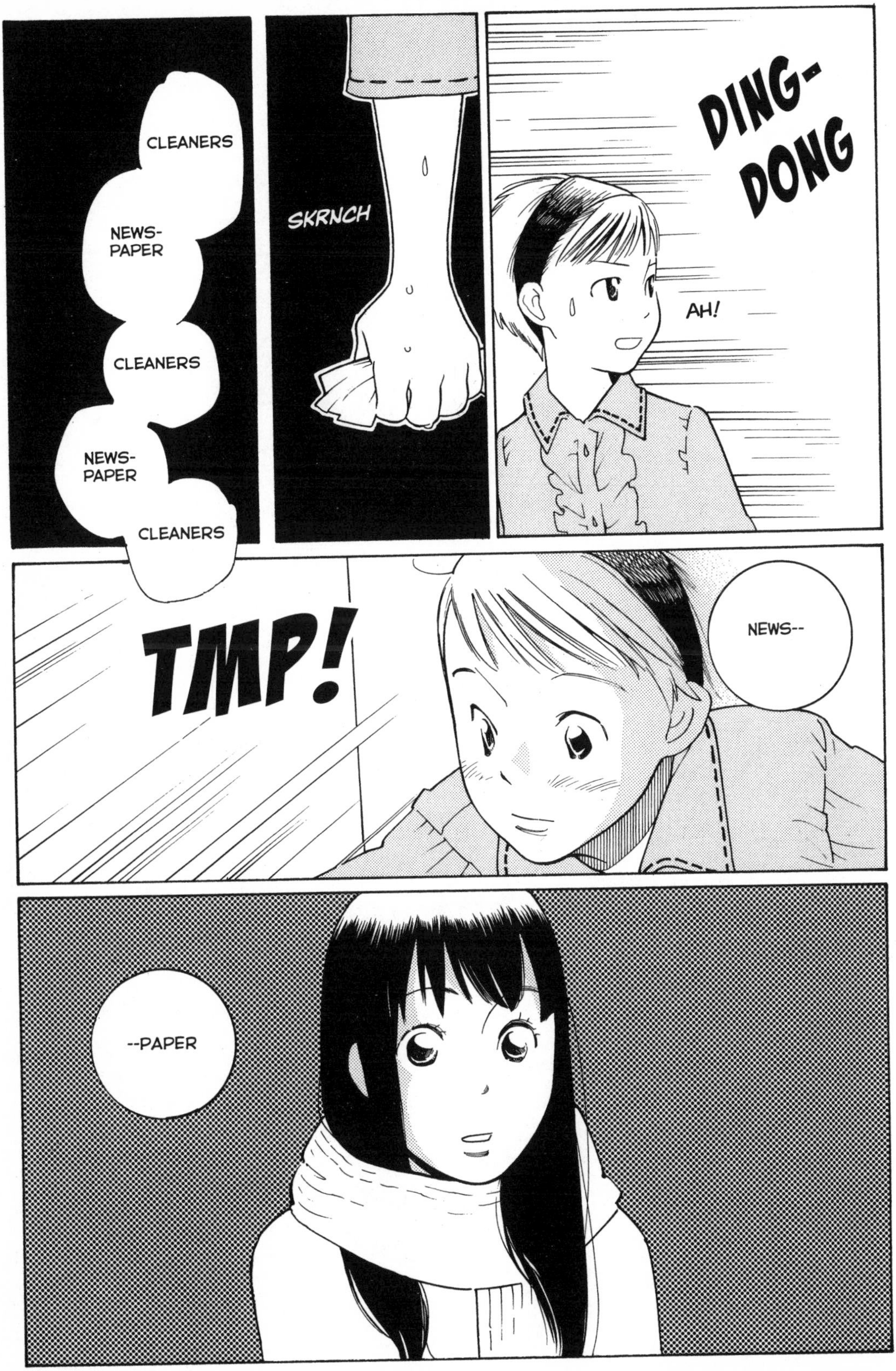
DING-DONG
AH!
SKRNCH
CLEANERS
NEWS-PAPER
CLEANERS
NEWS-PAPER
CLEANERS
NEWS--
TMP!
--PAPER

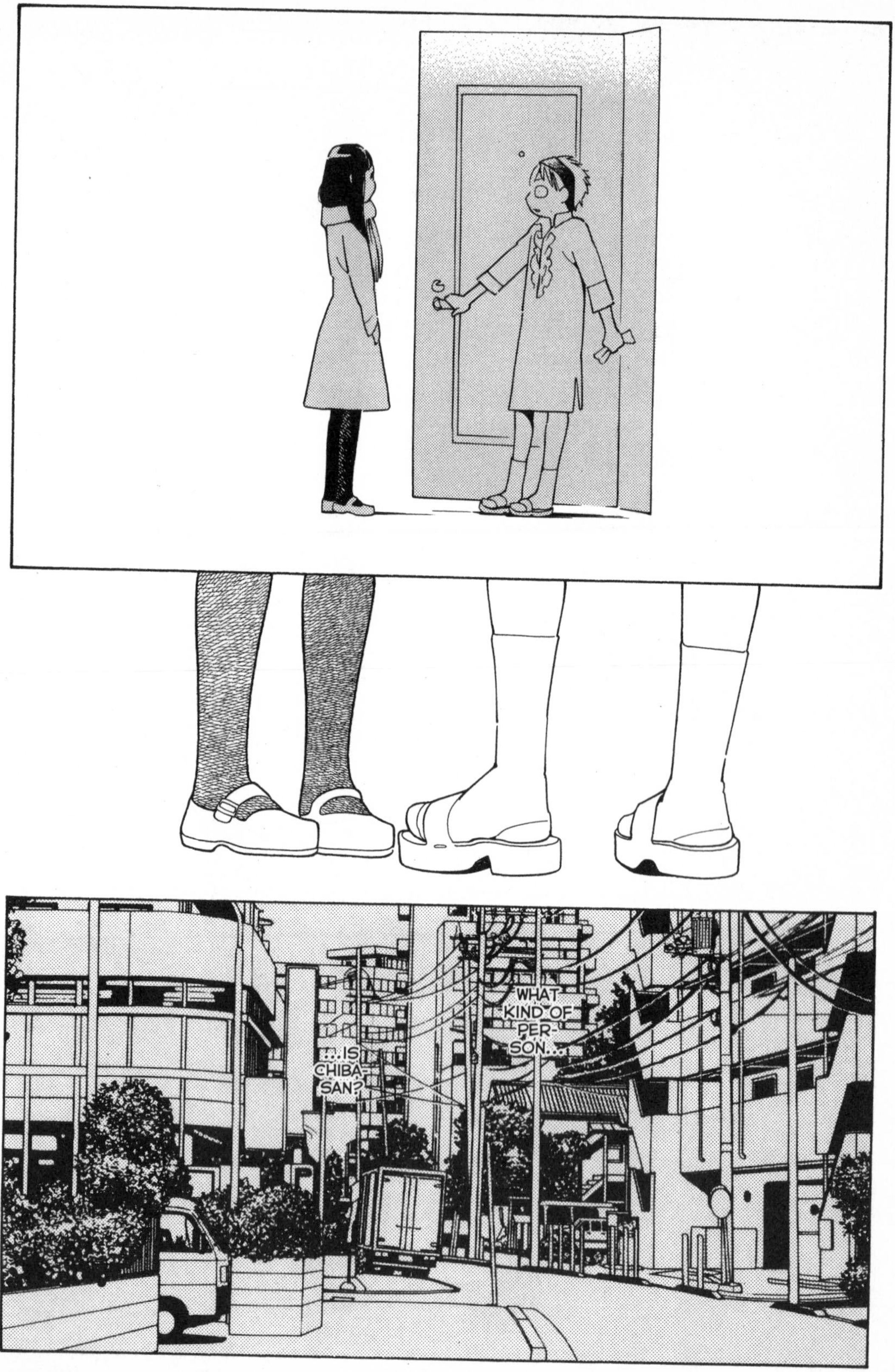
WHAT KIND OF PER-SON...
...IS CHIBA-SAN?

3

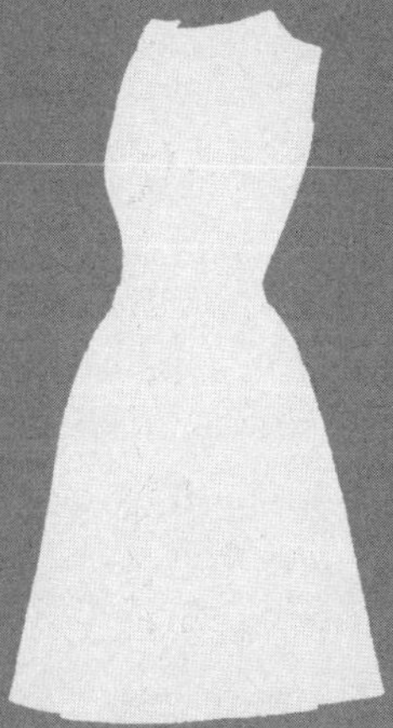

Oscar and André

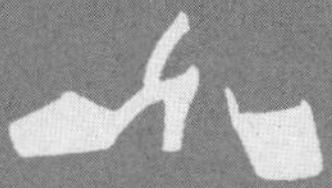

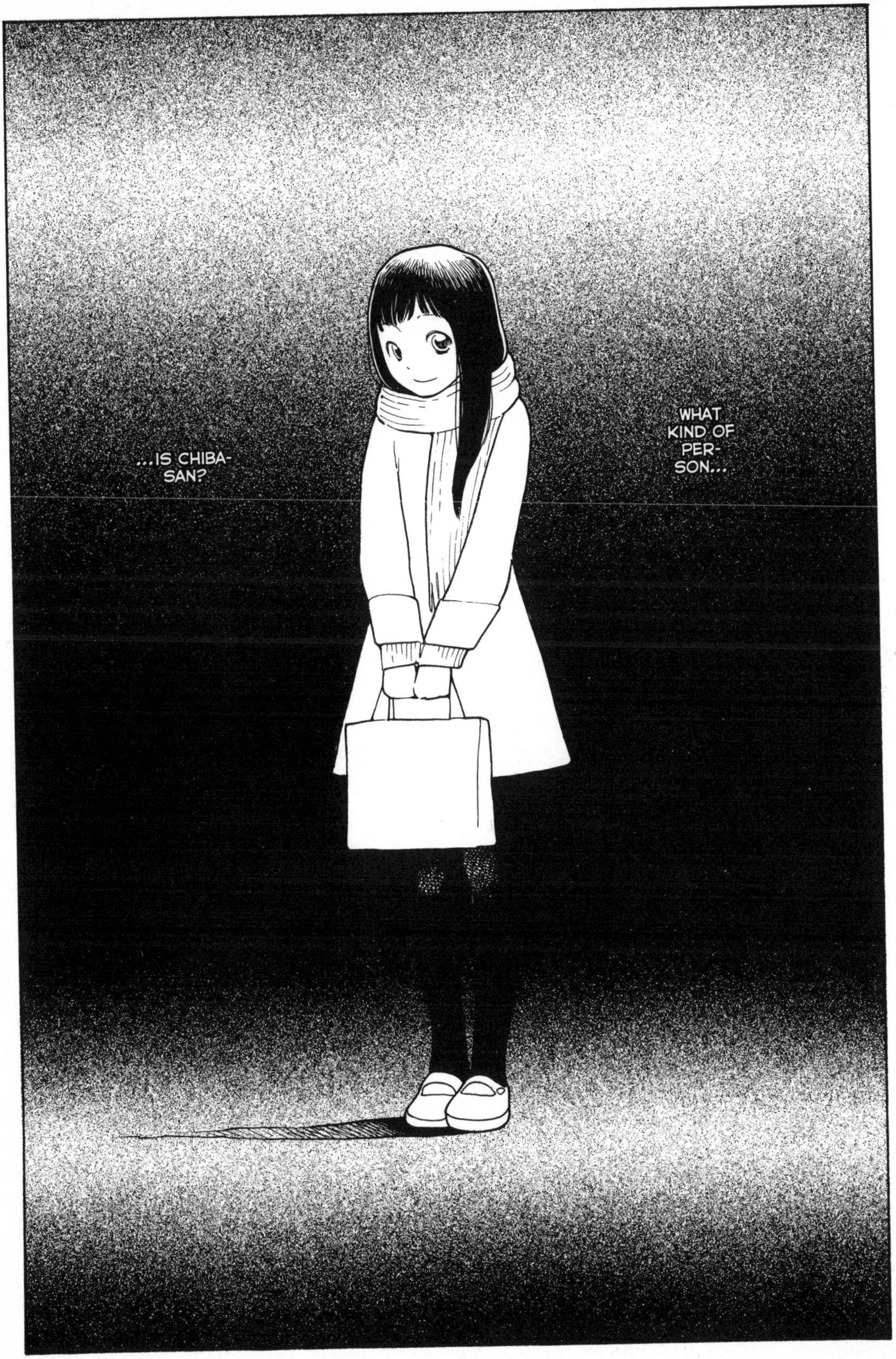
WHAT KIND OF PER-SON...
...IS CHIBA-SAN?

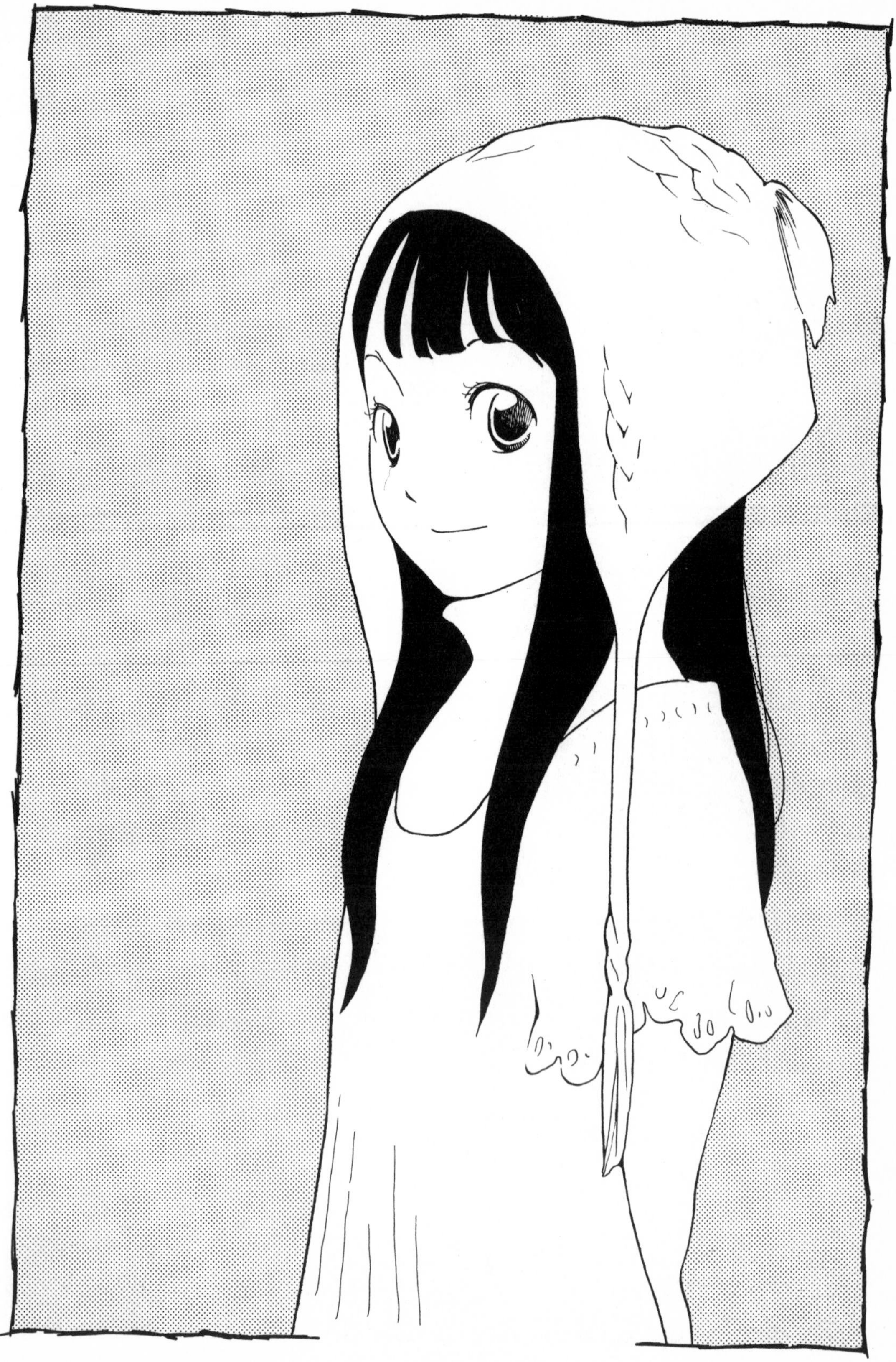

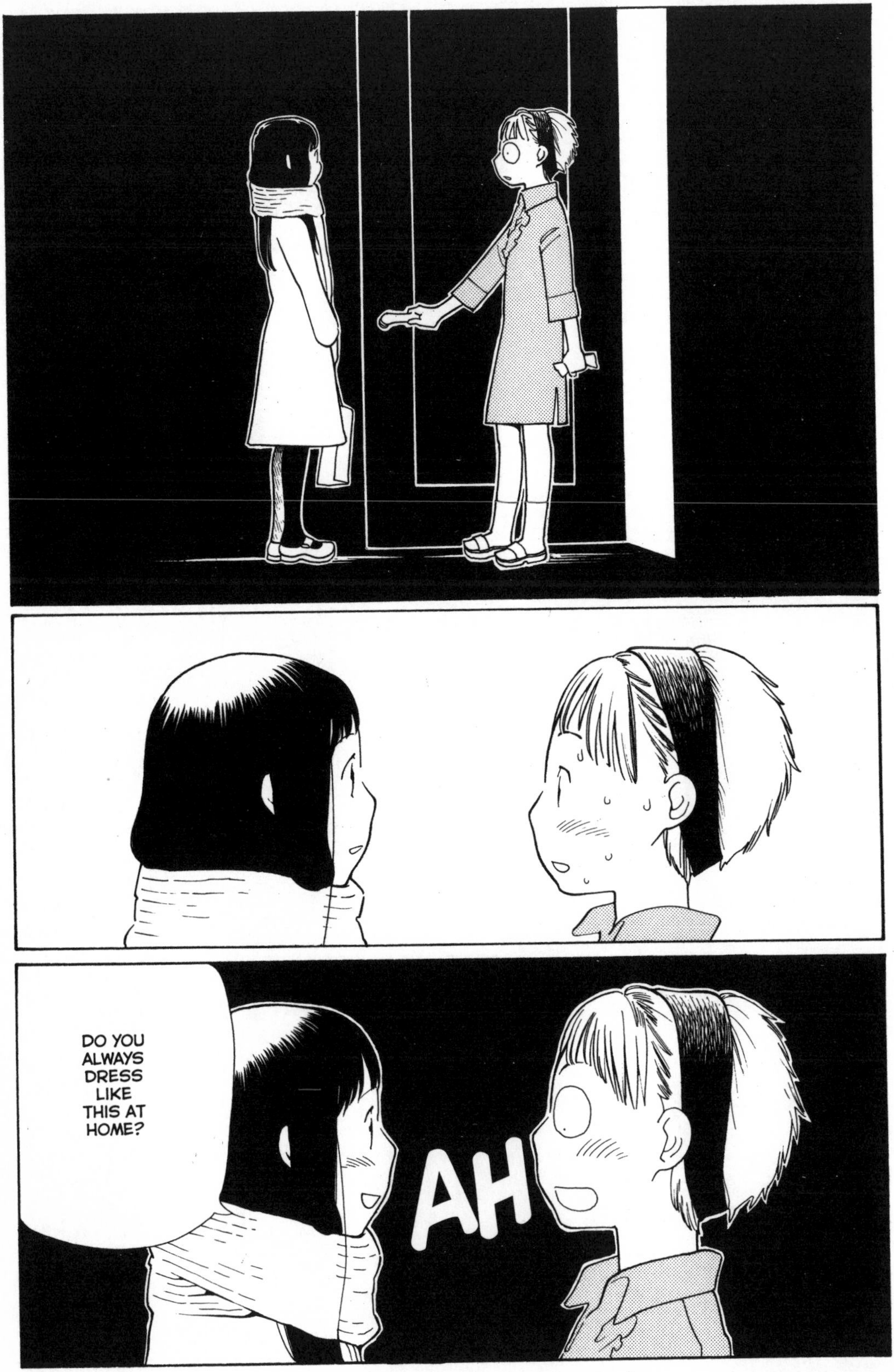
DO YOU ALWAYS DRESS LIKE THIS AT HOME?
AH

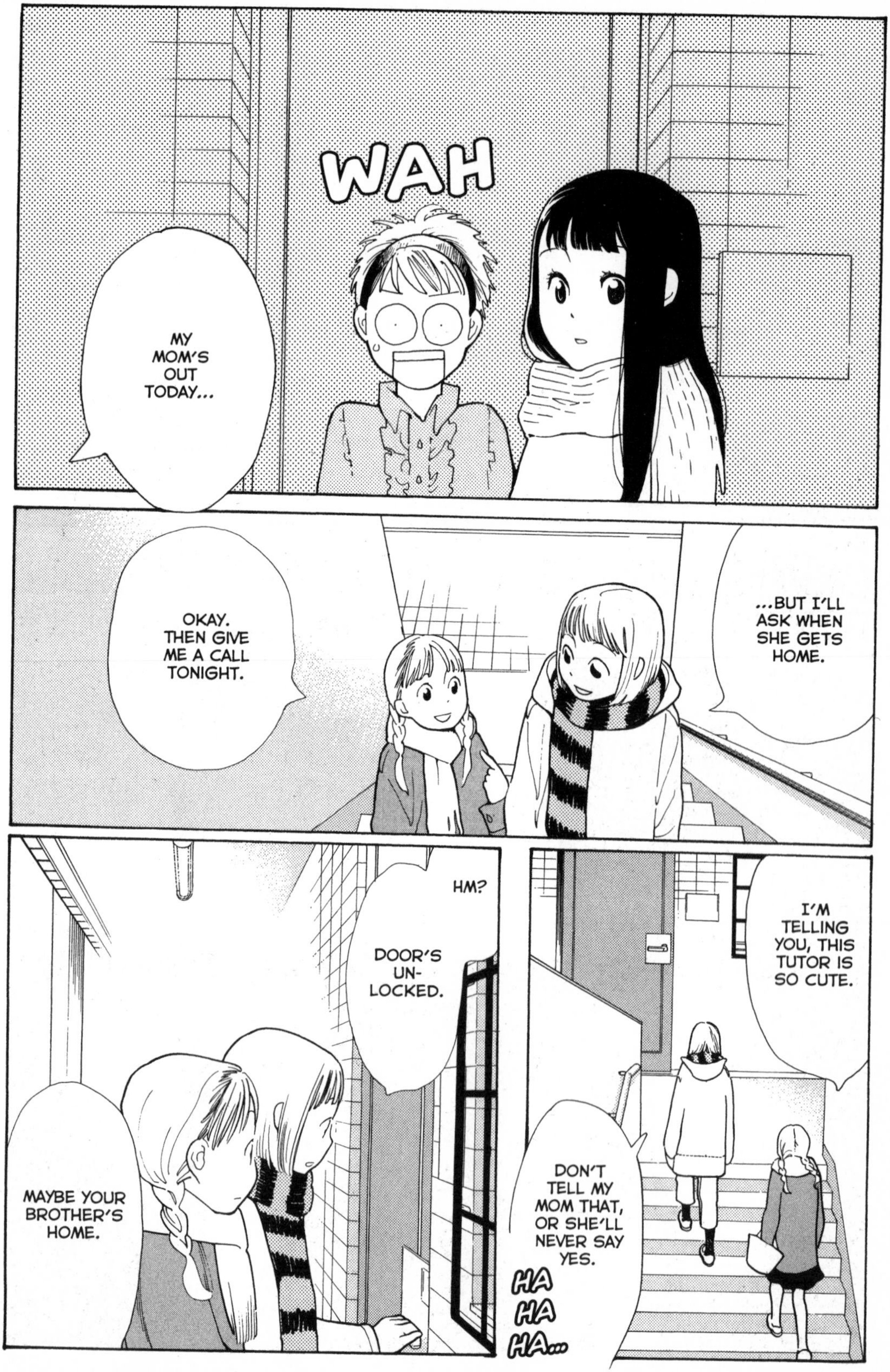
WAH
MY MOM'S OUT TODAY...
...BUT I'LL ASK WHEN SHE GETS HOME.
OKAY. THEN GIVE ME A CALL TONIGHT.
I'M TELLING YOU, THIS TUTOR IS SO CUTE.
DON'T TELL MY MOM THAT, OR SHE'LL NEVER SAY YES.
HA HA HA...
HM?
DOOR'S UN-LOCKED.
MAYBE YOUR BROTHER'S HOME.

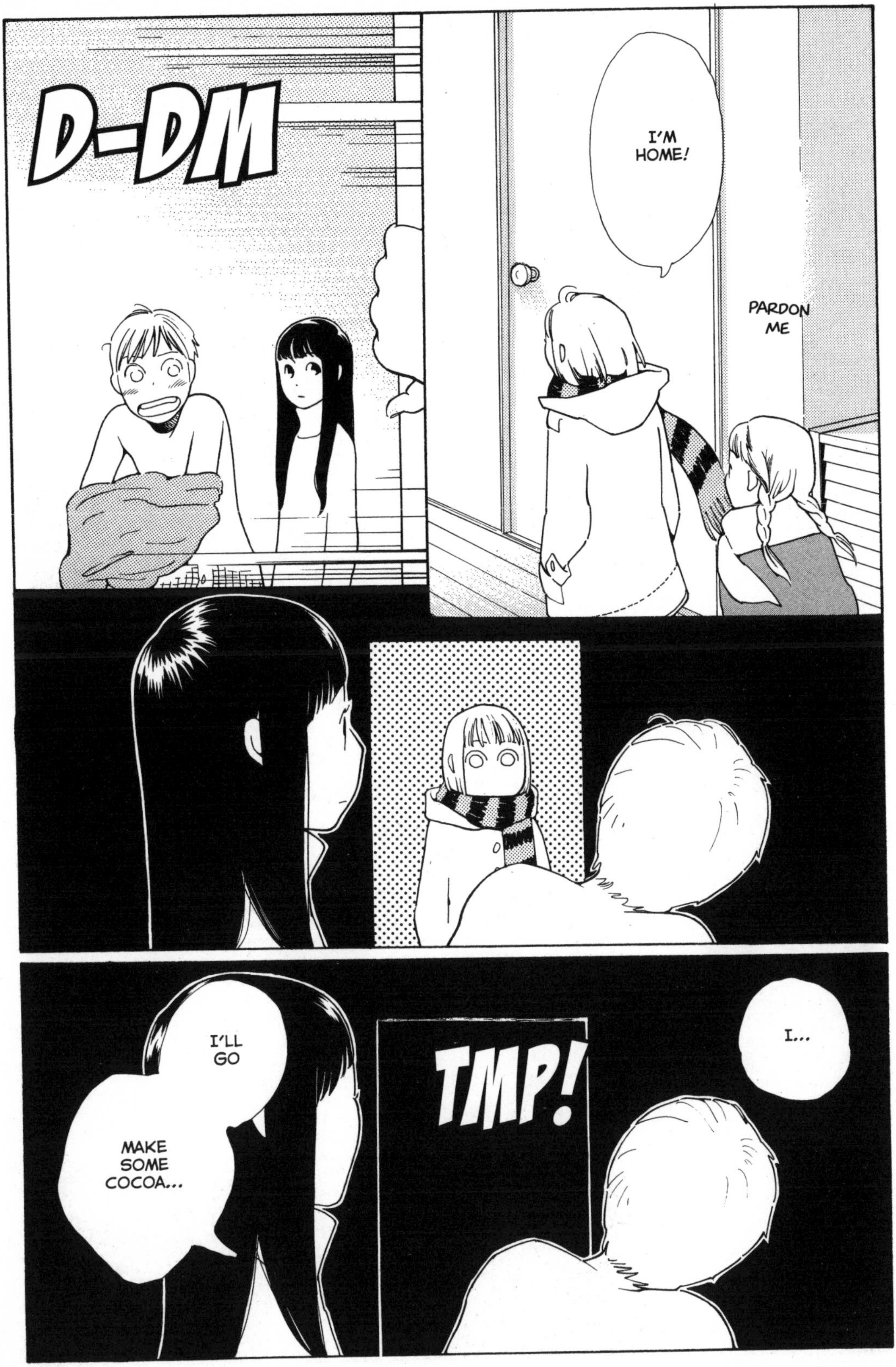
I'M HOME!
PARDON ME
D-DM
I...
TMP!
I'LL GO
MAKE SOME COCOA...

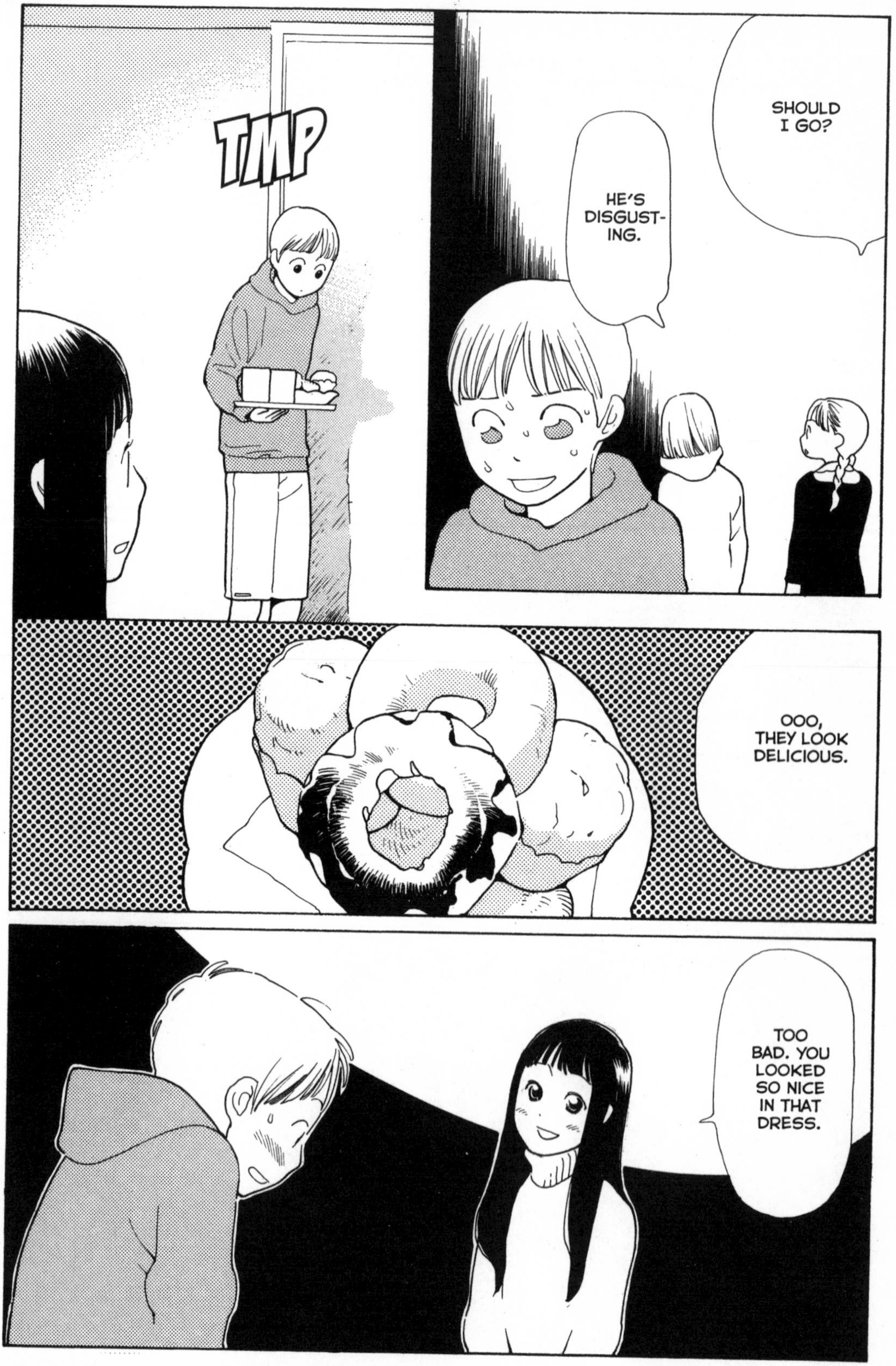
SHOULD I GO?
HE'S DISGUST-ING.
TMP
OOO, THEY LOOK DELICIOUS.
TOO BAD. YOU LOOKED SO NICE IN THAT DRESS.

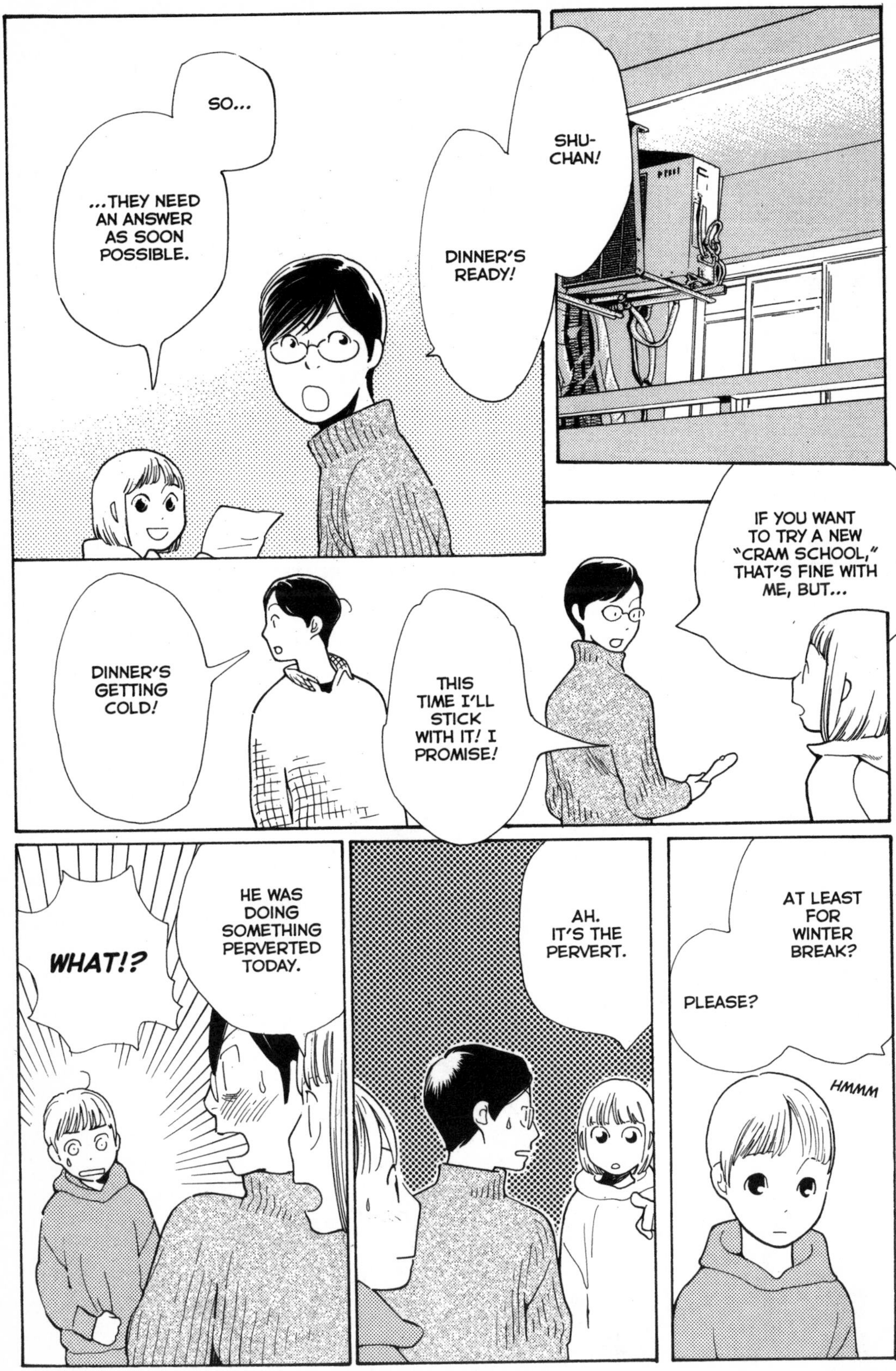
SHU-CHAN!
DINNER'S READY!
SO...
...THEY NEED AN ANSWER AS SOON POSSIBLE.
IF YOU WANT TO TRY A NEW "CRAM SCHOOL," THAT'S FINE WITH ME, BUT...
THIS TIME I'LL STICK WITH IT! I PROMISE!
DINNER'S GETTING COLD!
AT LEAST FOR WINTER BREAK?
PLEASE?
HMMM
AH. IT'S THE PERVERT.
HE WAS DOING SOMETHING PERVERTED TODAY.
WHAT!?

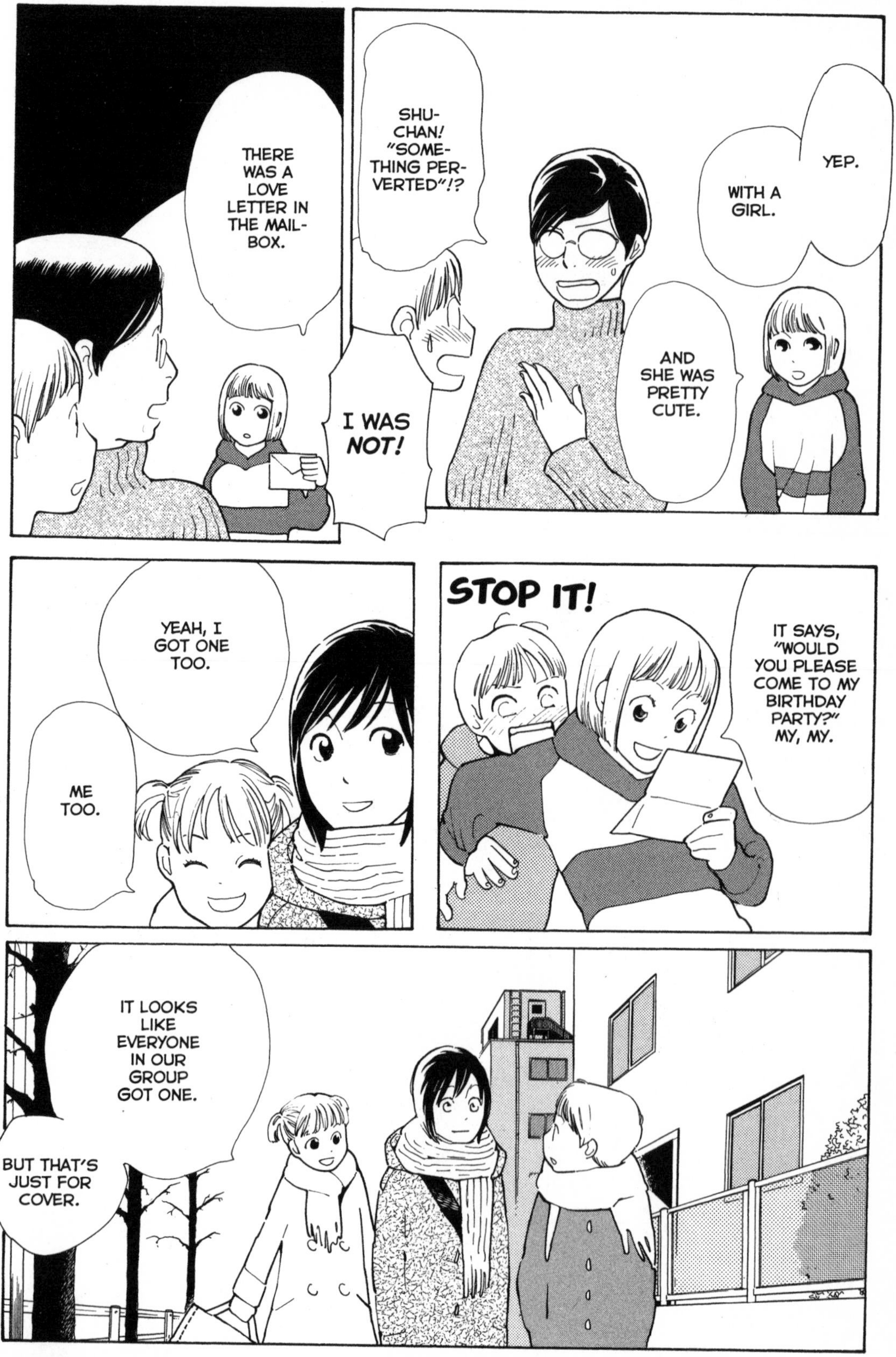
YEP.
WITH A GIRL.
SHU-CHAN! "SOMETHING PERVERTED"!?
AND SHE WAS PRETTY CUTE.
I WAS *NOT!*
THERE WAS A LOVE LETTER IN THE MAILBOX.
IT SAYS, "WOULD YOU PLEASE COME TO MY BIRTHDAY PARTY?" MY, MY.
STOP IT!
YEAH, I GOT ONE TOO.
ME TOO.
IT LOOKS LIKE EVERYONE IN OUR GROUP GOT ONE.
BUT THAT'S JUST FOR COVER.

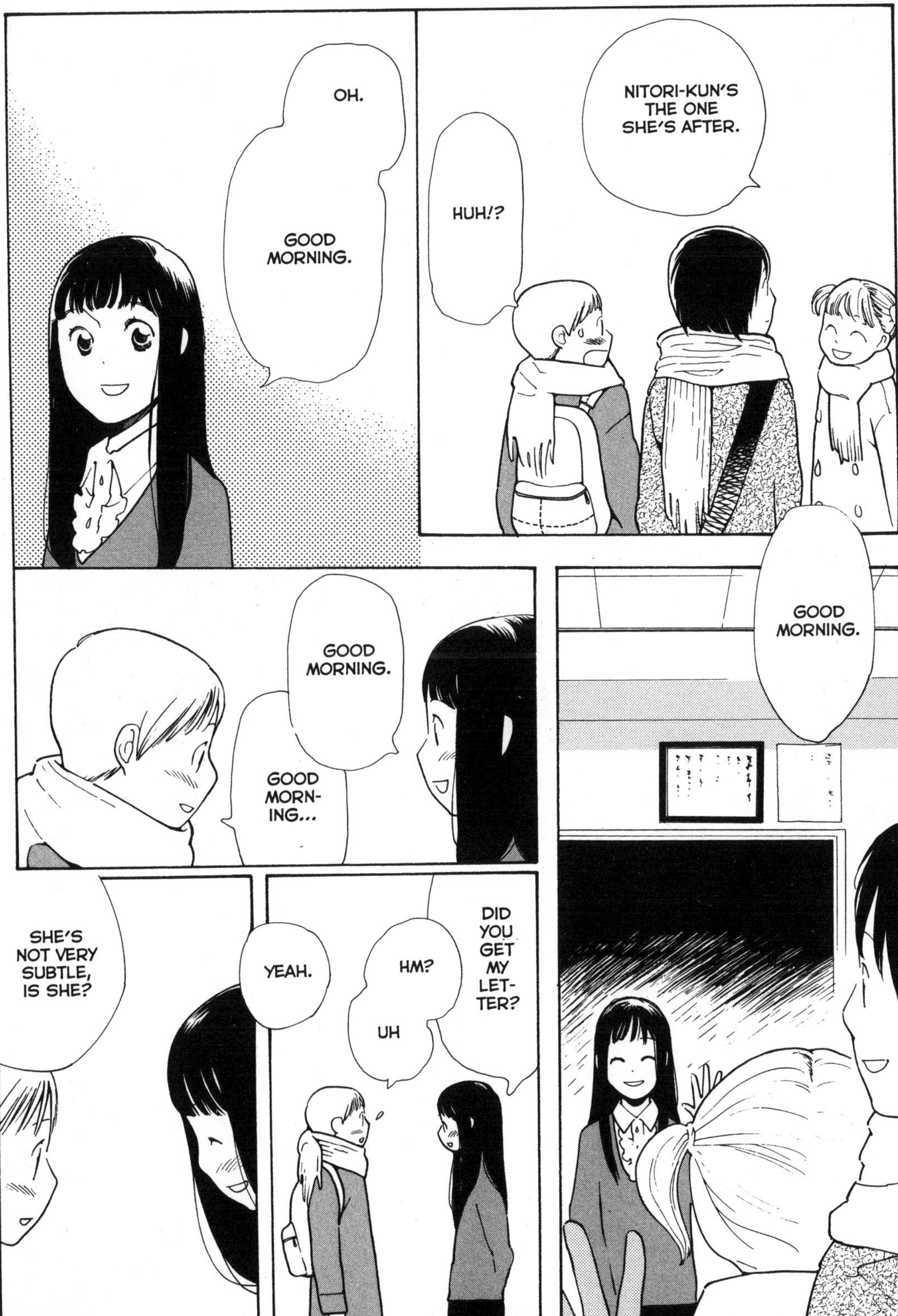
NITORI-KUN'S THE ONE SHE'S AFTER.
HUH!?
OH.
GOOD MORNING.
GOOD MORNING.
GOOD MORNING.
GOOD MORN-ING...
DID YOU GET MY LET-TER?
HM?
UH
YEAH.
SHE'S NOT VERY SUBTLE, IS SHE?

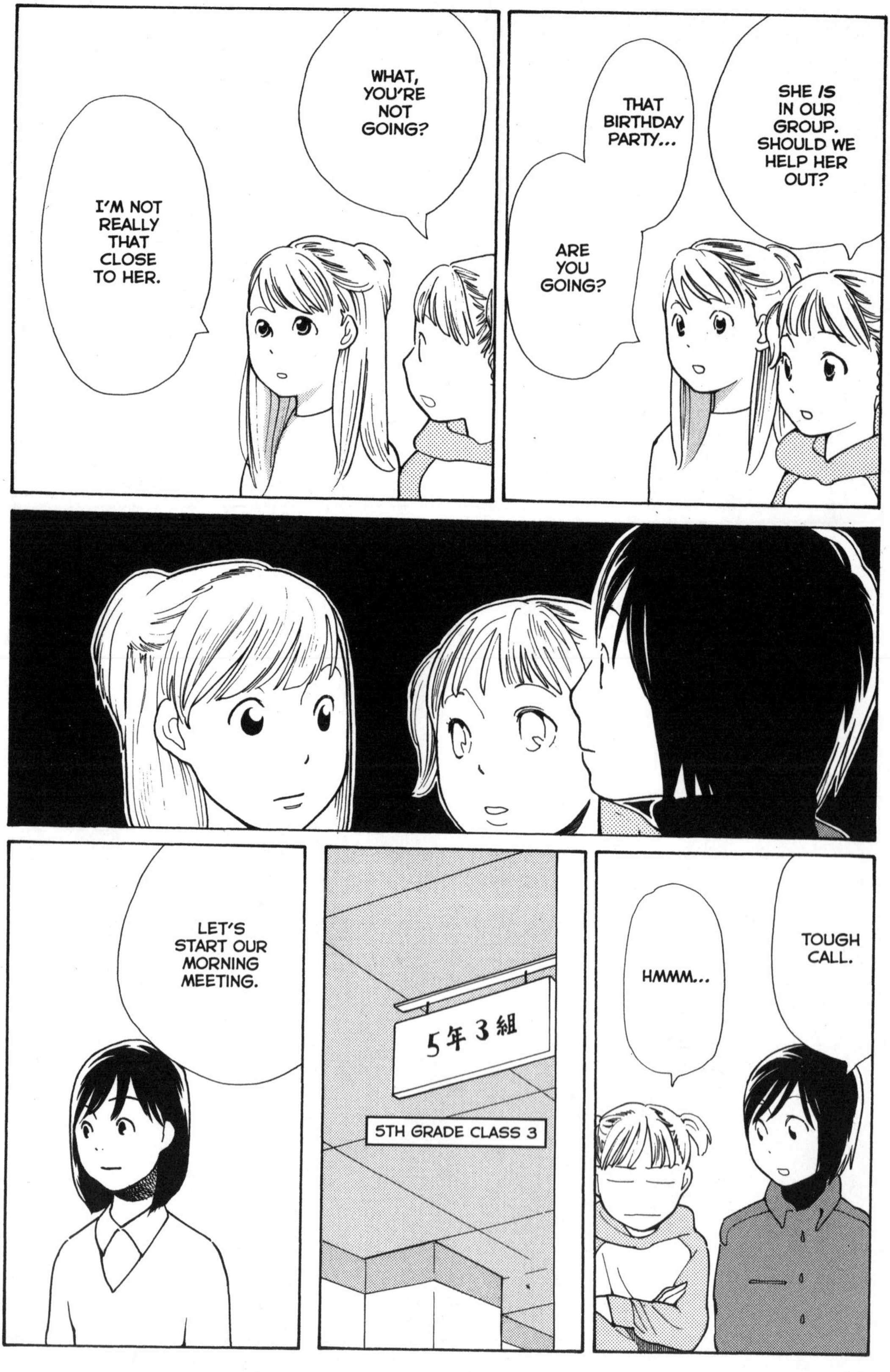
SHE *IS* IN OUR GROUP. SHOULD WE HELP HER OUT?
THAT BIRTHDAY PARTY...
ARE YOU GOING?
WHAT, YOU'RE NOT GOING?
I'M NOT REALLY THAT CLOSE TO HER.
TOUGH CALL.
HMMM...
5年3組
5TH GRADE CLASS 3
LET'S START OUR MORNING MEETING.

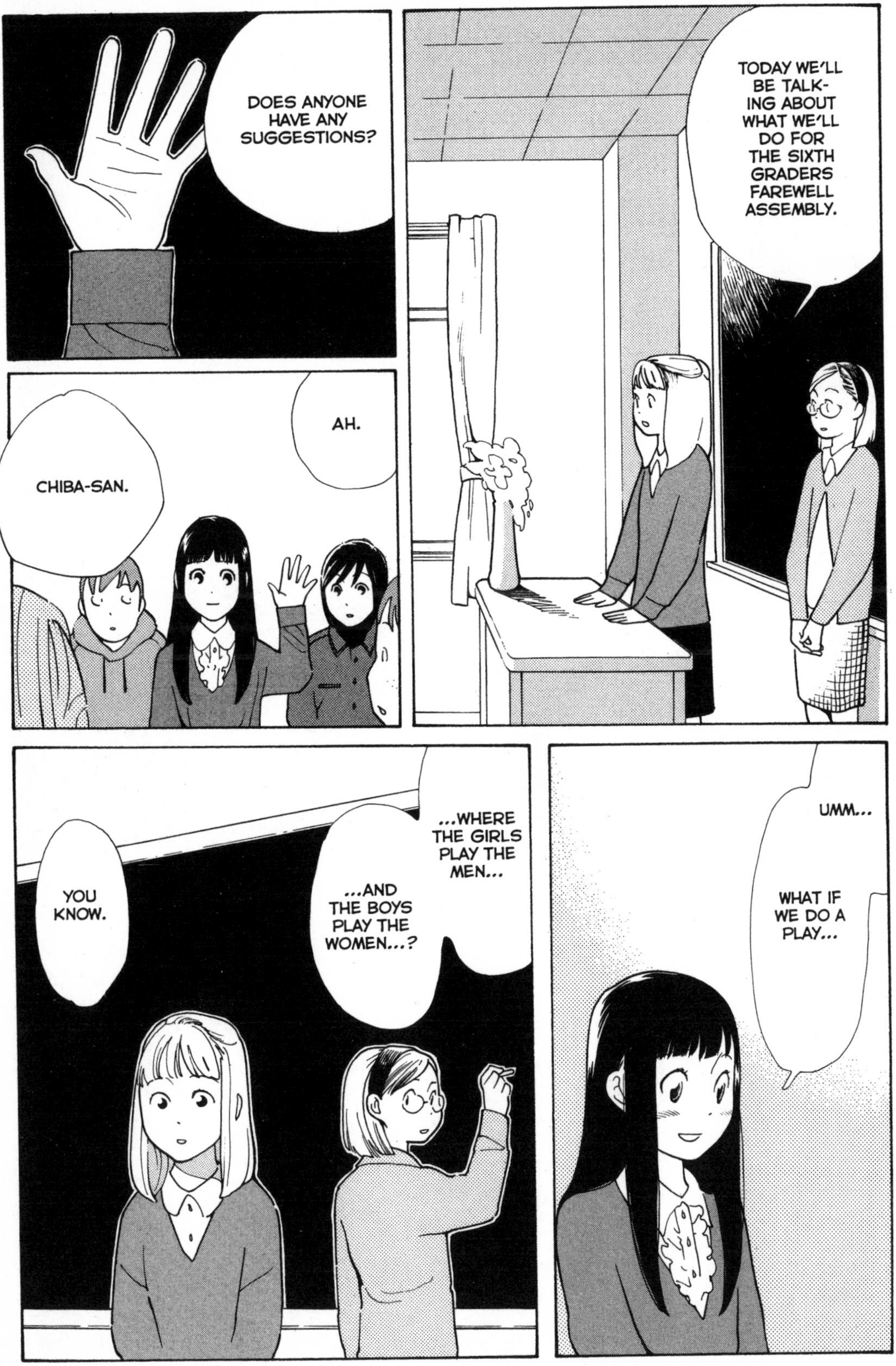
TODAY WE'LL BE TALK-ING ABOUT WHAT WE'LL DO FOR THE SIXTH GRADERS FAREWELL ASSEMBLY.
DOES ANYONE HAVE ANY SUGGESTIONS?
AH.
CHIBA-SAN.
UMM...
WHAT IF WE DO A PLAY...
...WHERE THE GIRLS PLAY THE MEN...
...AND THE BOYS PLAY THE WOMEN...?
YOU KNOW.

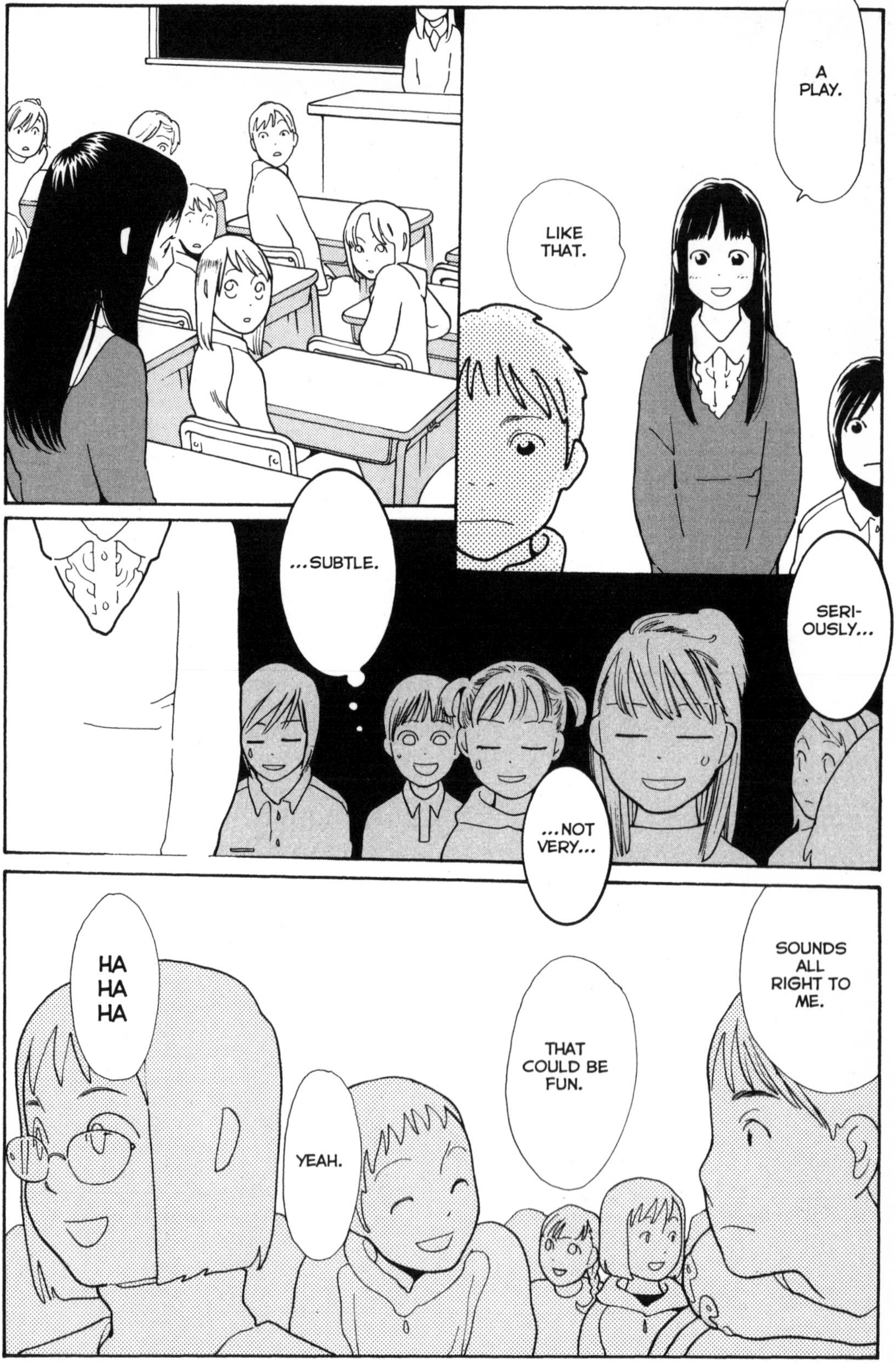
A PLAY.
LIKE THAT.
SERI-OUSLY...
...NOT VERY...
...SUBTLE.
SOUNDS ALL RIGHT TO ME.
THAT COULD BE FUN.
YEAH.
HA HA HA

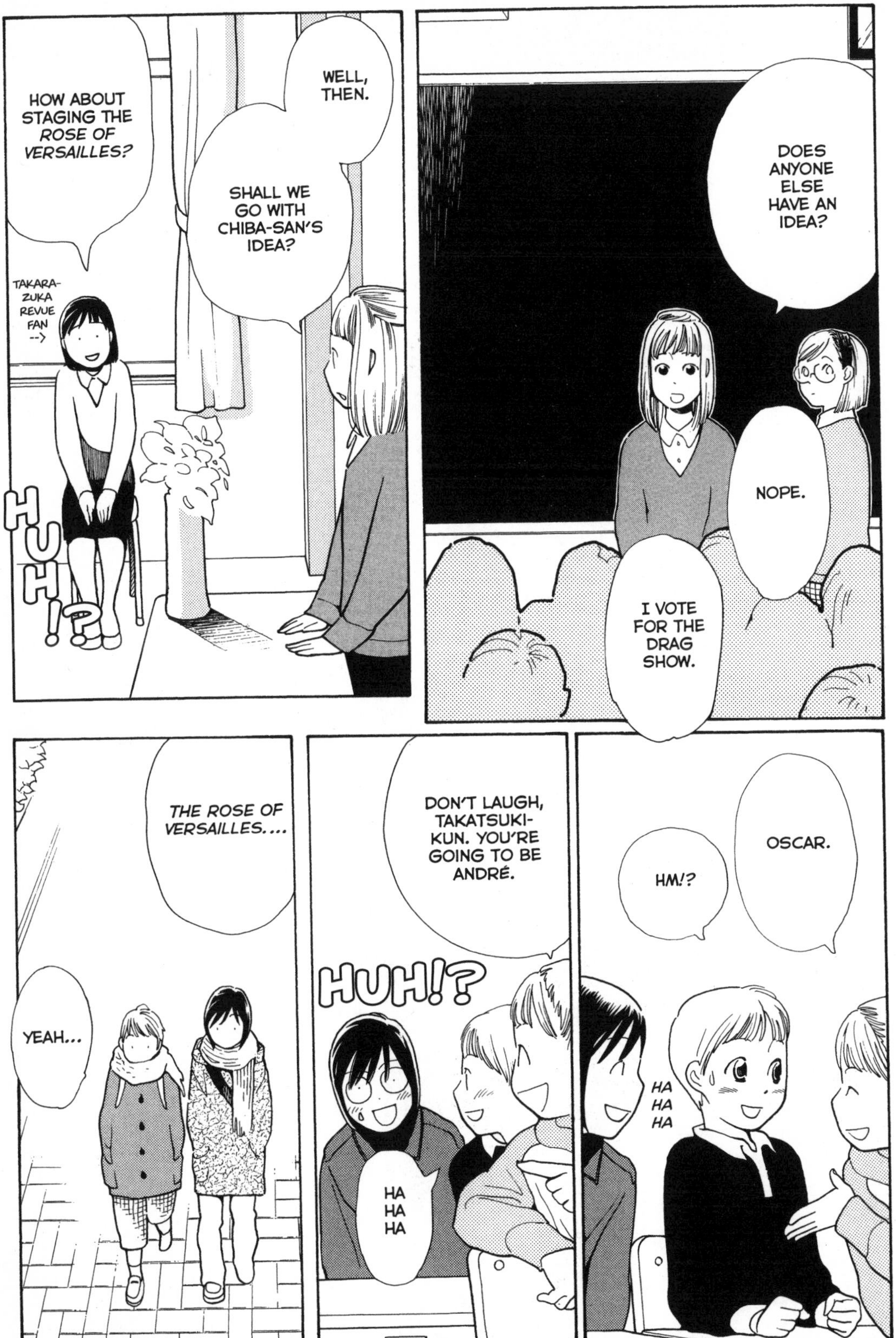
DOES ANYONE ELSE HAVE AN IDEA?
NOPE.
I VOTE FOR THE DRAG SHOW.
WELL, THEN.
SHALL WE GO WITH CHIBA-SAN'S IDEA?
HOW ABOUT STAGING THE *ROSE OF VERSAILLES?*
TAKARA-ZUKA REVUE FAN -->
HUH!?
OSCAR.
HM!?
HA HA HA
DON'T LAUGH, TAKATSUKI-KUN. YOU'RE GOING TO BE ANDRÉ.
HUH!?
HA HA HA
THE ROSE OF VERSAILLES....
YEAH...

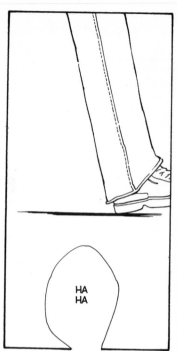

HA
HA

...HA
HA
HA

OR MAY-BE NOT.

I THINK YOU'D ACTUALLY BE BETTER AS MARIE ANTOI-NETTE.

....

BYE-BYE.

SEE YOU.

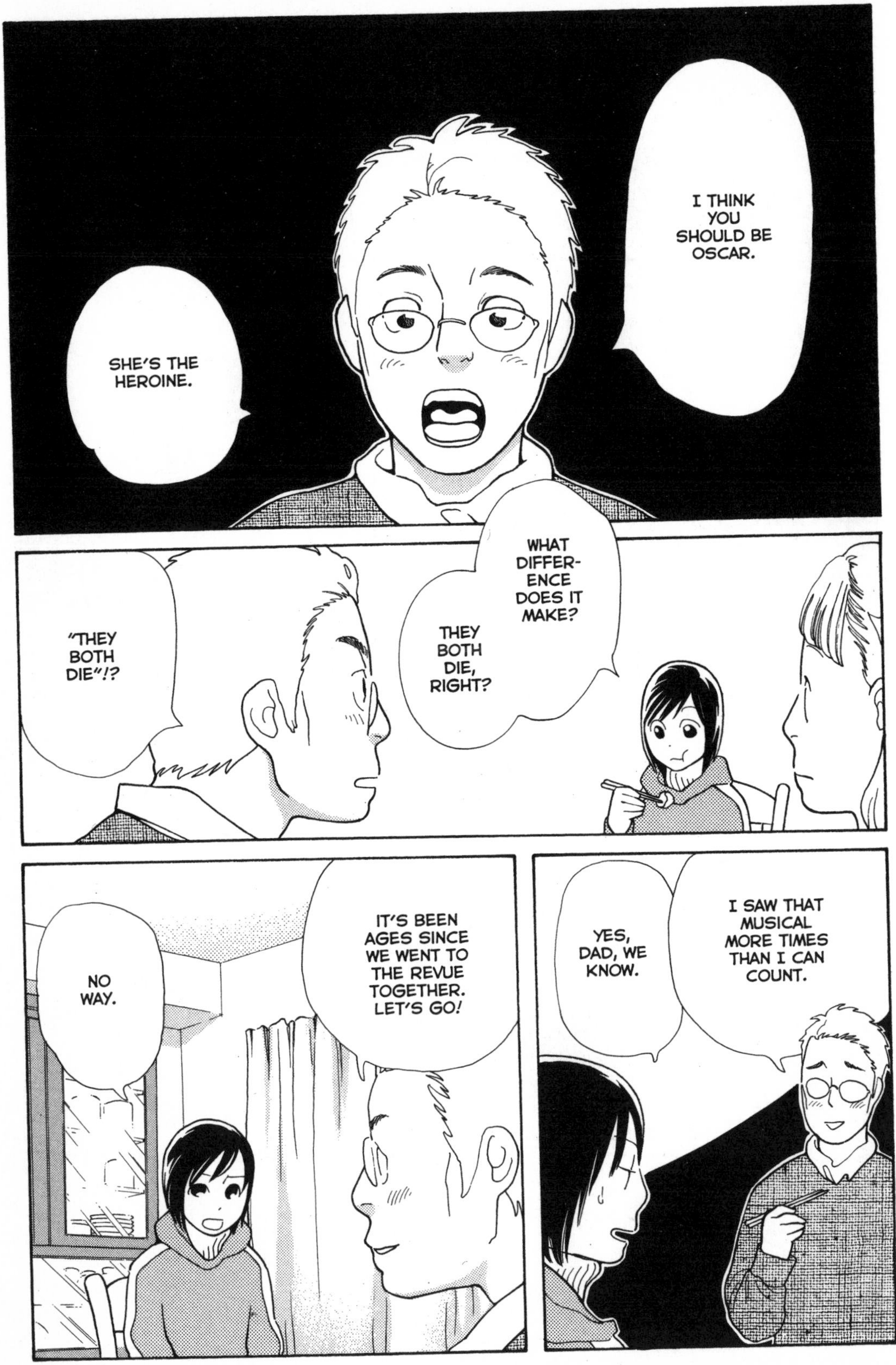
I THINK YOU SHOULD BE OSCAR.
SHE'S THE HEROINE.
WHAT DIFFER-ENCE DOES IT MAKE?
THEY BOTH DIE, RIGHT?
"THEY BOTH DIE"!?
I SAW THAT MUSICAL MORE TIMES THAN I CAN COUNT.
YES, DAD, WE KNOW.
IT'S BEEN AGES SINCE WE WENT TO THE REVUE TOGETHER. LET'S GO!
NO WAY.

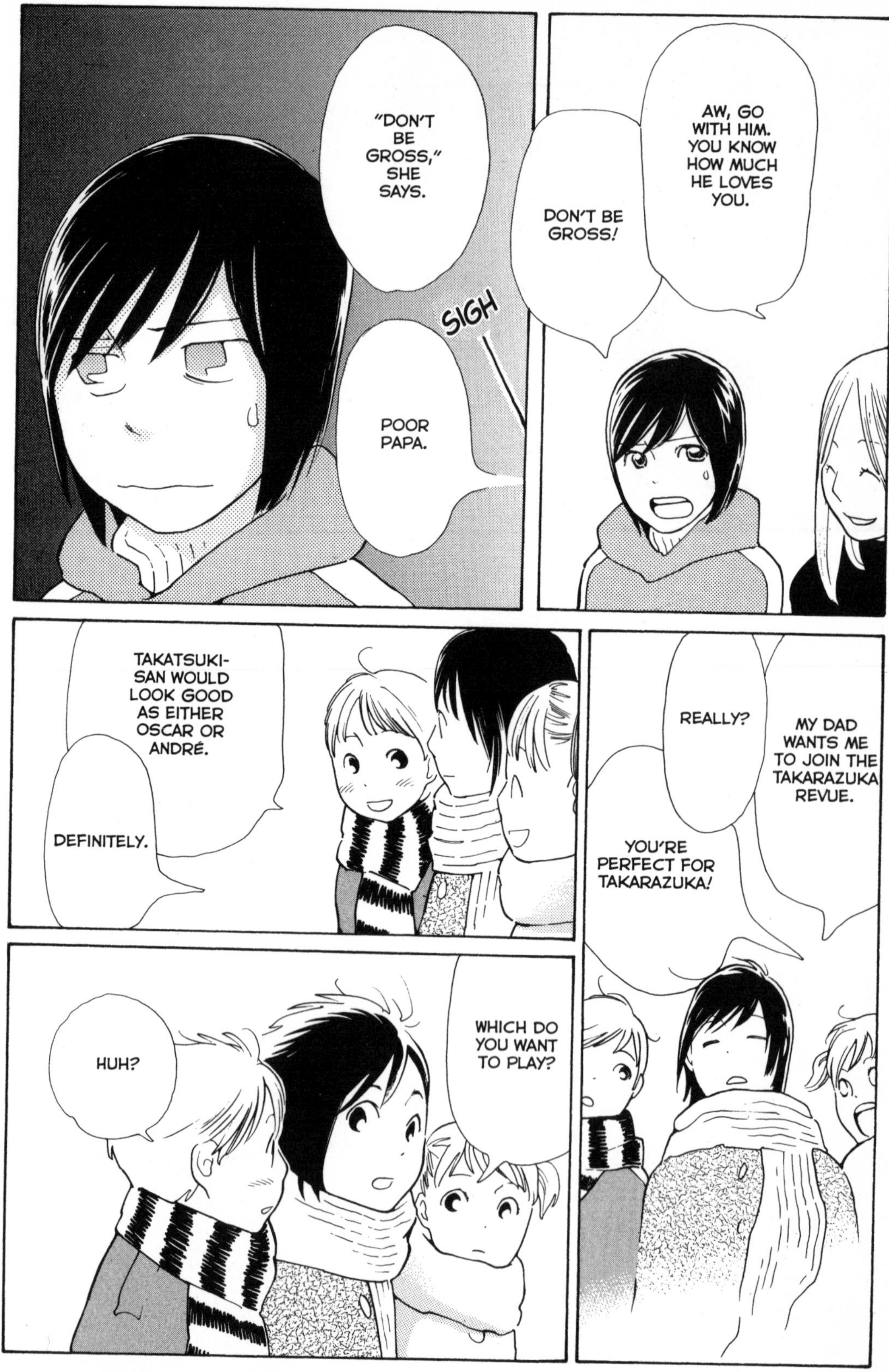
AW, GO WITH HIM. YOU KNOW HOW MUCH HE LOVES YOU.
DON'T BE GROSS!
"DON'T BE GROSS," SHE SAYS.
SIGH
POOR PAPA.
MY DAD WANTS ME TO JOIN THE TAKARAZUKA REVUE.
REALLY?
YOU'RE PERFECT FOR TAKARAZUKA!
TAKATSUKI-SAN WOULD LOOK GOOD AS EITHER OSCAR OR ANDRÉ.
DEFINITELY.
WHICH DO YOU WANT TO PLAY?
HUH?

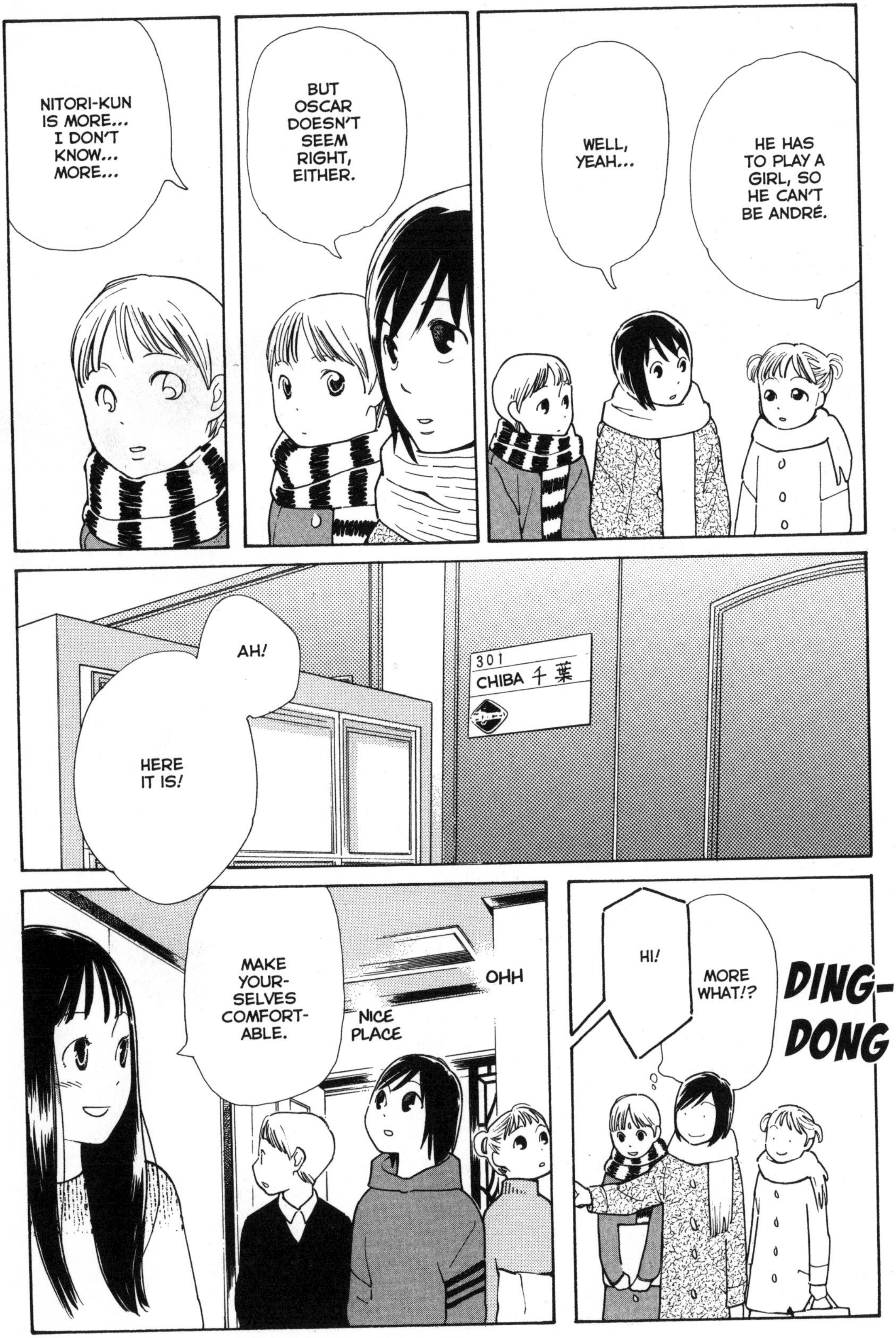
HE HAS TO PLAY A GIRL, SO HE CAN'T BE ANDRÉ.
WELL, YEAH...
BUT OSCAR DOESN'T SEEM RIGHT, EITHER.
NITORI-KUN IS MORE... I DON'T KNOW... MORE...
301
CHIBA 千葉
AH!
HERE IT IS!
DING-DONG
MORE WHAT!?
HI!
OHH
NICE PLACE
MAKE YOUR-SELVES COMFORT-ABLE.

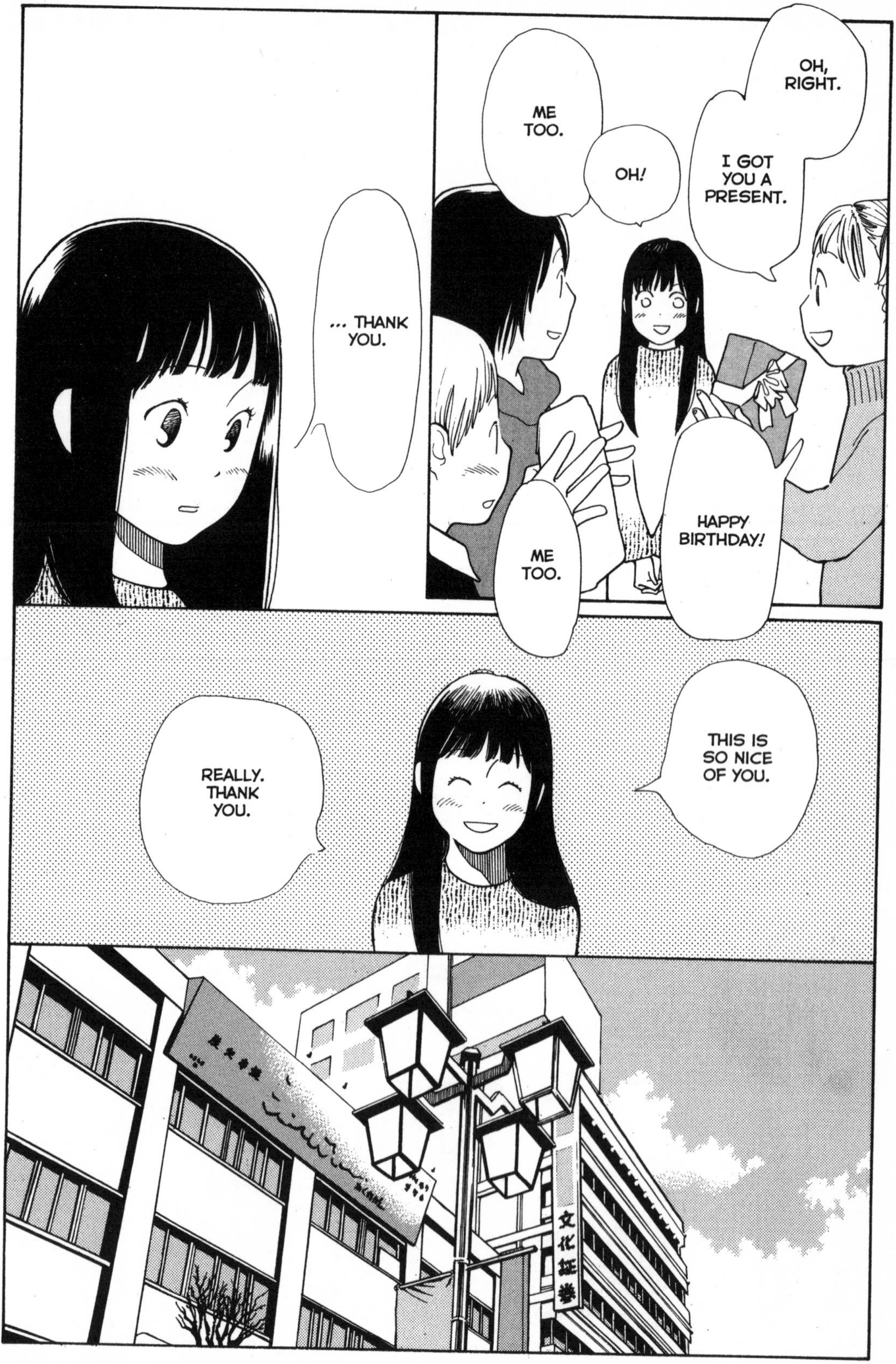
OH, RIGHT.
I GOT YOU A PRESENT.
OH!
ME TOO.
HAPPY BIRTHDAY!
ME TOO.
... THANK YOU.
THIS IS SO NICE OF YOU.
REALLY. THANK YOU.
文化証券

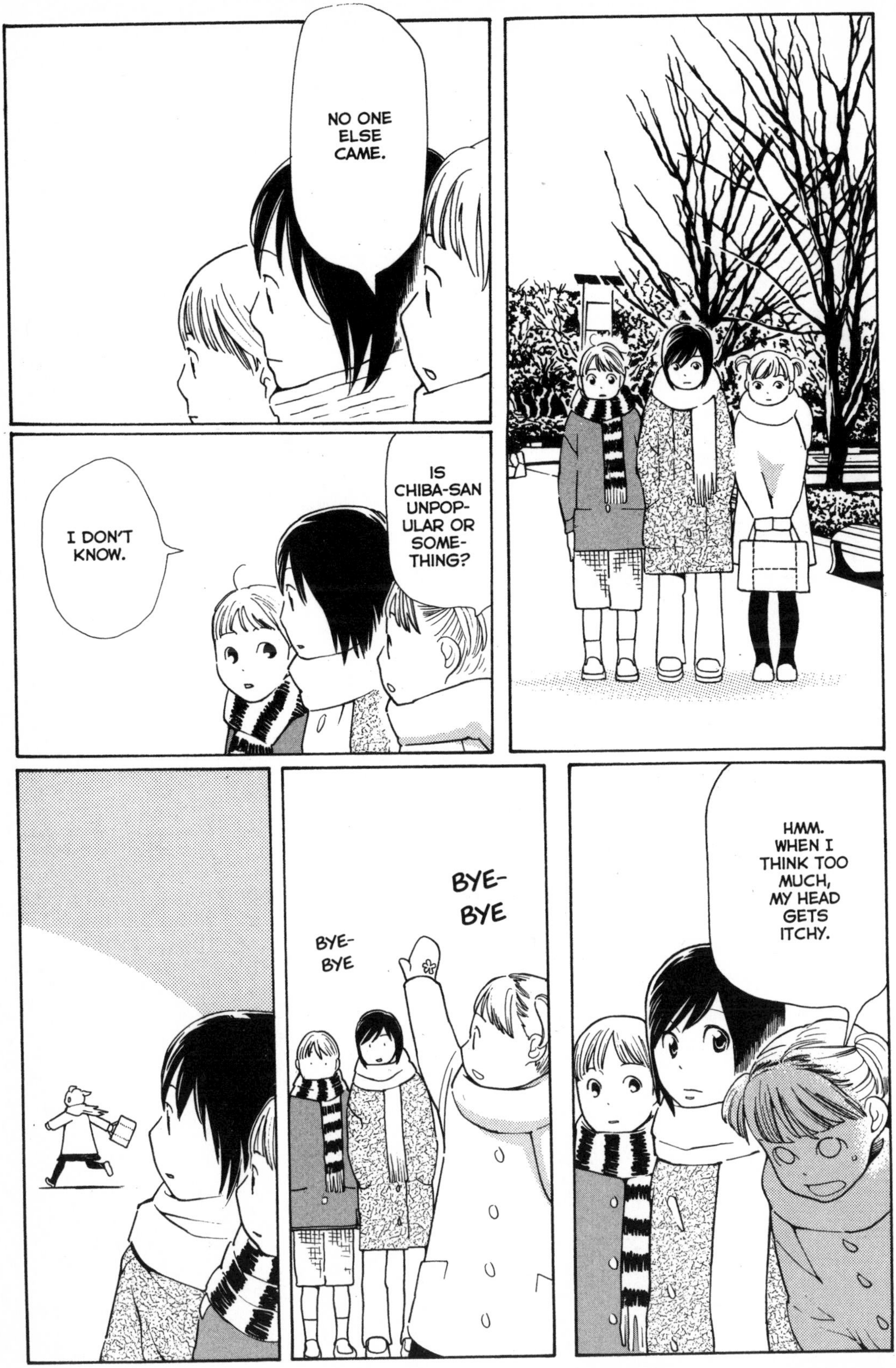
NO ONE ELSE CAME.
IS CHIBA-SAN UNPOPULAR OR SOMETHING?
I DON'T KNOW.
HMM. WHEN I THINK TOO MUCH, MY HEAD GETS ITCHY.
BYE-BYE
BYE-BYE

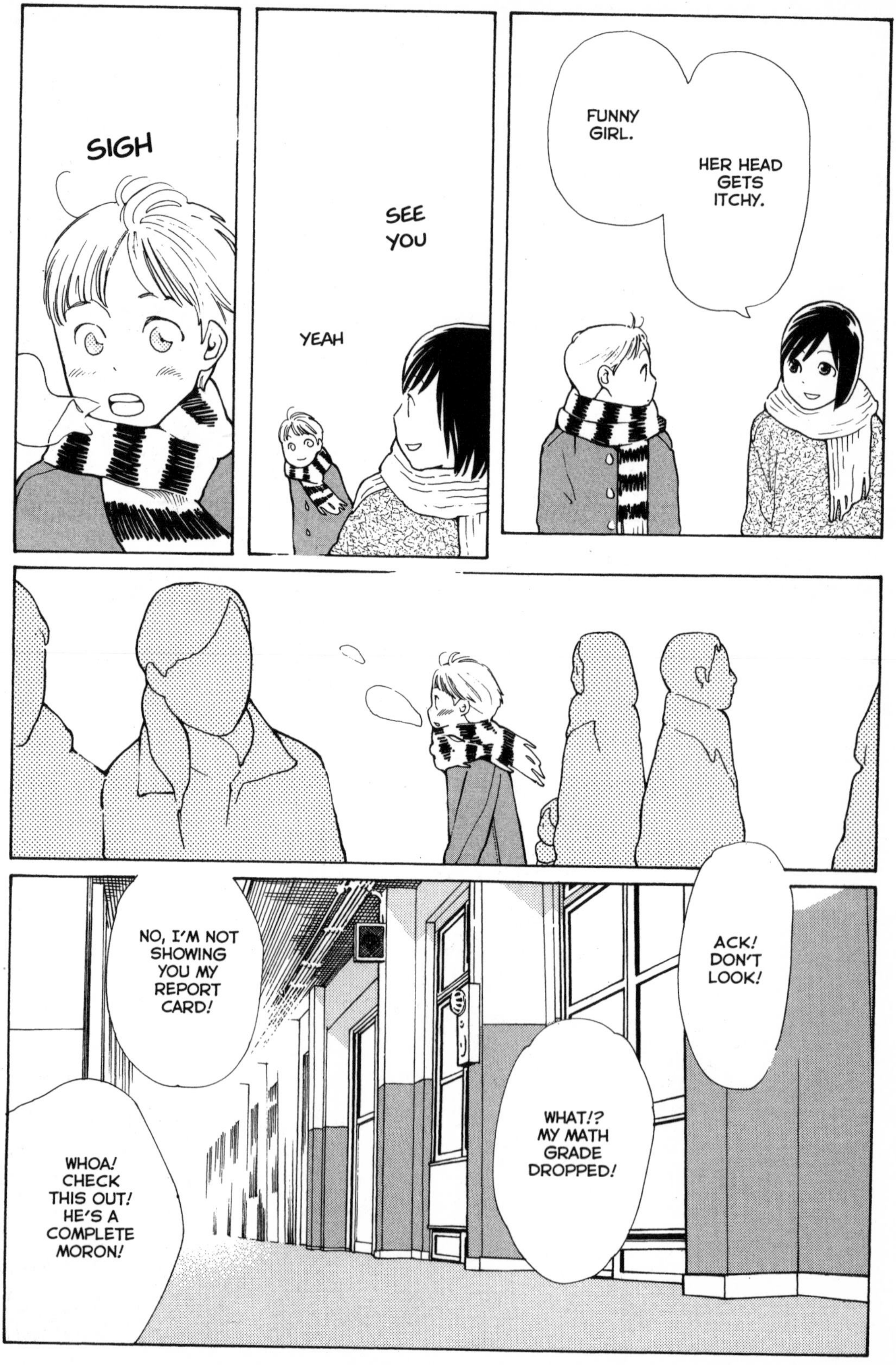
FUNNY GIRL.
HER HEAD GETS ITCHY.
SEE YOU
YEAH
SIGH
ACK! DON'T LOOK!
NO, I'M NOT SHOWING YOU MY REPORT CARD!
WHAT!? MY MATH GRADE DROPPED!
WHOA! CHECK THIS OUT! HE'S A COMPLETE MORON!

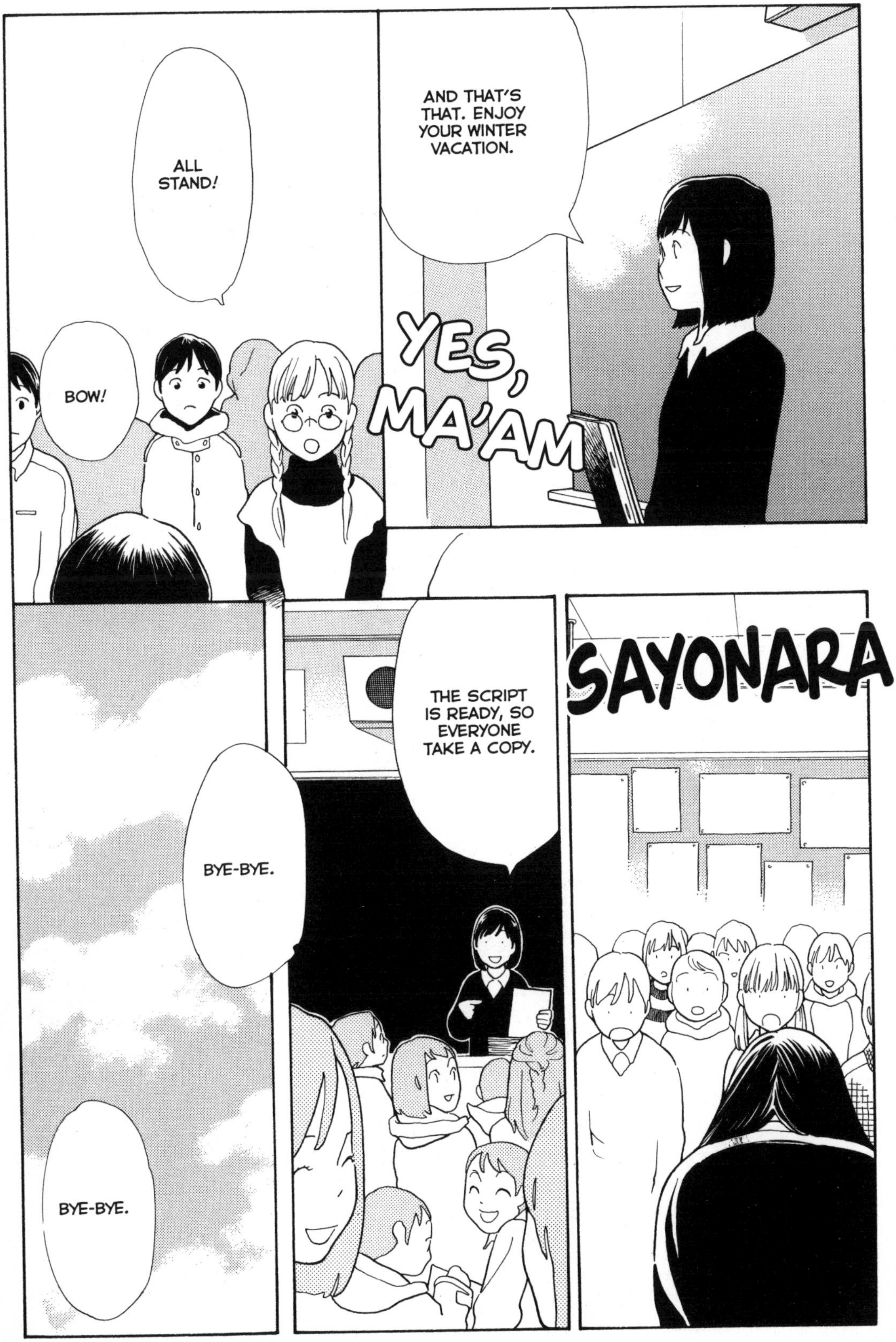
AND THAT'S THAT. ENJOY YOUR WINTER VACATION.
YES, MA'AM
ALL STAND!
BOW!
SAYONARA
THE SCRIPT IS READY, SO EVERYONE TAKE A COPY.
BYE-BYE.
BYE-BYE.

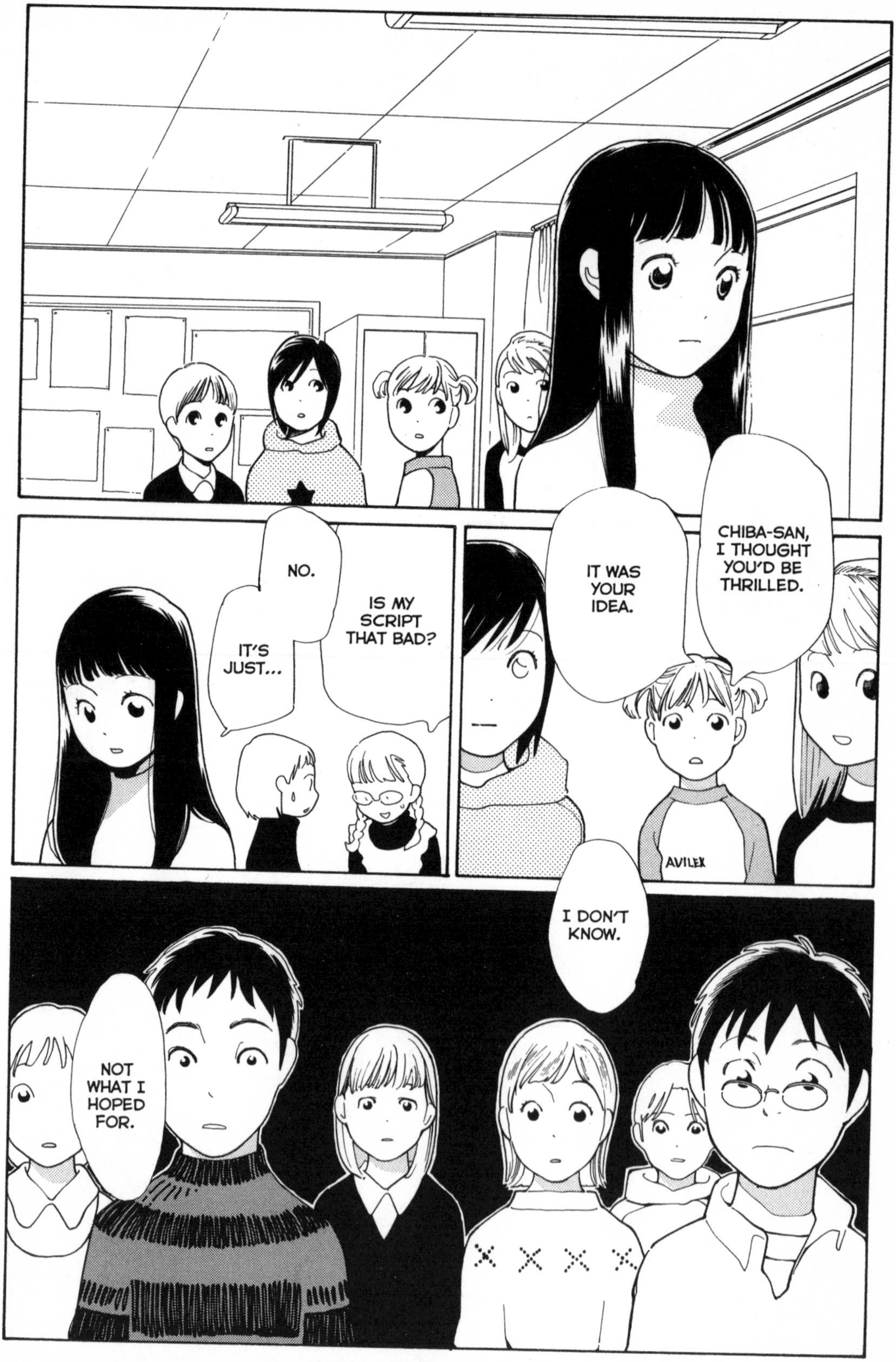
CHIBA-SAN, I THOUGHT YOU'D BE THRILLED.
IT WAS YOUR IDEA.
IS MY SCRIPT THAT BAD?
NO.
IT'S JUST...
I DON'T KNOW.
NOT WHAT I HOPED FOR.
AVILEX

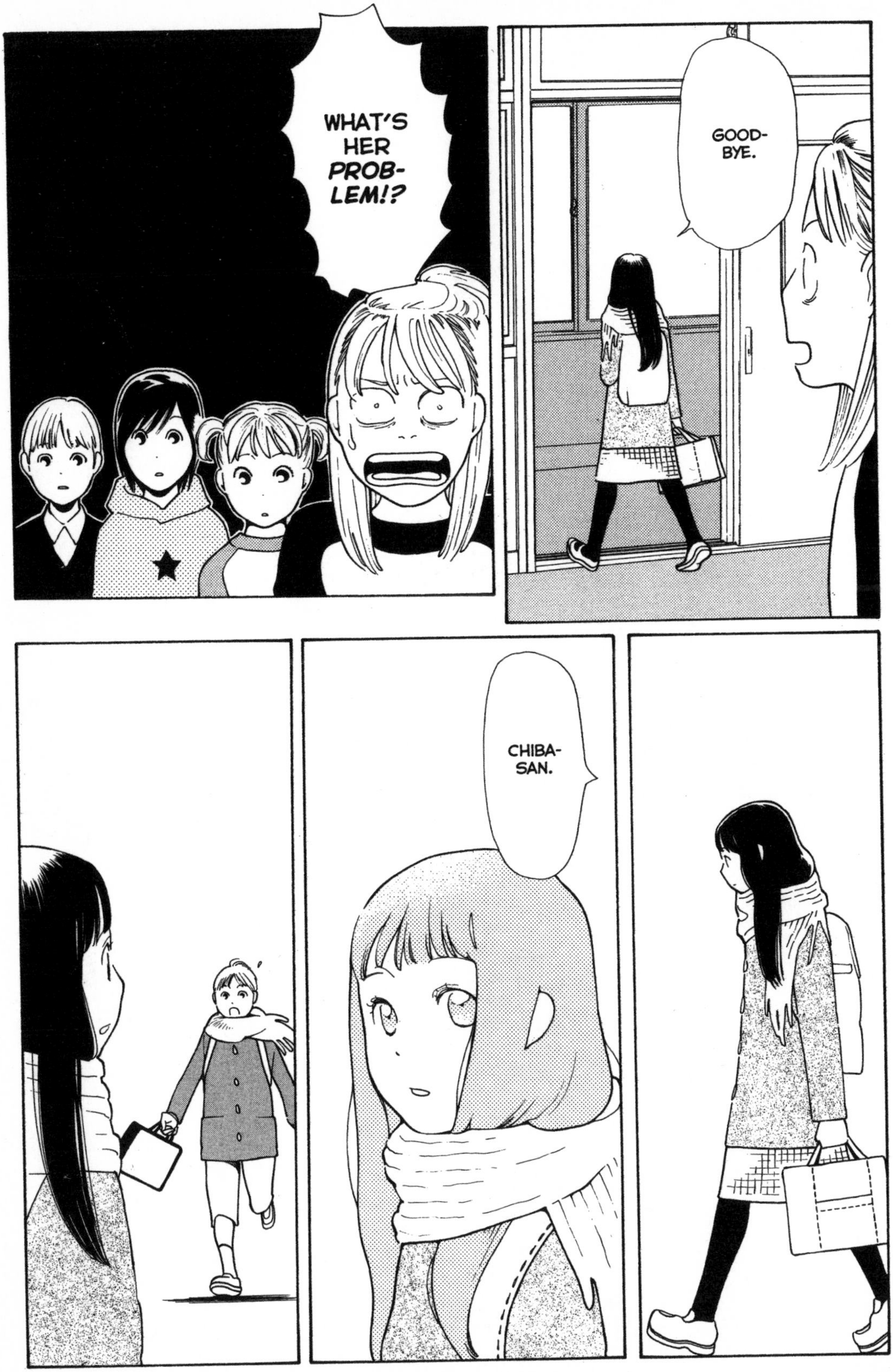
GOOD-BYE.
WHAT'S HER PROBLEM!?
CHIBA-SAN.

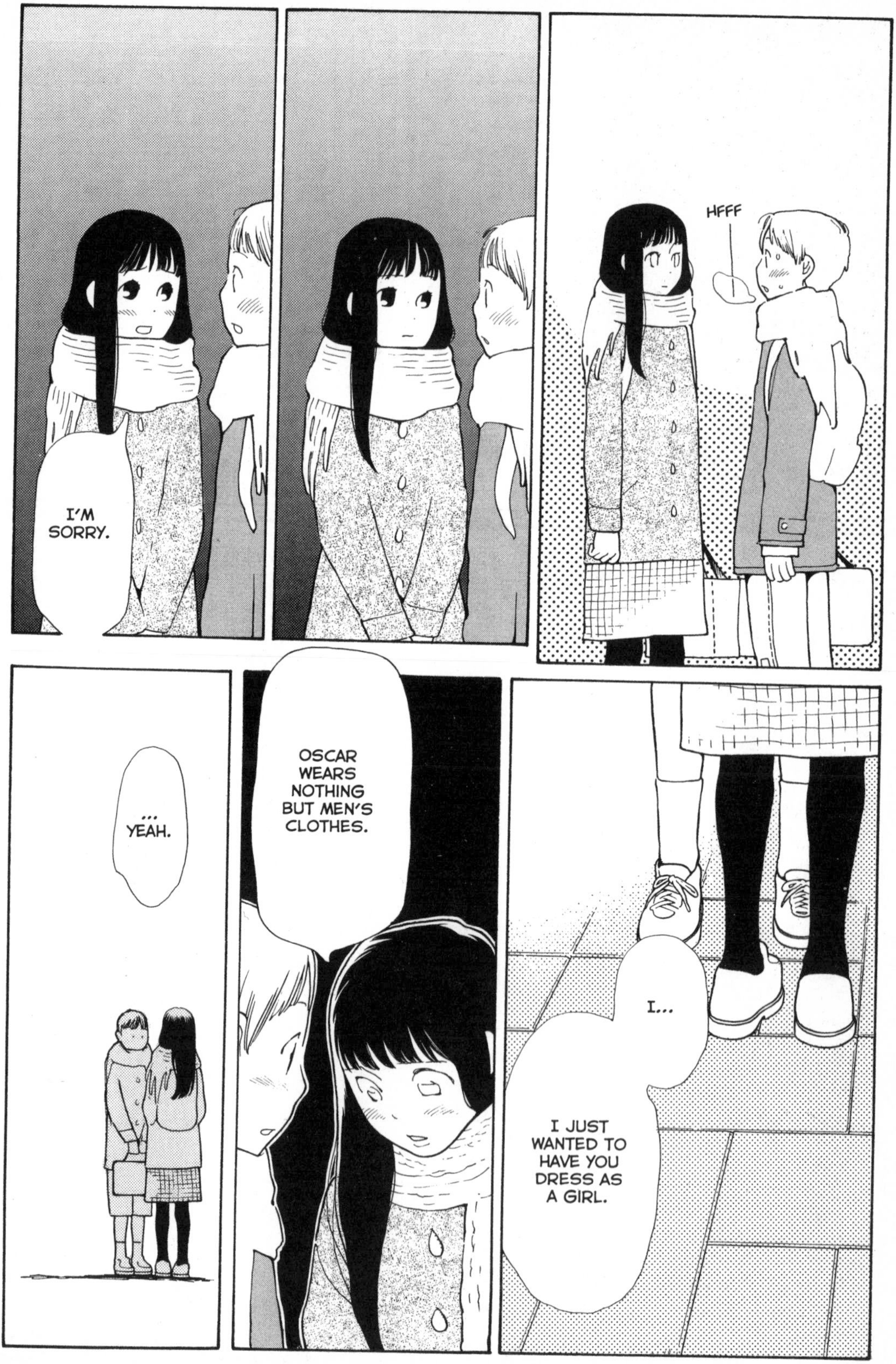
HFFF
I'M SORRY.
I...
I JUST WANTED TO HAVE YOU DRESS AS A GIRL.
OSCAR WEARS NOTHING BUT MEN'S CLOTHES.
... YEAH.

4

Wandering Daughter

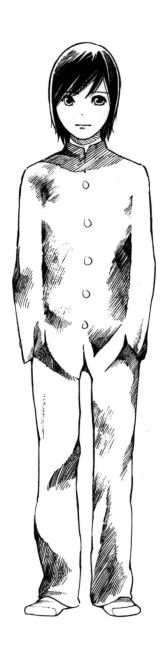

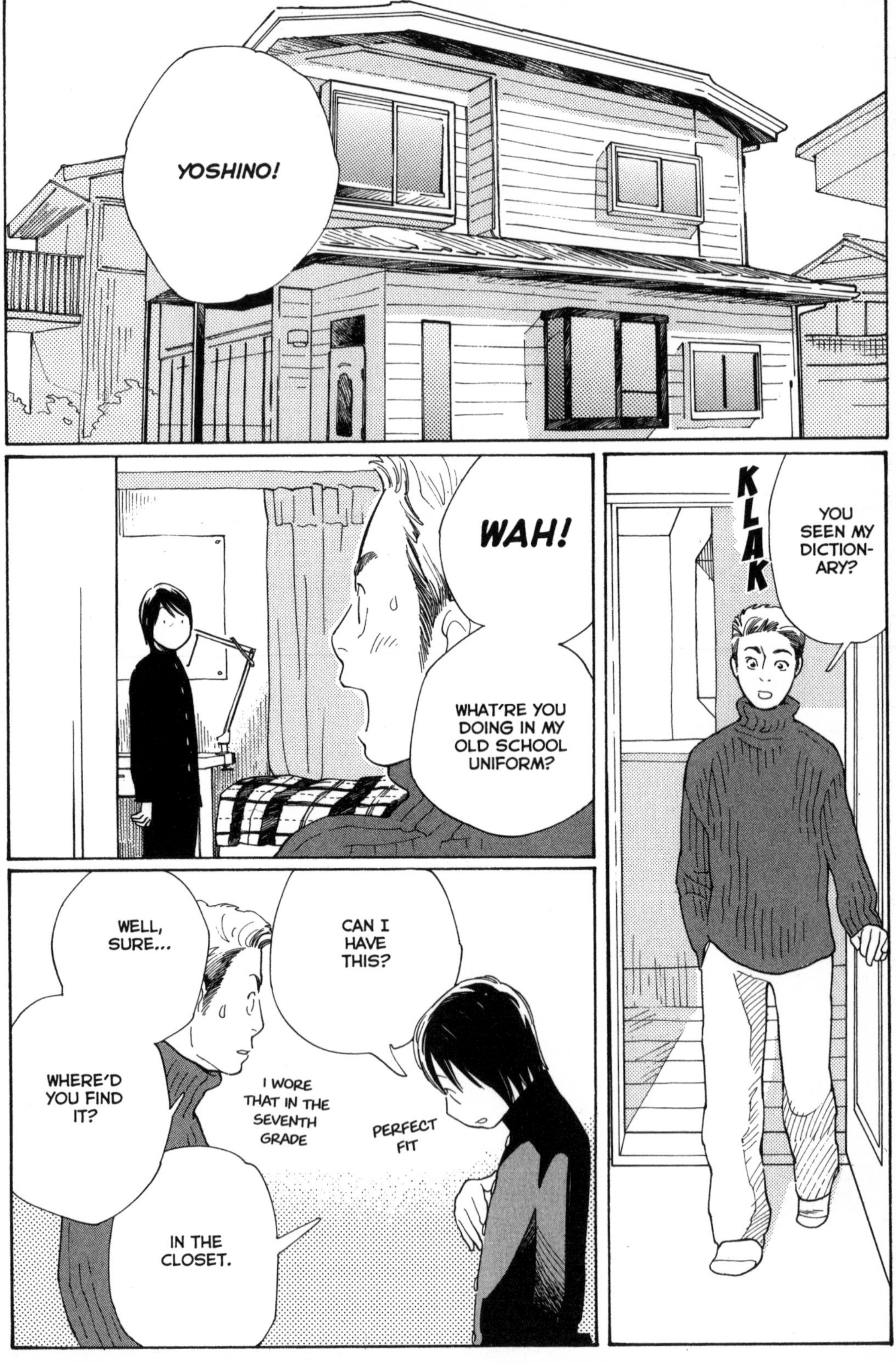

YOSHINO!
KLAK
YOU SEEN MY DICTIONARY?
WAH!
WHAT'RE YOU DOING IN MY OLD SCHOOL UNIFORM?
CAN I HAVE THIS?
WELL, SURE...
PERFECT FIT
I WORE THAT IN THE SEVENTH GRADE
WHERE'D YOU FIND IT?
IN THE CLOSET.

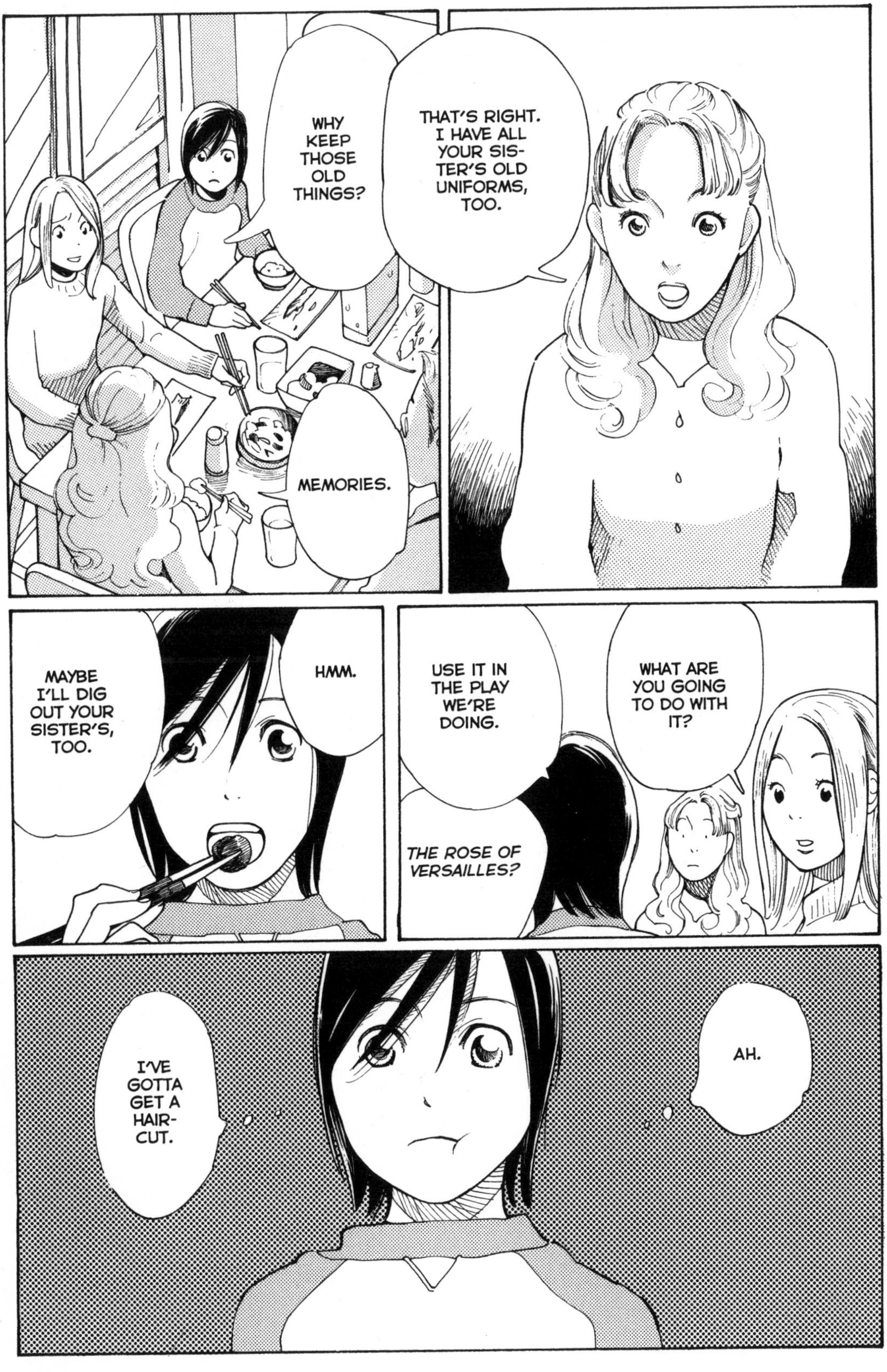
THAT'S RIGHT. I HAVE ALL YOUR SISTER'S OLD UNIFORMS, TOO.
WHY KEEP THOSE OLD THINGS?
MEMORIES.
WHAT ARE YOU GOING TO DO WITH IT?
USE IT IN THE PLAY WE'RE DOING.
THE ROSE OF VERSAILLES?
HMM.
MAYBE I'LL DIG OUT YOUR SISTER'S, TOO.
AH.
I'VE GOTTA GET A HAIR-CUT.

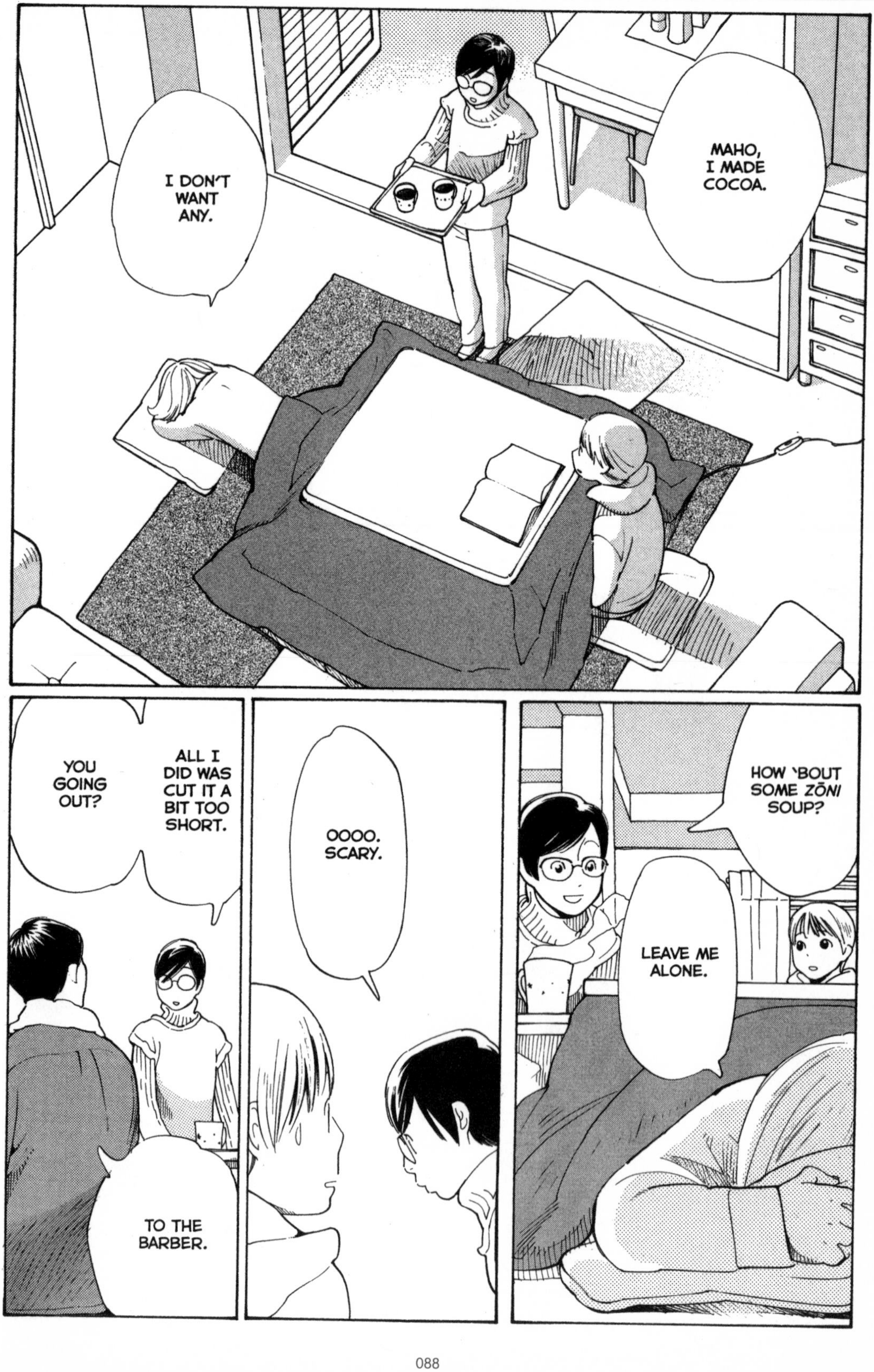
MAHO, I MADE COCOA.
I DON'T WANT ANY.
HOW 'BOUT SOME ZŌNI SOUP?
LEAVE ME ALONE.
OOOO. SCARY.
ALL I DID WAS CUT IT A BIT TOO SHORT.
YOU GOING OUT?
TO THE BARBER.

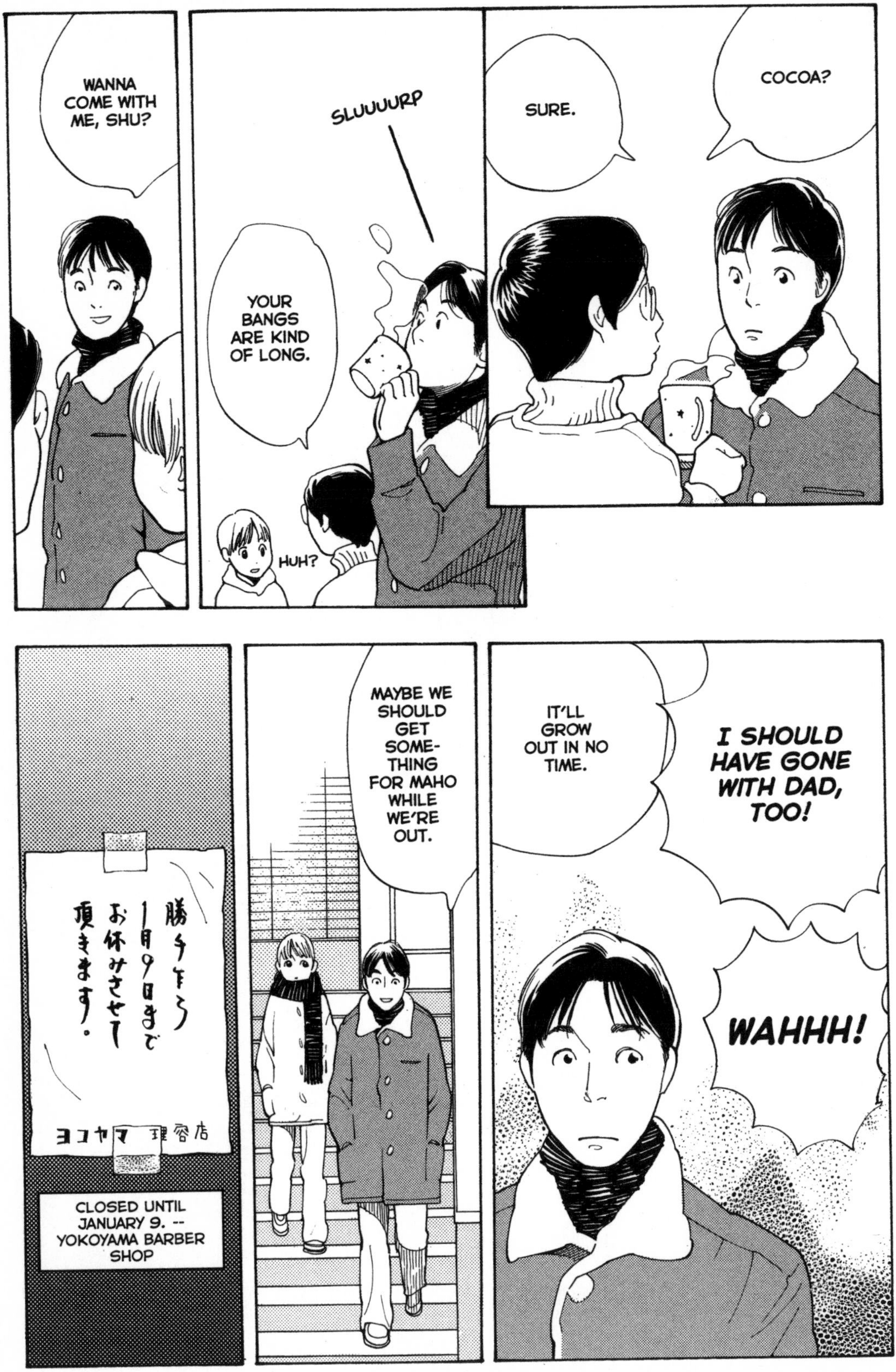
COCOA?
SURE.
SLUUUURP
YOUR BANGS ARE KIND OF LONG.
HUH?
WANNA COME WITH ME, SHU?
IT'LL GROW OUT IN NO TIME.
I SHOULD HAVE GONE WITH DAD, TOO!
WAHHH!
MAYBE WE SHOULD GET SOME-THING FOR MAHO WHILE WE'RE OUT.
勝手ながら 1月9日まで お休みさせて 頂きます。
ヨコヤマ 理容店
CLOSED UNTIL JANUARY 9. -- YOKOYAMA BARBER SHOP

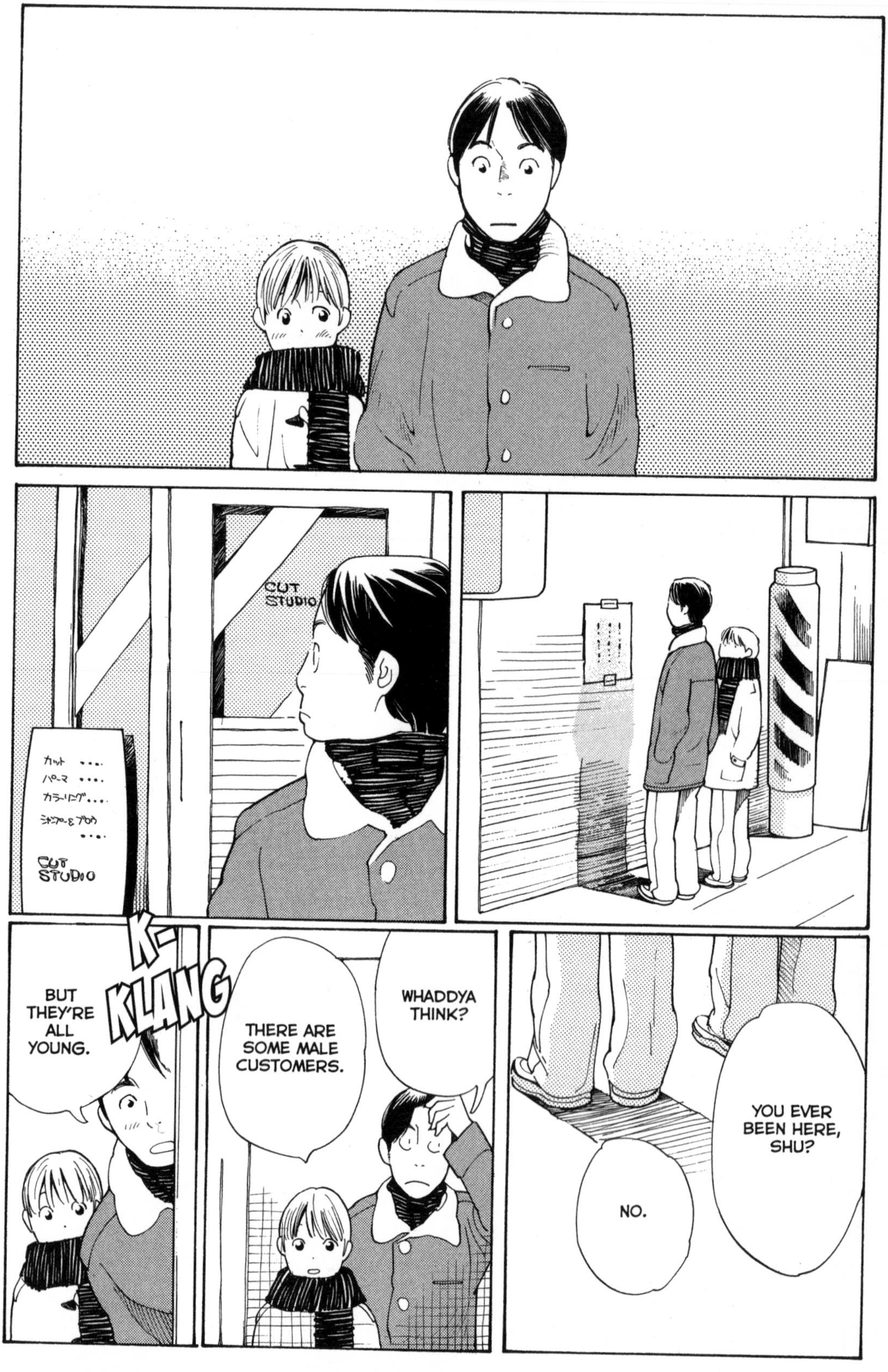
CUT STUDIO
カット ・・・
パーマ ・・・
カラーリング ・・・
シャンプー＆ブロウ ・・・
CUT STUDIO
YOU EVER BEEN HERE, SHU?
NO.
WHADDYA THINK?
THERE ARE SOME MALE CUSTOMERS.
K-KLANG
BUT THEY'RE ALL YOUNG.

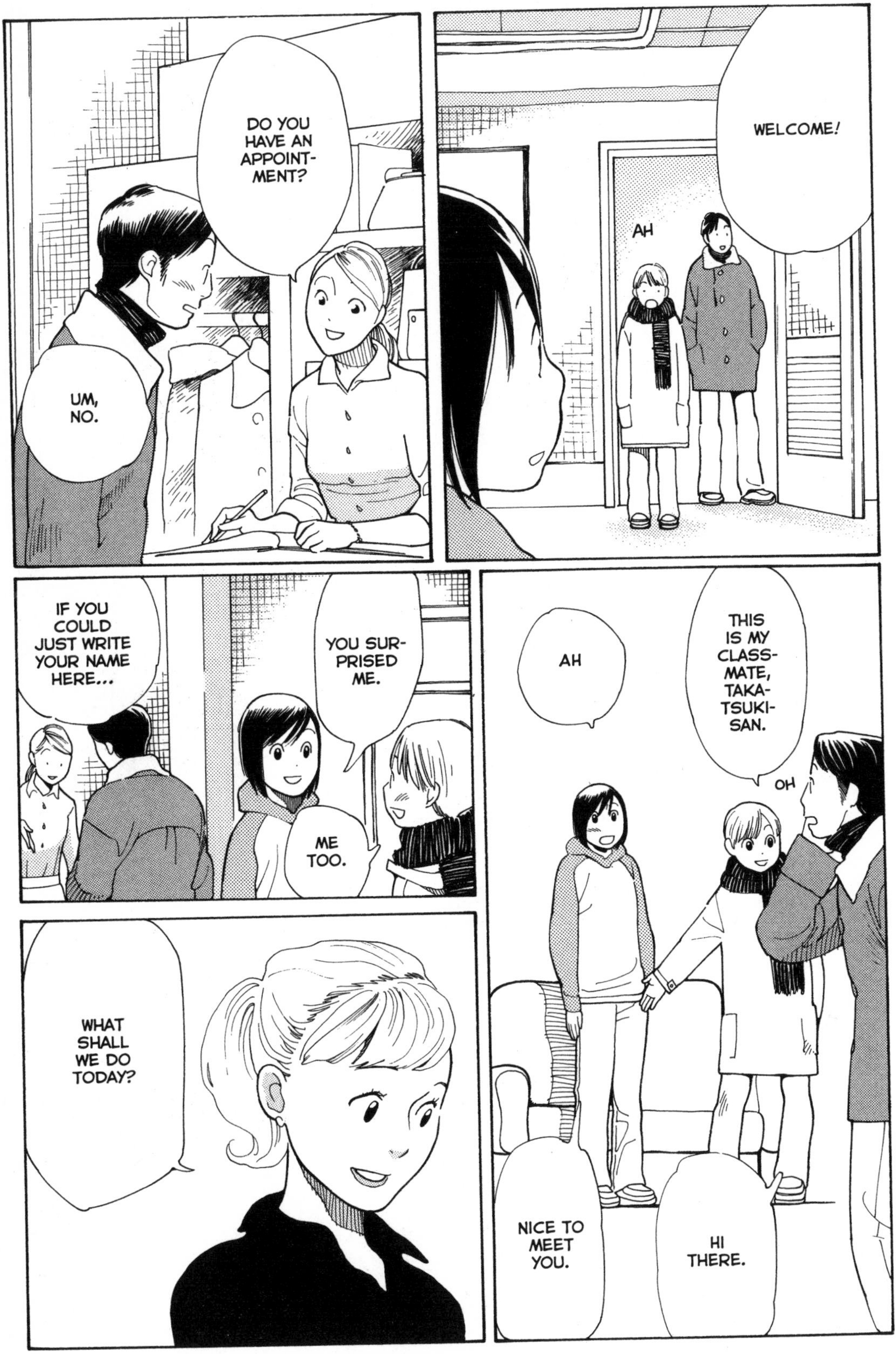
WELCOME!
AH
DO YOU HAVE AN APPOINTMENT?
UM, NO.
THIS IS MY CLASSMATE, TAKATSUKI-SAN.
AH
OH
HI THERE.
NICE TO MEET YOU.
YOU SURPRISED ME.
IF YOU COULD JUST WRITE YOUR NAME HERE...
ME TOO.
WHAT SHALL WE DO TODAY?

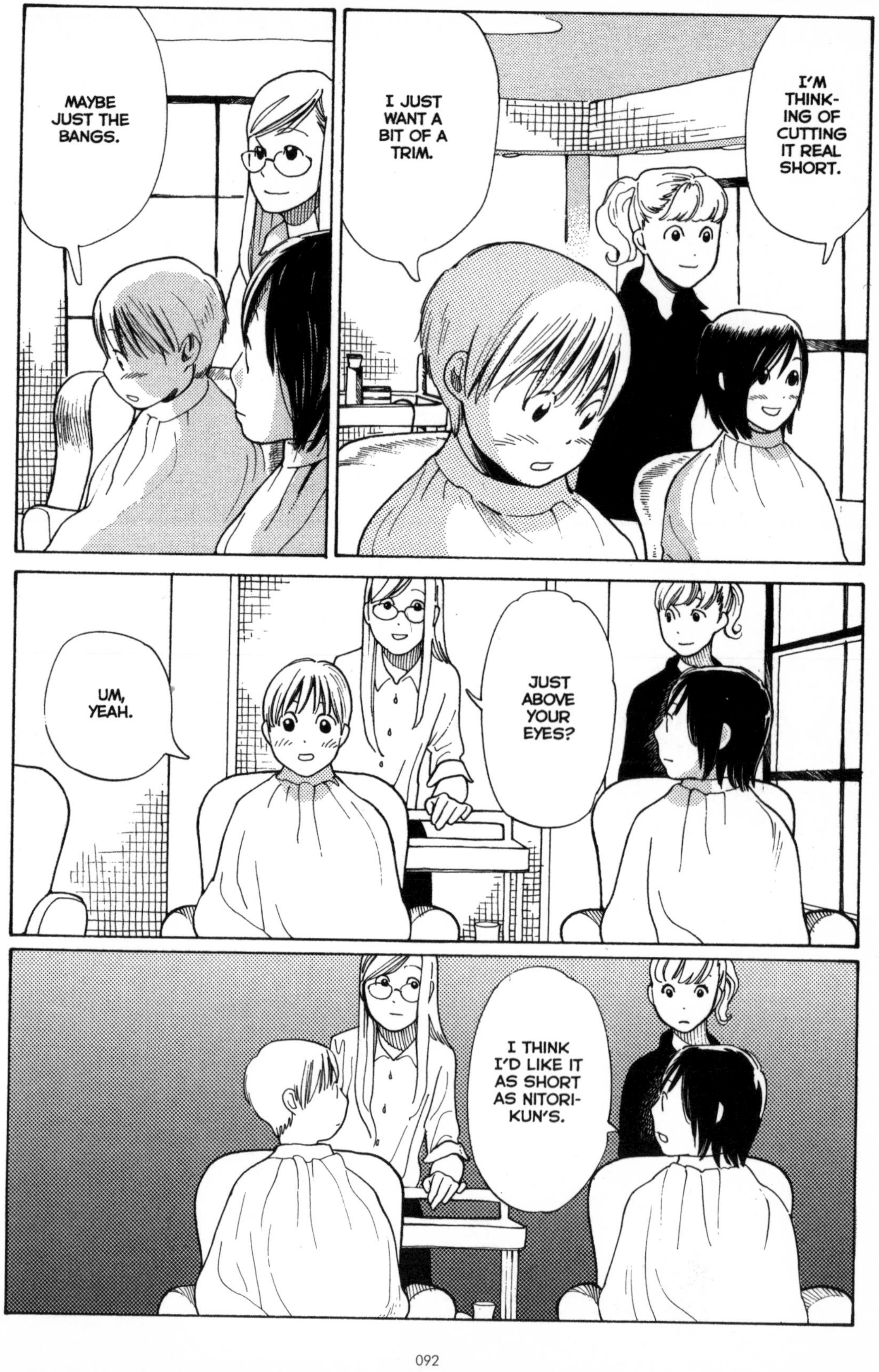
I'M THINKING OF CUTTING IT REAL SHORT.
I JUST WANT A BIT OF A TRIM.
MAYBE JUST THE BANGS.
JUST ABOVE YOUR EYES?
UM, YEAH.
I THINK I'D LIKE IT AS SHORT AS NITORI-KUN'S.

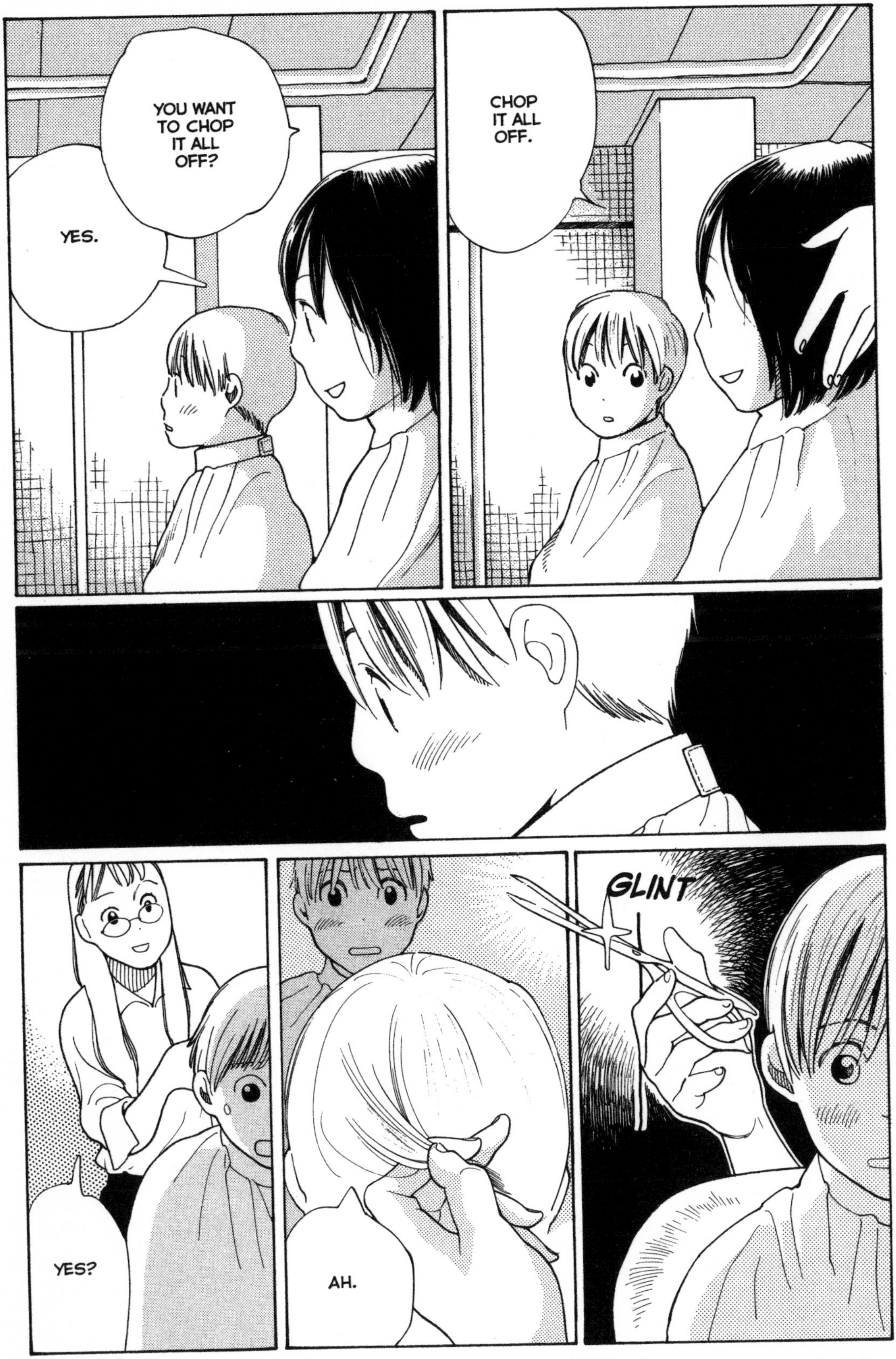
CHOP IT ALL OFF.
YOU WANT TO CHOP IT ALL OFF?
YES.
GLINT
AH.
YES?

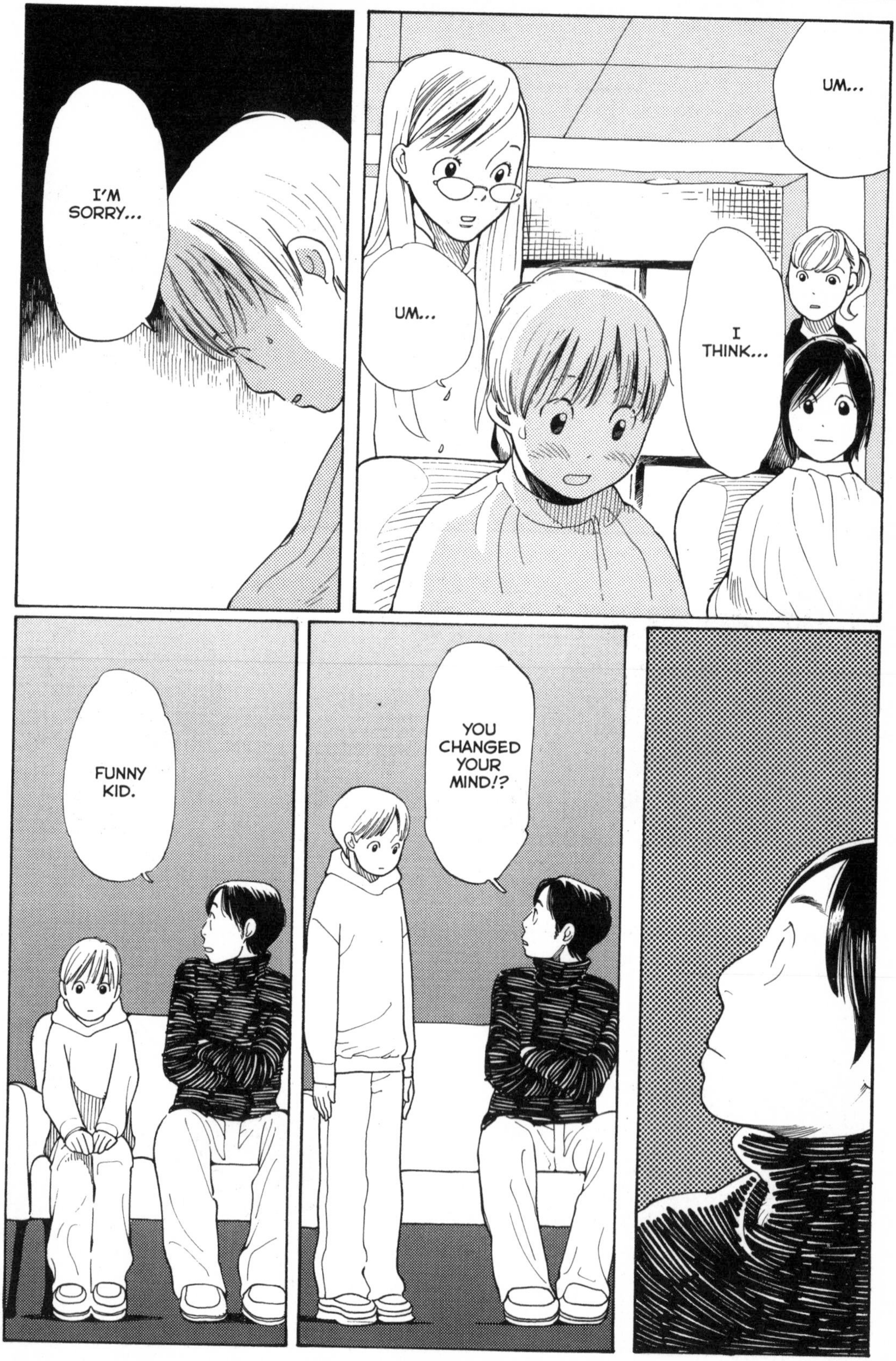
UM...
I THINK...
UM...
I'M SORRY...
YOU CHANGED YOUR MIND!?
FUNNY KID.

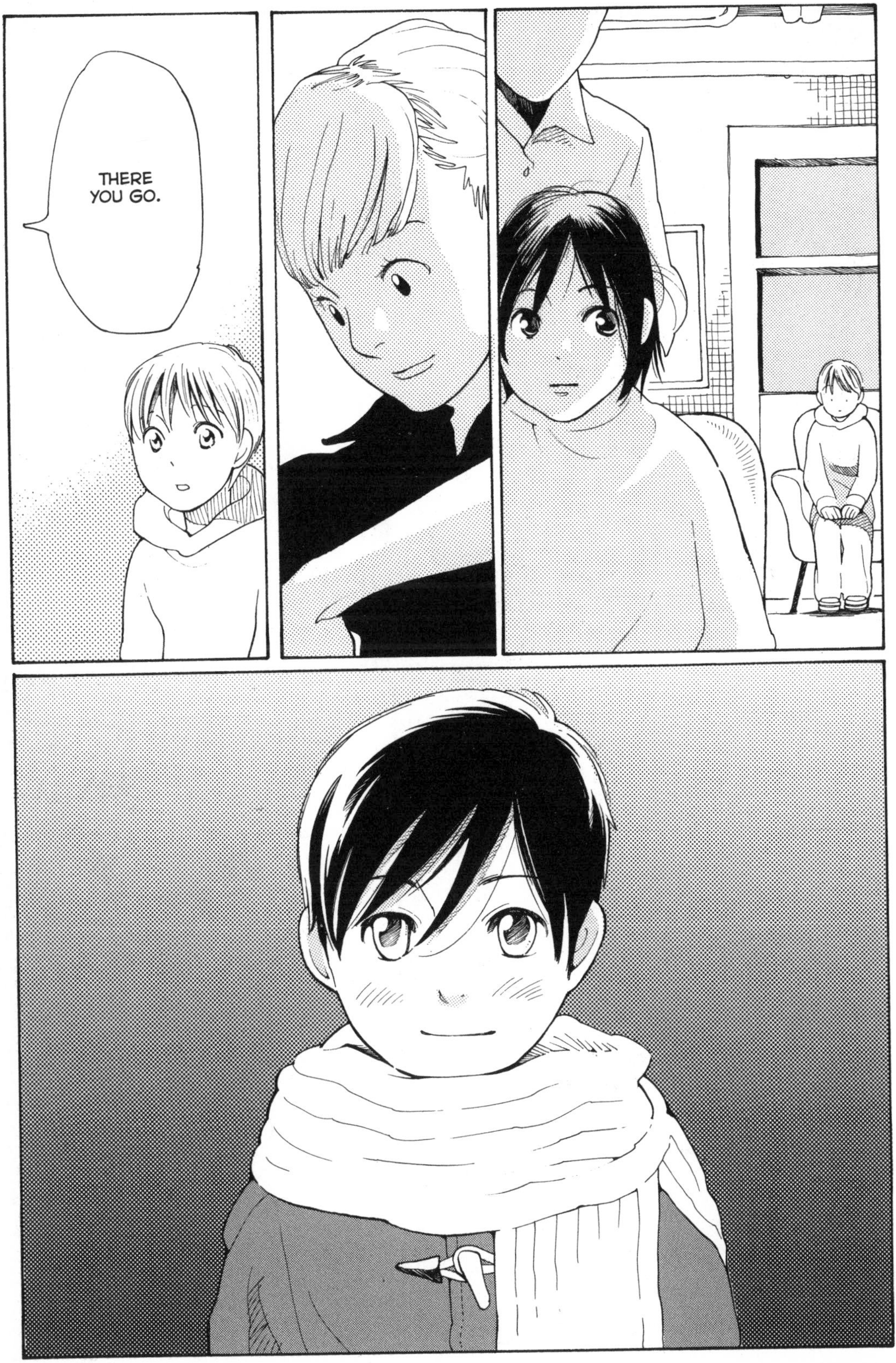
THERE YOU GO.

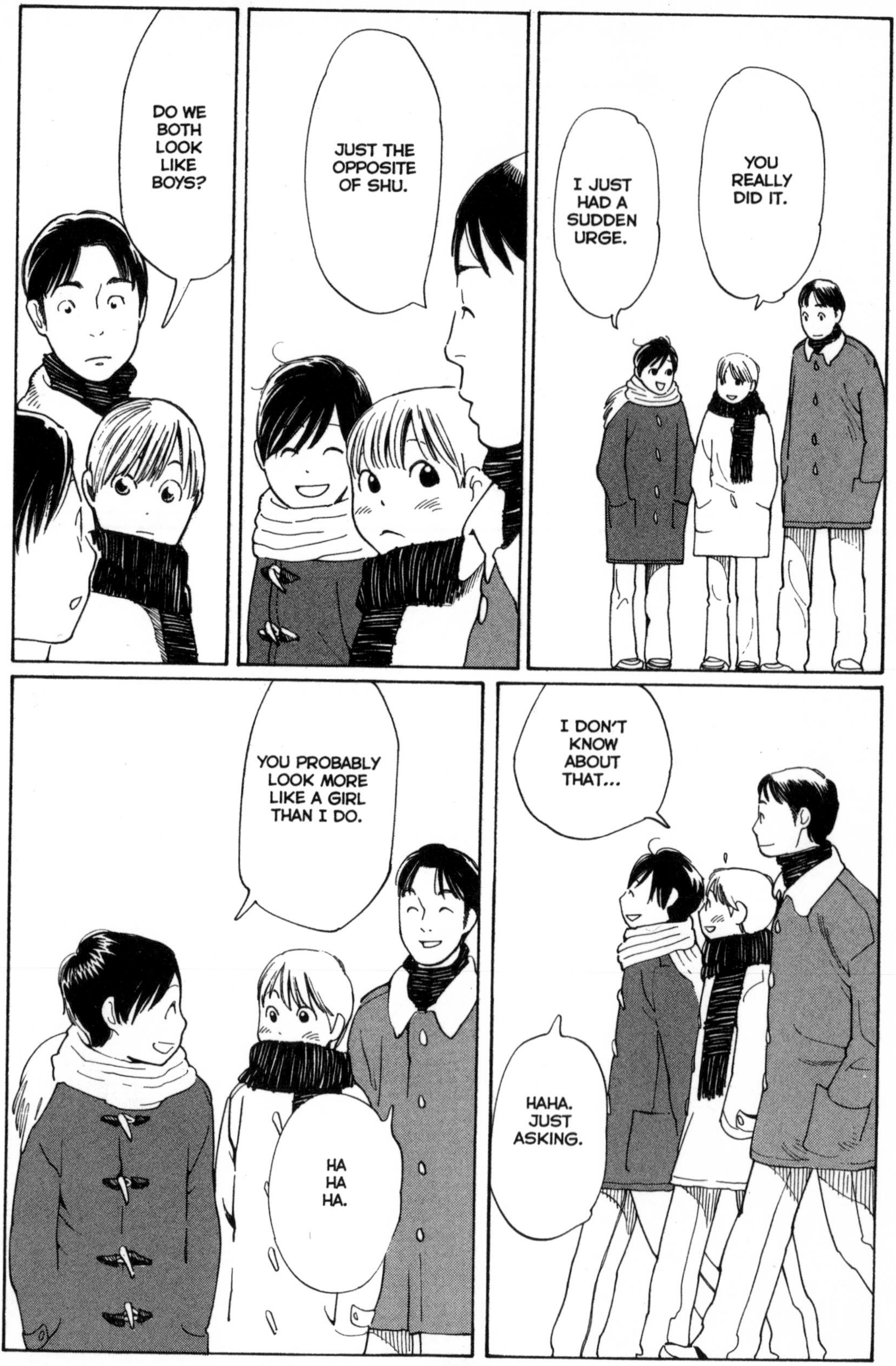
YOU REALLY DID IT.
I JUST HAD A SUDDEN URGE.
JUST THE OPPOSITE OF SHU.
DO WE BOTH LOOK LIKE BOYS?
I DON'T KNOW ABOUT THAT...
HAHA. JUST ASKING.
YOU PROBABLY LOOK MORE LIKE A GIRL THAN I DO.
HA HA HA.

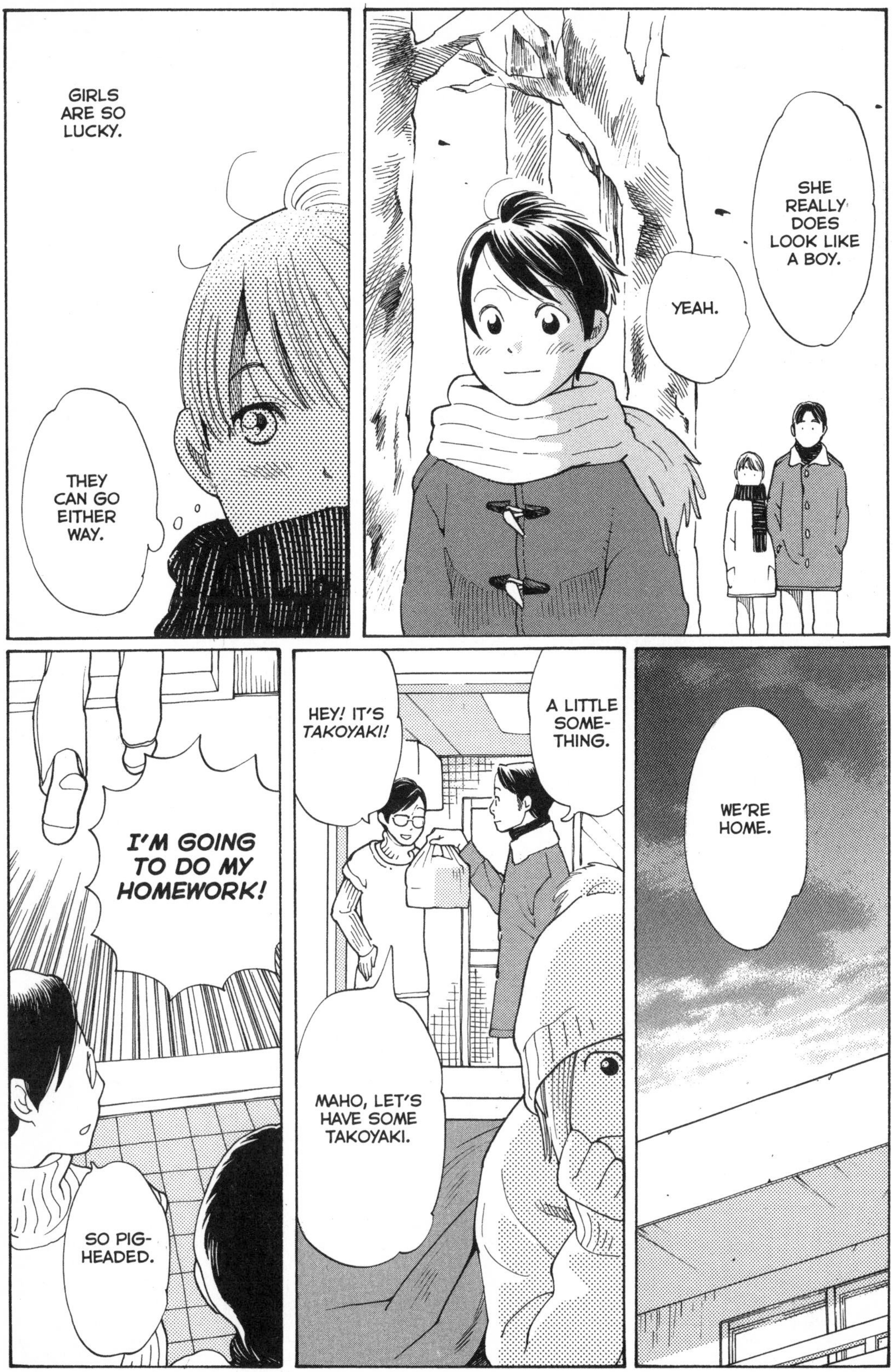
SHE REALLY DOES LOOK LIKE A BOY.
YEAH.
GIRLS ARE SO LUCKY.
THEY CAN GO EITHER WAY.
WE'RE HOME.
A LITTLE SOME-THING.
HEY! IT'S *TAKOYAKI!*
MAHO, LET'S HAVE SOME TAKOYAKI.
I'M GOING TO DO MY HOMEWORK!
SO PIG-HEADED.

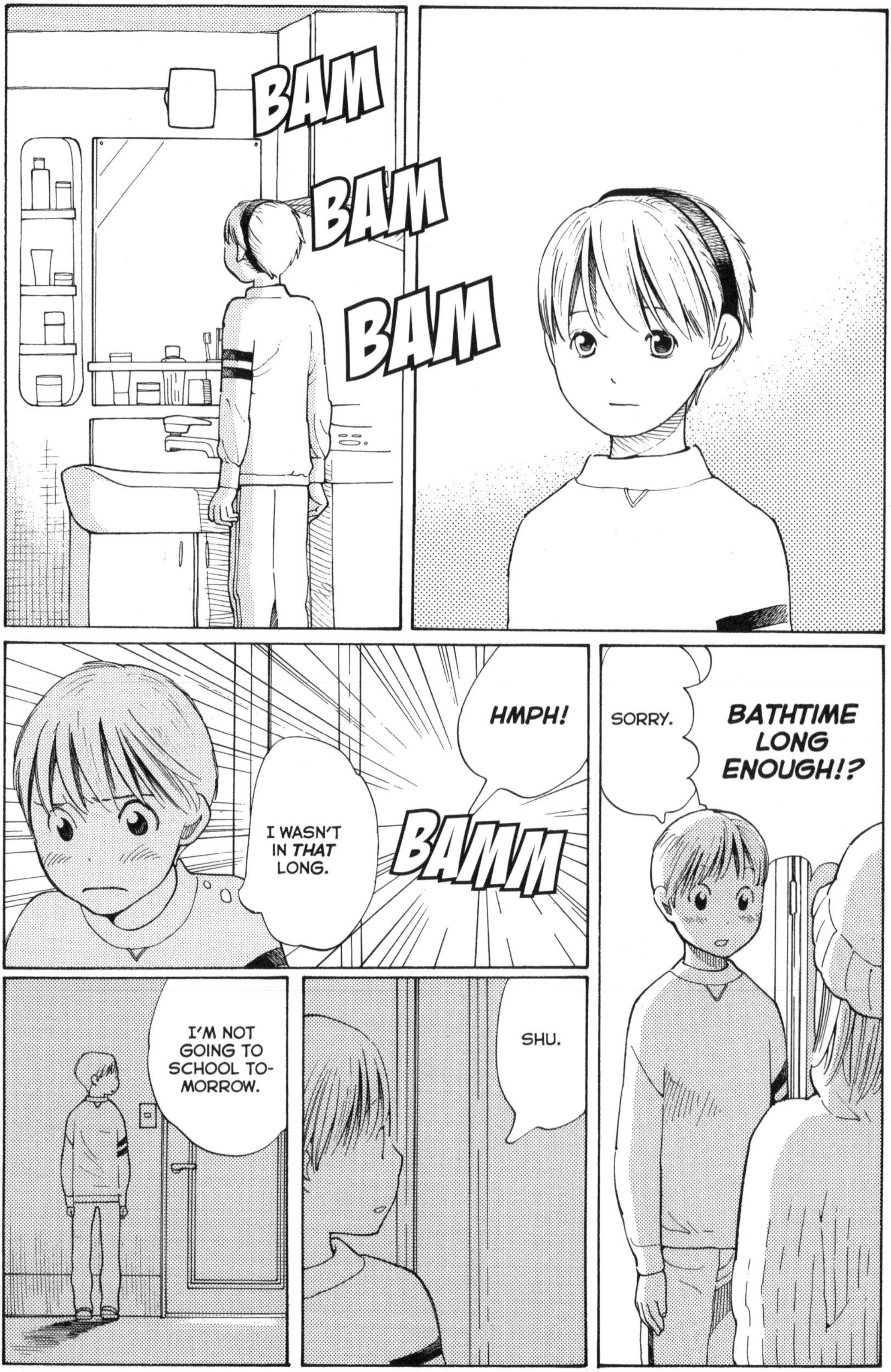
BAM
BAM
BAM
BATHTIME LONG ENOUGH!?
SORRY.
HMPH!
BAMM
I WASN'T IN *THAT* LONG.
SHU.
I'M NOT GOING TO SCHOOL TO-MORROW.

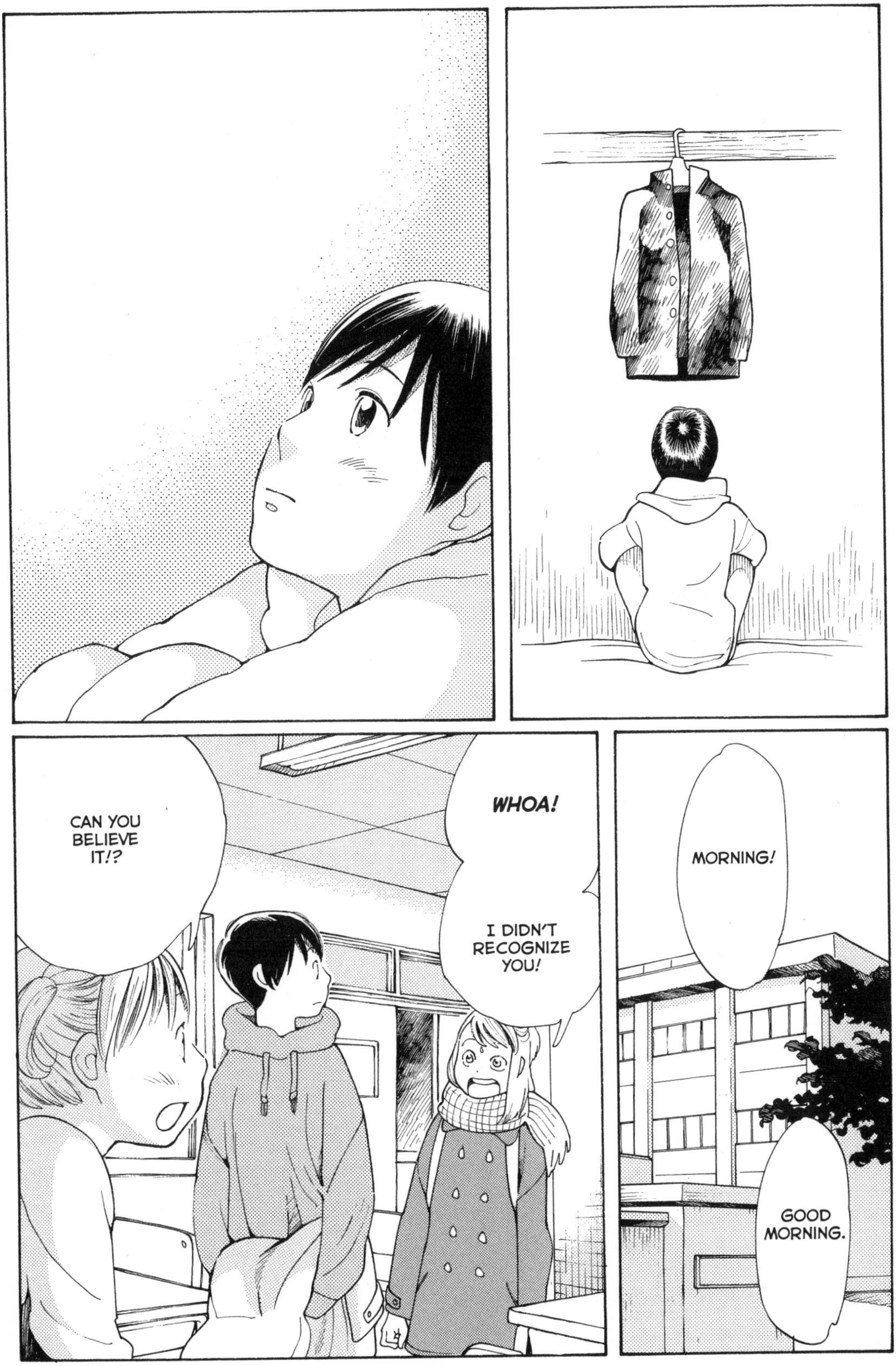
MORNING!
GOOD MORNING.
WHOA!
I DIDN'T RECOGNIZE YOU!
CAN YOU BELIEVE IT!?

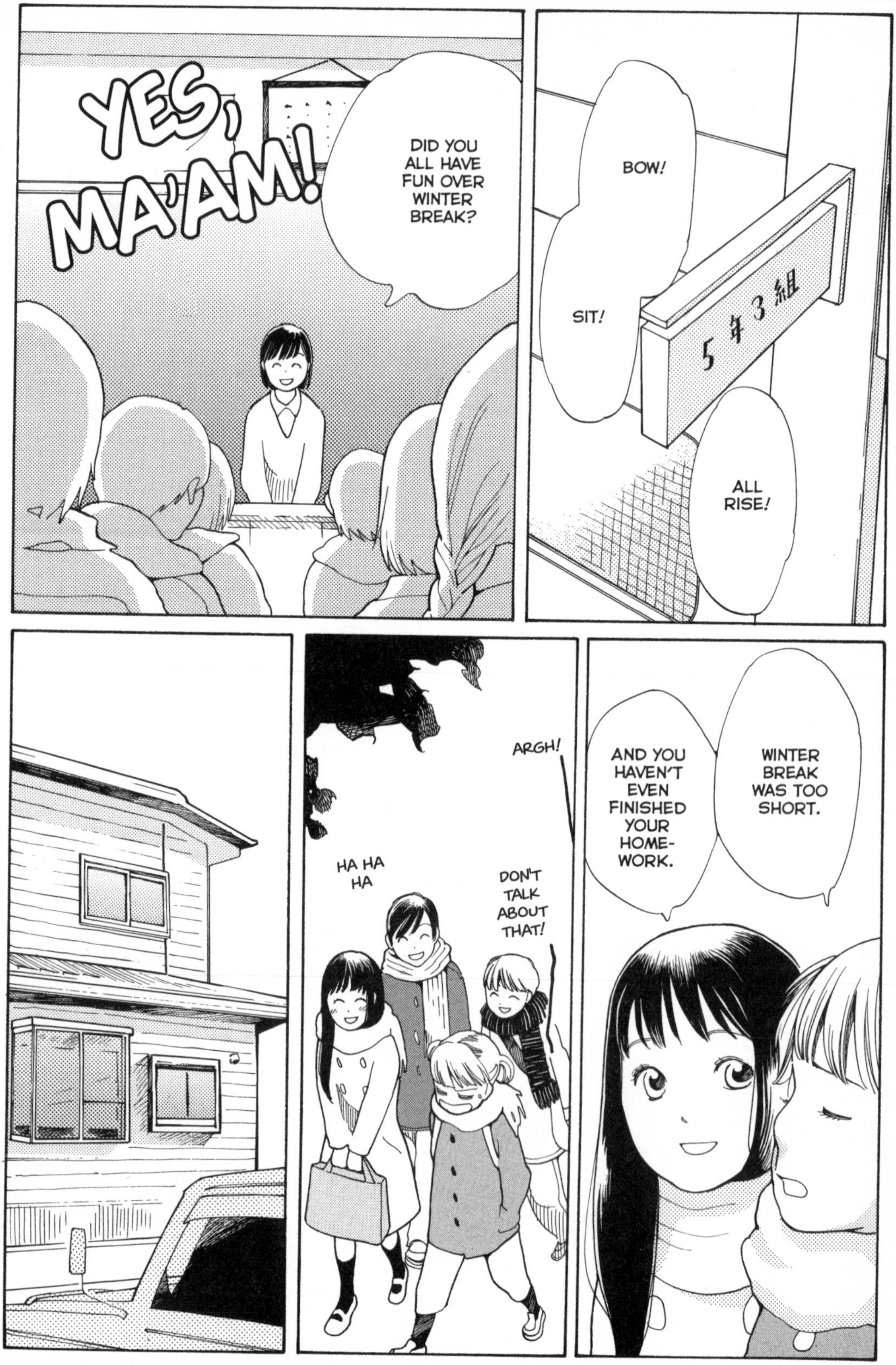
ALL RISE!
BOW!
SIT!
DID YOU ALL HAVE FUN OVER WINTER BREAK?
YES, MA'AM!
WINTER BREAK WAS TOO SHORT.
AND YOU HAVEN'T EVEN FINISHED YOUR HOME-WORK.
ARGH!
DON'T TALK ABOUT THAT!
HA HA HA

YOCCHAN!

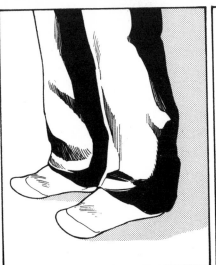

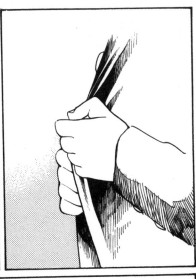

WHAT ABOUT LUNCH?

OH

I'LL GET SOMETHING WHILE I'M OUT.

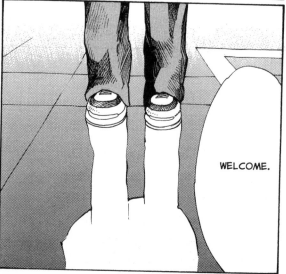

WELCOME.

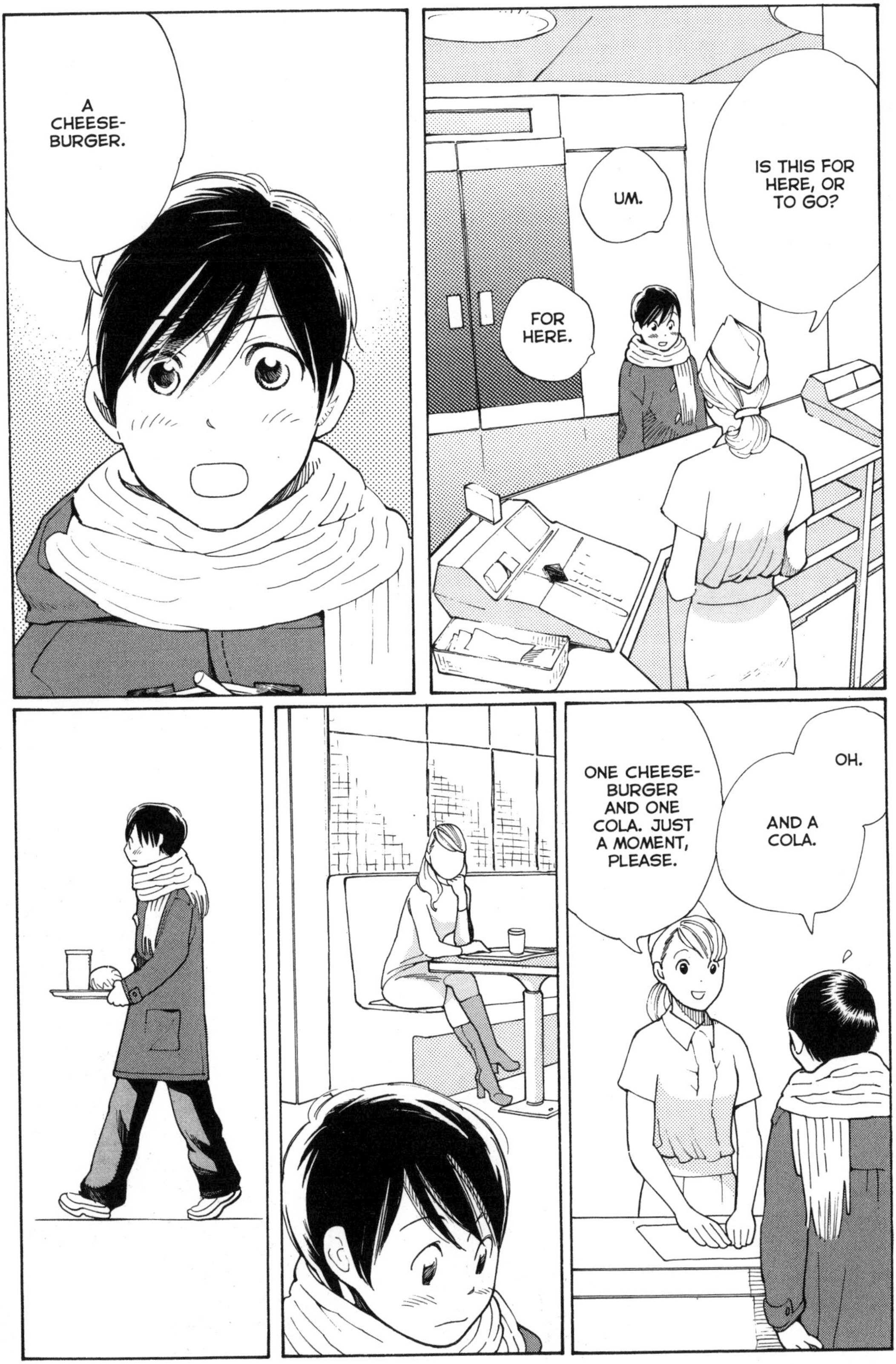
IS THIS FOR HERE, OR TO GO?
UM.
FOR HERE.
A CHEESE-BURGER.
OH.
AND A COLA.
ONE CHEESE-BURGER AND ONE COLA. JUST A MOMENT, PLEASE.

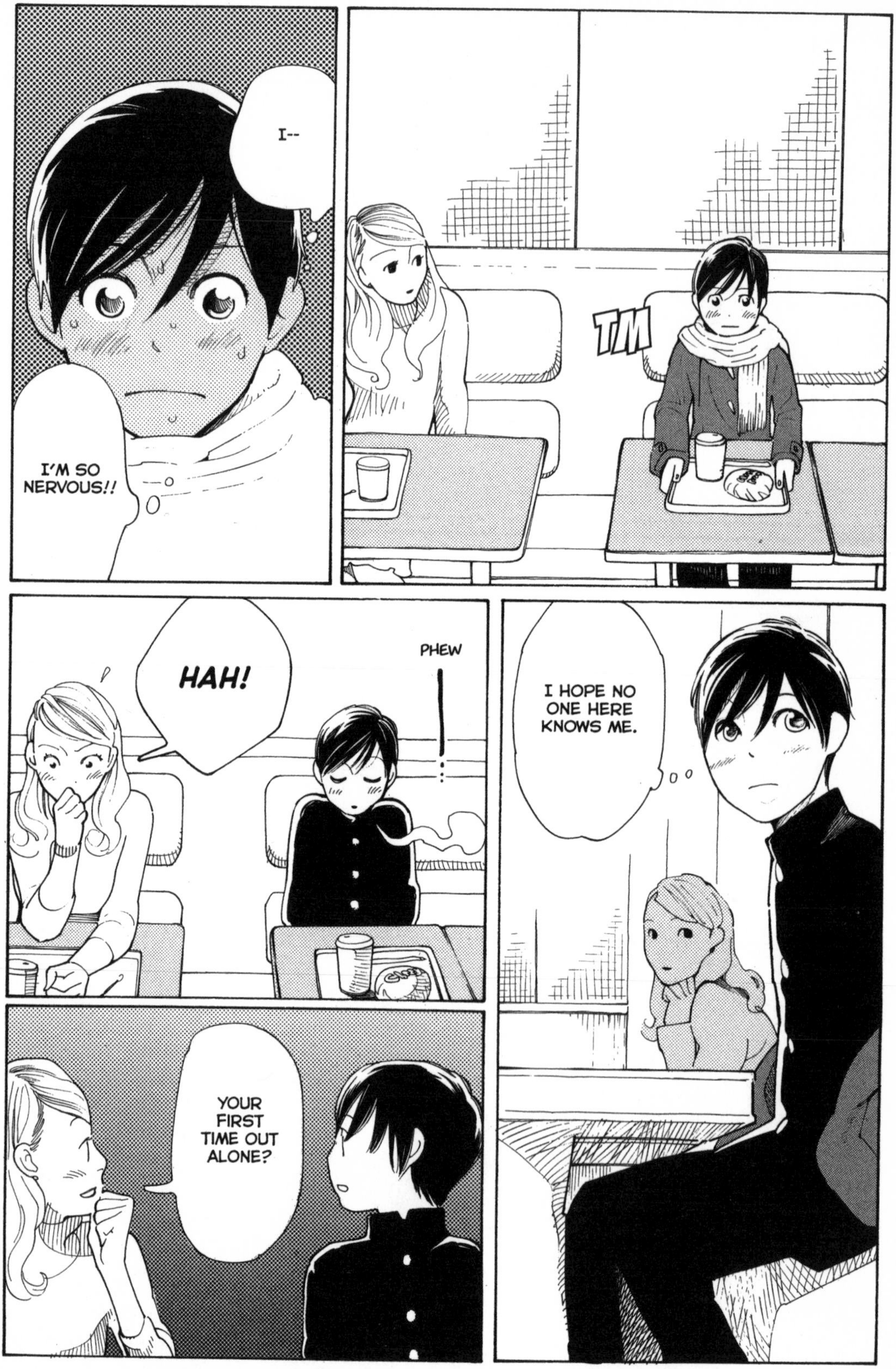
TM
I--
I'M SO NERVOUS!!
I HOPE NO ONE HERE KNOWS ME.
PHEW
HAH!
YOUR FIRST TIME OUT ALONE?

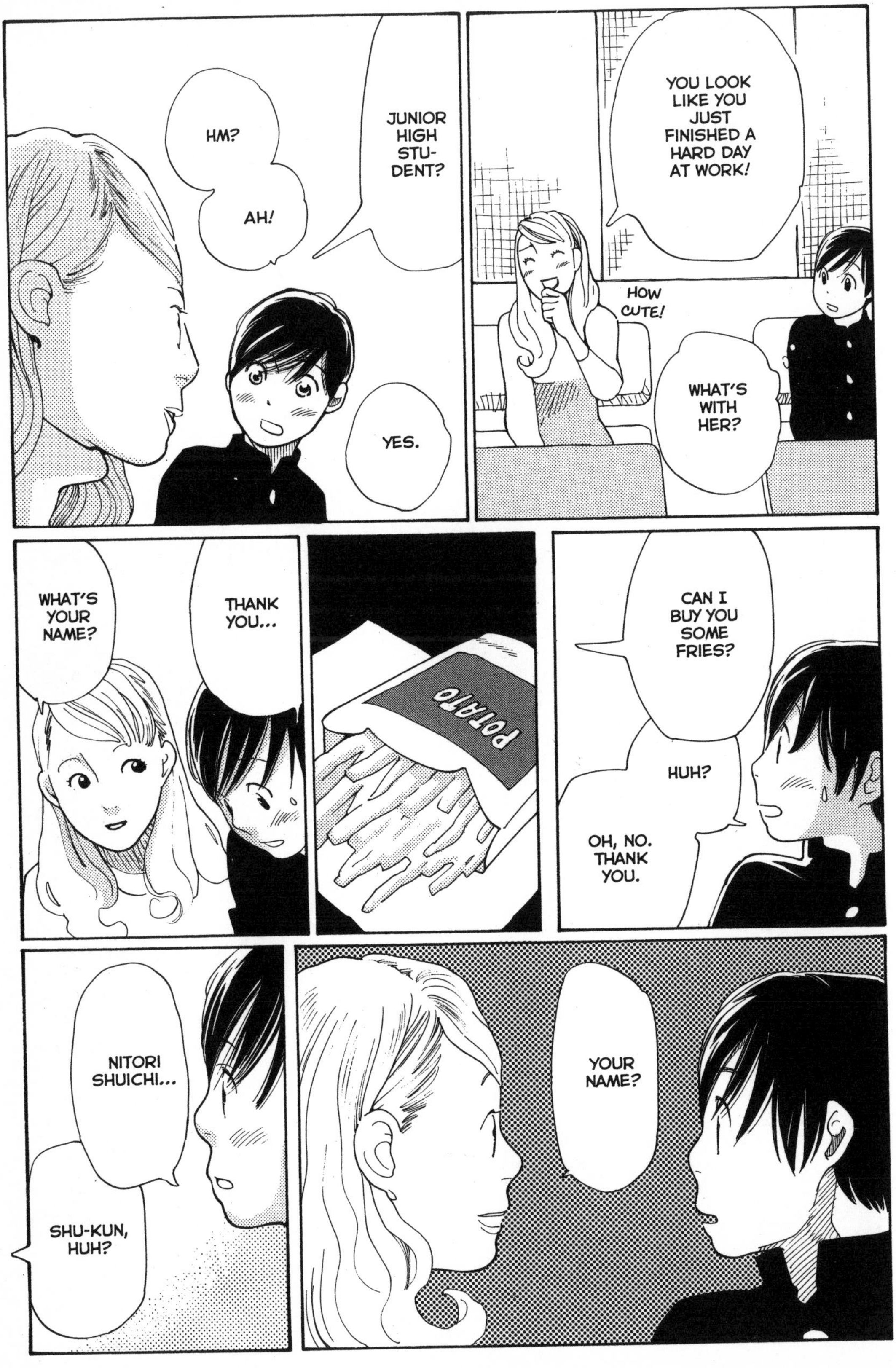
YOU LOOK LIKE YOU JUST FINISHED A HARD DAY AT WORK!
HOW CUTE!
WHAT'S WITH HER?
JUNIOR HIGH STU-DENT?
HM?
AH!
YES.
CAN I BUY YOU SOME FRIES?
HUH?
OH, NO. THANK YOU.
POTATO
THANK YOU...
WHAT'S YOUR NAME?
YOUR NAME?
NITORI SHUICHI...
SHU-KUN, HUH?

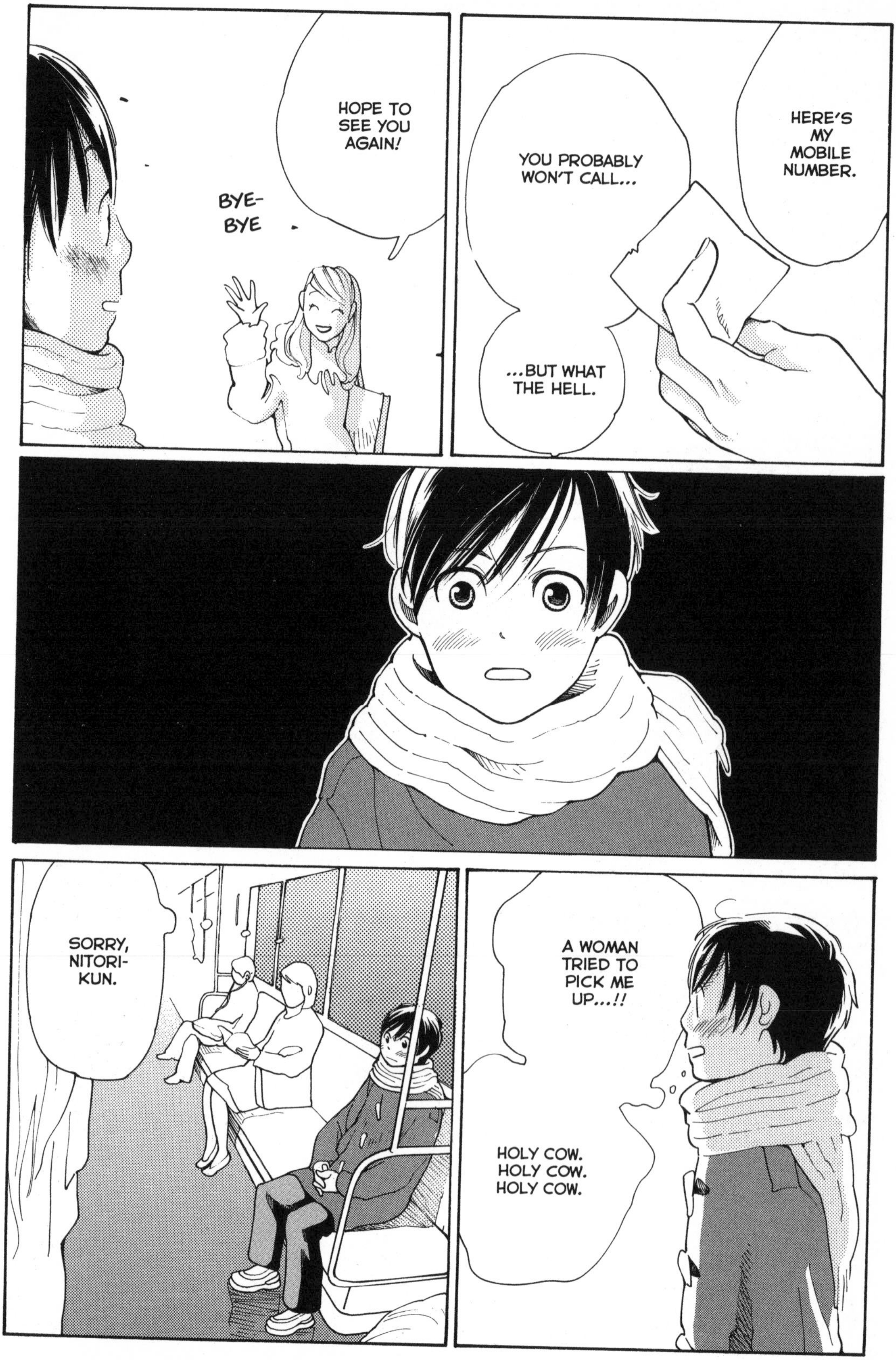
HERE'S MY MOBILE NUMBER.
YOU PROBABLY WON'T CALL...
...BUT WHAT THE HELL.
HOPE TO SEE YOU AGAIN!
BYE-BYE
A WOMAN TRIED TO PICK ME UP...!!
HOLY COW. HOLY COW. HOLY COW.
SORRY, NITORI-KUN.

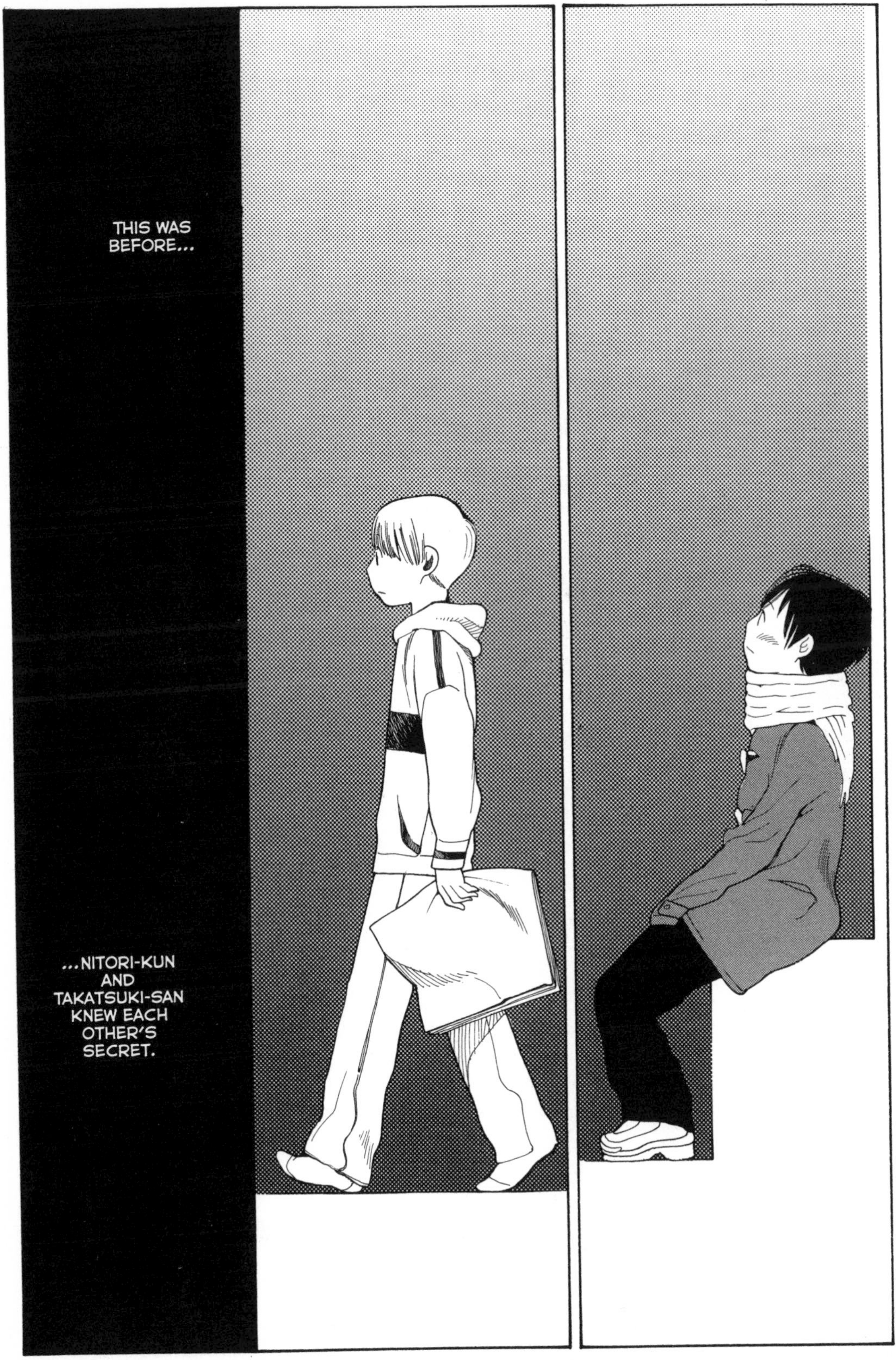
THIS WAS BEFORE...
...NITORI-KUN AND TAKATSUKI-SAN KNEW EACH OTHER'S SECRET.

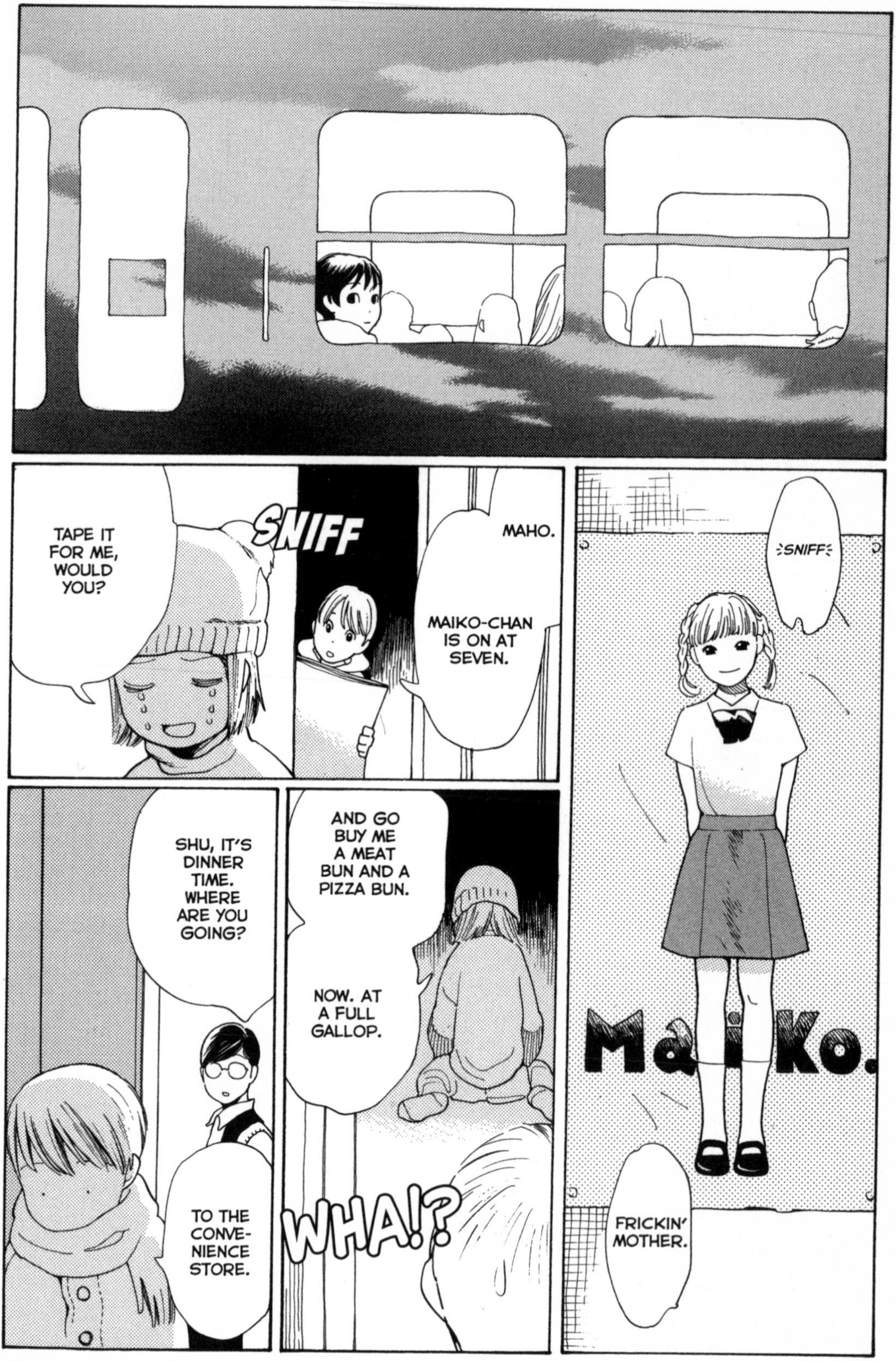
SNIFF
Maiko.
FRICKIN' MOTHER.
MAHO.
MAIKO-CHAN IS ON AT SEVEN.
SNIFF
TAPE IT FOR ME, WOULD YOU?
AND GO BUY ME A MEAT BUN AND A PIZZA BUN.
NOW. AT A FULL GALLOP.
WHA!?
SHU, IT'S DINNER TIME. WHERE ARE YOU GOING?
TO THE CONVE-NIENCE STORE.

5

Nitori-kun's Birthday

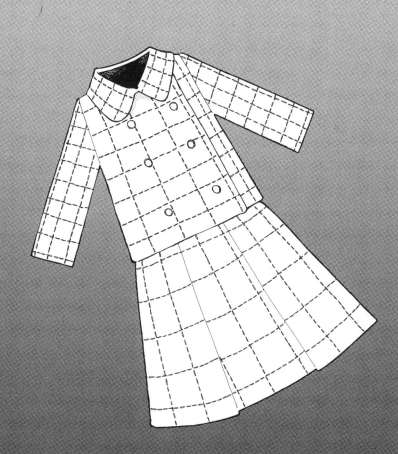

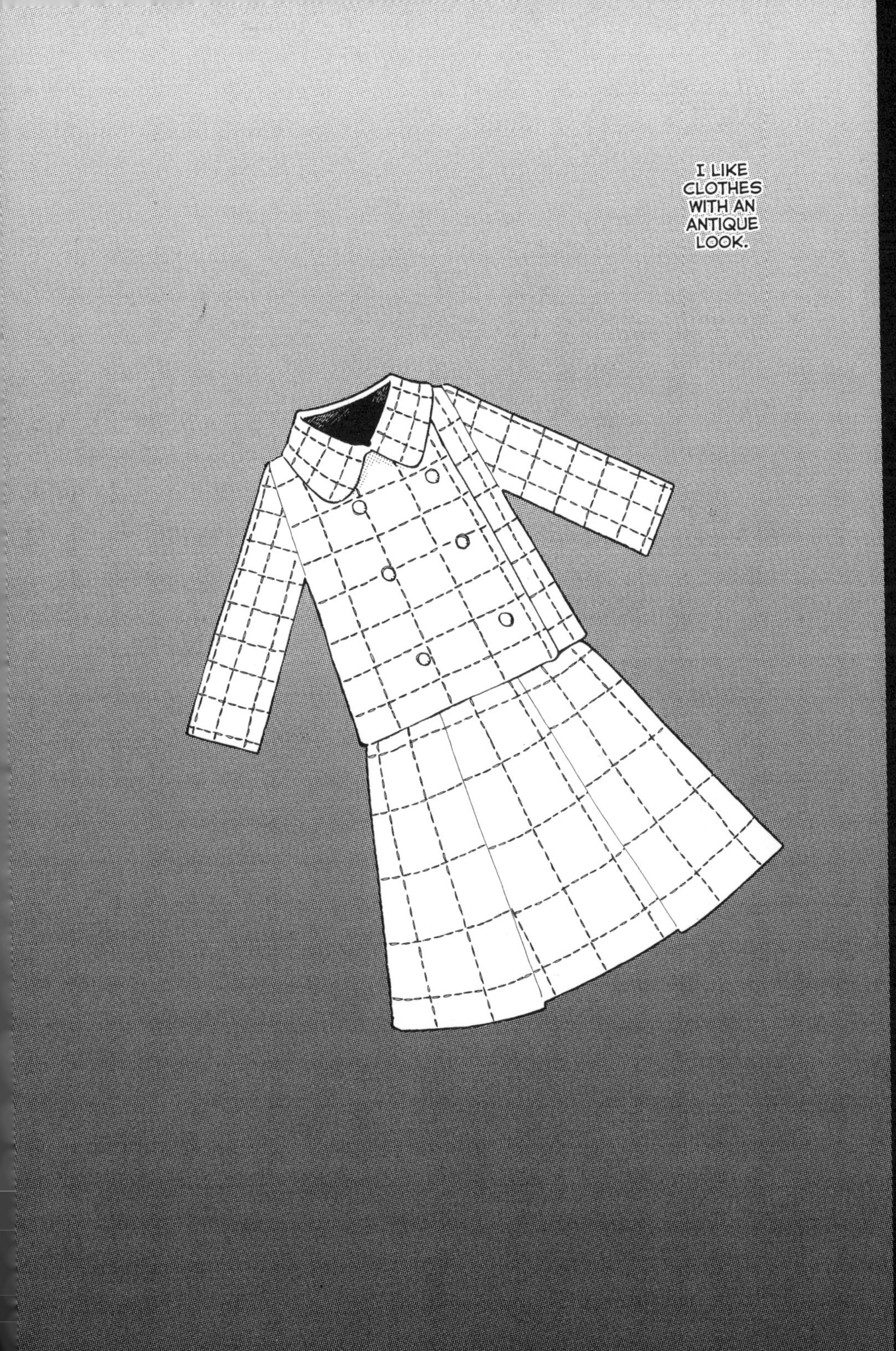

I LIKE CLOTHES WITH AN ANTIQUE LOOK.

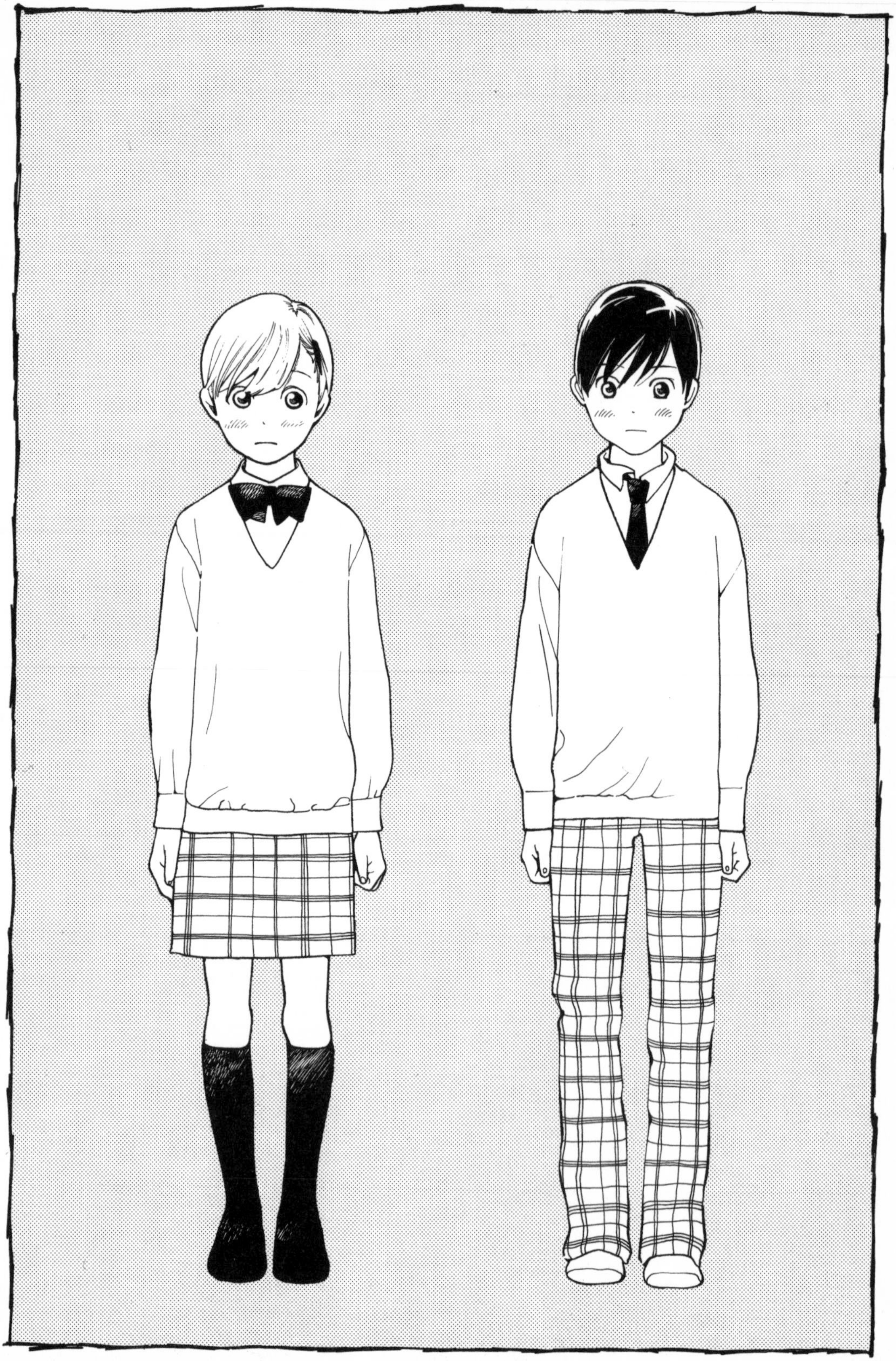

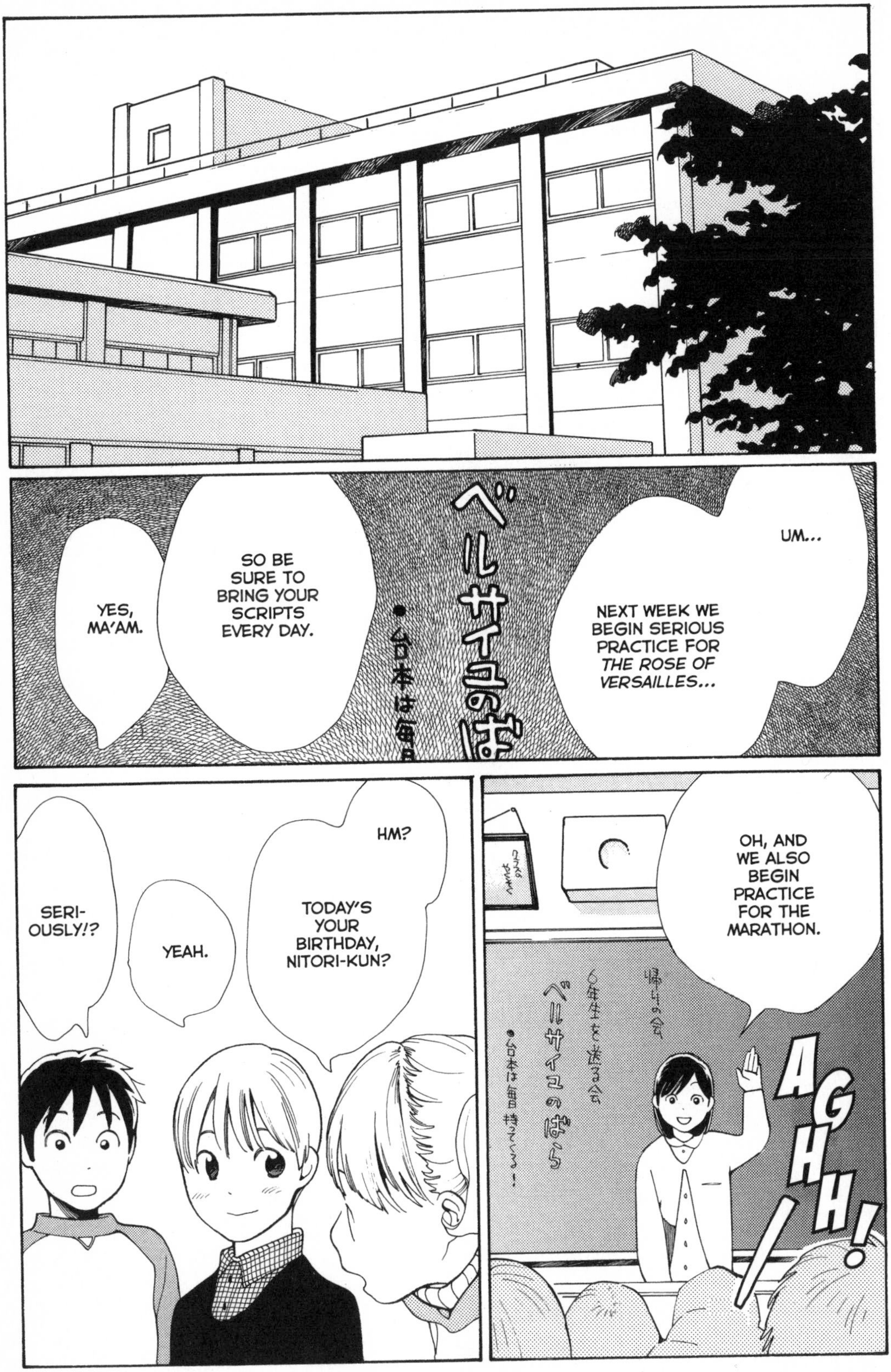

UM...
NEXT WEEK WE BEGIN SERIOUS PRACTICE FOR *THE ROSE OF VERSAILLES*...
SO BE SURE TO BRING YOUR SCRIPTS EVERY DAY.
YES, MA'AM.
OH, AND WE ALSO BEGIN PRACTICE FOR THE MARATHON.
AGHH!
帰りの会
6年生を送る会
ベルサイユのばら
●台本は毎日持ってくる！
HM?
TODAY'S YOUR BIRTHDAY, NITORI-KUN?
YEAH.
SERI-OUSLY!?

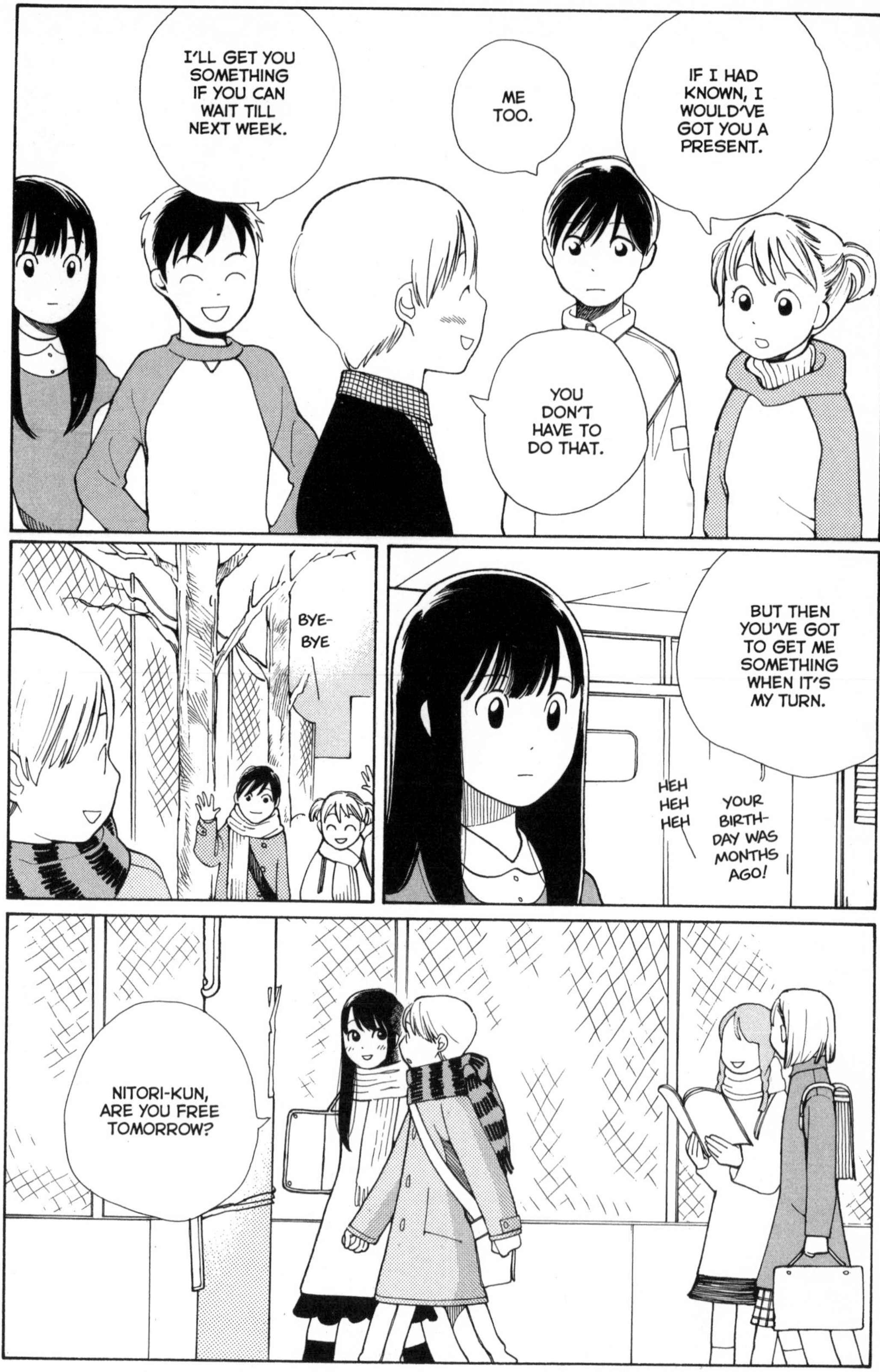
IF I HAD KNOWN, I WOULD'VE GOT YOU A PRESENT.
ME TOO.
I'LL GET YOU SOMETHING IF YOU CAN WAIT TILL NEXT WEEK.
YOU DON'T HAVE TO DO THAT.
BUT THEN YOU'VE GOT TO GET ME SOMETHING WHEN IT'S MY TURN.
YOUR BIRTH-DAY WAS MONTHS AGO!
HEH HEH HEH
BYE-BYE
NITORI-KUN, ARE YOU FREE TOMORROW?

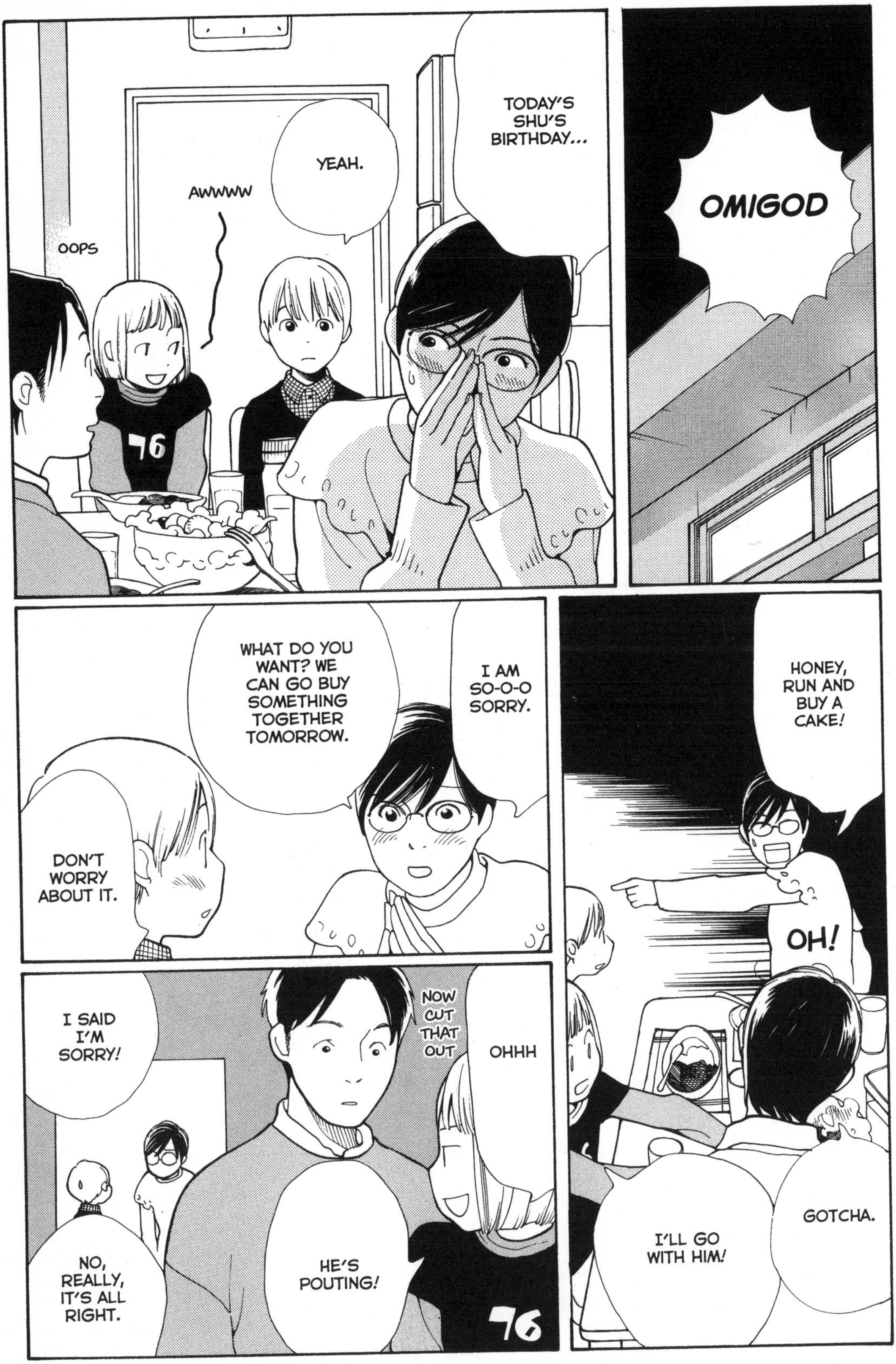
OMIGOD
TODAY'S SHU'S BIRTHDAY...
YEAH.
AWWWW
OOPS
HONEY, RUN AND BUY A CAKE!
OH!
GOTCHA.
I'LL GO WITH HIM!
I AM SO-O-O SORRY.
WHAT DO YOU WANT? WE CAN GO BUY SOMETHING TOGETHER TOMORROW.
DON'T WORRY ABOUT IT.
OHHH
NOW CUT THAT OUT
I SAID I'M SORRY!
HE'S POUTING!
NO, REALLY, IT'S ALL RIGHT.

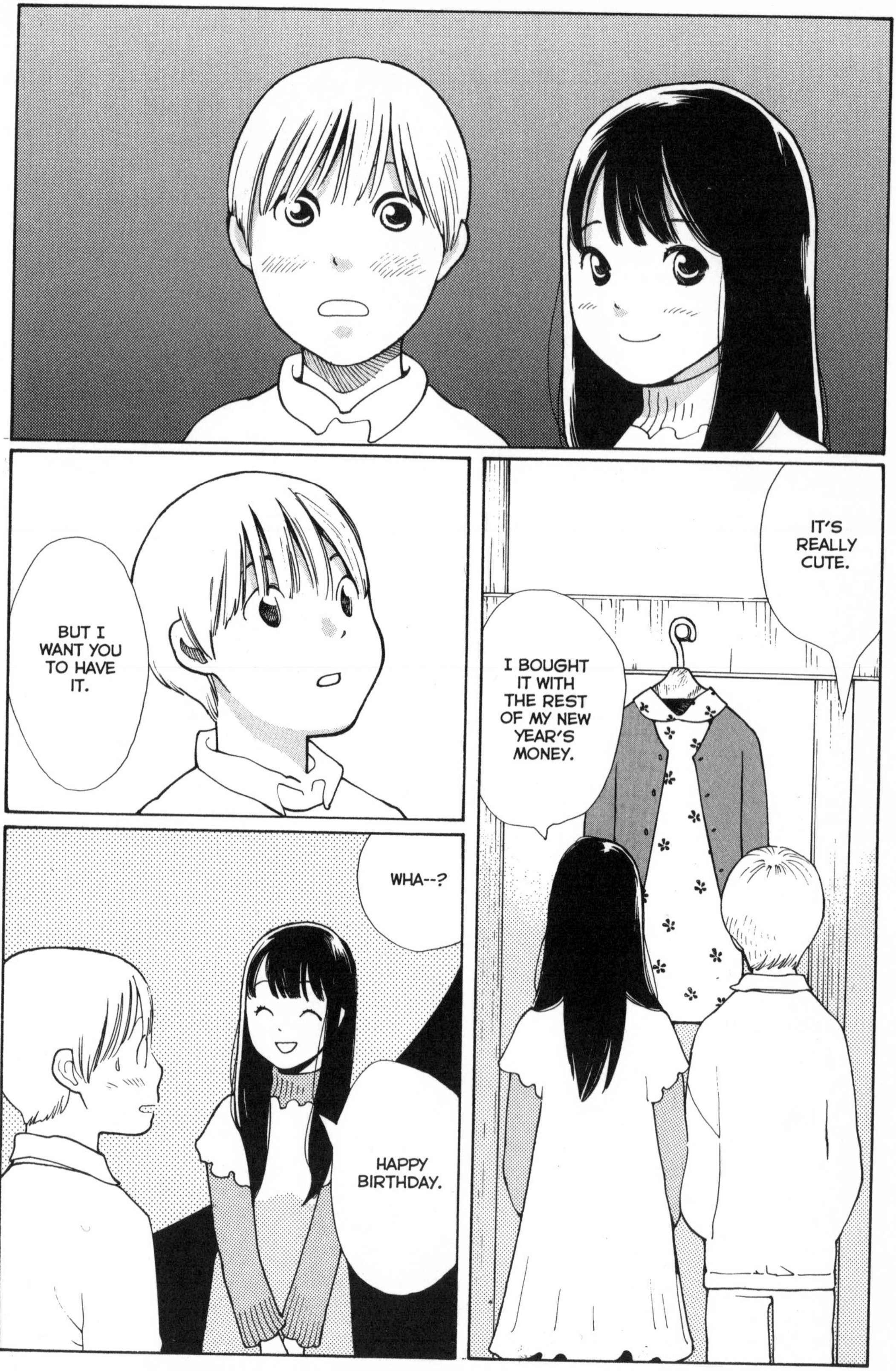
IT'S REALLY CUTE.
I BOUGHT IT WITH THE REST OF MY NEW YEAR'S MONEY.
BUT I WANT YOU TO HAVE IT.
WHA--?
HAPPY BIRTHDAY.

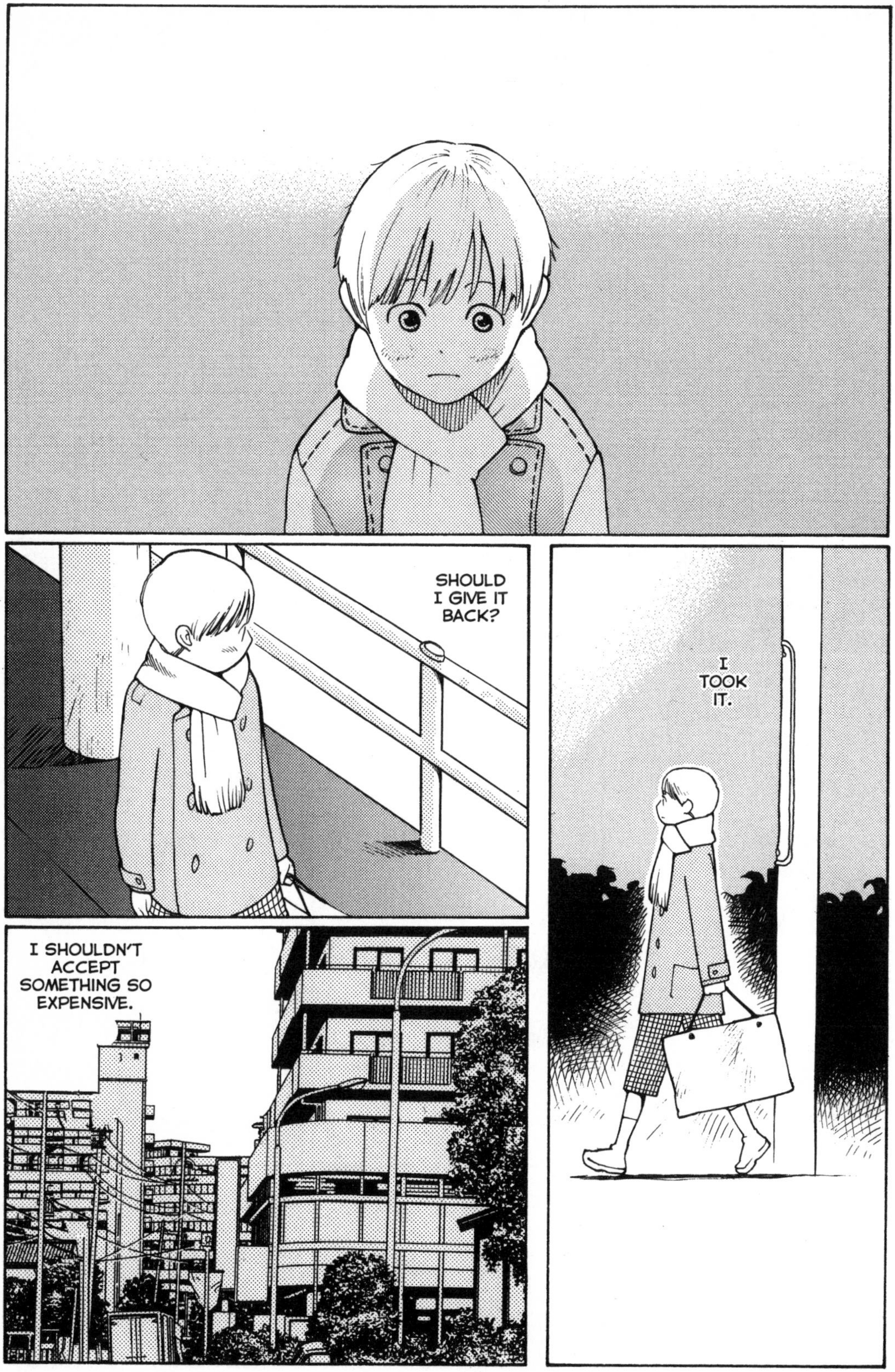
I TOOK IT.
SHOULD I GIVE IT BACK?
I SHOULDN'T ACCEPT SOMETHING SO EXPENSIVE.

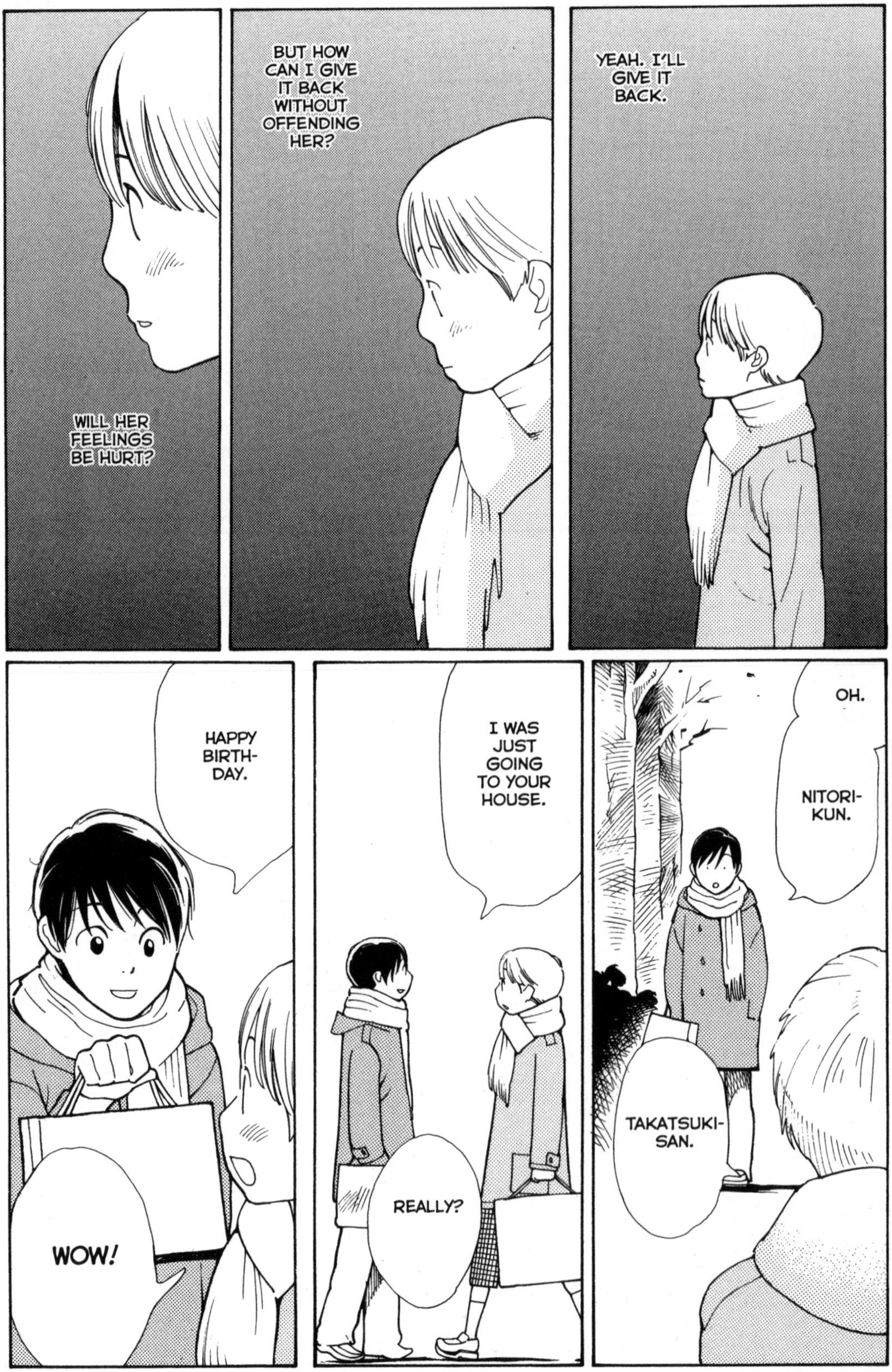
YEAH. I'LL GIVE IT BACK.
BUT HOW CAN I GIVE IT BACK WITHOUT OFFENDING HER?
WILL HER FEELINGS BE HURT?
OH.
NITORI-KUN.
TAKATSUKI-SAN.
I WAS JUST GOING TO YOUR HOUSE.
REALLY?
HAPPY BIRTH-DAY.
WOW!

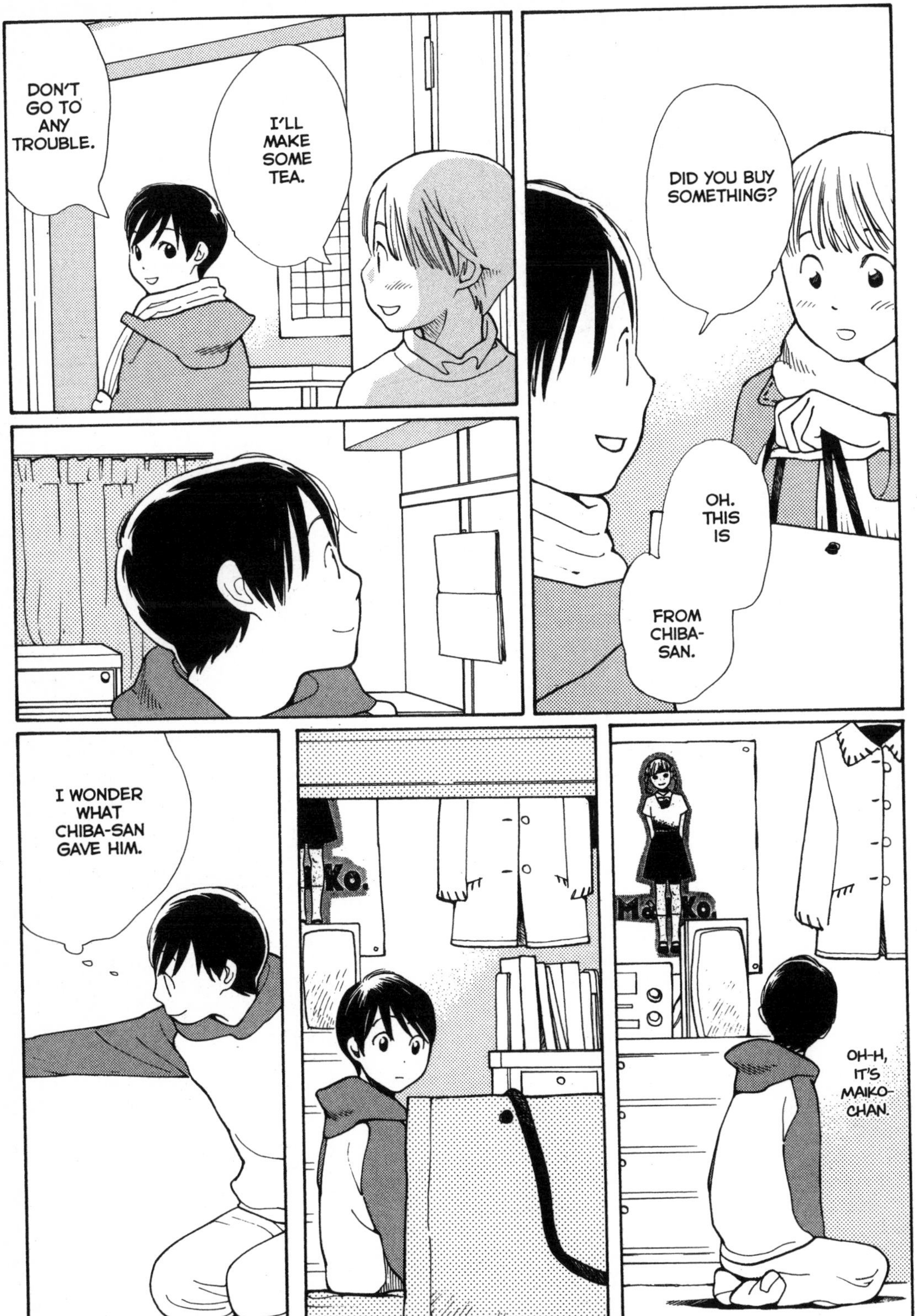
DID YOU BUY SOMETHING?
OH. THIS IS
FROM CHIBA-SAN.
I'LL MAKE SOME TEA.
DON'T GO TO ANY TROUBLE.
OH-H, IT'S MAIKO-CHAN.
I WONDER WHAT CHIBA-SAN GAVE HIM.

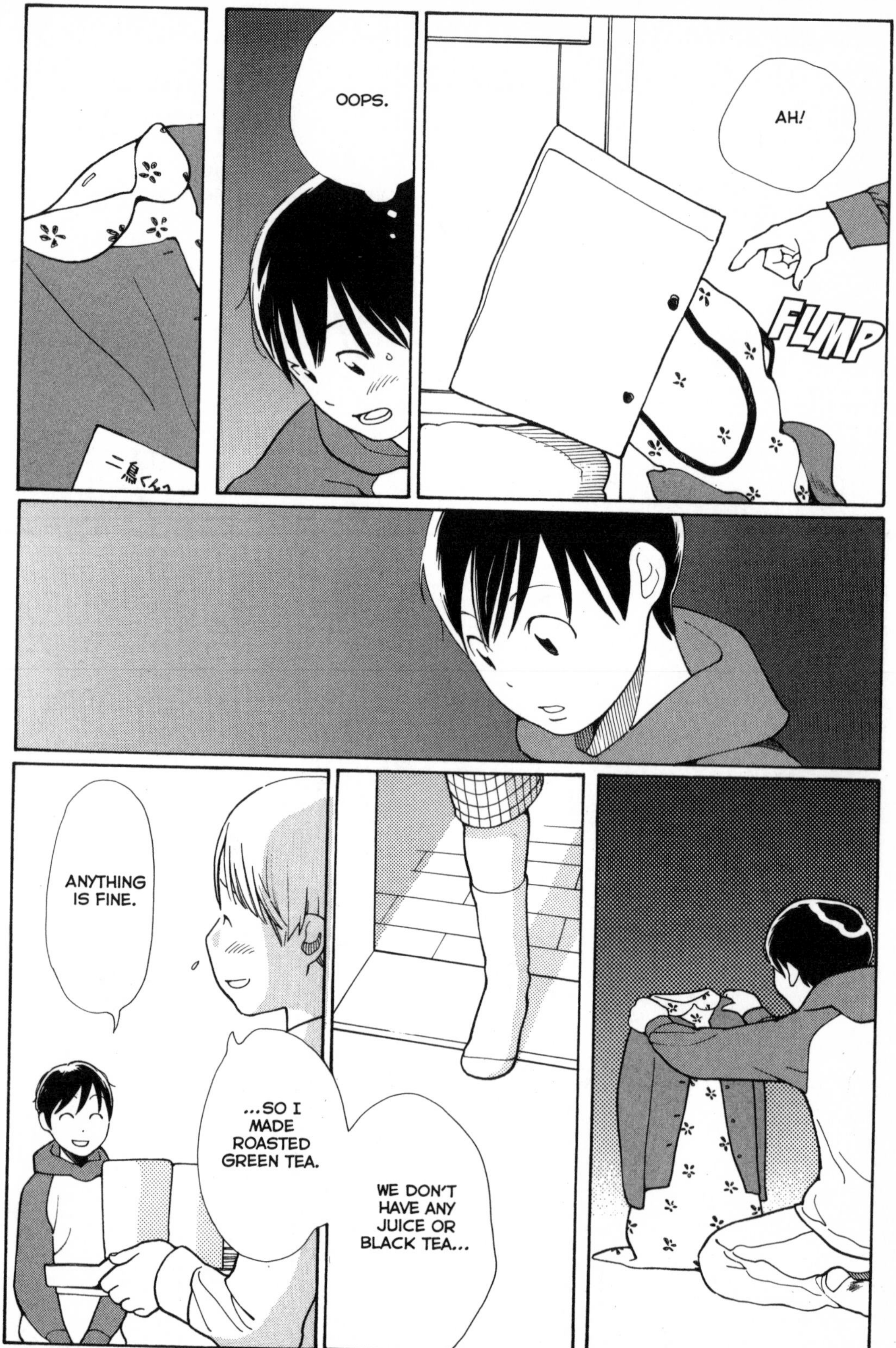
AH!
FLMP
OOPS.
WE DON'T HAVE ANY JUICE OR BLACK TEA...
...SO I MADE ROASTED GREEN TEA.
ANYTHING IS FINE.

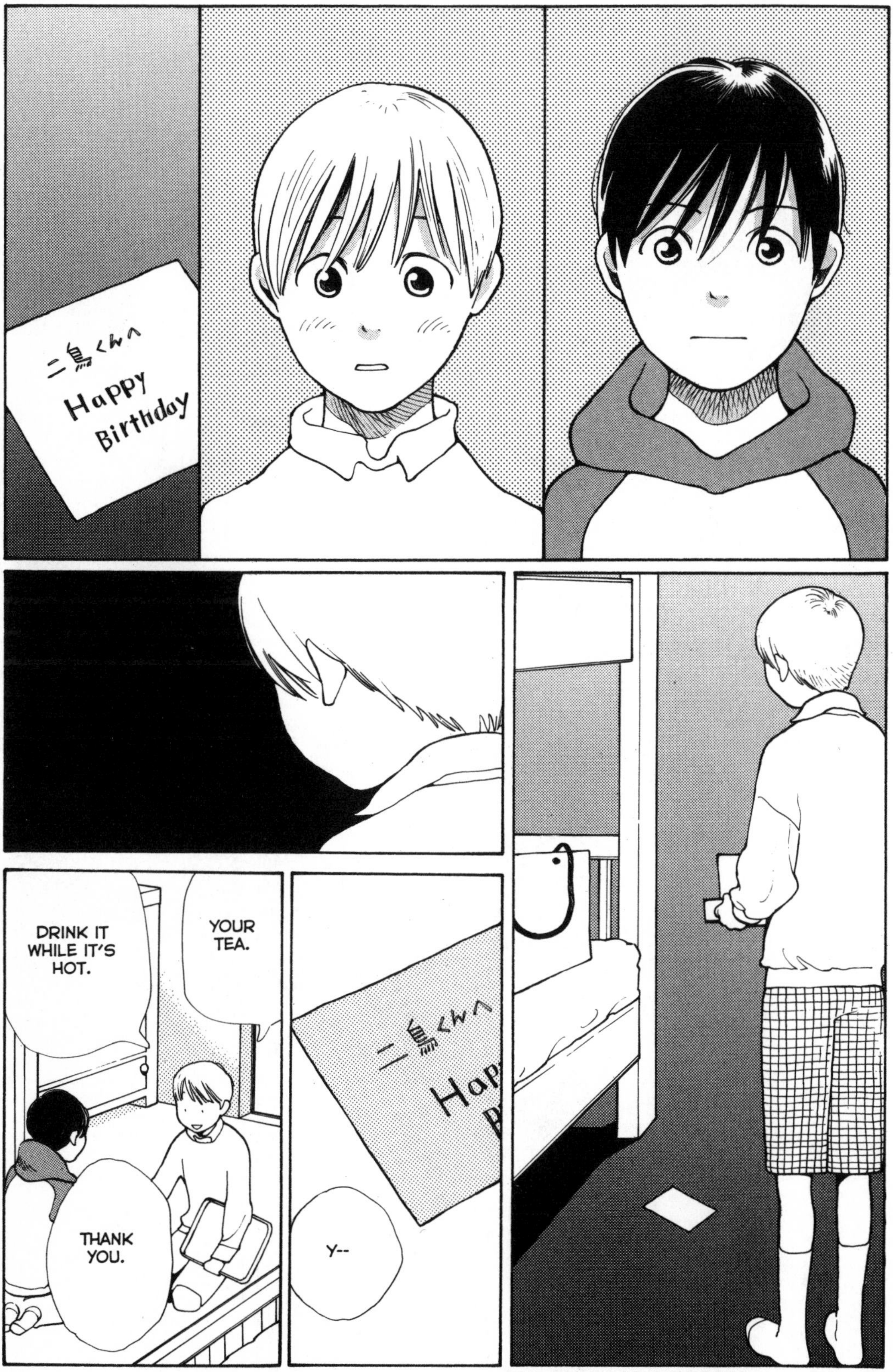
二鳥くんへ
Happy Birthday
二鳥くんへ
Y--
YOUR TEA.
DRINK IT WHILE IT'S HOT.
THANK YOU.

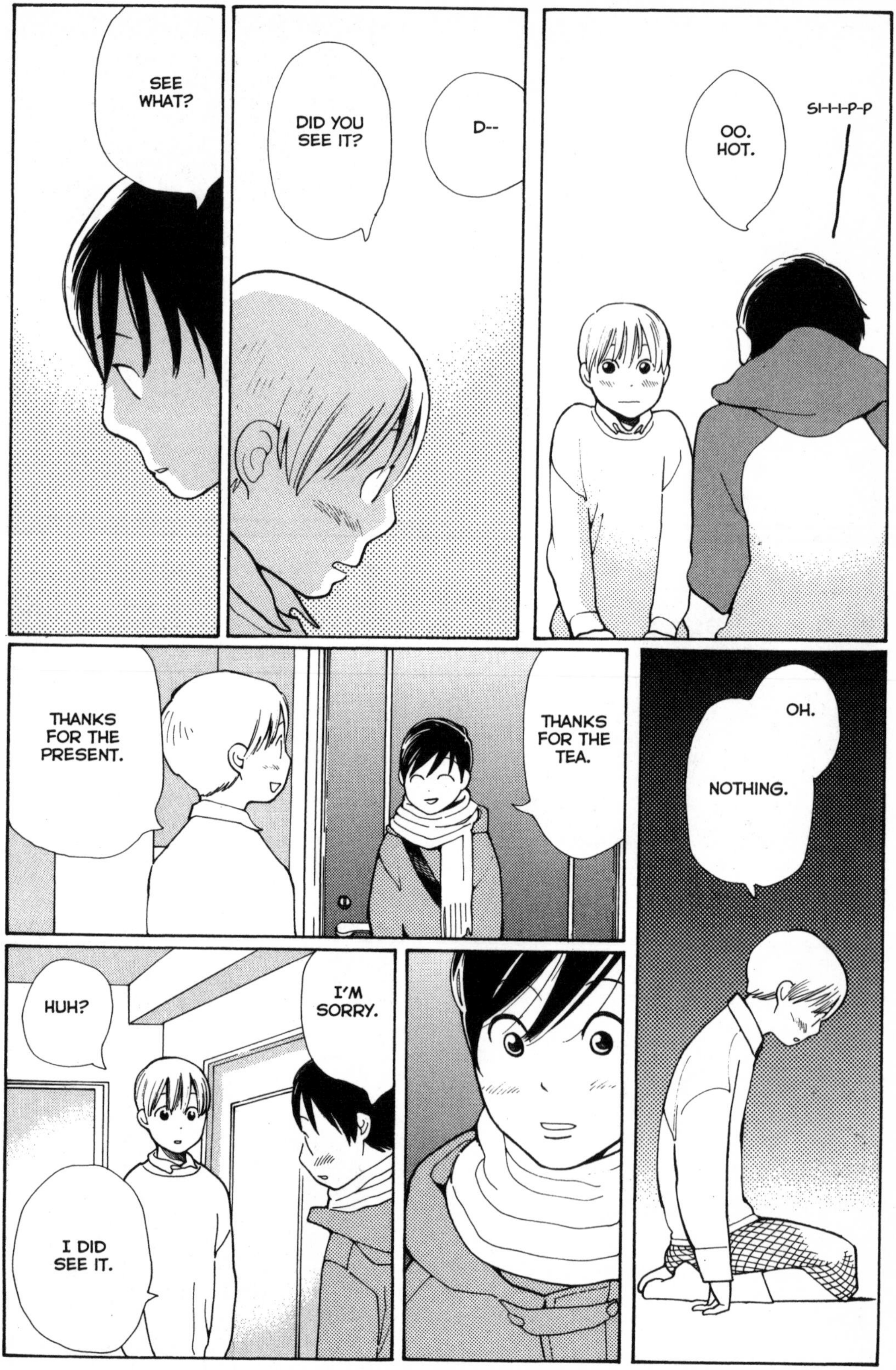
SI-I-I-P-P
OO. HOT.
D--
DID YOU SEE IT?
SEE WHAT?
OH.
NOTHING.
THANKS FOR THE TEA.
THANKS FOR THE PRESENT.
I'M SORRY.
HUH?
I DID SEE IT.

SHU-CHAN. TELEPHONE.

TMP

SOMEONE NAMED CHIBA-SAN.

I FORGOT TO GIVE YOU THESE.

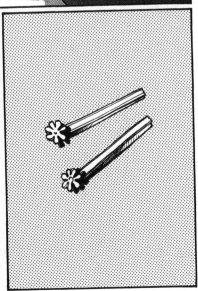

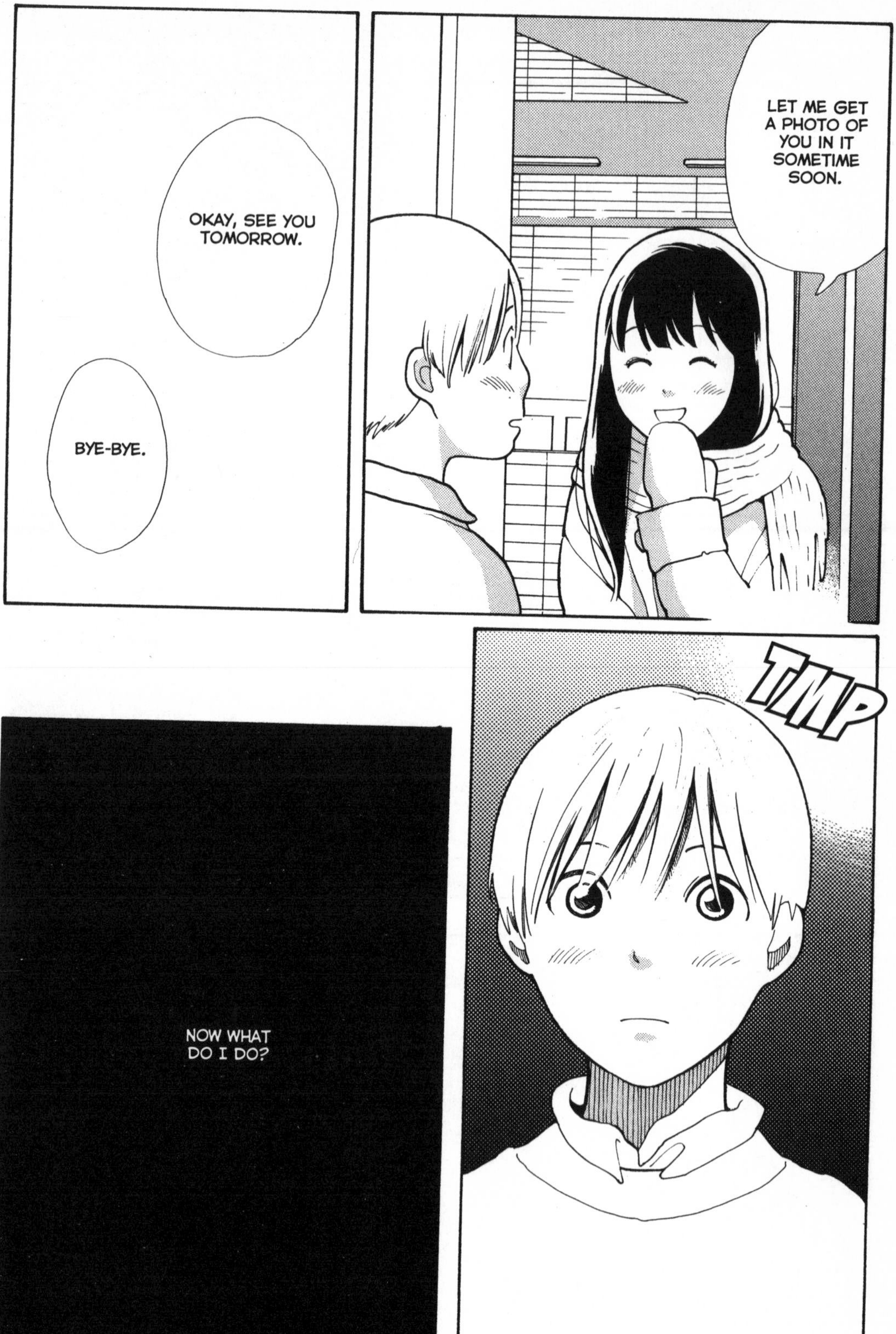
LET ME GET A PHOTO OF YOU IN IT SOMETIME SOON.
OKAY, SEE YOU TOMORROW.
BYE-BYE.
TMP
NOW WHAT DO I DO?

6

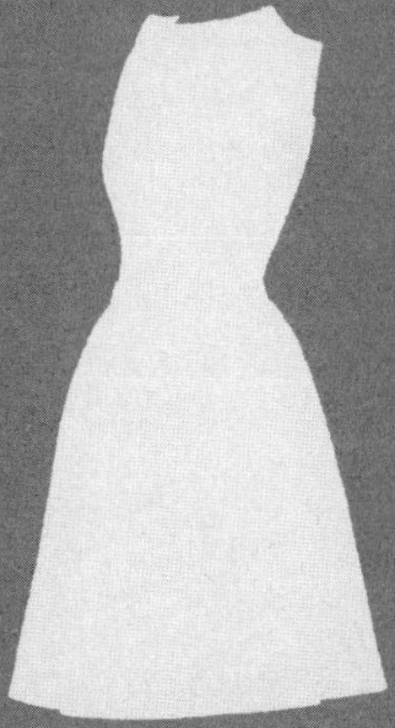

Friends and Their Words

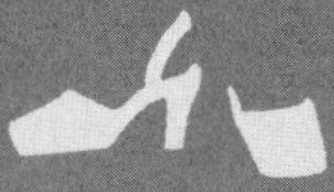

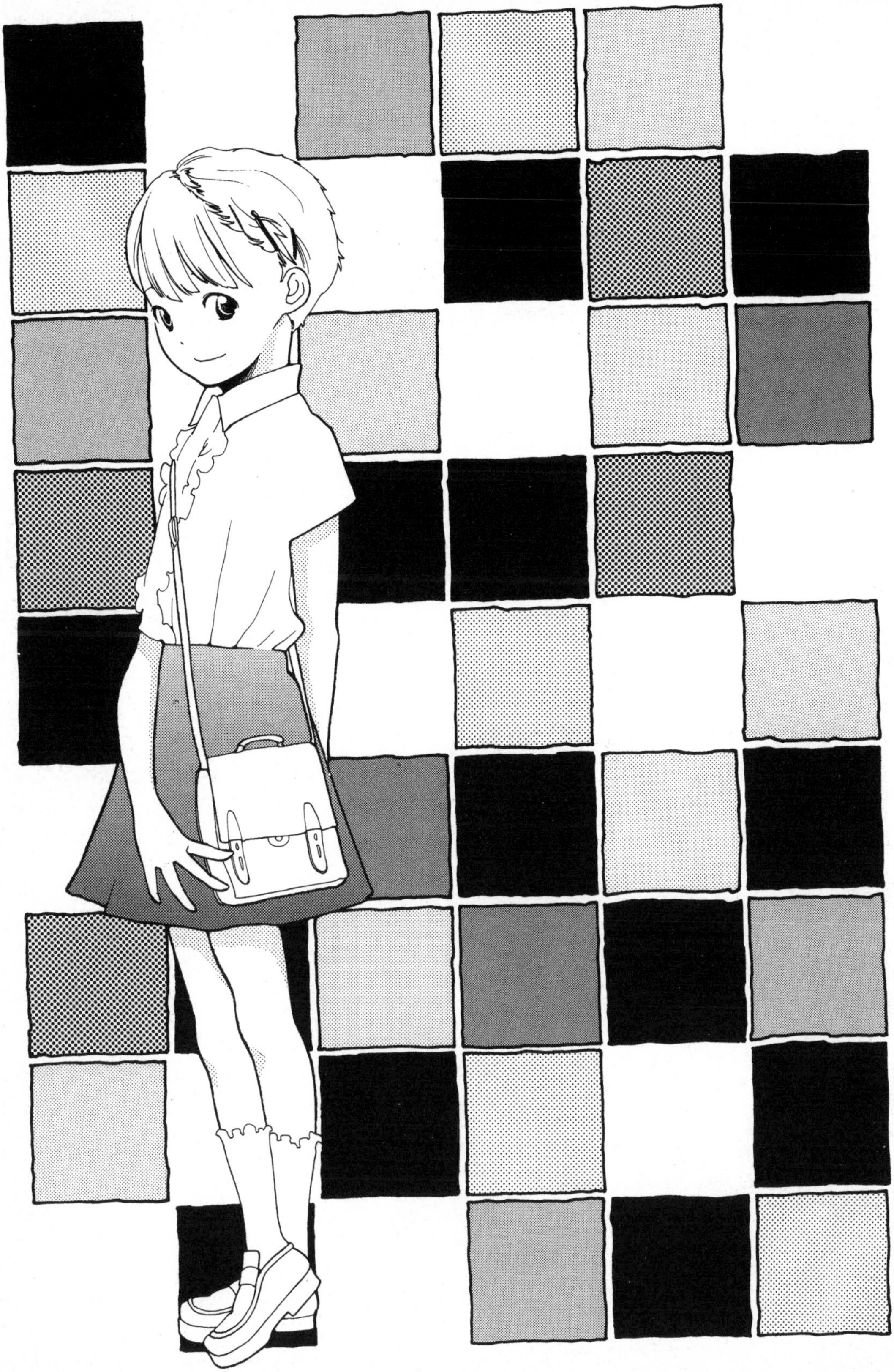

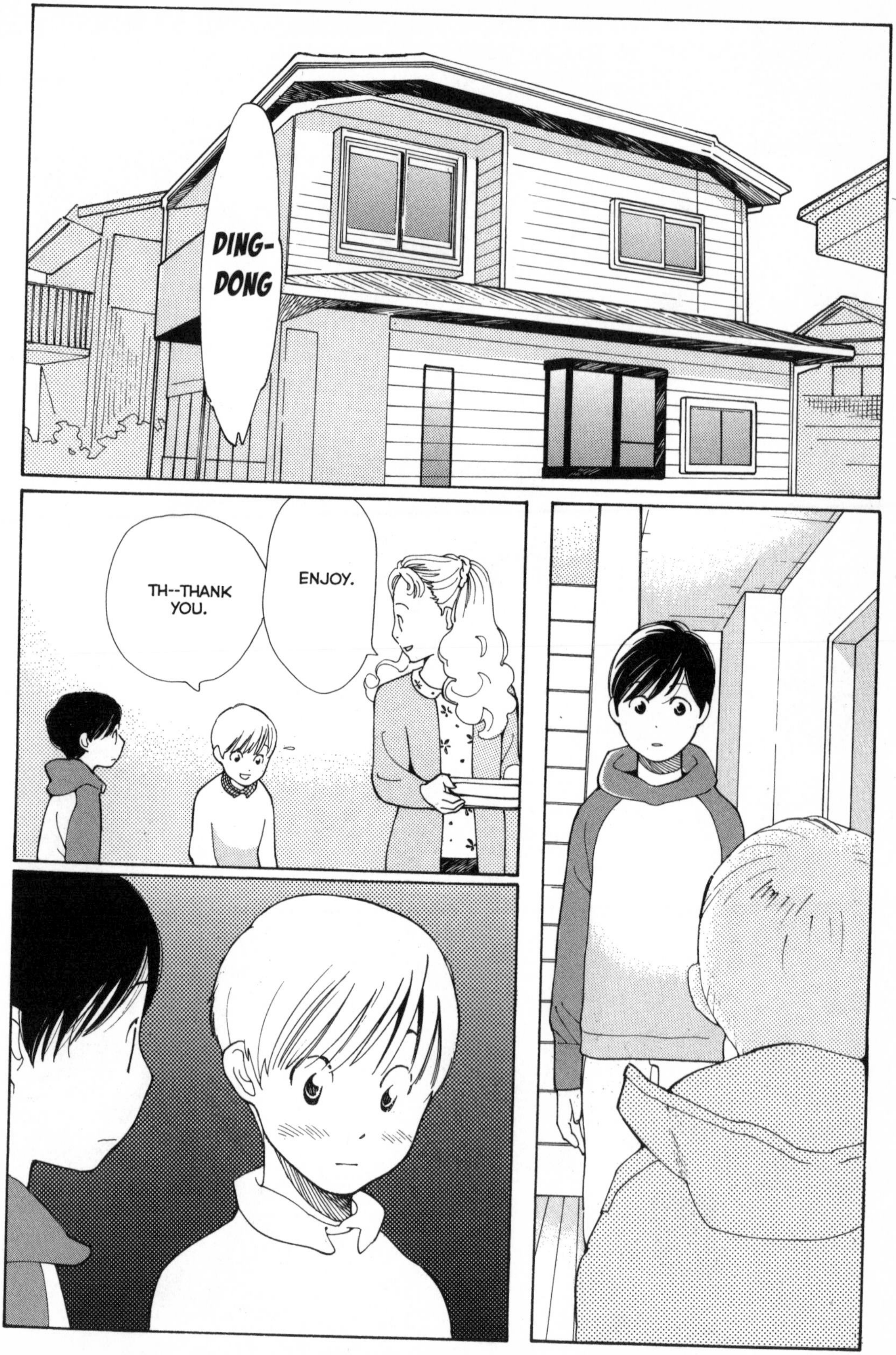
DING-DONG
ENJOY.
TH--THANK YOU.

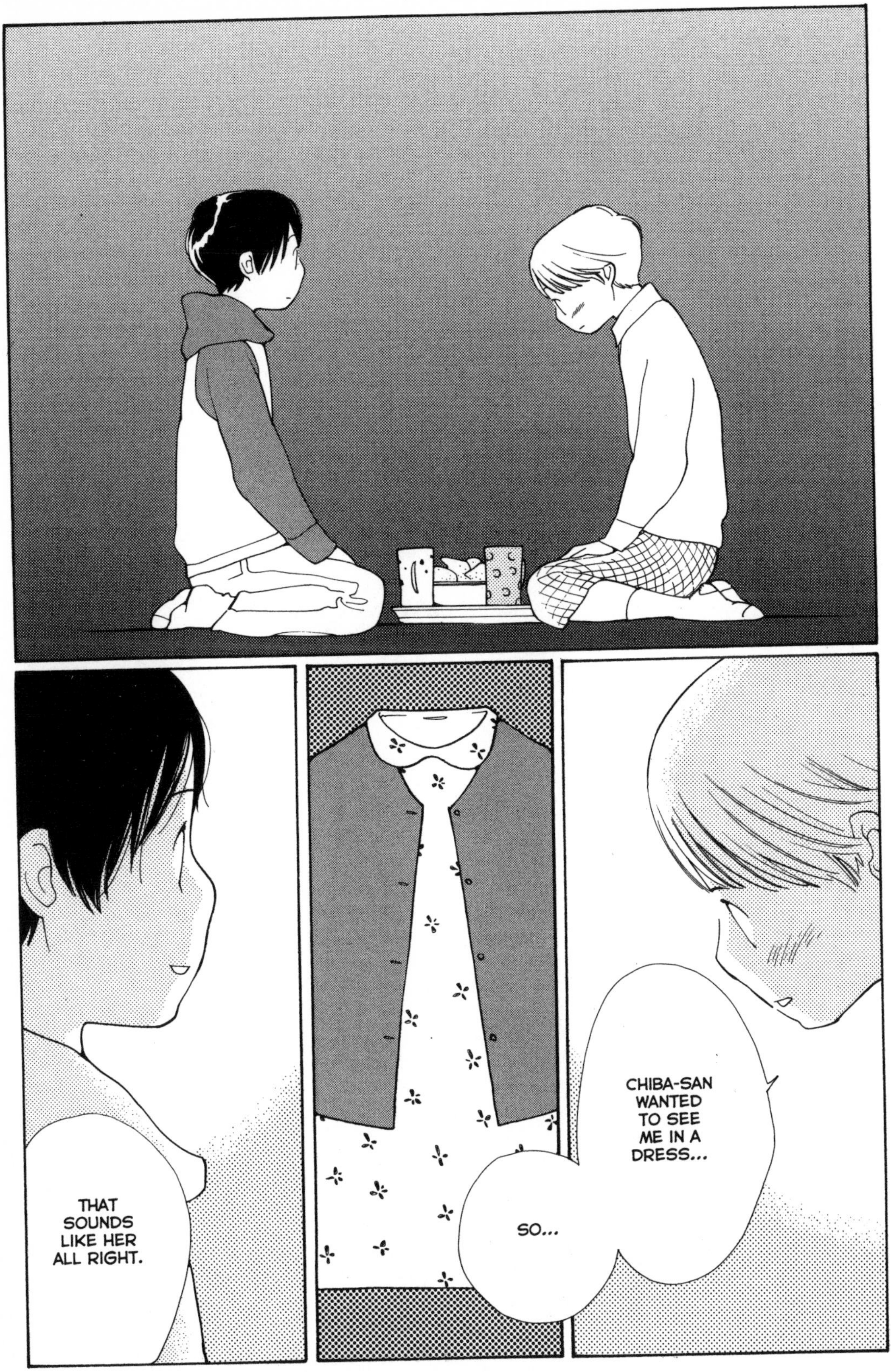
CHIBA-SAN WANTED TO SEE ME IN A DRESS...
SO...
THAT SOUNDS LIKE HER ALL RIGHT.

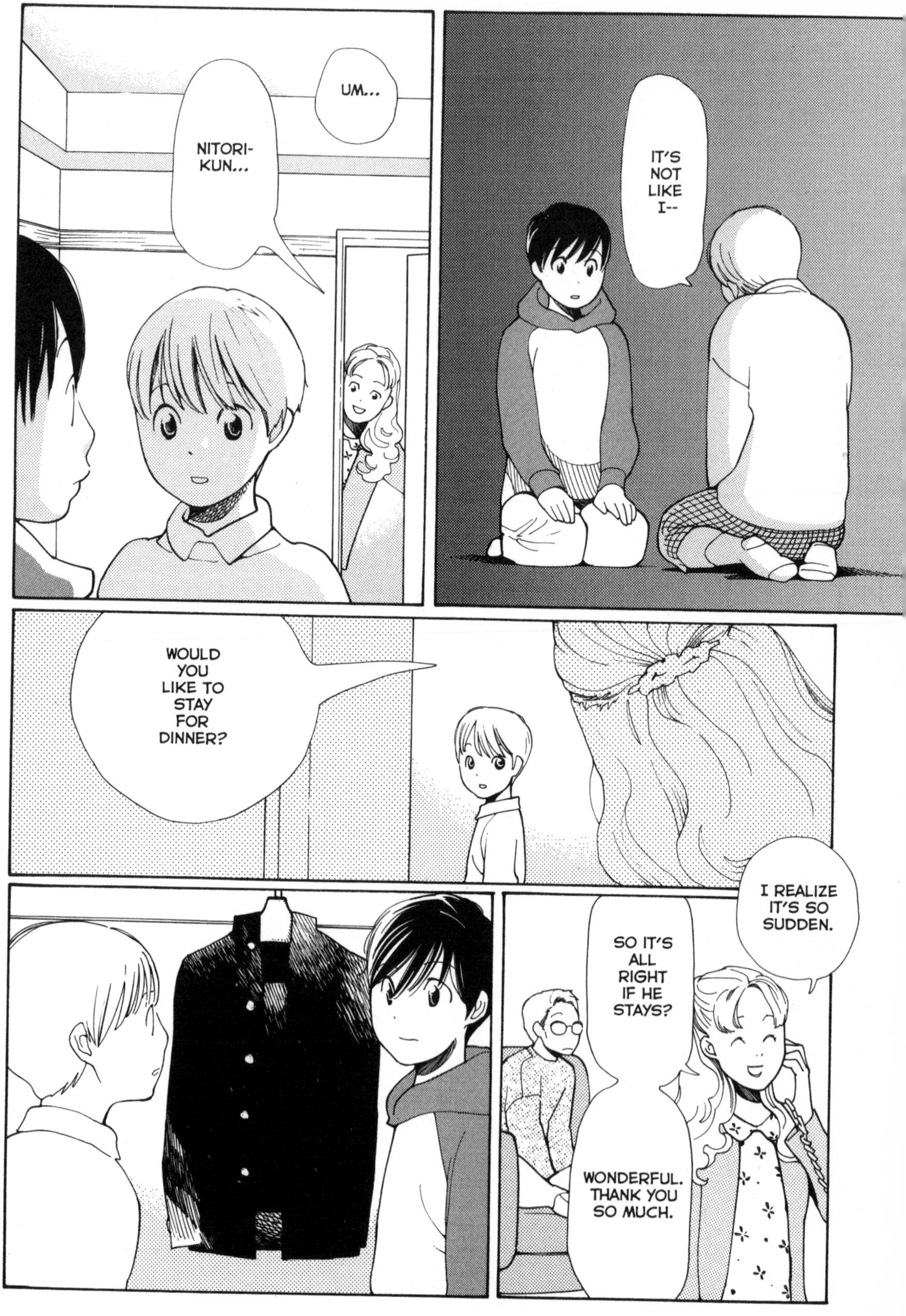
IT'S NOT LIKE I--
UM...
NITORI-KUN...
WOULD YOU LIKE TO STAY FOR DINNER?
I REALIZE IT'S SO SUDDEN.
SO IT'S ALL RIGHT IF HE STAYS?
WONDERFUL. THANK YOU SO MUCH.

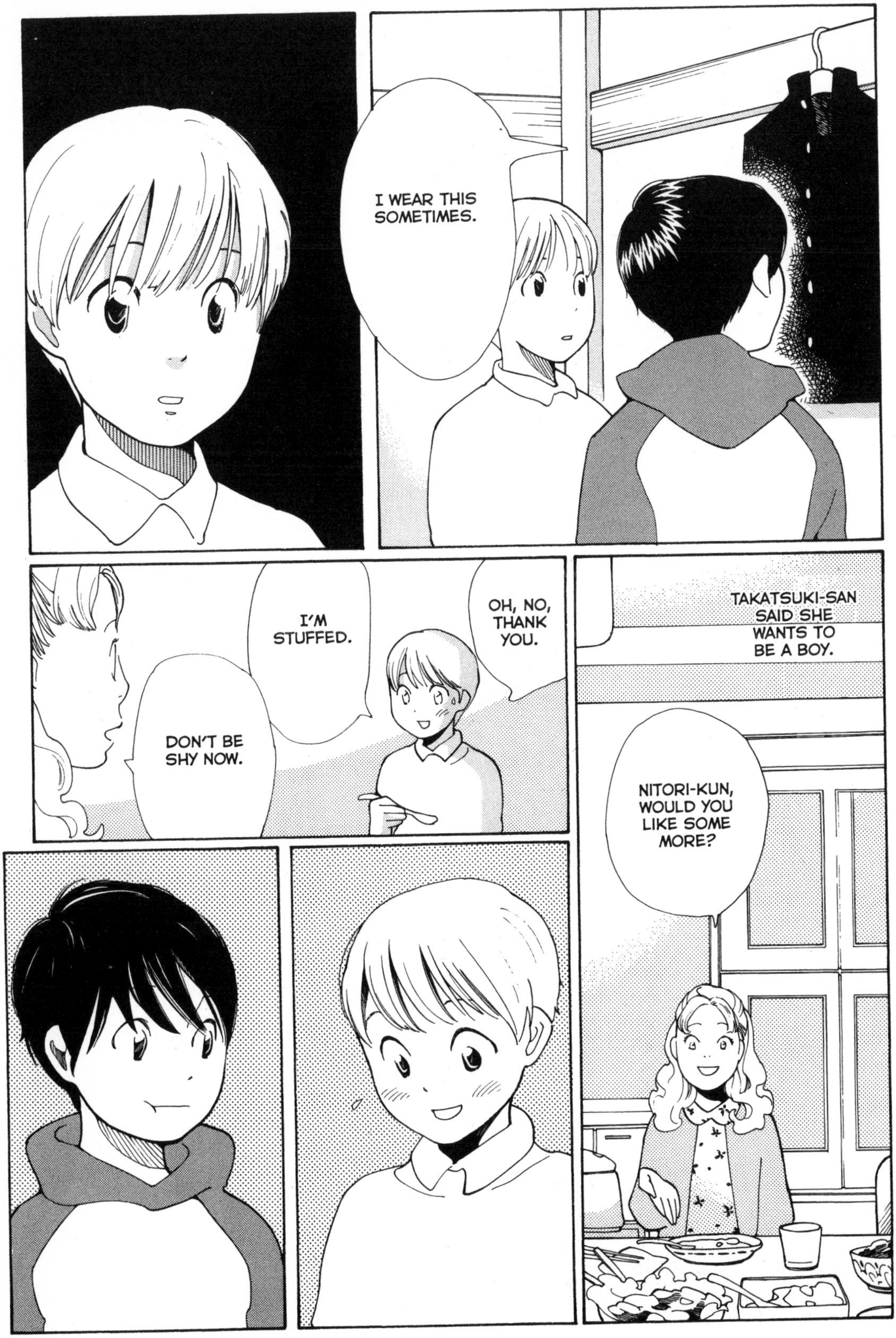
I WEAR THIS SOMETIMES.
TAKATSUKI-SAN SAID SHE WANTS TO BE A BOY.
NITORI-KUN, WOULD YOU LIKE SOME MORE?
OH, NO, THANK YOU.
I'M STUFFED.
DON'T BE SHY NOW.

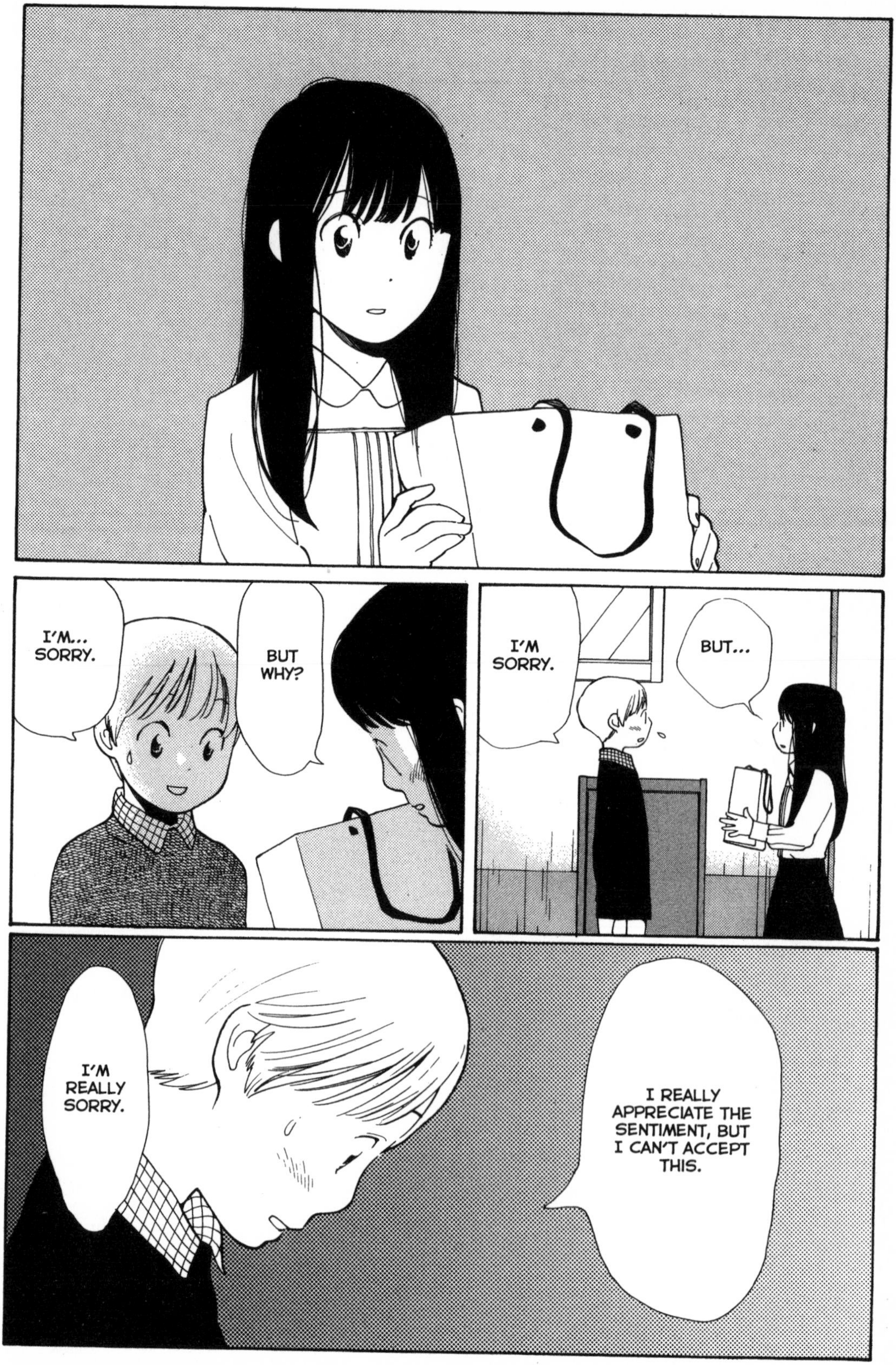
BUT...
I'M SORRY.
BUT WHY?
I'M... SORRY.
I REALLY APPRECIATE THE SENTIMENT, BUT I CAN'T ACCEPT THIS.
I'M REALLY SORRY.

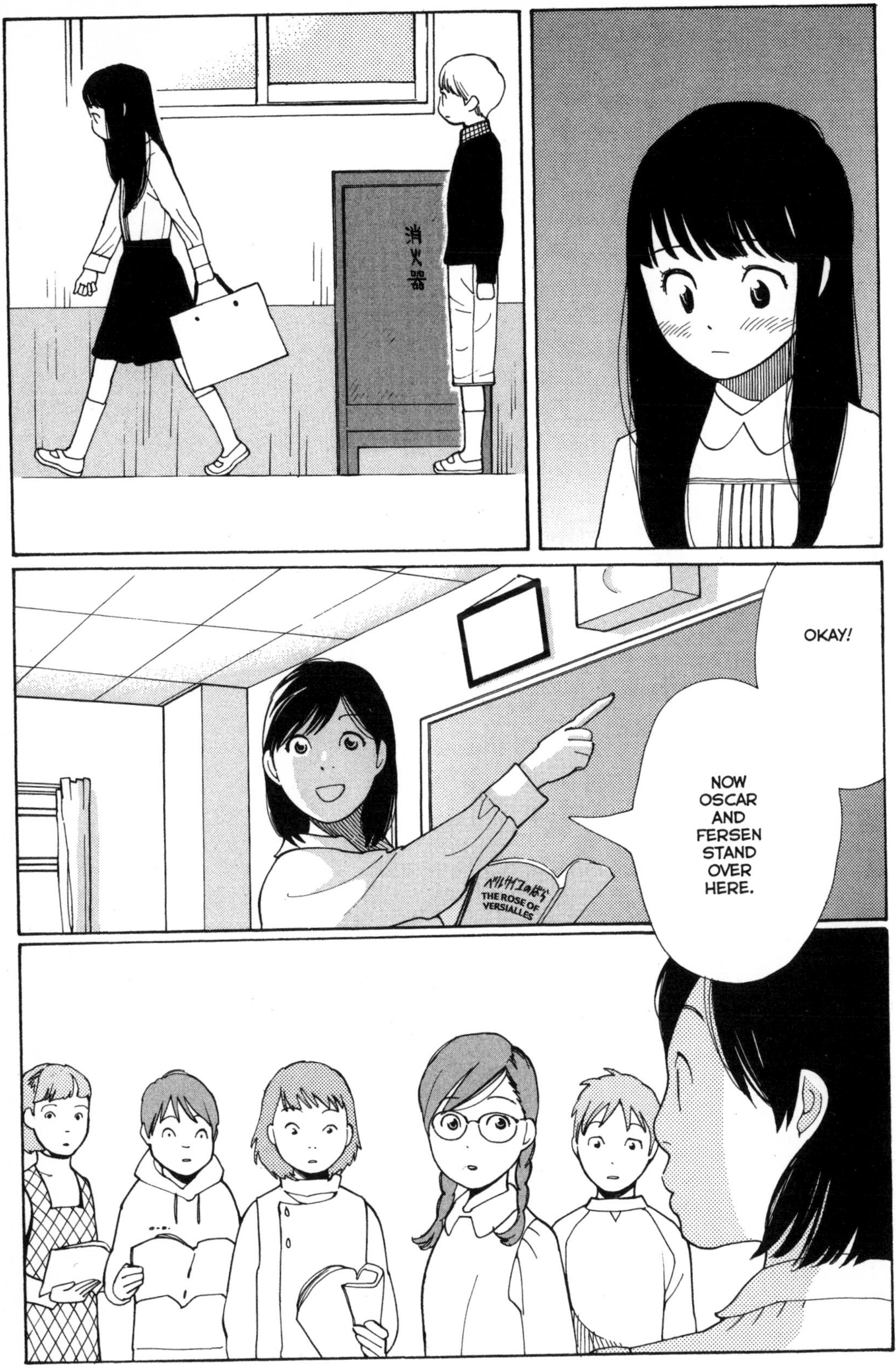
消火器
OKAY!
NOW OSCAR AND FERSEN STAND OVER HERE.
ベルサイユのばら
THE ROSE OF VERSIALLES

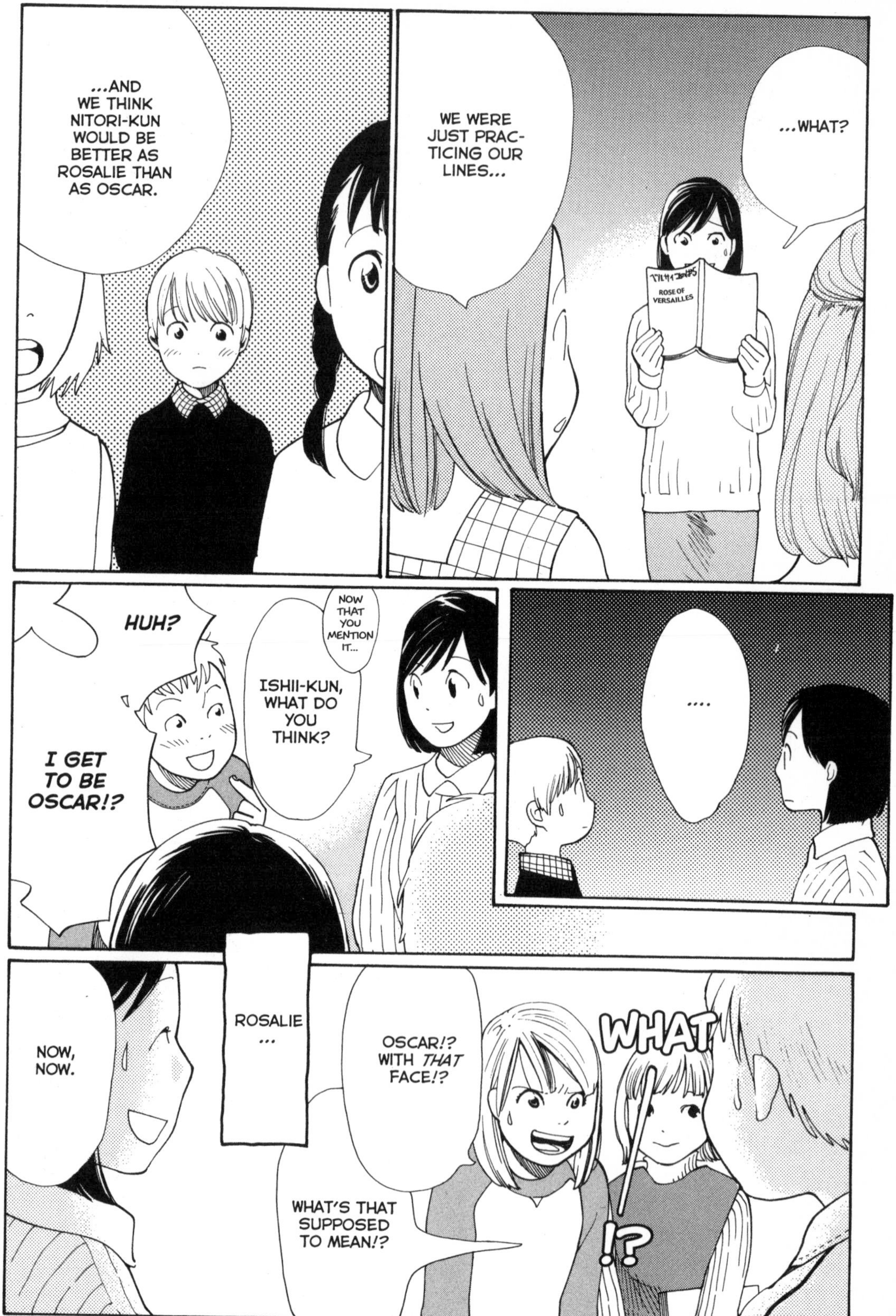
...WHAT?
WE WERE JUST PRAC-TICING OUR LINES...
ベルサイユのばら
ROSE OF VERSAILLES
...AND WE THINK NITORI-KUN WOULD BE BETTER AS ROSALIE THAN AS OSCAR.
....
NOW THAT YOU MENTION IT...
ISHII-KUN, WHAT DO YOU THINK?
HUH?
I GET TO BE OSCAR!?
WHAT
!?
OSCAR!? WITH *THAT* FACE!?
WHAT'S THAT SUPPOSED TO MEAN!?
ROSALIE ...
NOW, NOW.

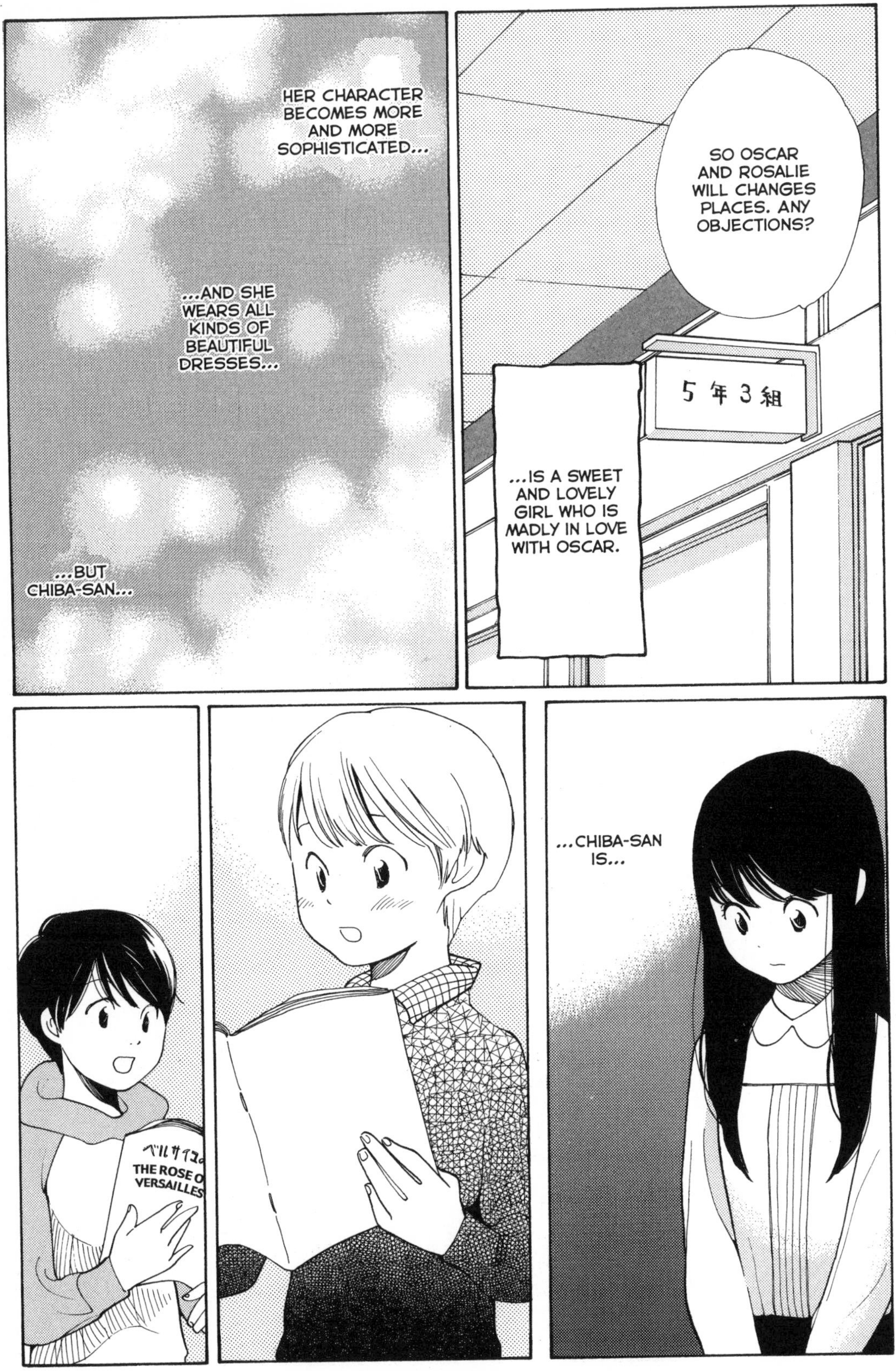
HER CHARACTER BECOMES MORE AND MORE SOPHISTICATED...
...AND SHE WEARS ALL KINDS OF BEAUTIFUL DRESSES...
...BUT CHIBA-SAN...
SO OSCAR AND ROSALIE WILL CHANGES PLACES. ANY OBJECTIONS?
5年3組
...IS A SWEET AND LOVELY GIRL WHO IS MADLY IN LOVE WITH OSCAR.
THE ROSE O
VERSAILLES
...CHIBA-SAN IS...

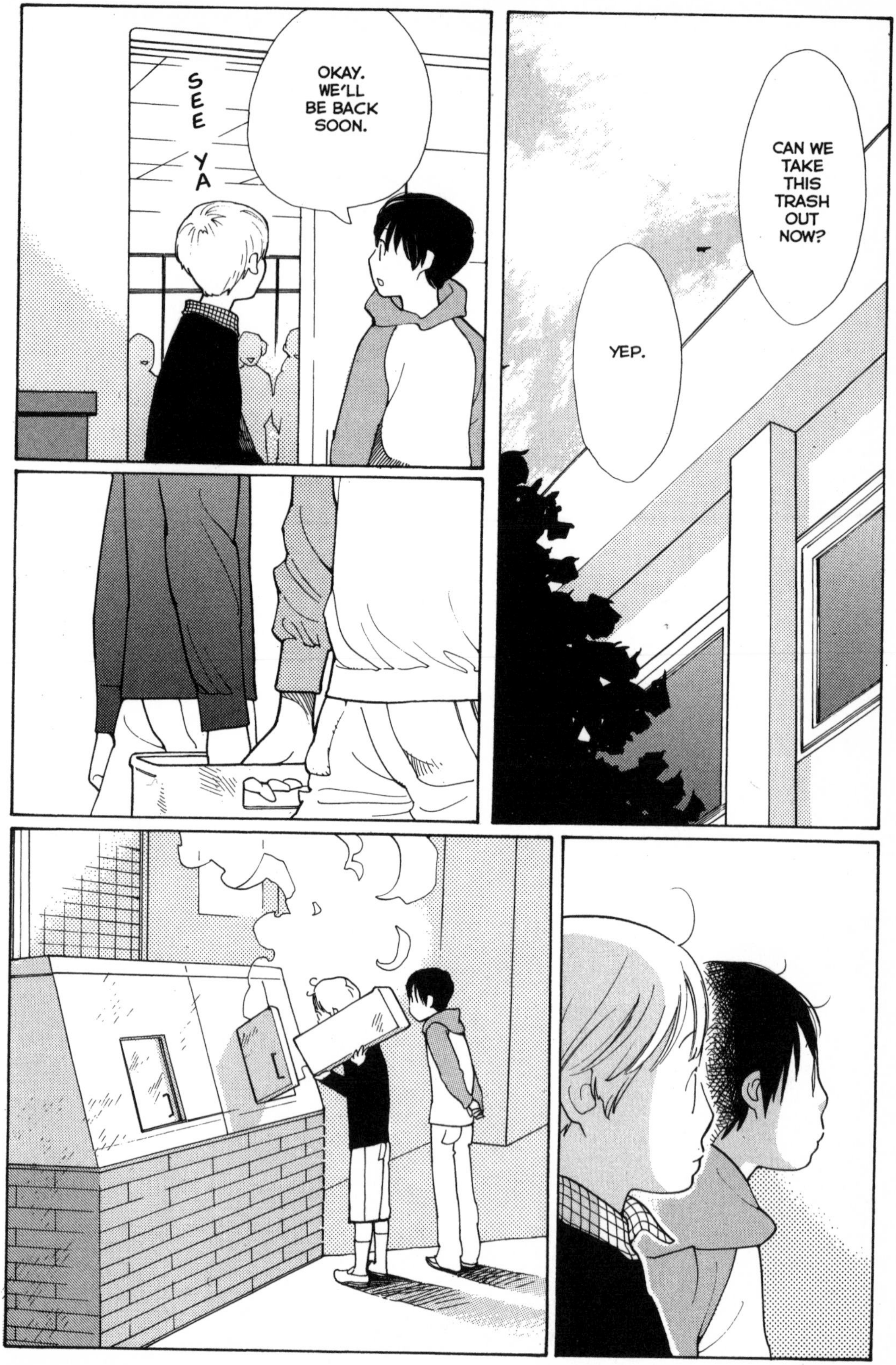
CAN WE TAKE THIS TRASH OUT NOW?
YEP.
OKAY. WE'LL BE BACK SOON.
SEE YA

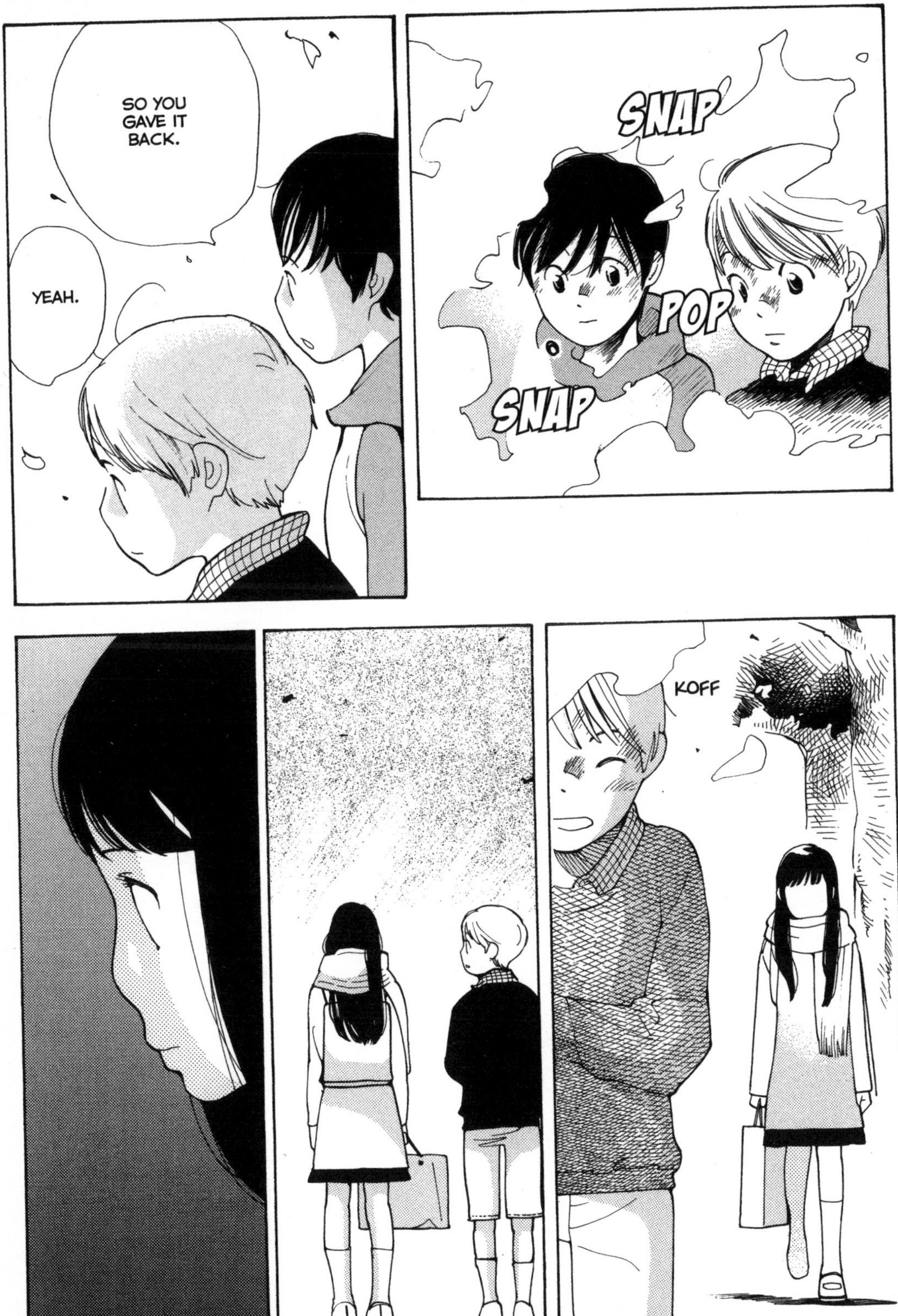
SNAP
POP
SNAP
SO YOU GAVE IT BACK.
YEAH.
KOFF

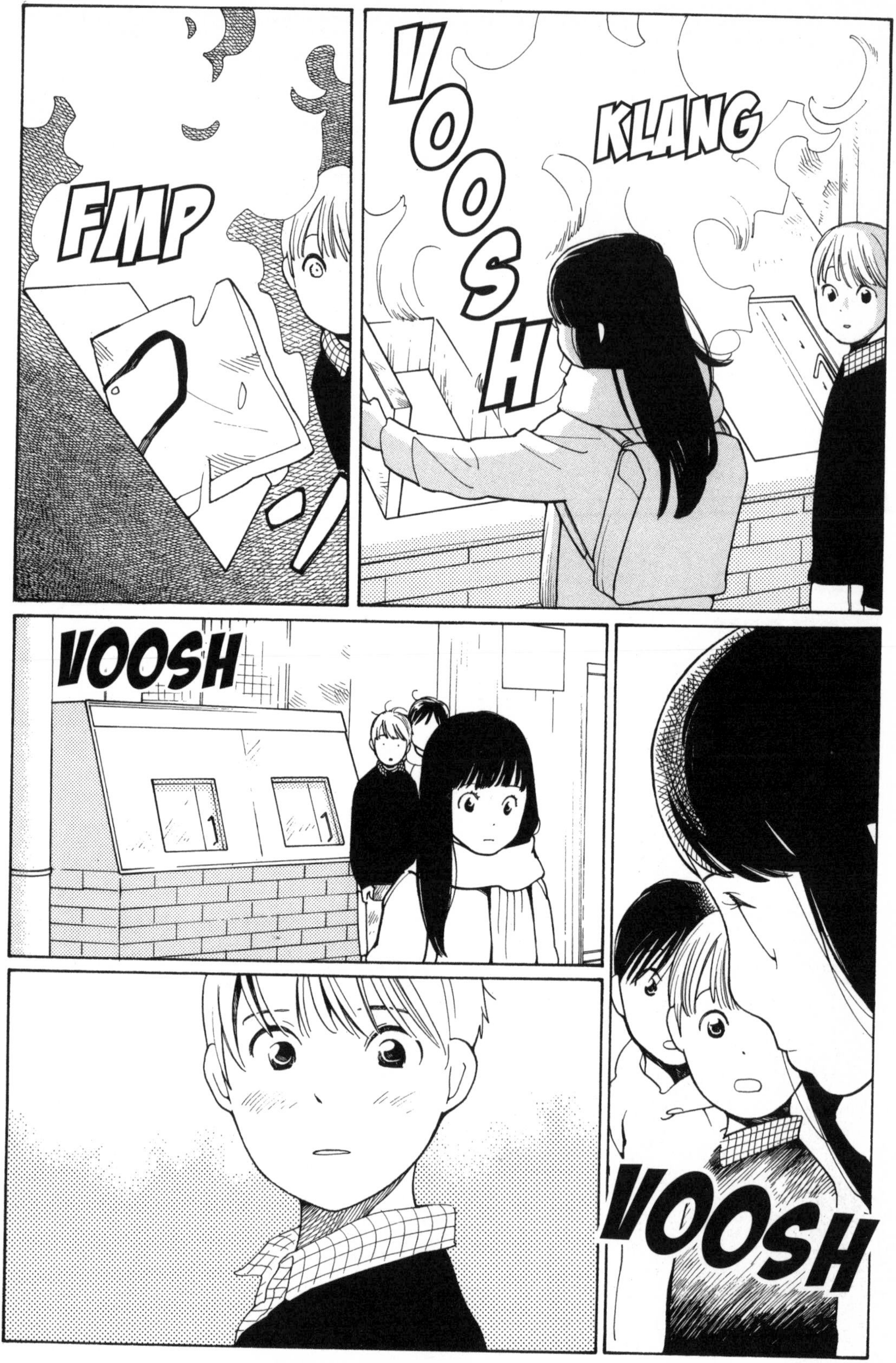
VOOSH
KLANG
FMP
VOOSH
VOOSH

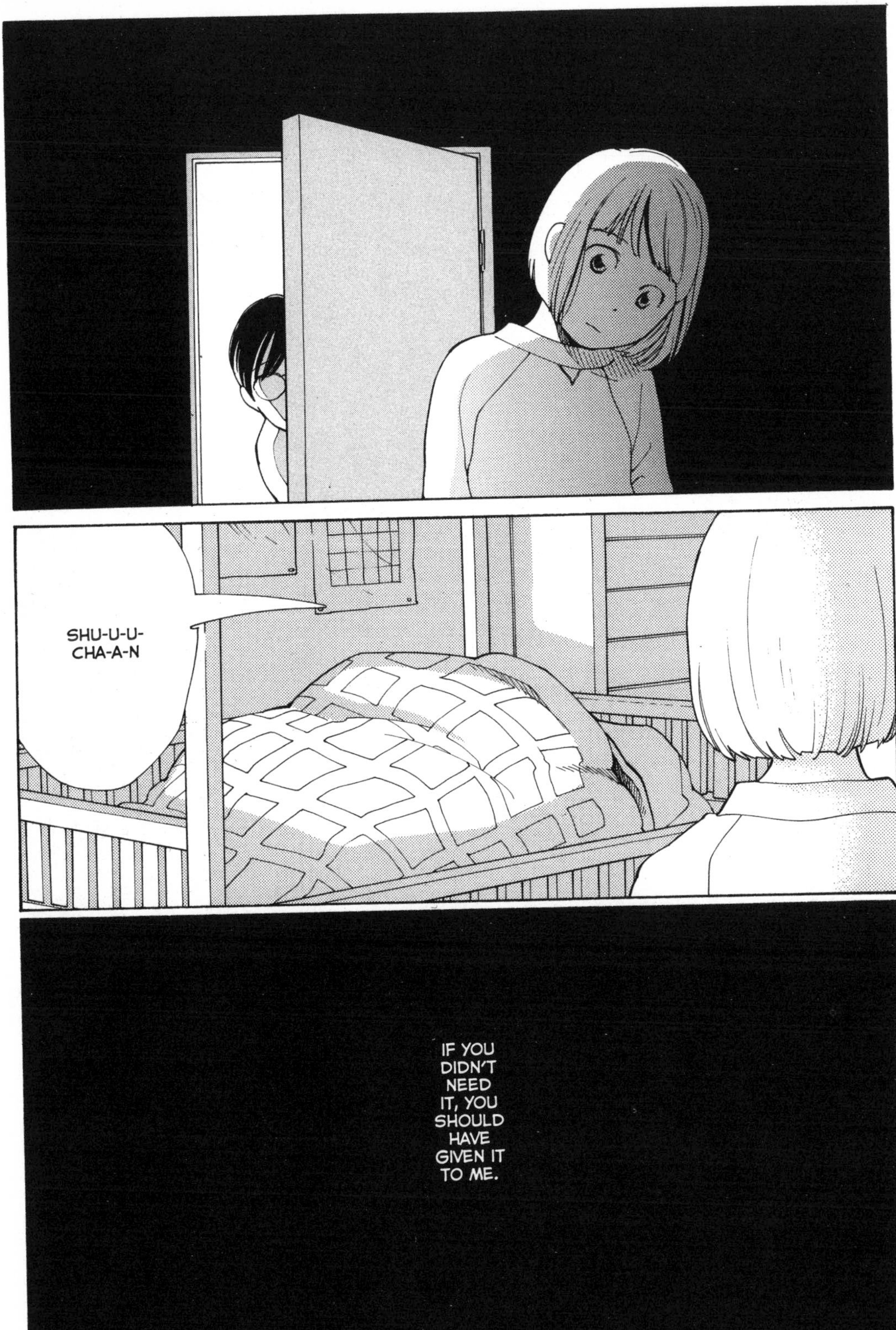
SHU-U-U-
CHA-A-N
IF YOU DIDN'T NEED IT, YOU SHOULD HAVE GIVEN IT TO ME.

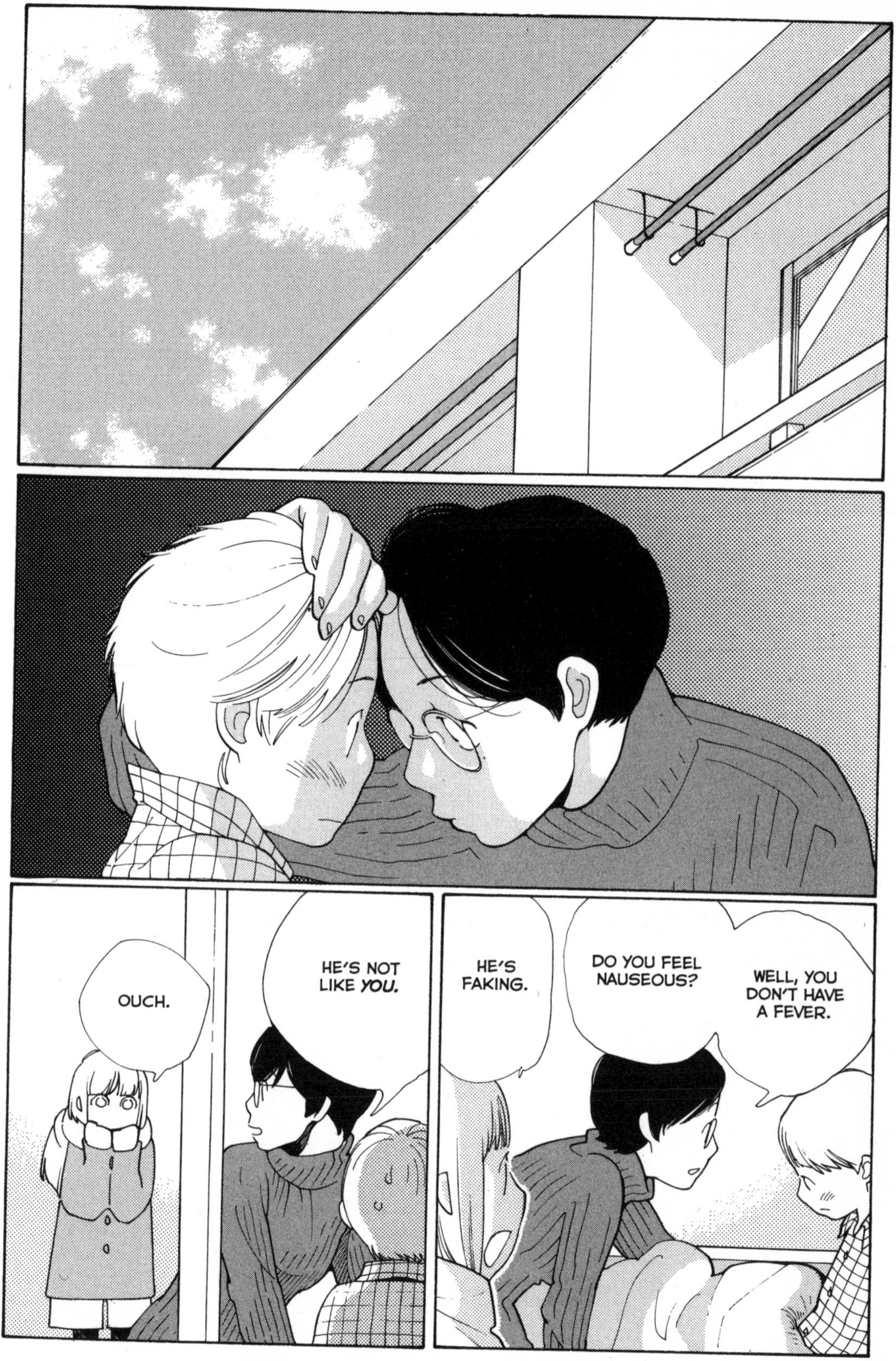
WELL, YOU DON'T HAVE A FEVER.
DO YOU FEEL NAUSEOUS?
HE'S FAKING.
HE'S NOT LIKE *YOU.*
OUCH.

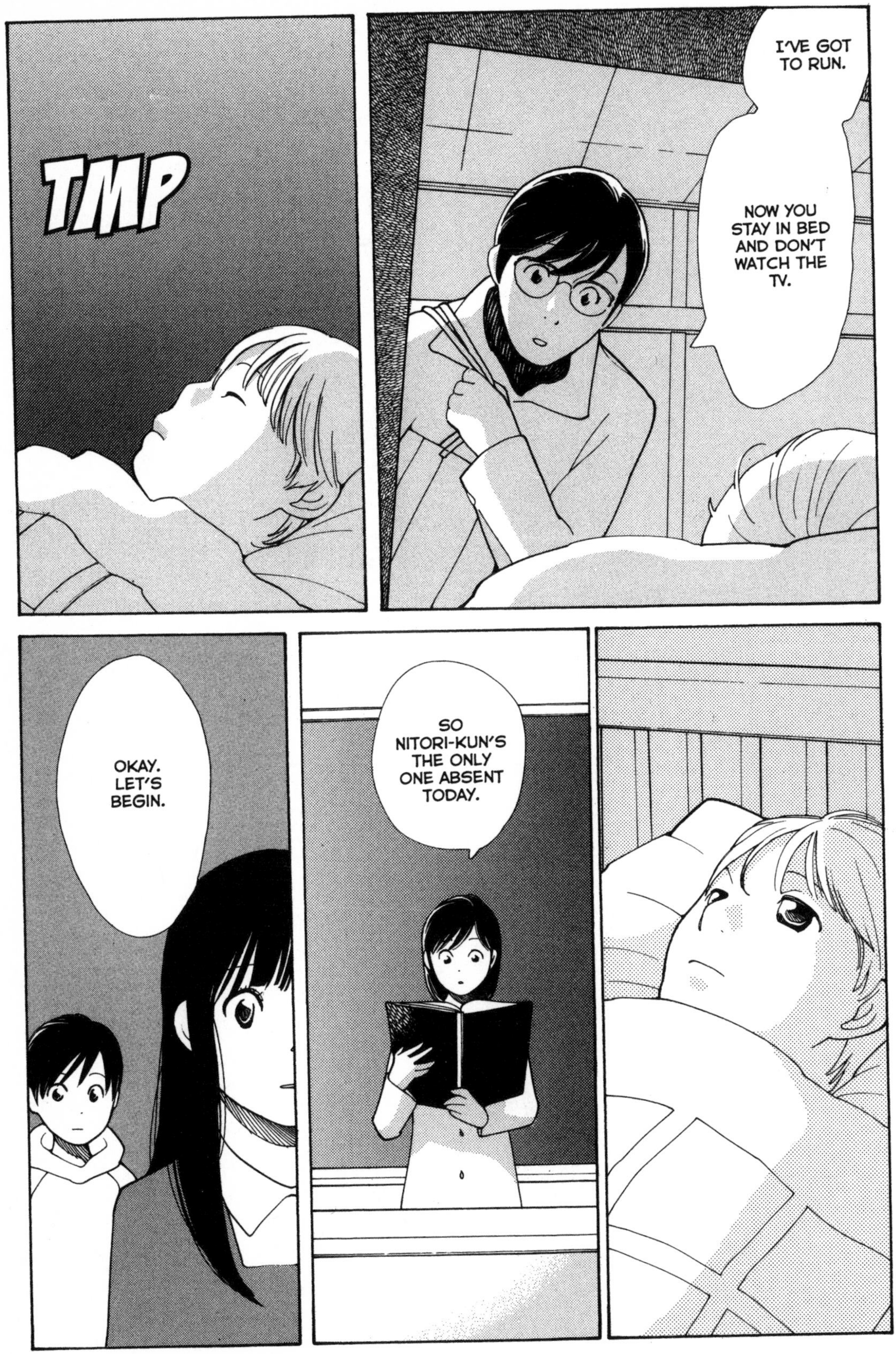
I'VE GOT TO RUN.
NOW YOU STAY IN BED AND DON'T WATCH THE TV.
TMP
SO NITORI-KUN'S THE ONLY ONE ABSENT TODAY.
OKAY. LET'S BEGIN.

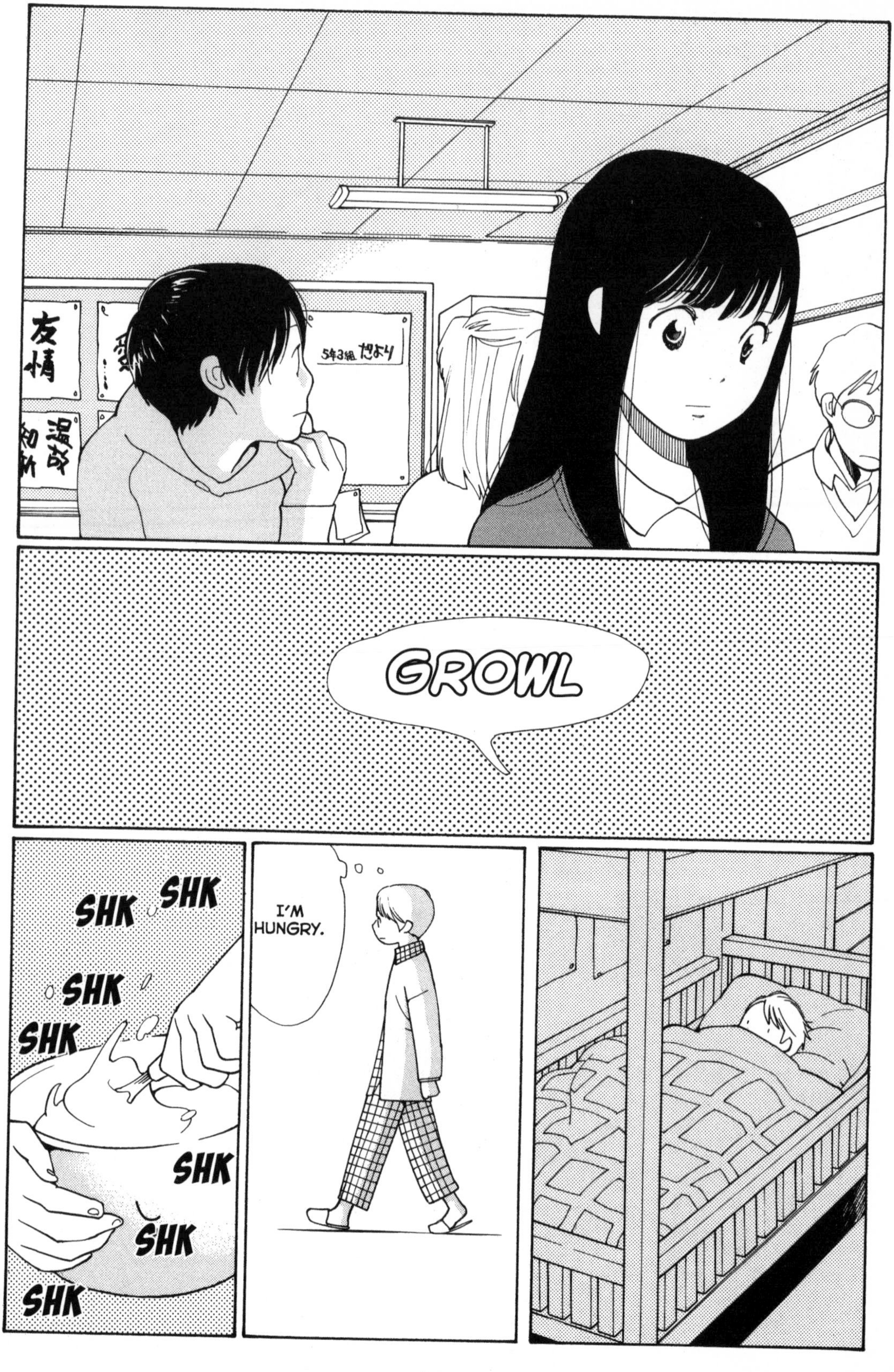
友情
温故知新
5年3組 だより
GROWL
I'M HUNGRY.
SHK SHK
SHK
SHK
SHK
SHK
SHK

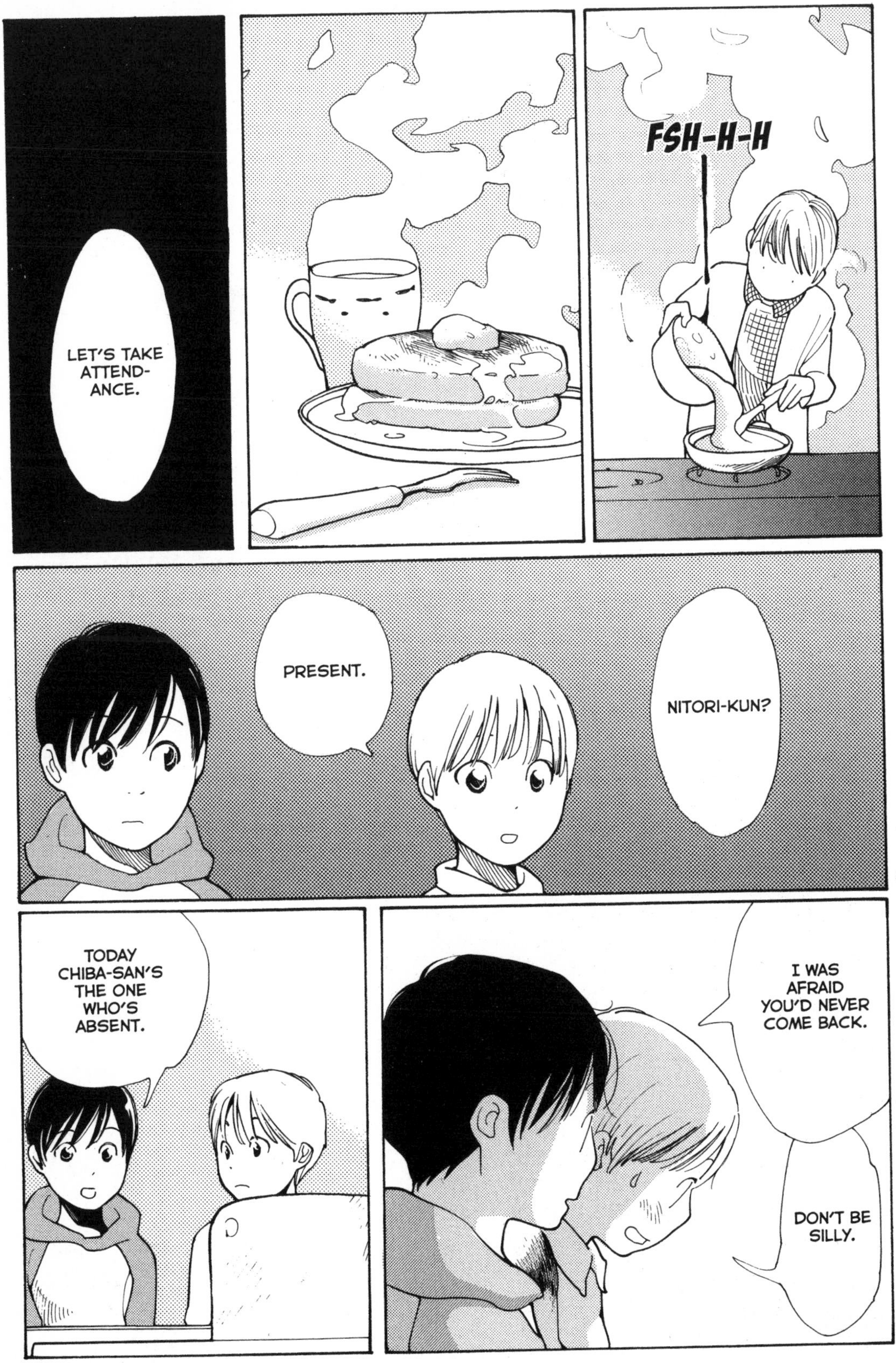
FSH-H-H
LET'S TAKE ATTENDANCE.
NITORI-KUN?
PRESENT.
I WAS AFRAID YOU'D NEVER COME BACK.
DON'T BE SILLY.
TODAY CHIBA-SAN'S THE ONE WHO'S ABSENT.

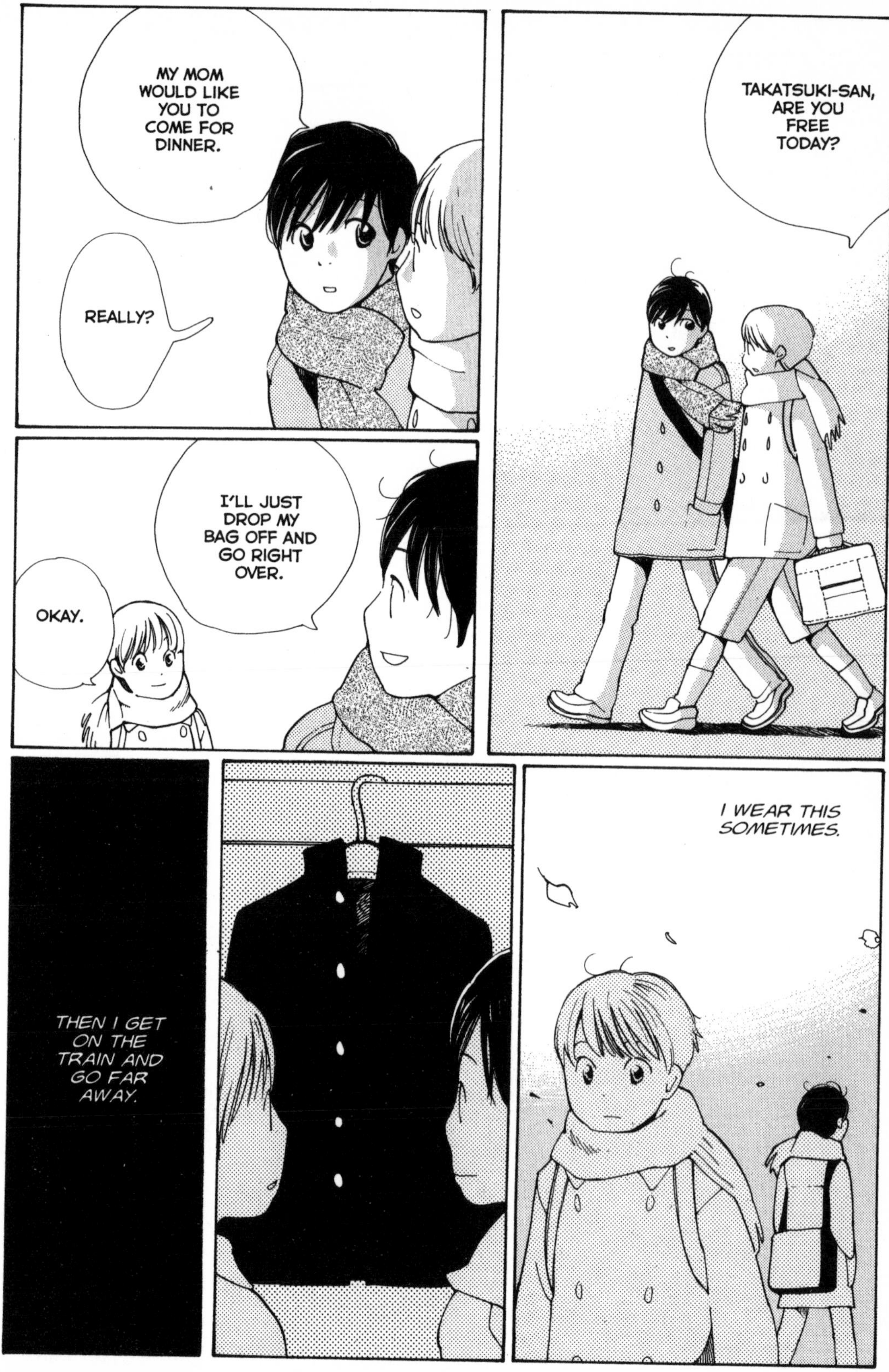
TAKATSUKI-SAN, ARE YOU FREE TODAY?
MY MOM WOULD LIKE YOU TO COME FOR DINNER.
REALLY?
I'LL JUST DROP MY BAG OFF AND GO RIGHT OVER.
OKAY.
I WEAR THIS SOMETIMES.
THEN I GET ON THE TRAIN AND GO FAR AWAY.

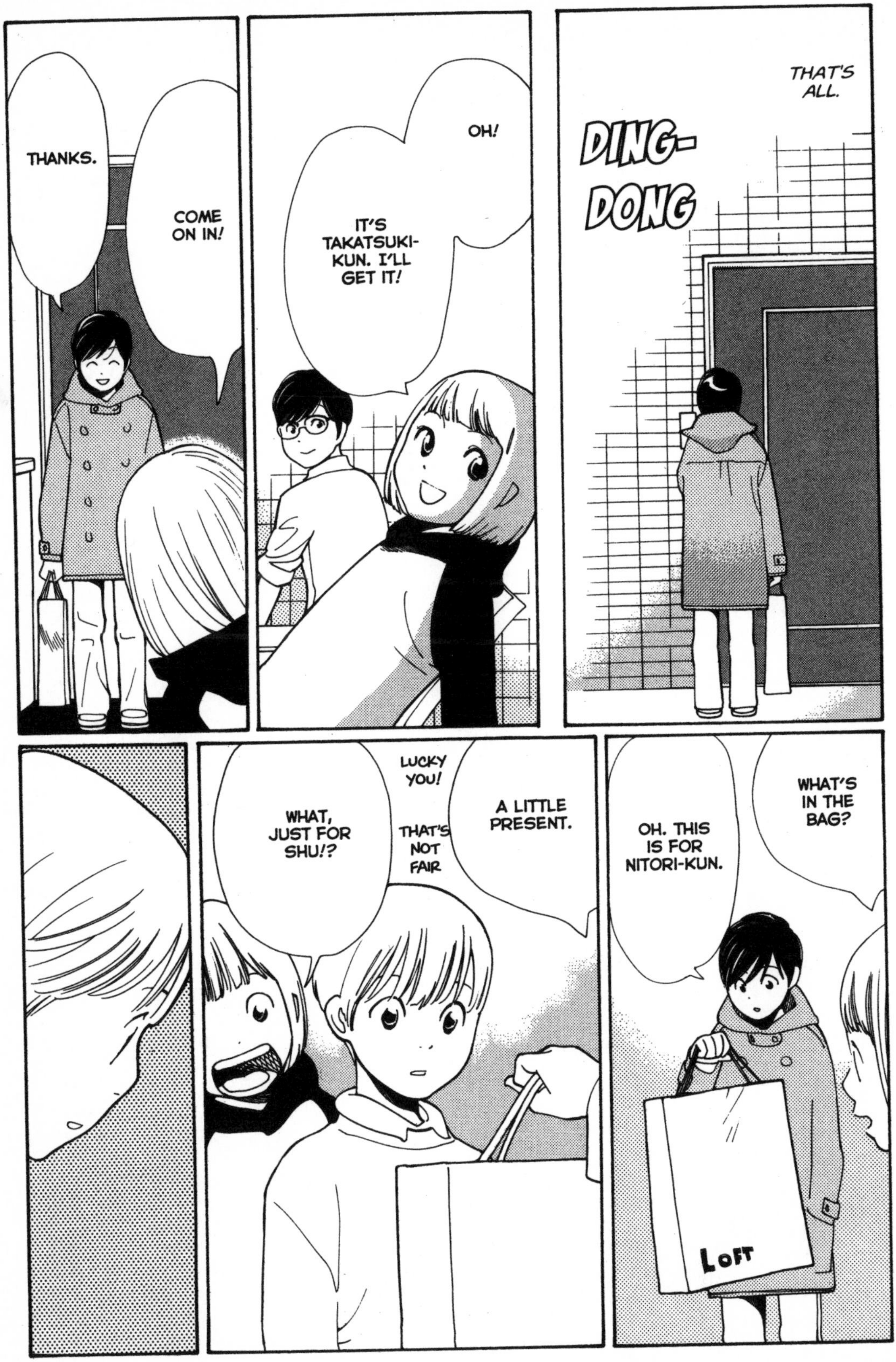
THAT'S ALL.
DING-DONG
OH!
IT'S TAKATSUKI-KUN. I'LL GET IT!
COME ON IN!
THANKS.
WHAT'S IN THE BAG?
OH. THIS IS FOR NITORI-KUN.
LOFT
A LITTLE PRESENT.
LUCKY YOU!
THAT'S NOT FAIR
WHAT, JUST FOR SHU!?

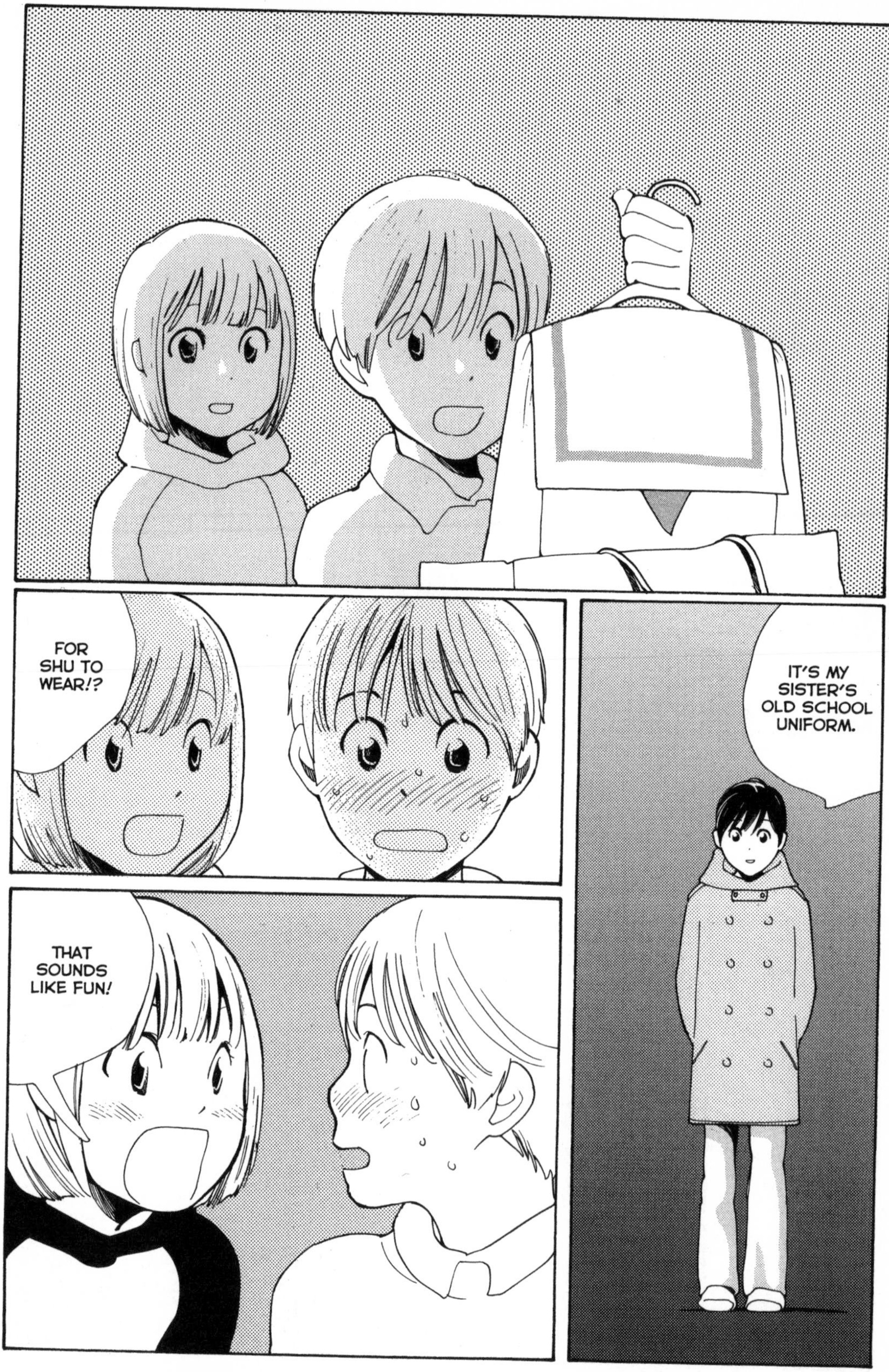
IT'S MY SISTER'S OLD SCHOOL UNIFORM.
FOR SHU TO WEAR!?
THAT SOUNDS LIKE FUN!

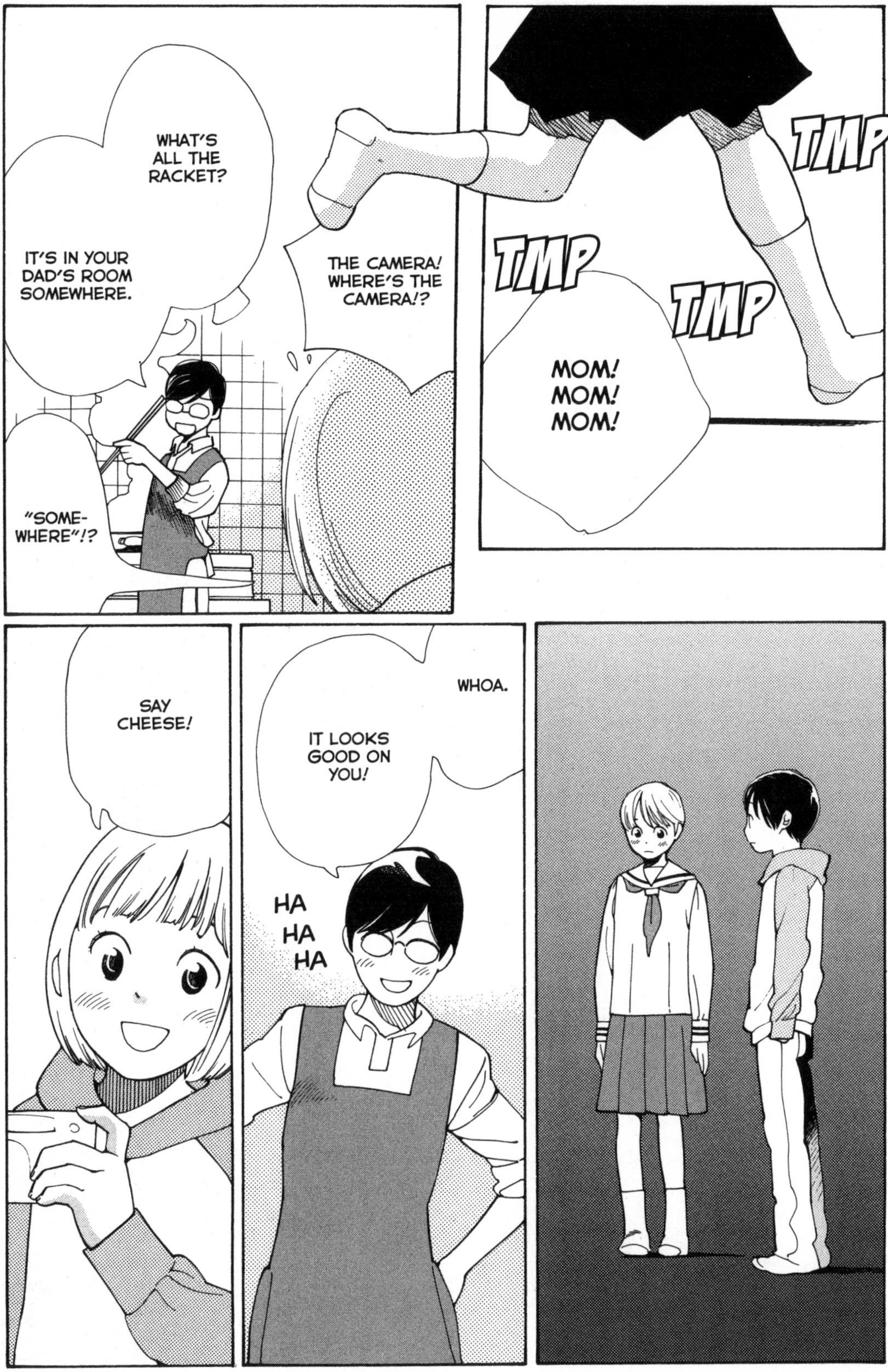
TMP
TMP
TMP
MOM! MOM! MOM!
THE CAMERA! WHERE'S THE CAMERA!?
WHAT'S ALL THE RACKET?
IT'S IN YOUR DAD'S ROOM SOMEWHERE.
"SOME-WHERE"!?
WHOA.
IT LOOKS GOOD ON YOU!
HA HA HA
SAY CHEESE!

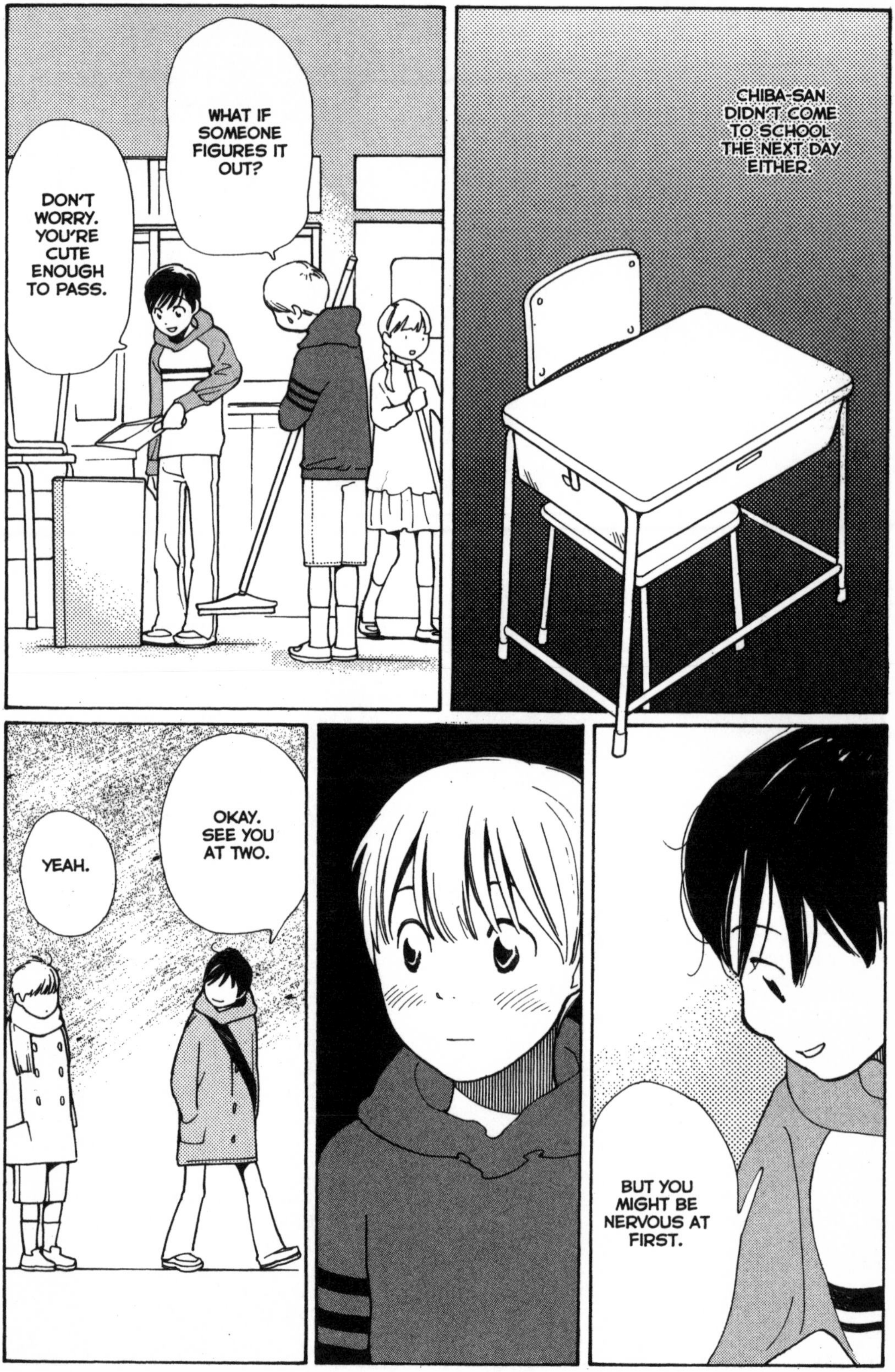
CHIBA-SAN DIDN'T COME TO SCHOOL THE NEXT DAY EITHER.
WHAT IF SOMEONE FIGURES IT OUT?
DON'T WORRY. YOU'RE CUTE ENOUGH TO PASS.
BUT YOU MIGHT BE NERVOUS AT FIRST.
OKAY. SEE YOU AT TWO.
YEAH.

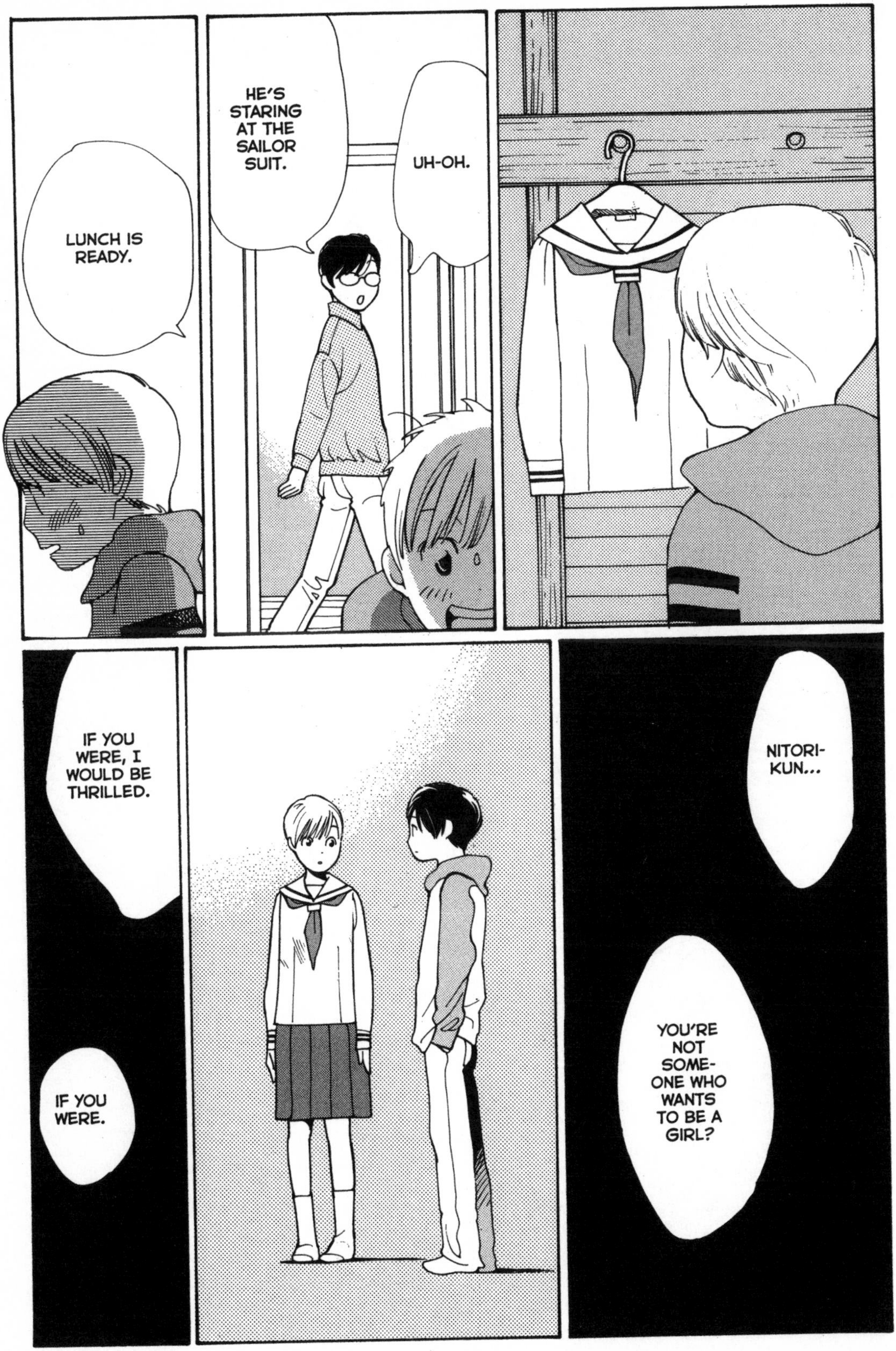
UH-OH.
HE'S STARING AT THE SAILOR SUIT.
LUNCH IS READY.
NITORI-KUN...
YOU'RE NOT SOME-ONE WHO WANTS TO BE A GIRL?
IF YOU WERE, I WOULD BE THRILLED.
IF YOU WERE.

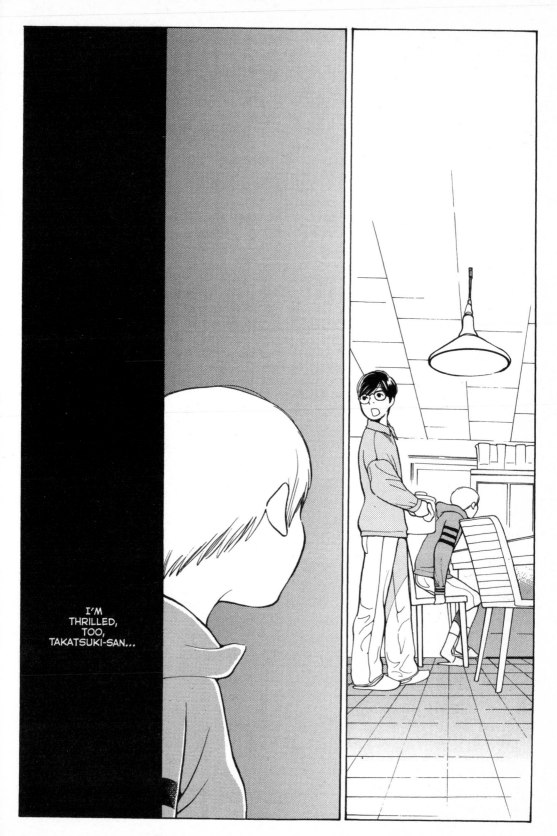

I'M
THRILLED,
TOO,
TAKATSUKI-SAN...

7

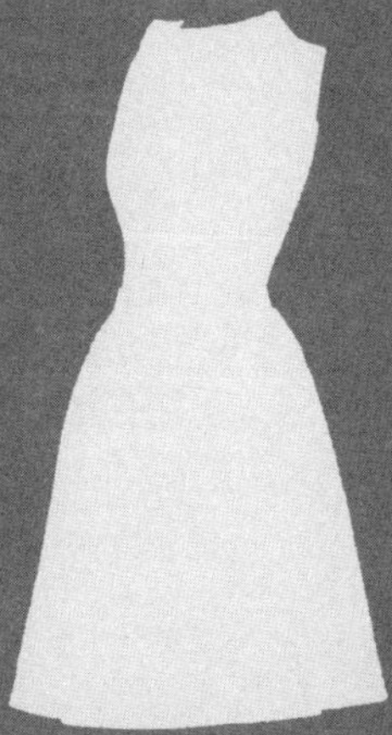

Takatsuki-san's Calamity

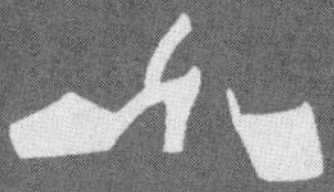

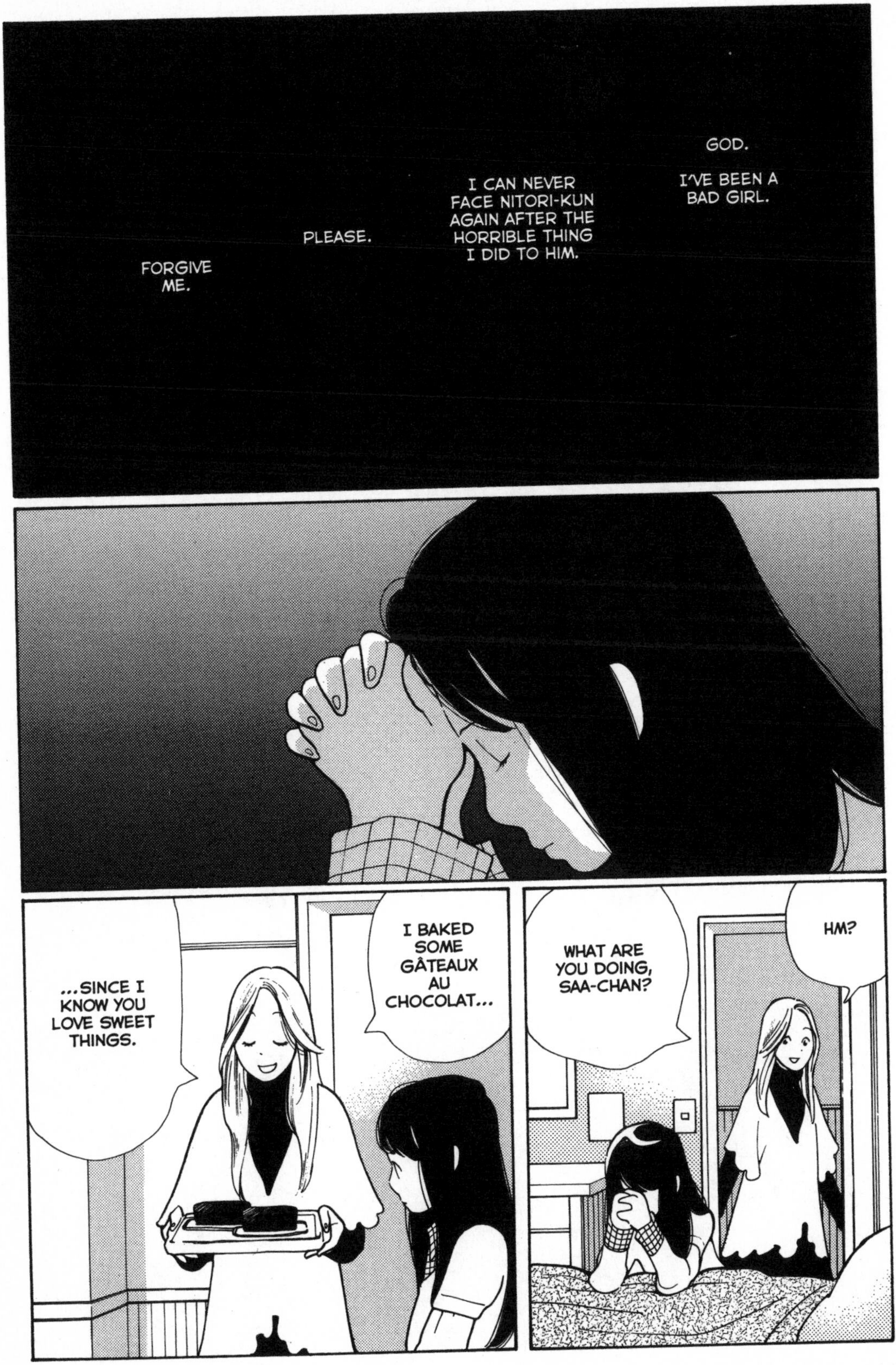
GOD.
I'VE BEEN A BAD GIRL.
I CAN NEVER FACE NITORI-KUN AGAIN AFTER THE HORRIBLE THING I DID TO HIM.
PLEASE.
FORGIVE ME.
HM?
WHAT ARE YOU DOING, SAA-CHAN?
I BAKED SOME GÂTEAUX AU CHOCOLAT...
...SINCE I KNOW YOU LOVE SWEET THINGS.

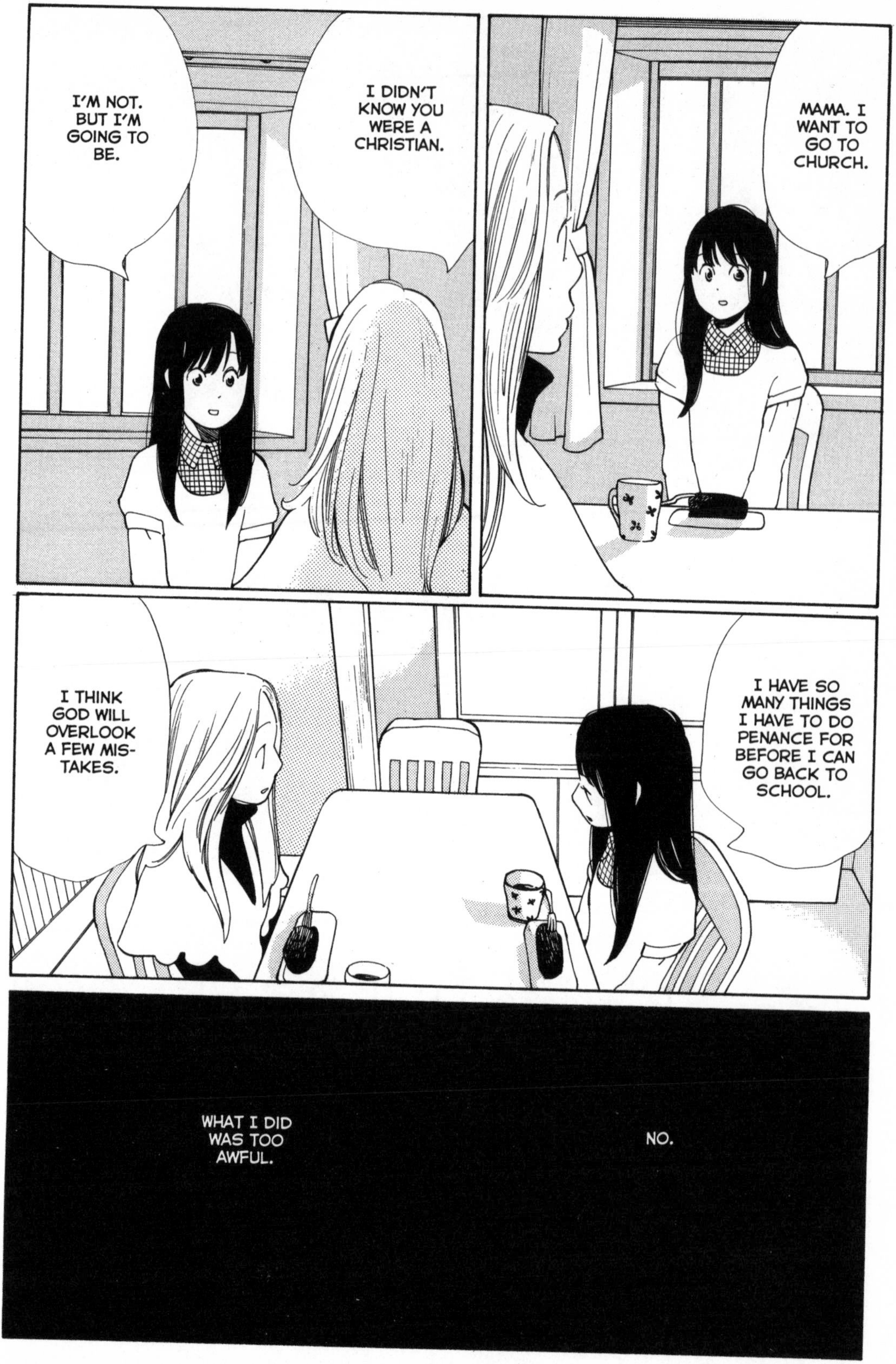
MAMA. I WANT TO GO TO CHURCH.
I DIDN'T KNOW YOU WERE A CHRISTIAN.
I'M NOT. BUT I'M GOING TO BE.
I HAVE SO MANY THINGS I HAVE TO DO PENANCE FOR BEFORE I CAN GO BACK TO SCHOOL.
I THINK GOD WILL OVERLOOK A FEW MIS-TAKES.
NO.
WHAT I DID WAS TOO AWFUL.

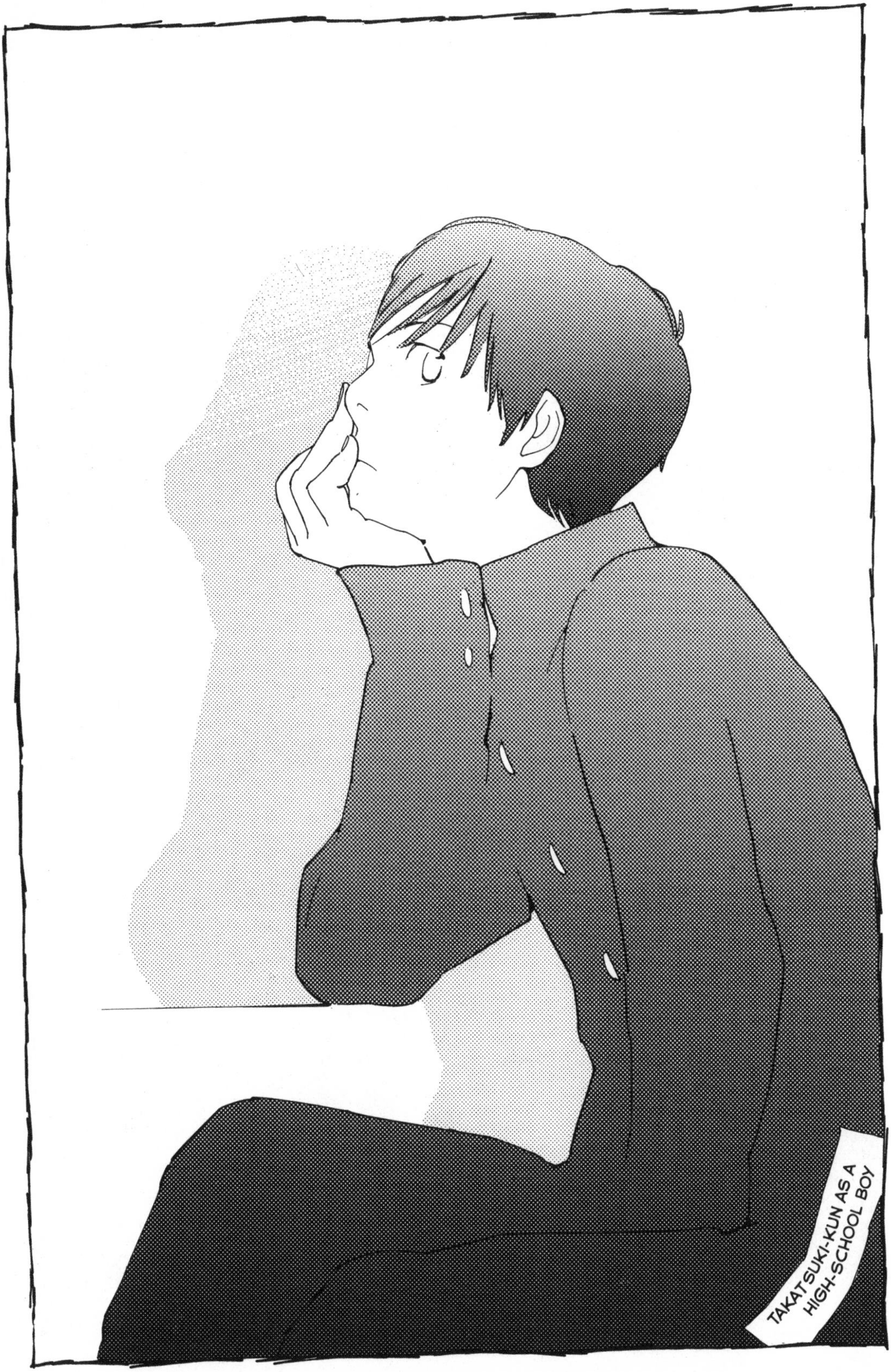
TAKATSUKI-KUN AS A HIGH-SCHOOL BOY

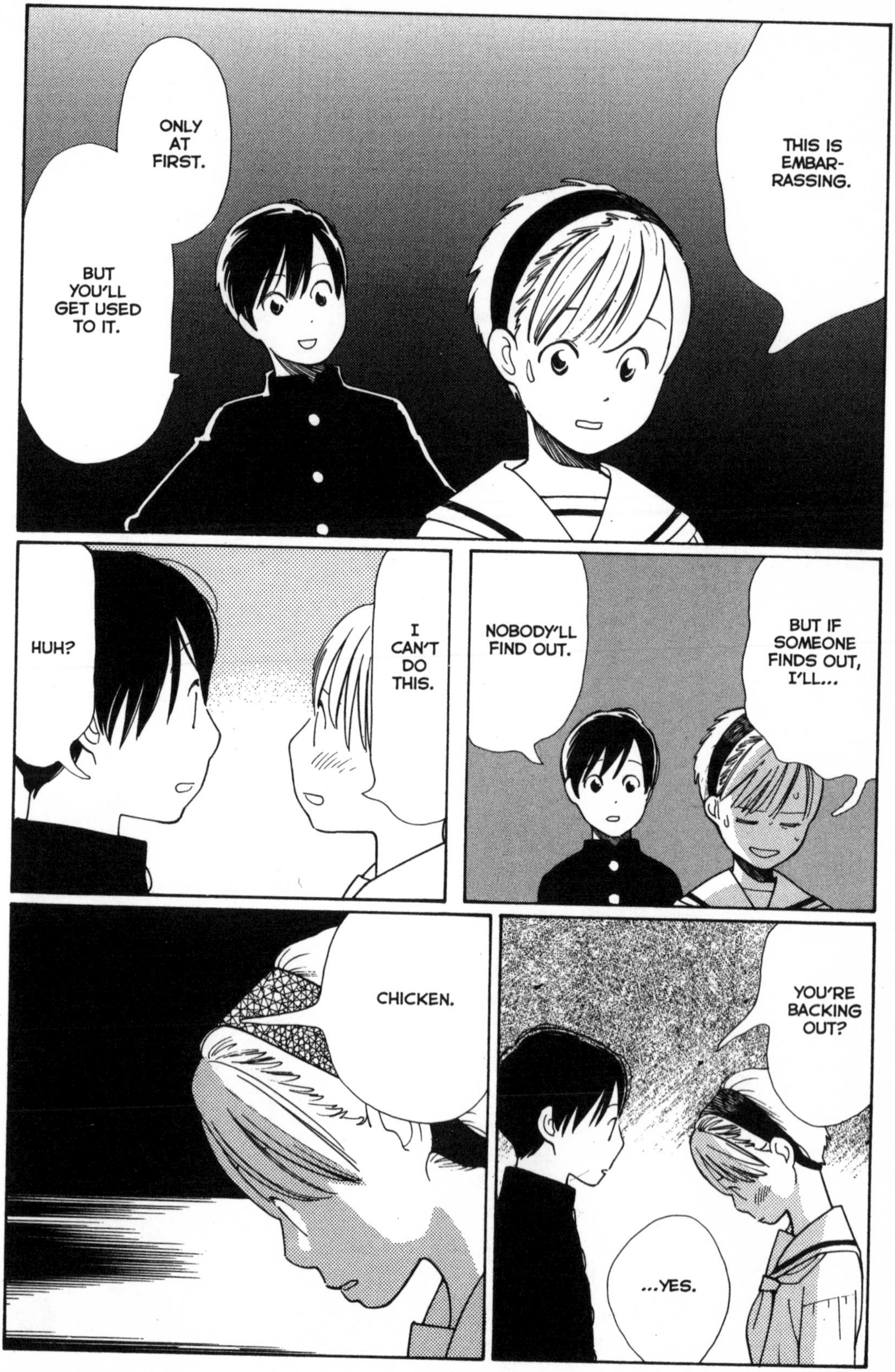
THIS IS EMBARRASSING.
ONLY AT FIRST.
BUT YOU'LL GET USED TO IT.
BUT IF SOMEONE FINDS OUT, I'LL...
NOBODY'LL FIND OUT.
I CAN'T DO THIS.
HUH?
YOU'RE BACKING OUT?
...YES.
CHICKEN.

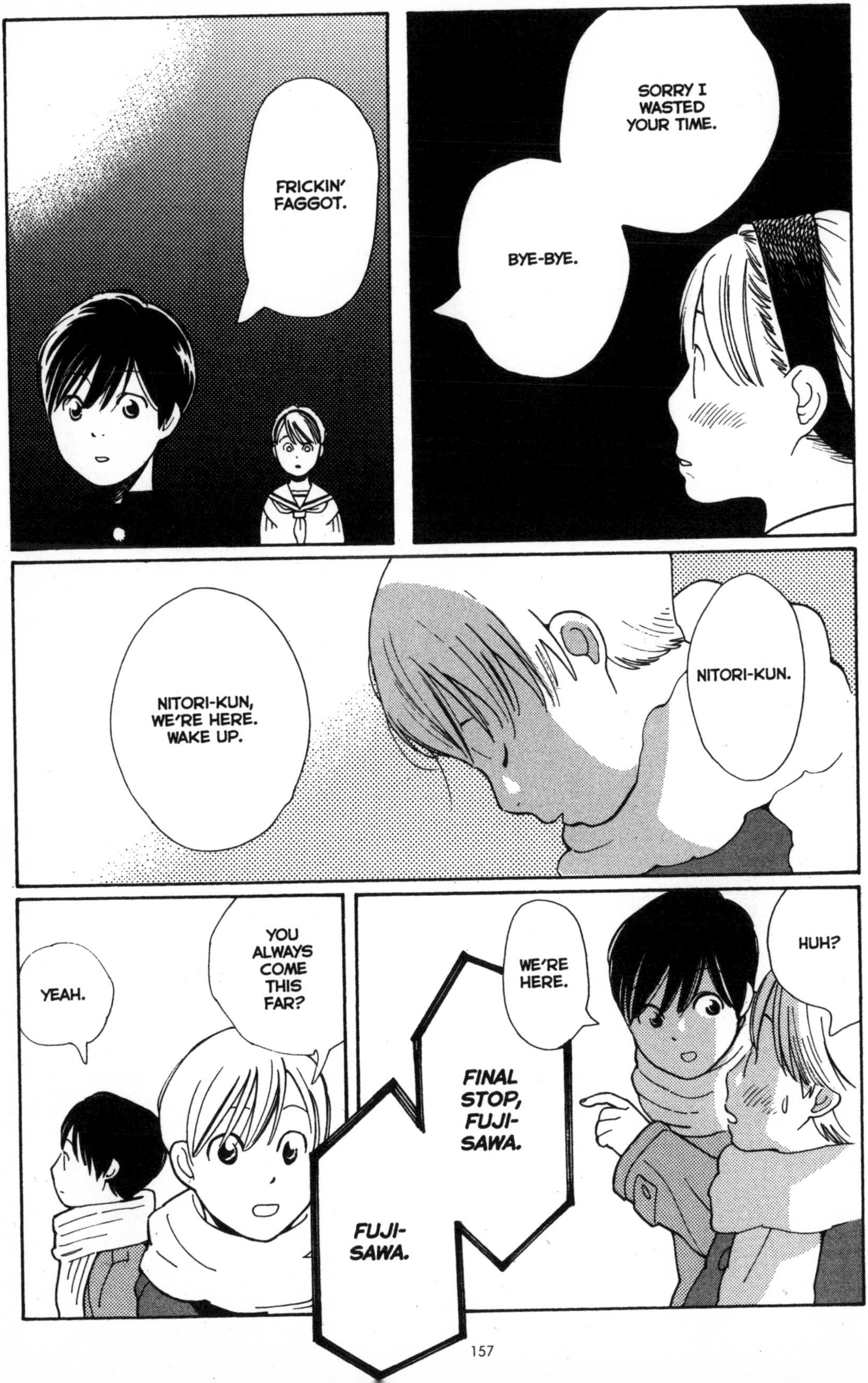
SORRY I WASTED YOUR TIME.
BYE-BYE.
FRICKIN' FAGGOT.
NITORI-KUN.
NITORI-KUN, WE'RE HERE. WAKE UP.
HUH?
WE'RE HERE.
FINAL STOP, FUJI-SAWA.
FUJI-SAWA.
YOU ALWAYS COME THIS FAR?
YEAH.

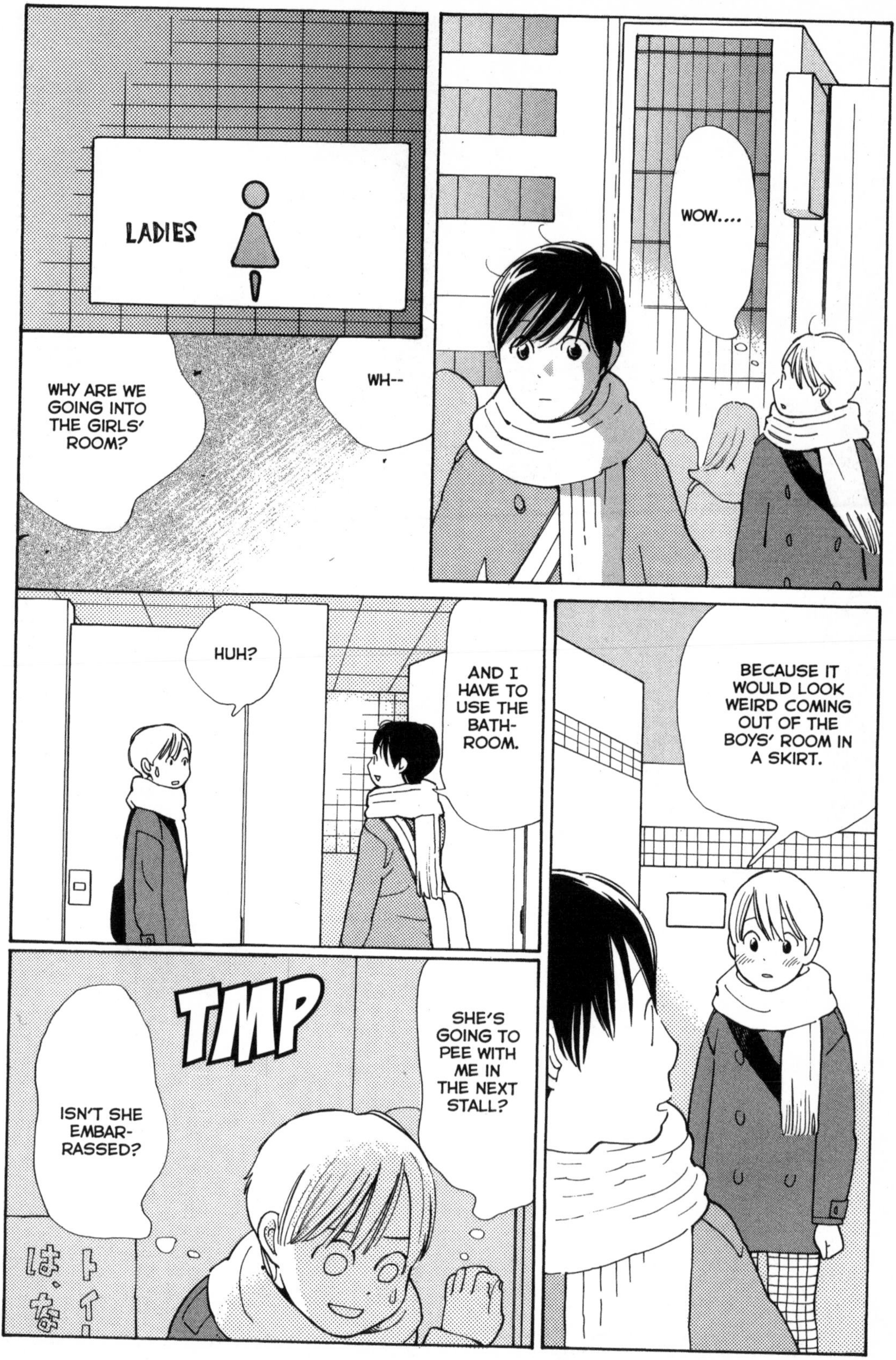
WOW....
LADIES
WH--
WHY ARE WE GOING INTO THE GIRLS' ROOM?
BECAUSE IT WOULD LOOK WEIRD COMING OUT OF THE BOYS' ROOM IN A SKIRT.
AND I HAVE TO USE THE BATH-ROOM.
HUH?
TMP
SHE'S GOING TO PEE WITH ME IN THE NEXT STALL?
ISN'T SHE EMBAR-RASSED?

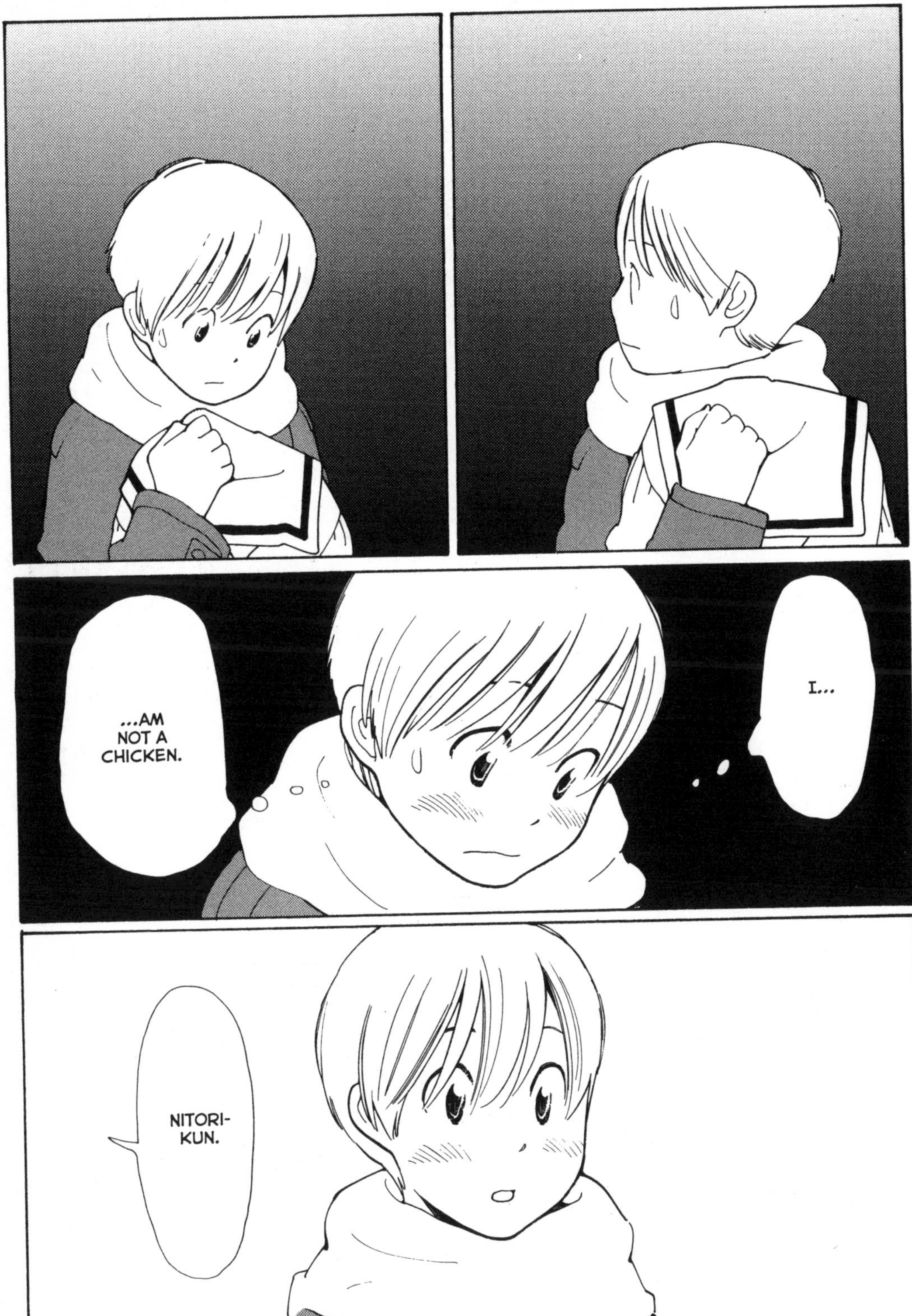
I...
...AM NOT A CHICKEN.
NITORI-KUN.

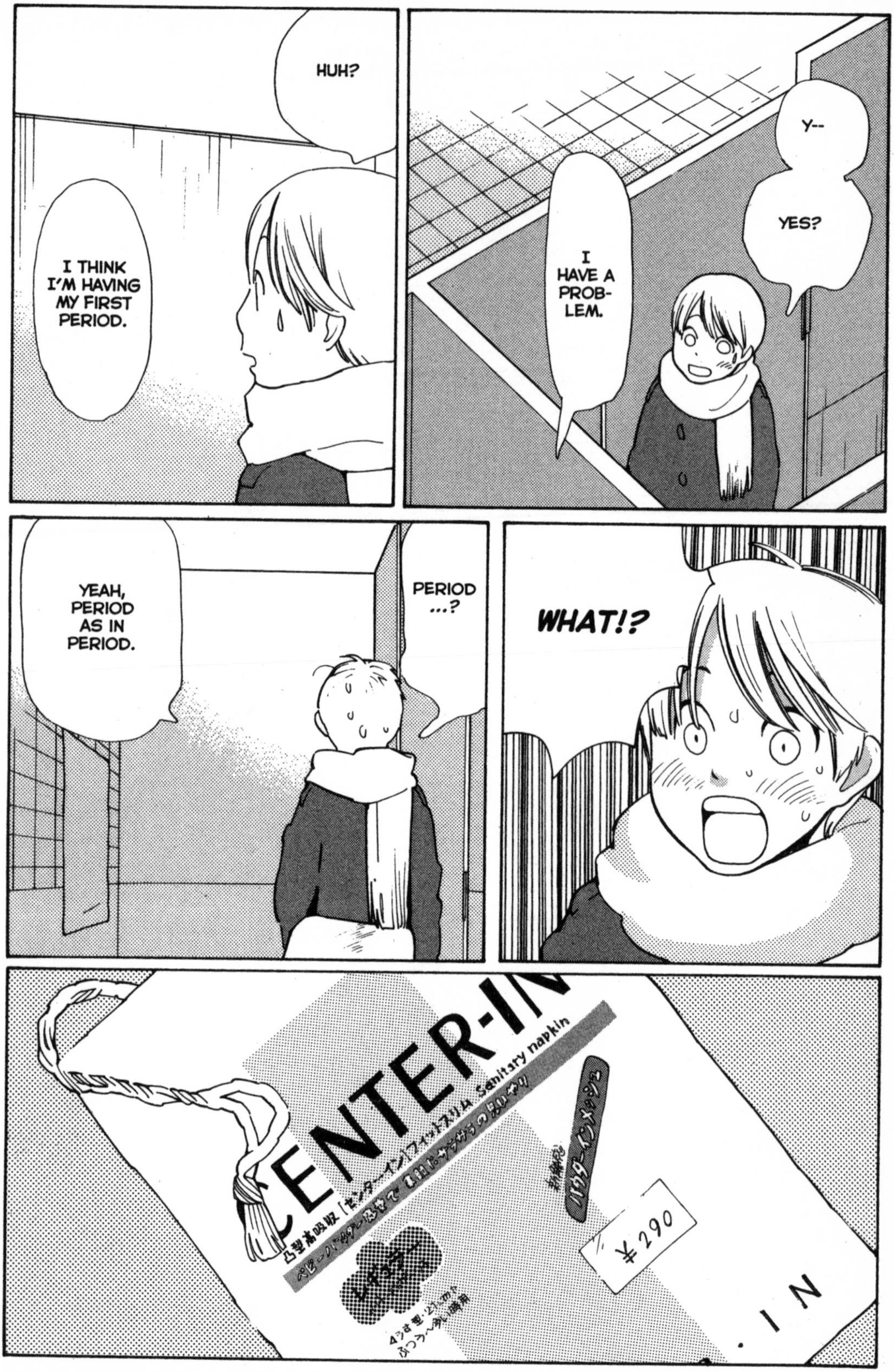
Y--
YES?
I HAVE A PROBLEM.
HUH?
I THINK I'M HAVING MY FIRST PERIOD.
WHAT!?
PERIOD ...?
YEAH, PERIOD AS IN PERIOD.
CENTER-IN
Sanitary napkin
¥290
IN

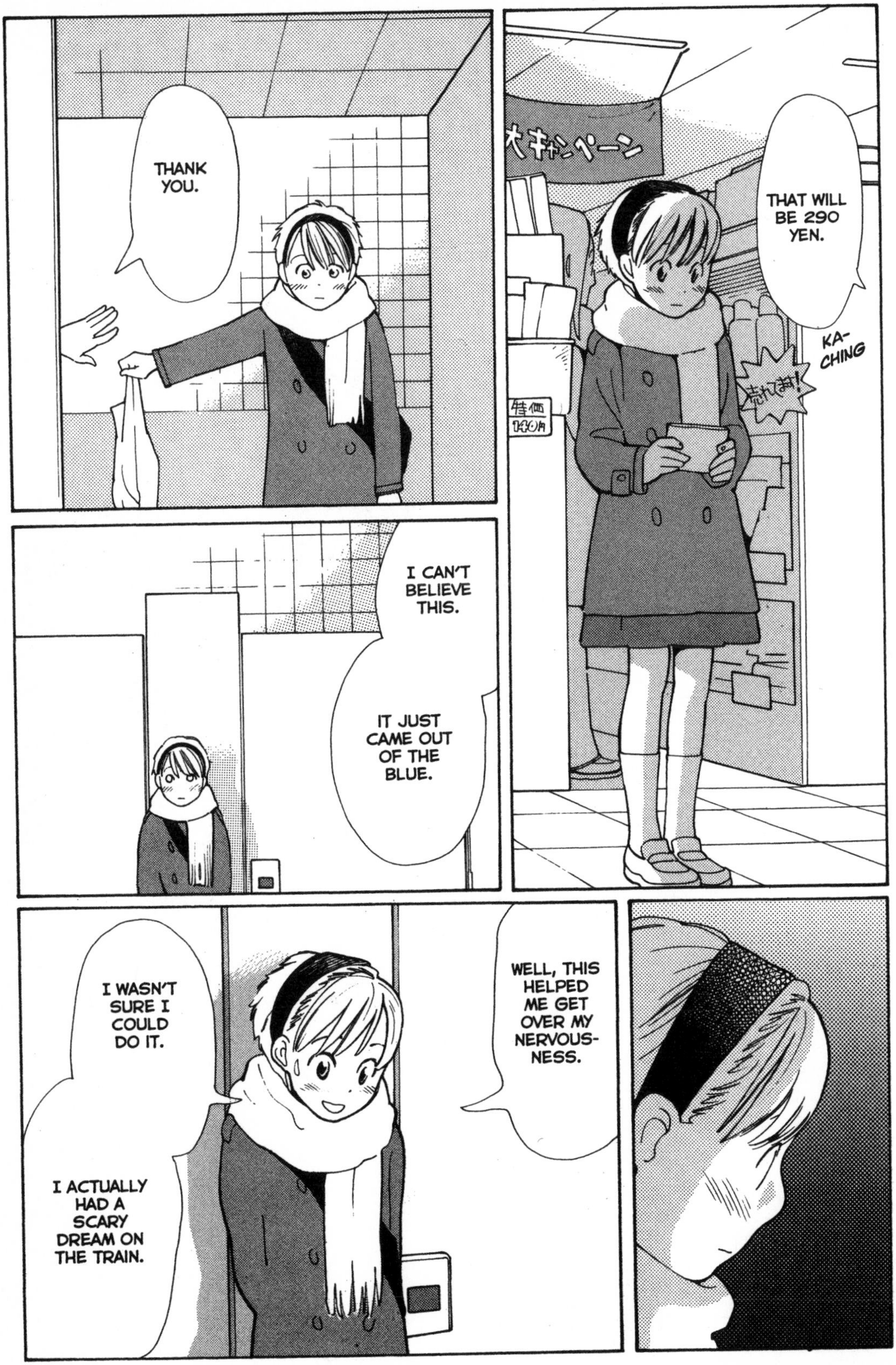

大キャンペーン
THAT WILL BE 290 YEN.
KA-CHING
特価 140円
THANK YOU.
I CAN'T BELIEVE THIS.
IT JUST CAME OUT OF THE BLUE.
WELL, THIS HELPED ME GET OVER MY NERVOUS-NESS.
I WASN'T SURE I COULD DO IT.
I ACTUALLY HAD A SCARY DREAM ON THE TRAIN.

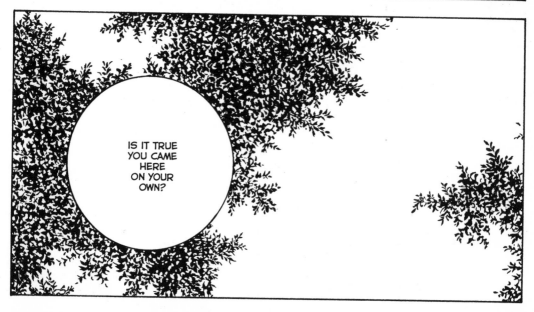

IS IT TRUE
YOU CAME
HERE
ON YOUR
OWN?

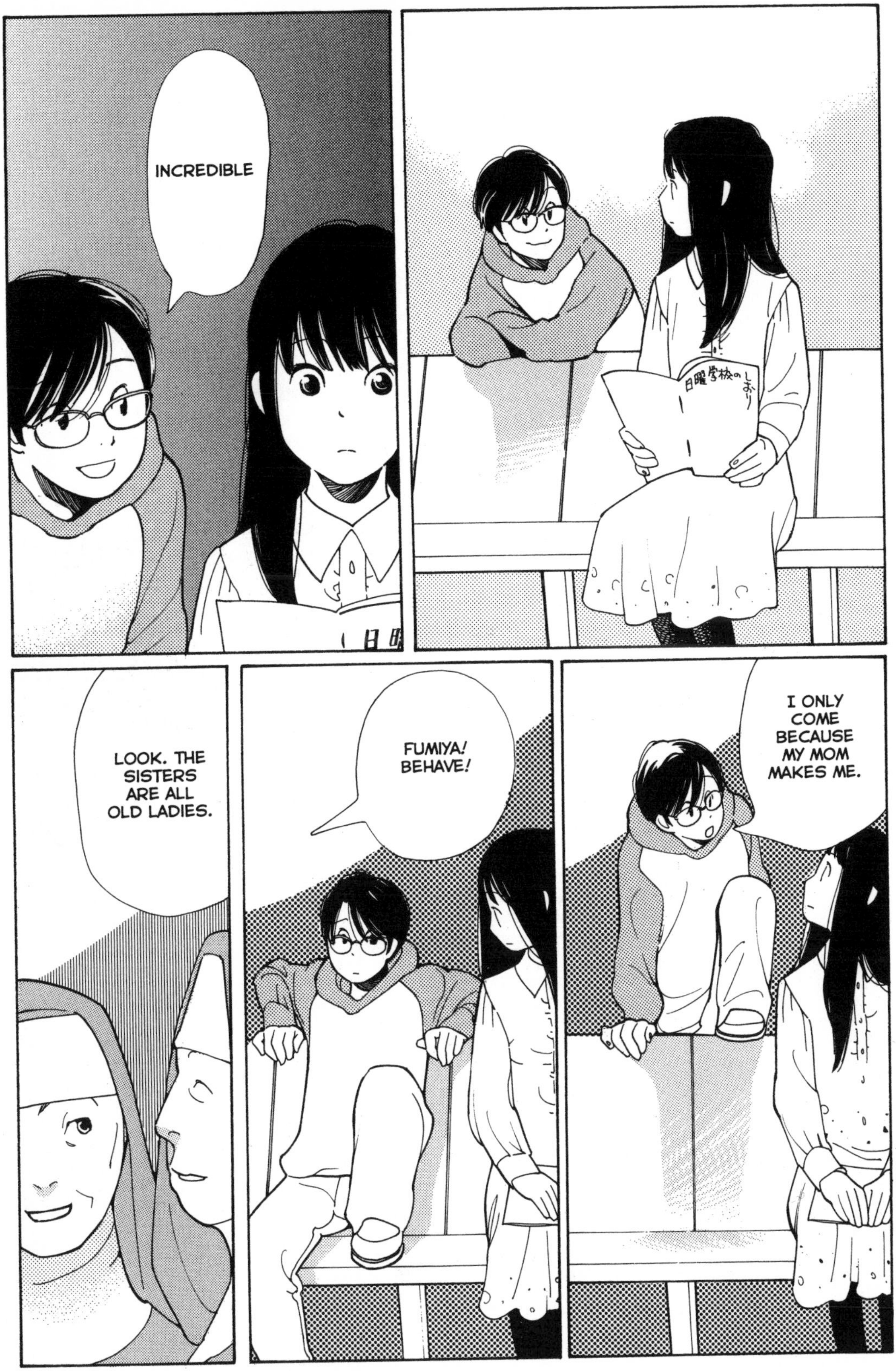
日曜学校のしおり
INCREDIBLE
I ONLY COME BECAUSE MY MOM MAKES ME.
FUMIYA! BEHAVE!
LOOK. THE SISTERS ARE ALL OLD LADIES.

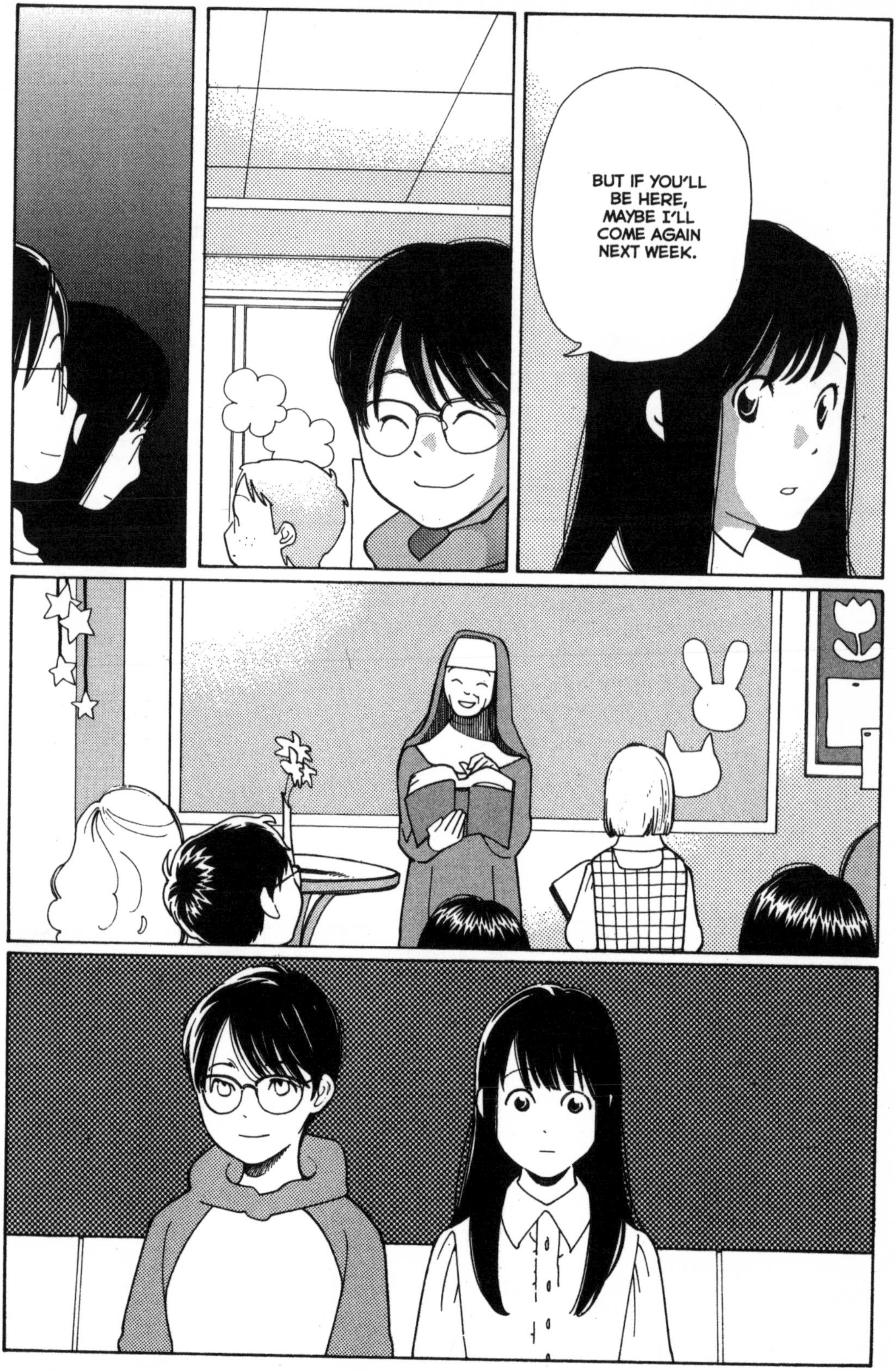
BUT IF YOU'LL BE HERE, MAYBE I'LL COME AGAIN NEXT WEEK.

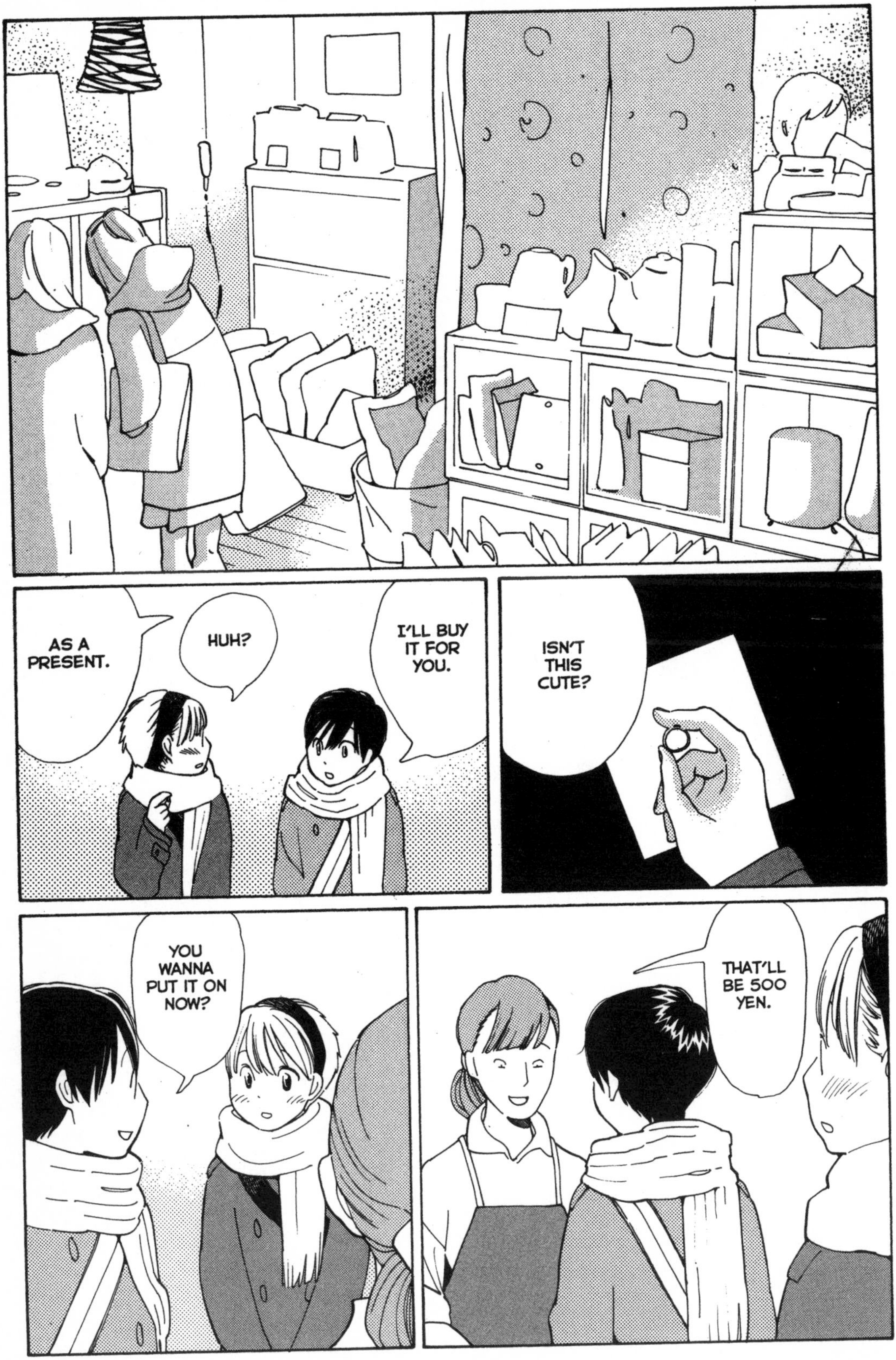
ISN'T THIS CUTE?
I'LL BUY IT FOR YOU.
HUH?
AS A PRESENT.
THAT'LL BE 500 YEN.
YOU WANNA PUT IT ON NOW?

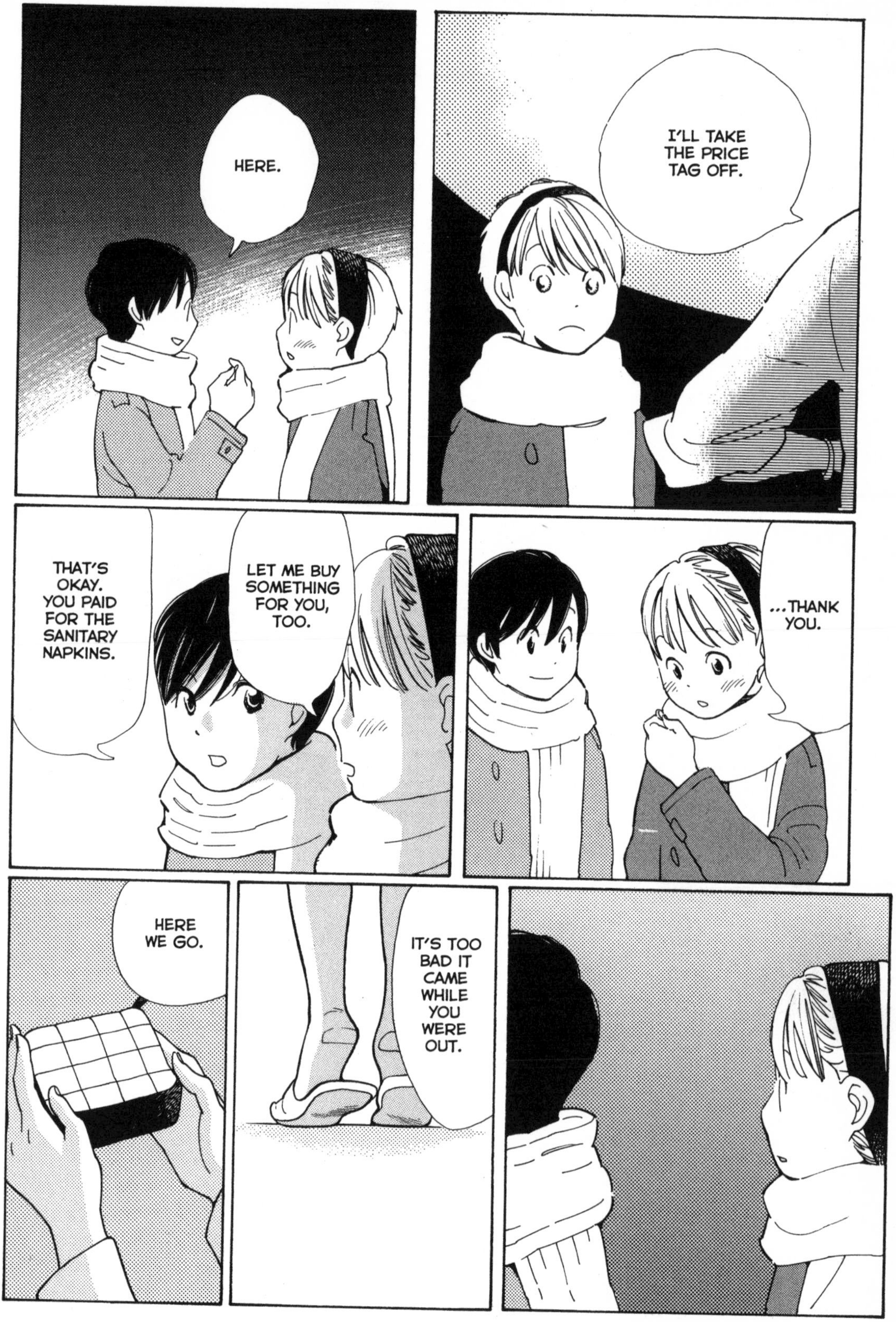
I'LL TAKE THE PRICE TAG OFF.
HERE.
...THANK YOU.
LET ME BUY SOMETHING FOR YOU, TOO.
THAT'S OKAY. YOU PAID FOR THE SANITARY NAPKINS.
IT'S TOO BAD IT CAME WHILE YOU WERE OUT.
HERE WE GO.

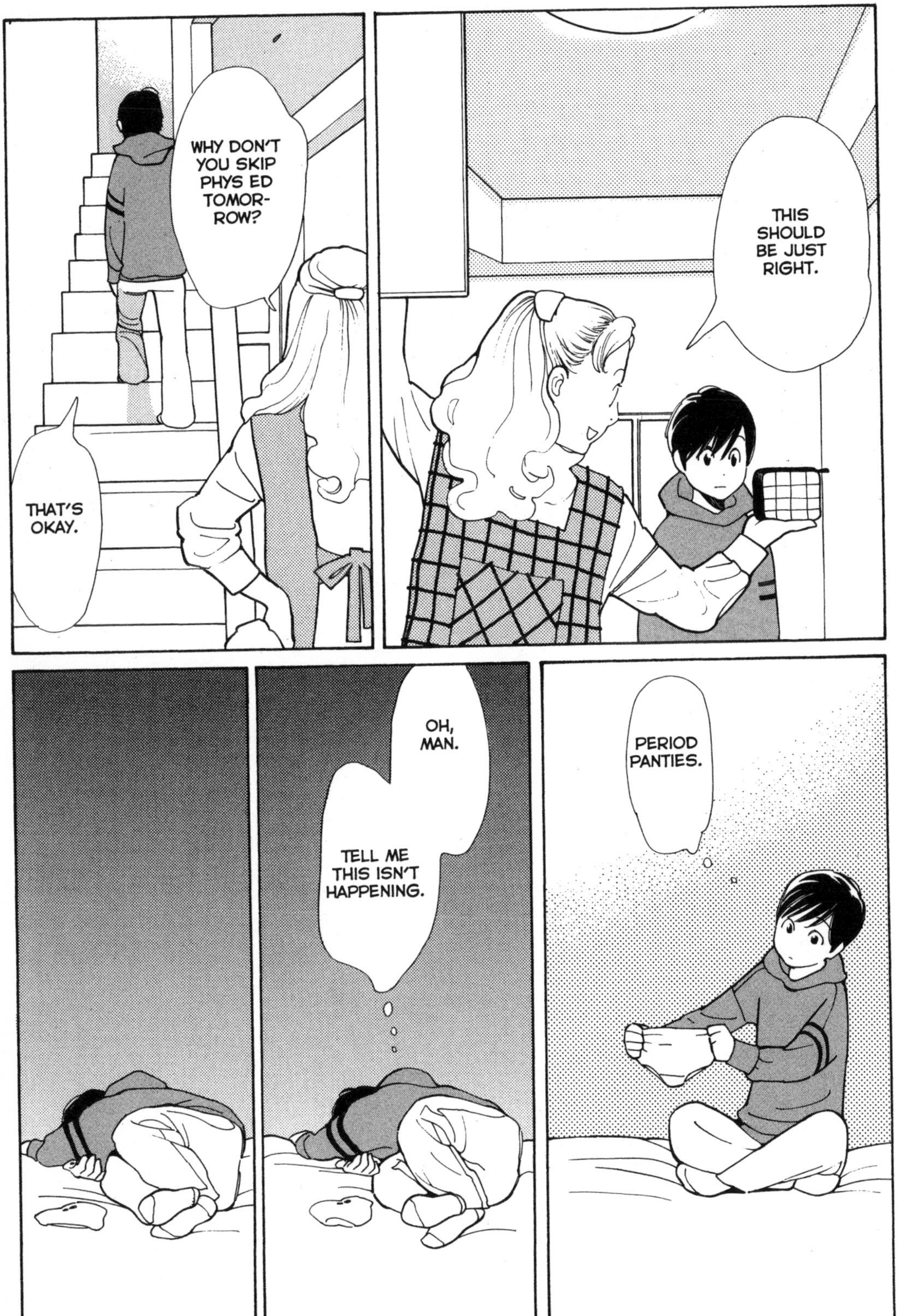
THIS SHOULD BE JUST RIGHT.
WHY DON'T YOU SKIP PHYS ED TOMOR-ROW?
THAT'S OKAY.
PERIOD PANTIES.
OH, MAN.
TELL ME THIS ISN'T HAPPENING.

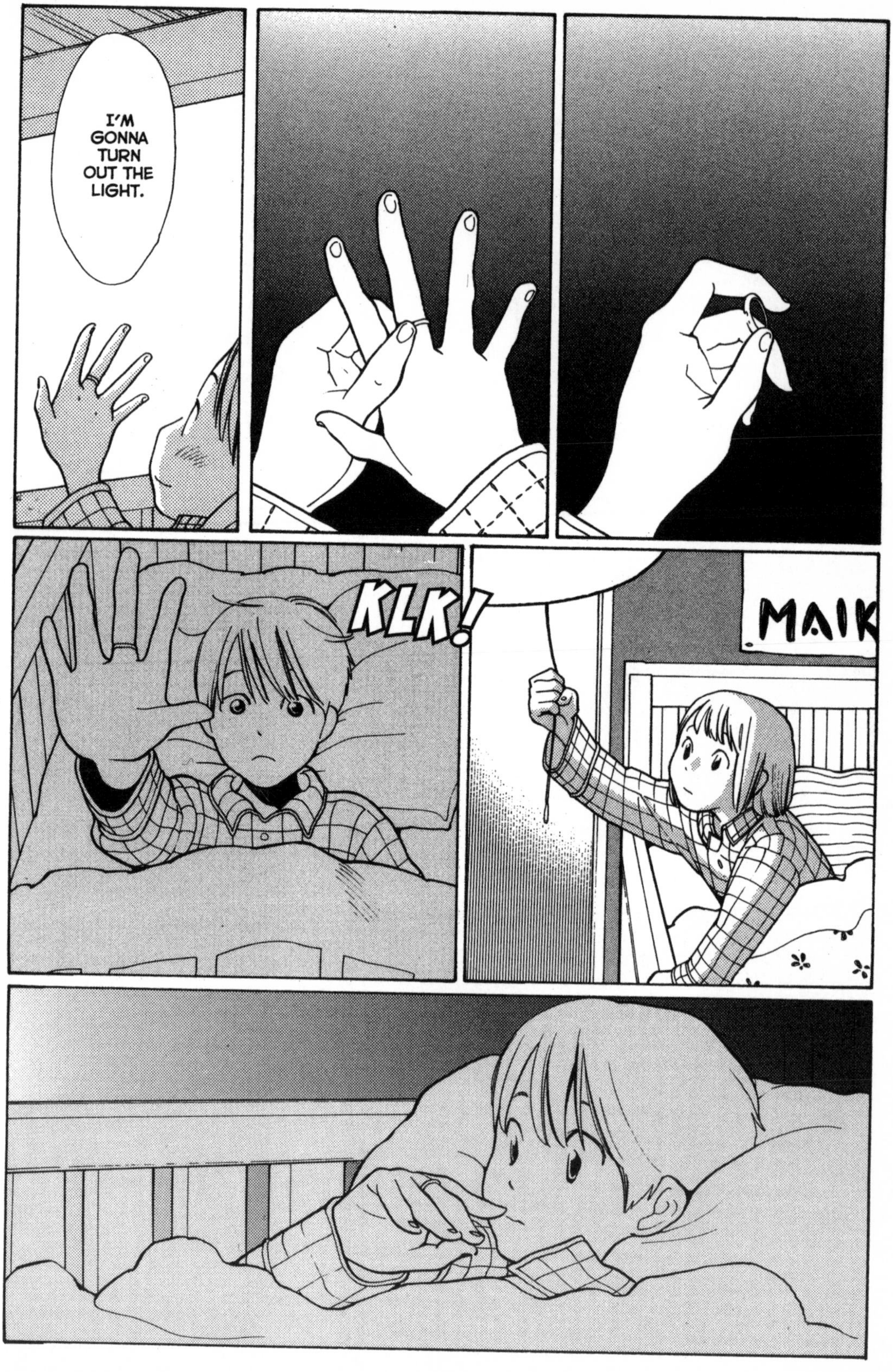
I'M GONNA TURN OUT THE LIGHT.
MAIK
KLK!

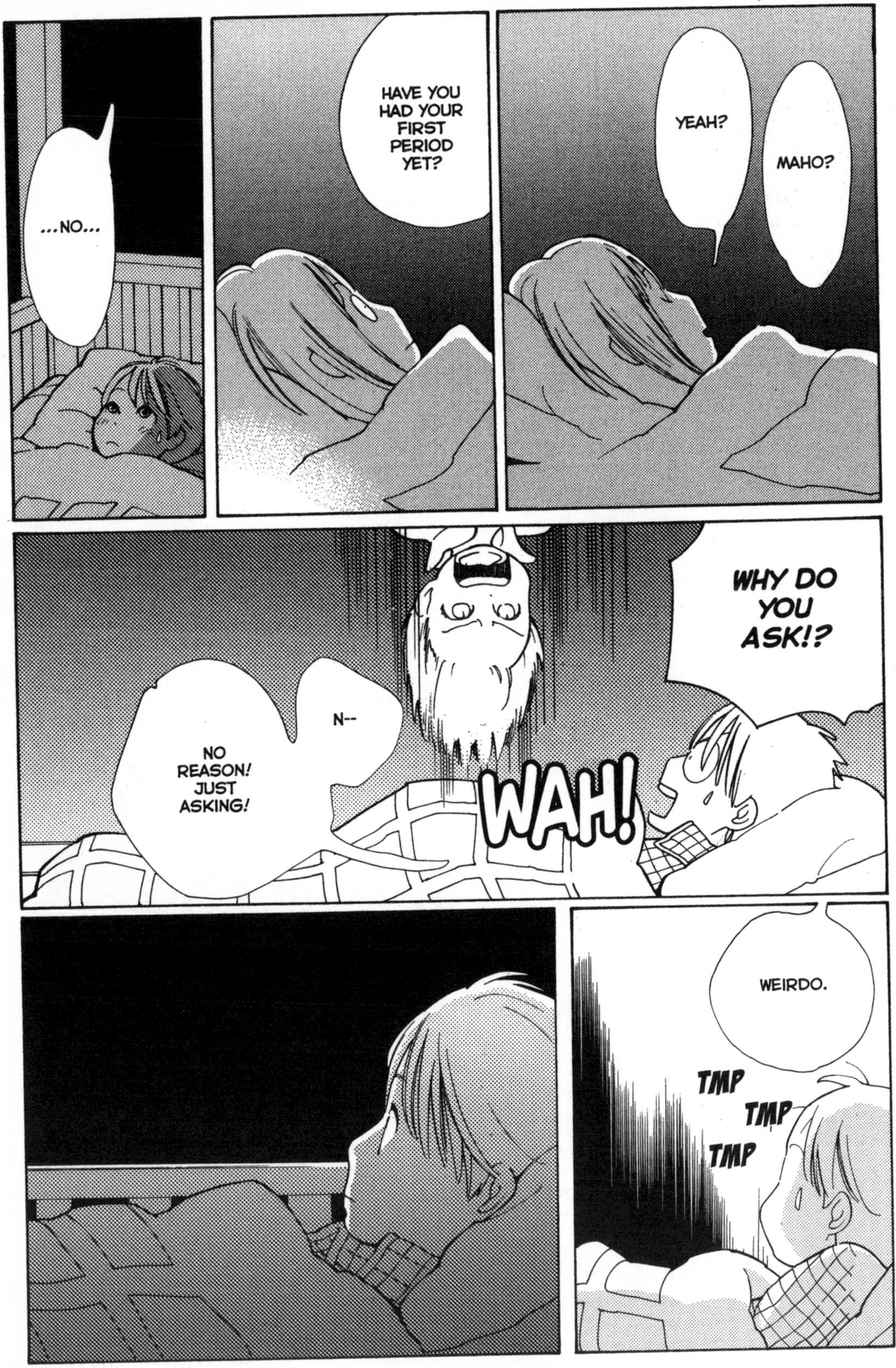
MAHO?
YEAH?
HAVE YOU HAD YOUR FIRST PERIOD YET?
...NO...
WHY DO YOU ASK!?
WAH!
N--
NO REASON! JUST ASKING!
WEIRDO.
TMP
TMP
TMP

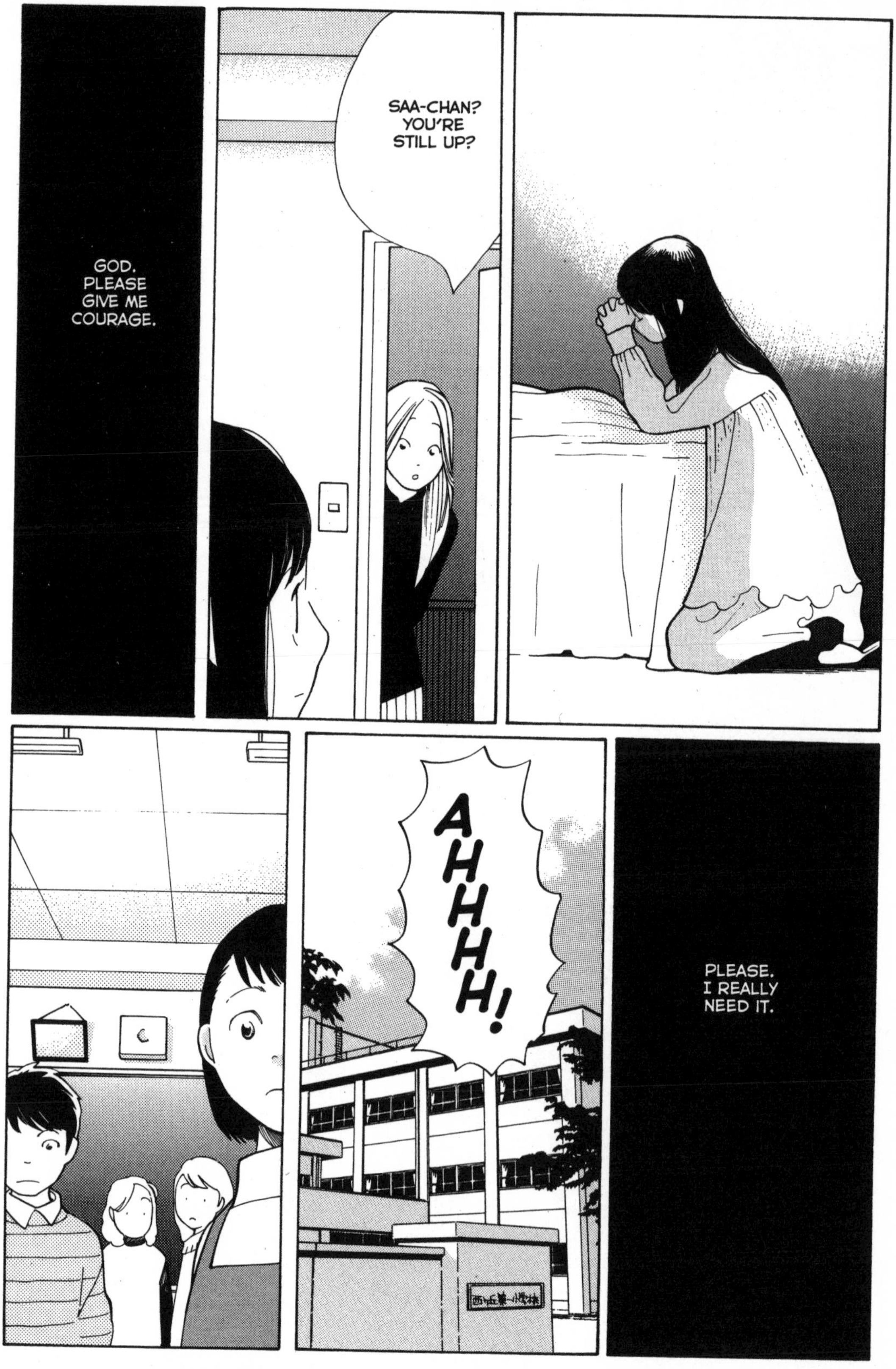
SAA-CHAN? YOU'RE STILL UP?
GOD. PLEASE GIVE ME COURAGE.
PLEASE. I REALLY NEED IT.
AHHHH!

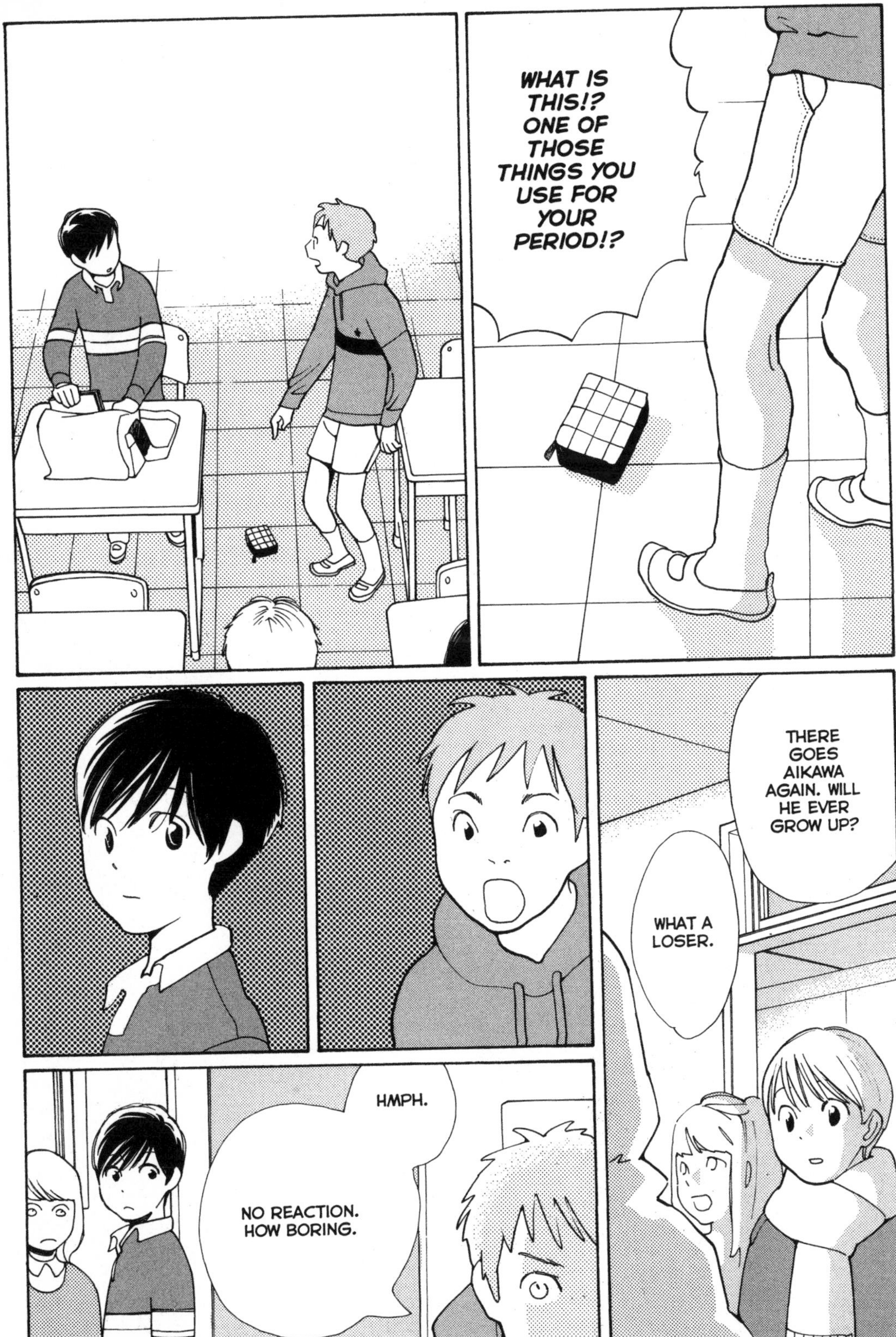
WHAT IS THIS!? ONE OF THOSE THINGS YOU USE FOR YOUR PERIOD!?
THERE GOES AIKAWA AGAIN. WILL HE EVER GROW UP?
WHAT A LOSER.
HMPH.
NO REACTION. HOW BORING.

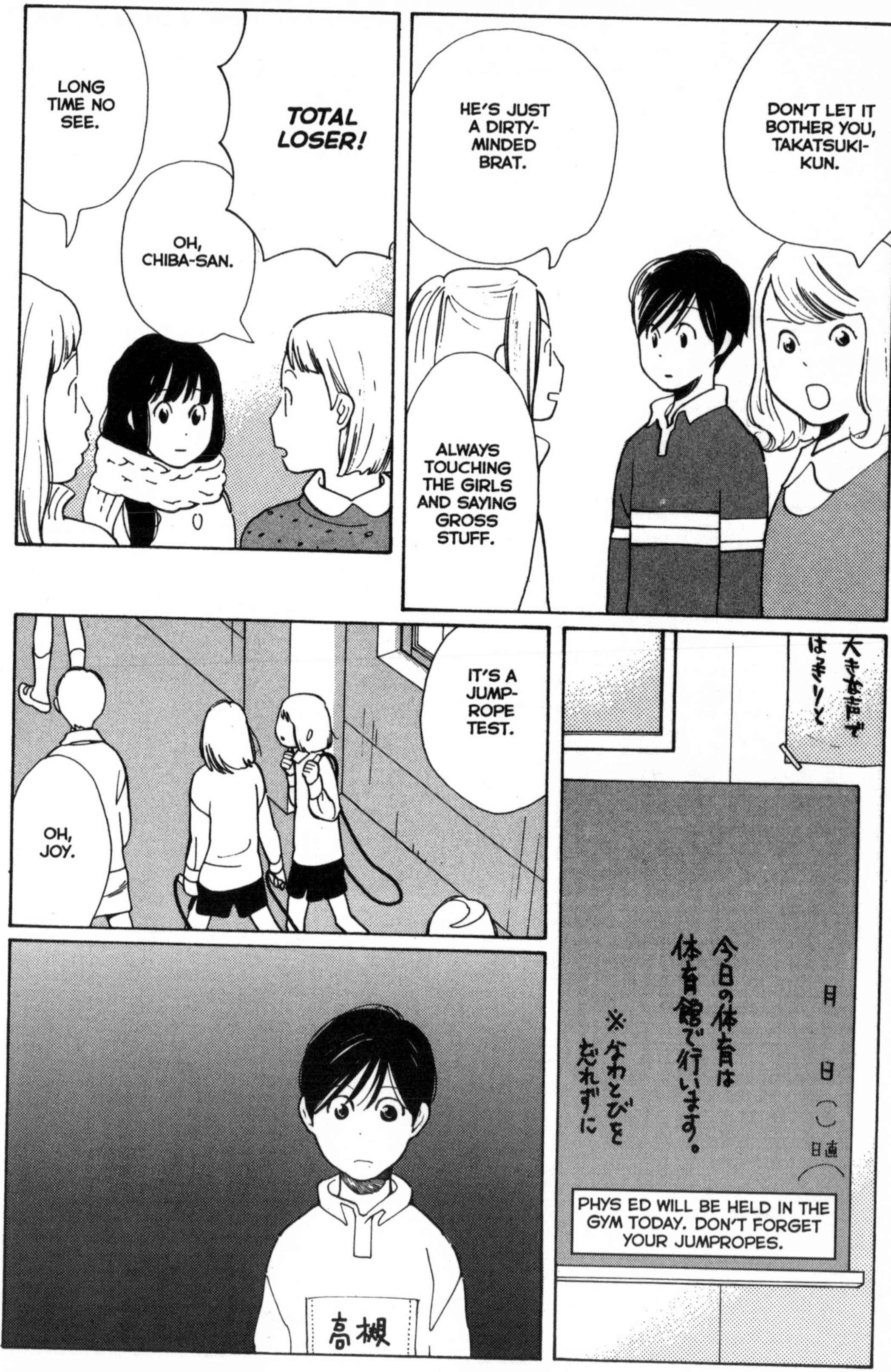
DON'T LET IT BOTHER YOU, TAKATSUKI-KUN.
HE'S JUST A DIRTY-MINDED BRAT.
ALWAYS TOUCHING THE GIRLS AND SAYING GROSS STUFF.
TOTAL LOSER!
LONG TIME NO SEE.
OH, CHIBA-SAN.
大きな声ではっきりと
月 日（ ） 日直
今日の体育は体育館で行います。
※なわとびを忘れずに
PHYS ED WILL BE HELD IN THE GYM TODAY. DON'T FORGET YOUR JUMPROPES.
IT'S A JUMP-ROPE TEST.
OH, JOY.
高槻

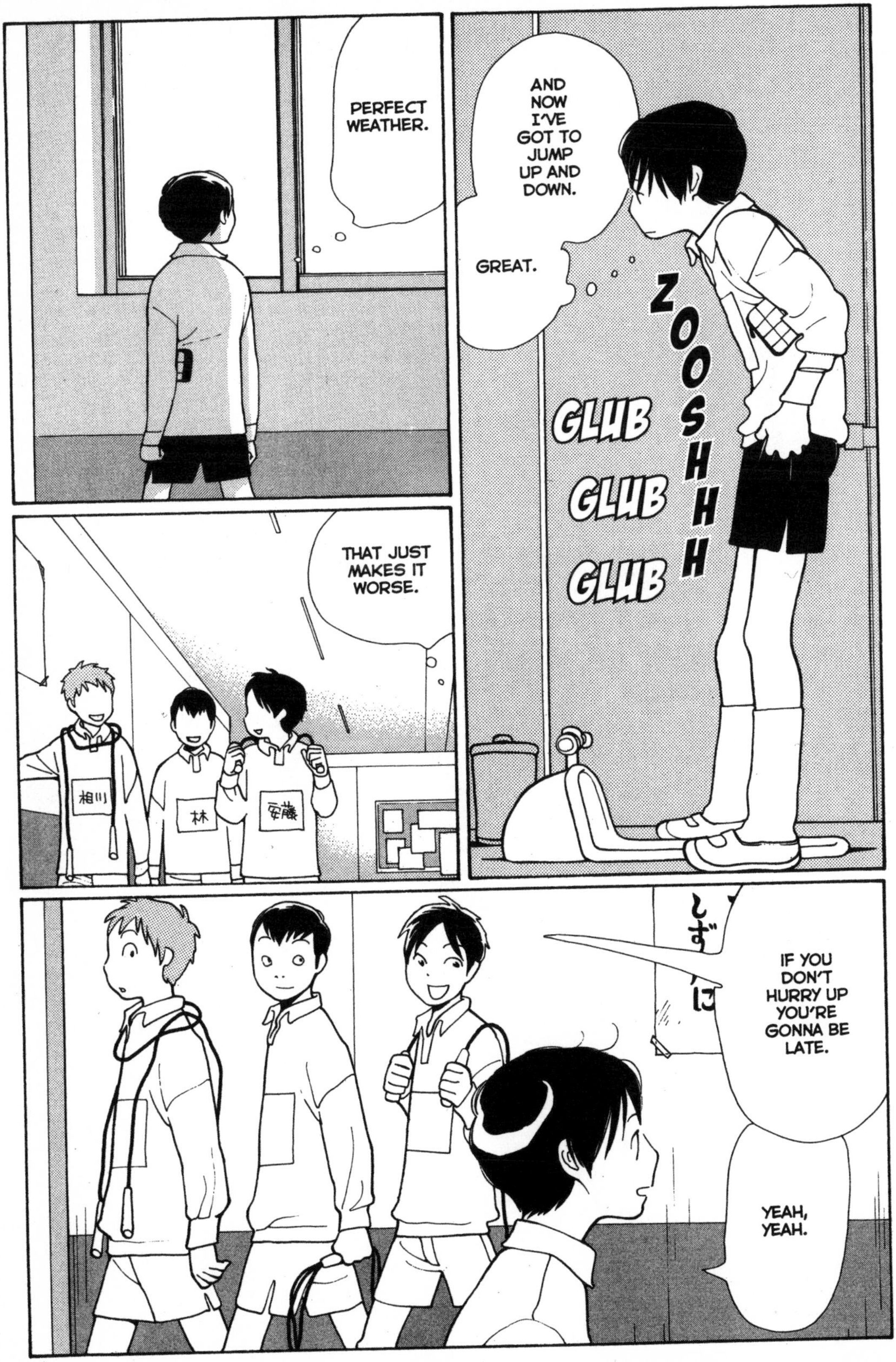
AND NOW I'VE GOT TO JUMP UP AND DOWN.
GREAT.
ZOOSHHH
GLUB GLUB GLUB
PERFECT WEATHER.
THAT JUST MAKES IT WORSE.
安藤
林
相川
IF YOU DON'T HURRY UP YOU'RE GONNA BE LATE.
YEAH, YEAH.

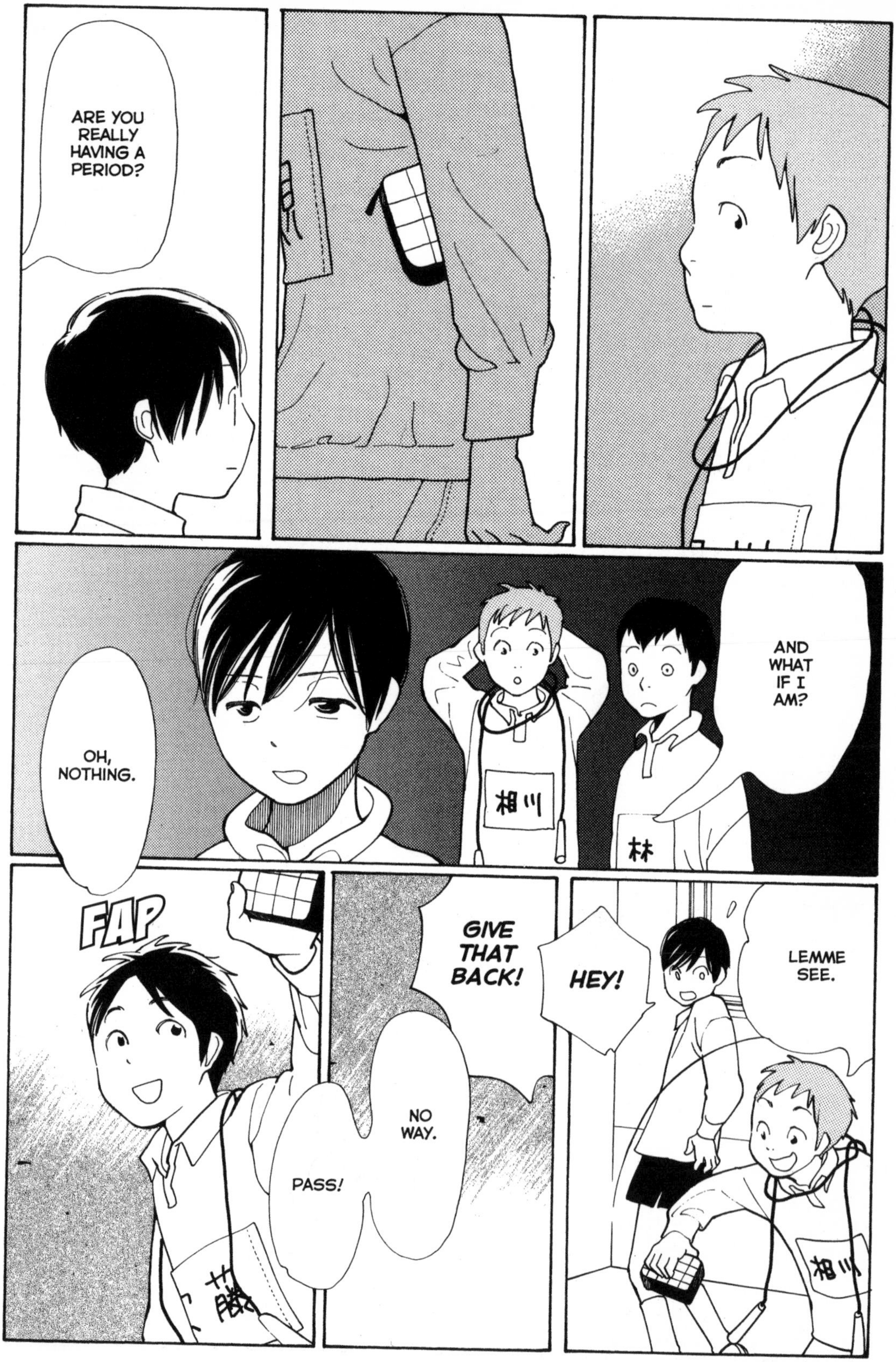
ARE YOU REALLY HAVING A PERIOD?
AND WHAT IF I AM?
相川
林
OH, NOTHING.
LEMME SEE.
HEY!
相川
GIVE THAT BACK!
NO WAY.
PASS!
FAP

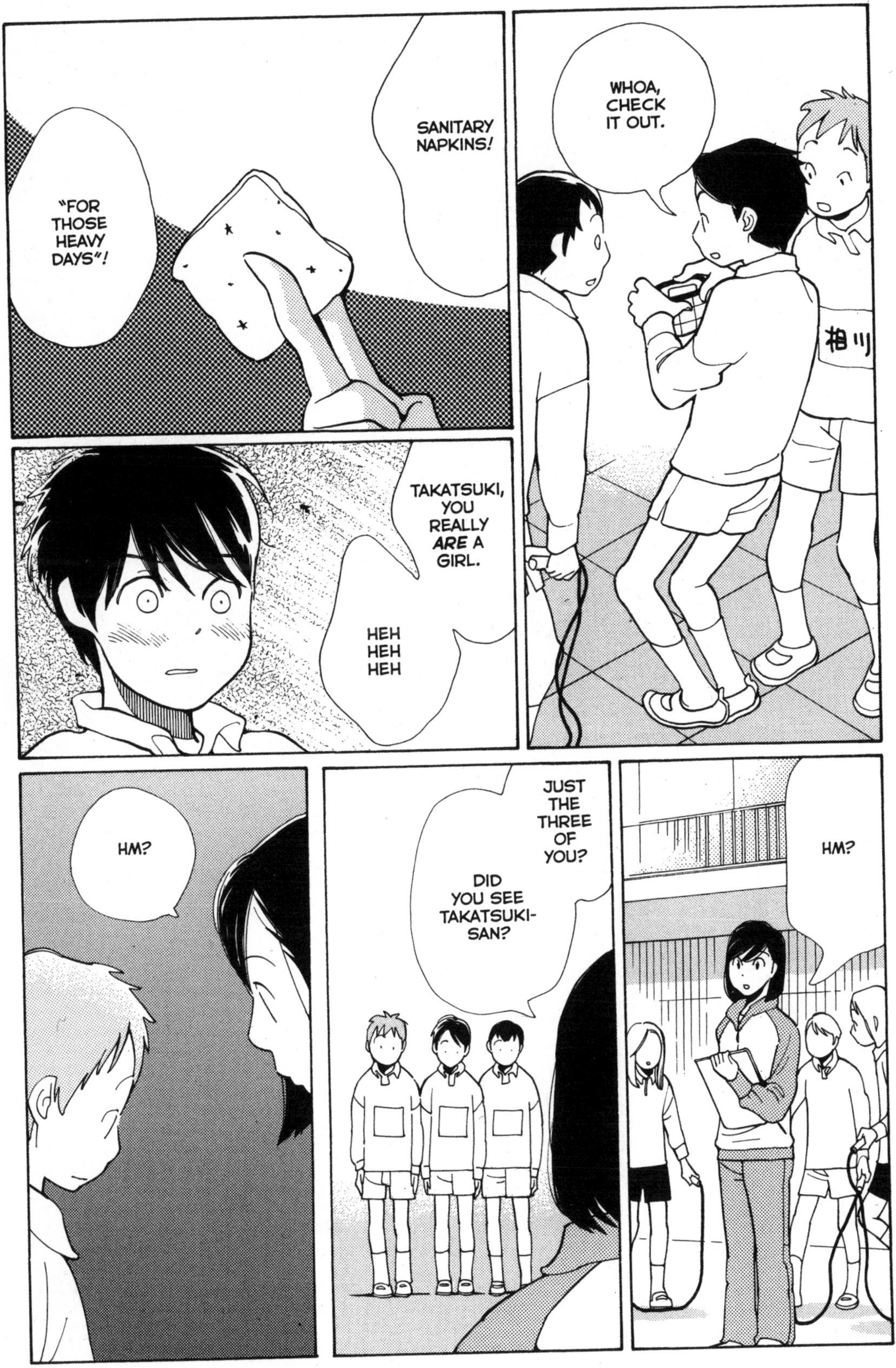
WHOA, CHECK IT OUT.
SANITARY NAPKINS!
"FOR THOSE HEAVY DAYS"!
TAKATSUKI, YOU REALLY *ARE* A GIRL.
HEH HEH HEH
HM?
JUST THE THREE OF YOU?
DID YOU SEE TAKATSUKI-SAN?
HM?

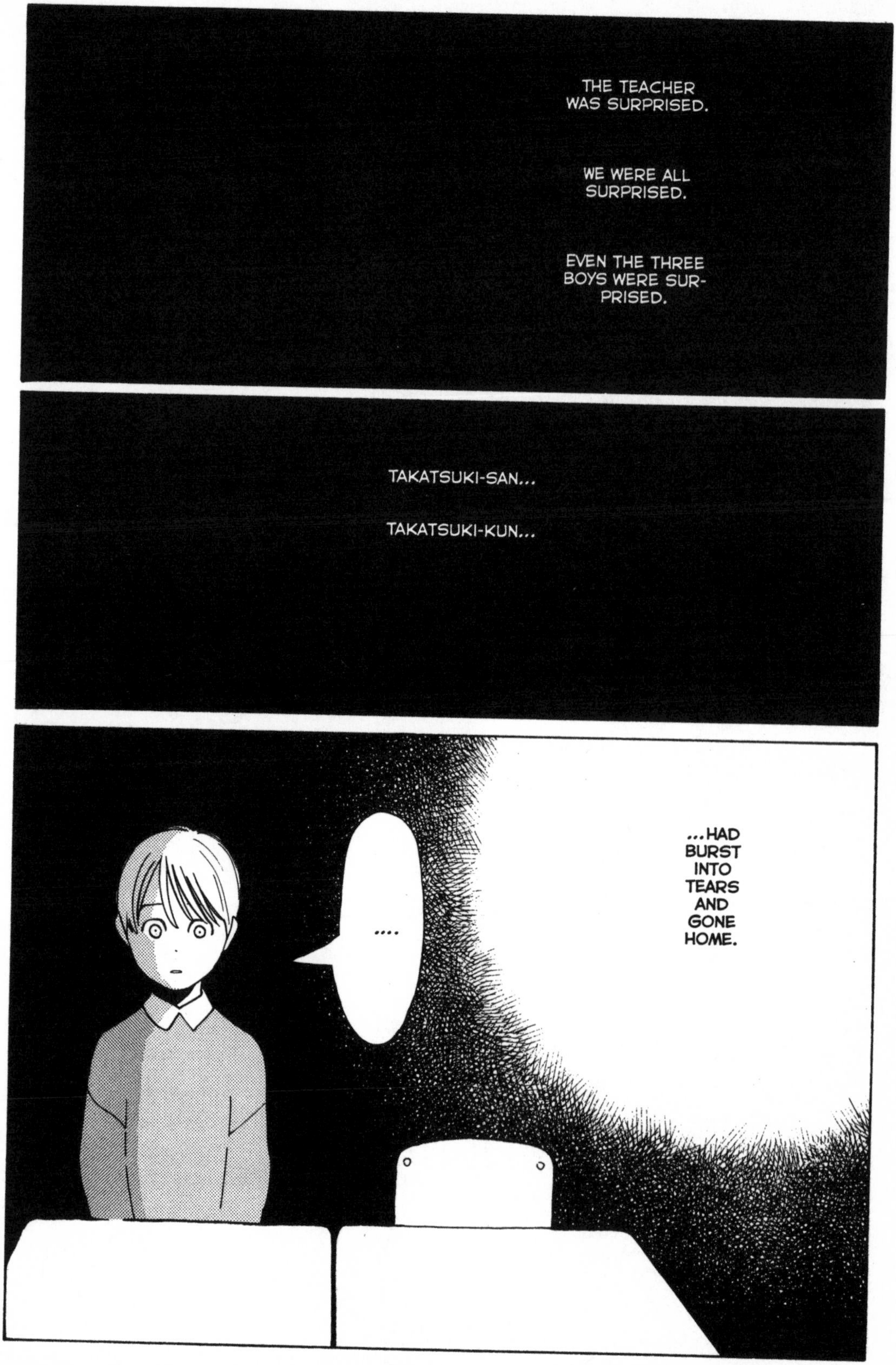
THE TEACHER WAS SURPRISED.
WE WERE ALL SURPRISED.
EVEN THE THREE BOYS WERE SURPRISED.
TAKATSUKI-SAN...
TAKATSUKI-KUN...
...HAD BURST INTO TEARS AND GONE HOME.
....

8

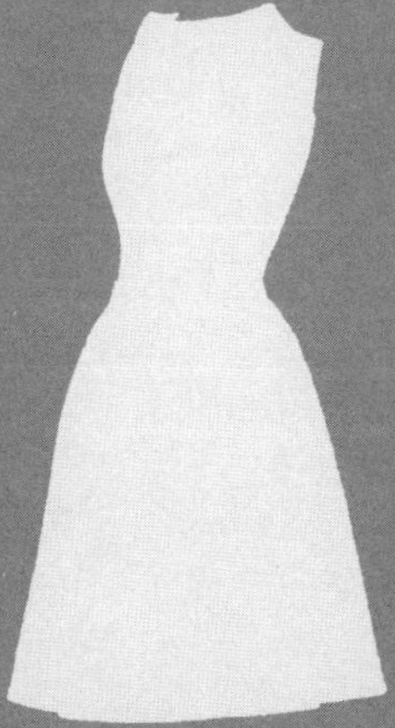

Everything I Want

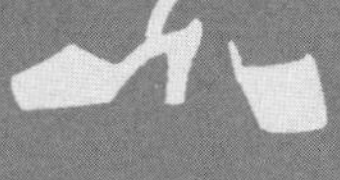

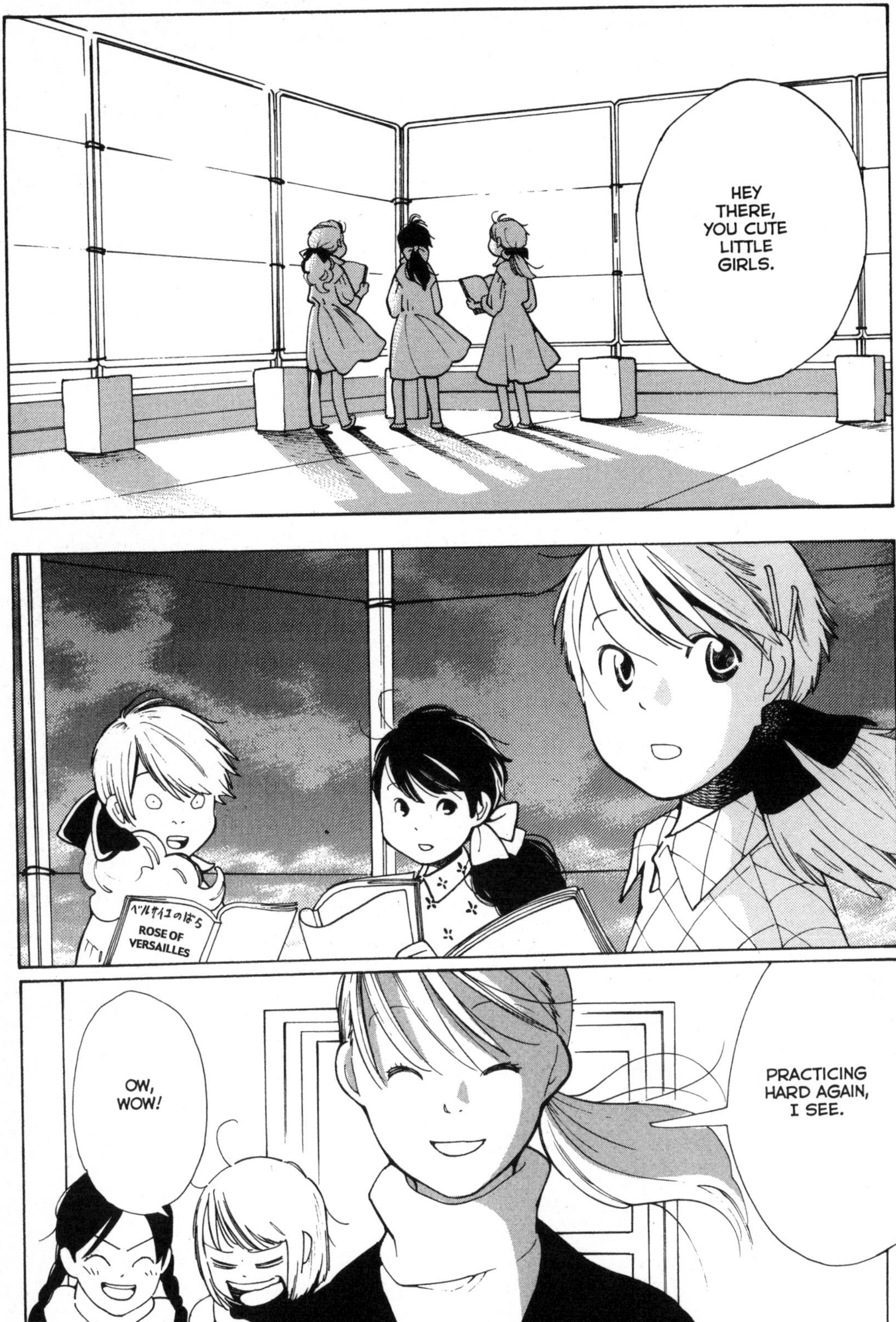
HEY THERE, YOU CUTE LITTLE GIRLS.
ベルサイユのばら
ROSE OF VERSAILLES
PRACTICING HARD AGAIN, I SEE.
OW, WOW!

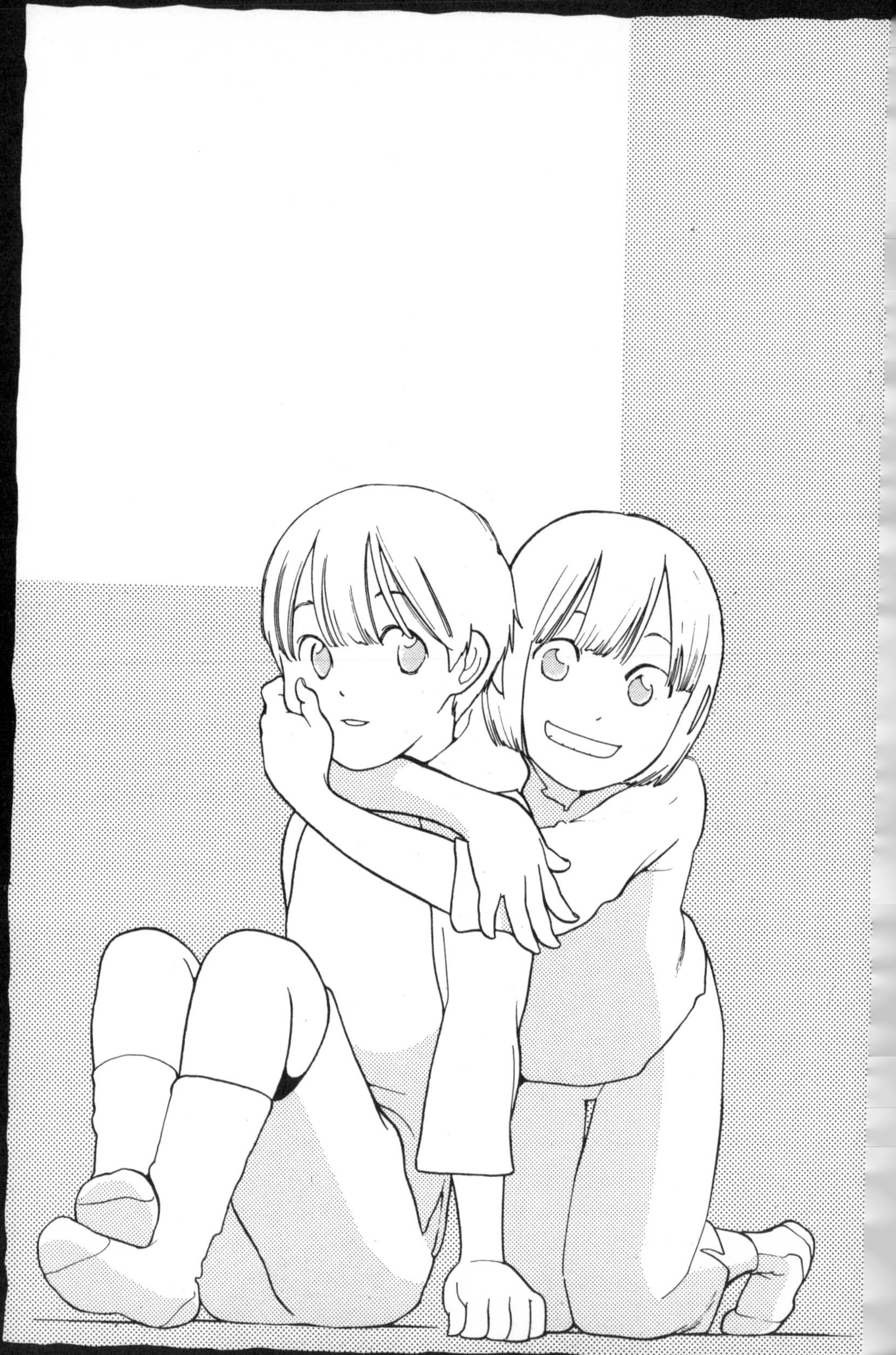

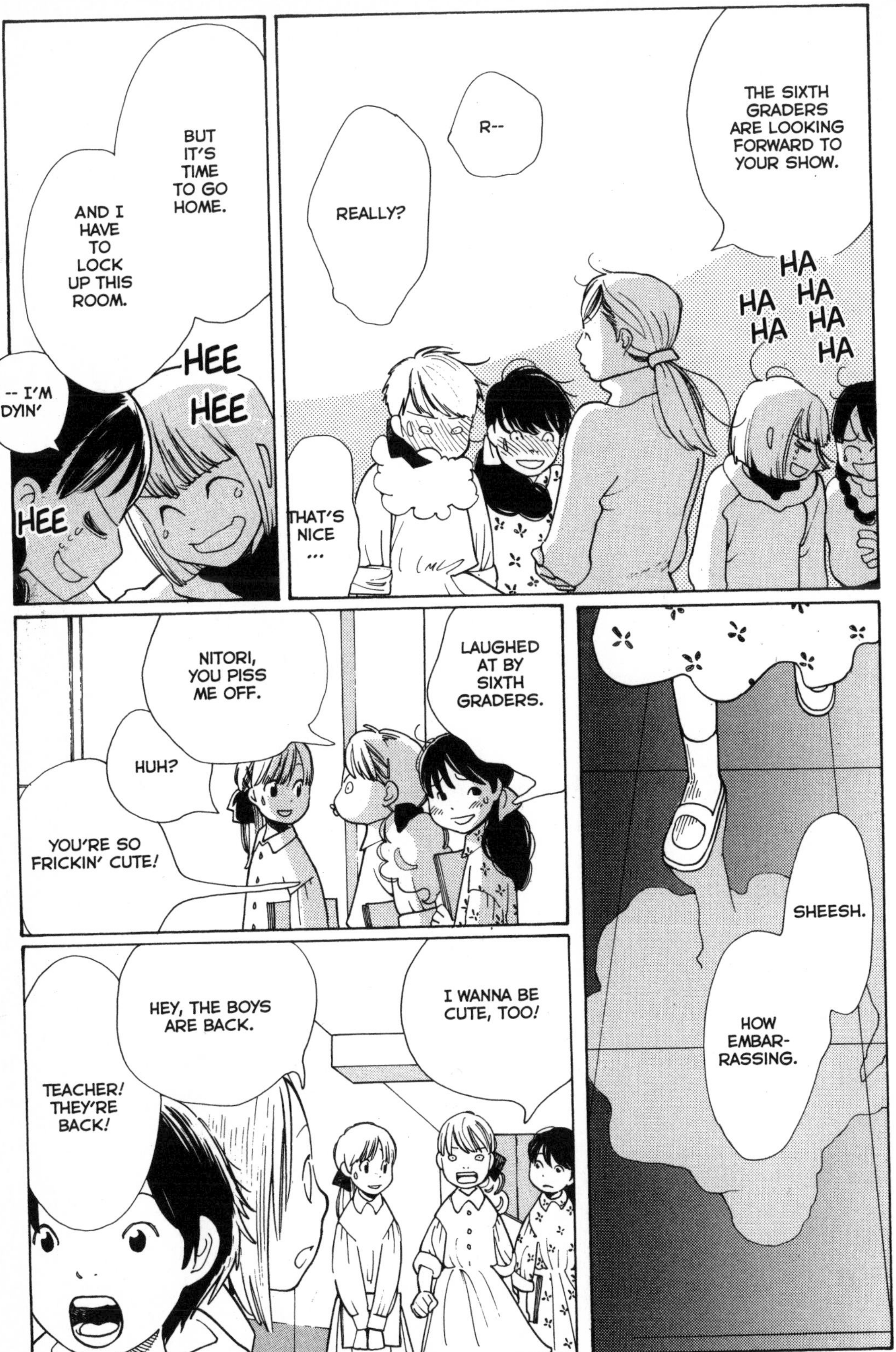
THE SIXTH GRADERS ARE LOOKING FORWARD TO YOUR SHOW.
HA HA HA HA HA HA
R--
REALLY?
THAT'S NICE ...
BUT IT'S TIME TO GO HOME.
AND I HAVE TO LOCK UP THIS ROOM.
HEE HEE
I -- I'M DYIN'
HEE
SHEESH.
HOW EMBAR-RASSING.
LAUGHED AT BY SIXTH GRADERS.
NITORI, YOU PISS ME OFF.
HUH?
YOU'RE SO FRICKIN' CUTE!
I WANNA BE CUTE, TOO!
HEY, THE BOYS ARE BACK.
TEACHER! THEY'RE BACK!

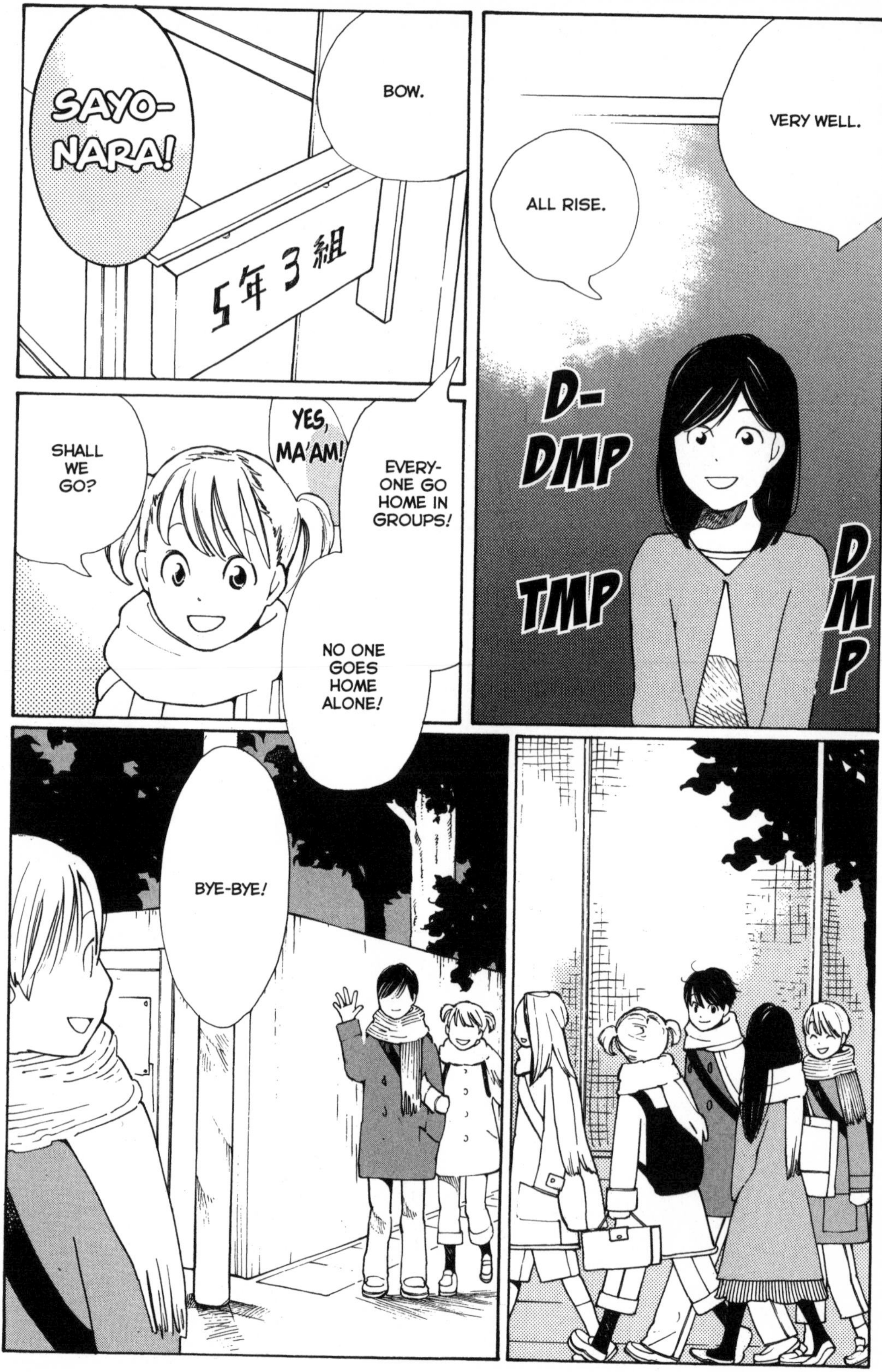
VERY WELL.
ALL RISE.
D-DMP
DMP
TMP
BOW.
SAYO-NARA!
EVERY-ONE GO HOME IN GROUPS!
YES, MA'AM!
SHALL WE GO?
NO ONE GOES HOME ALONE!
BYE-BYE!

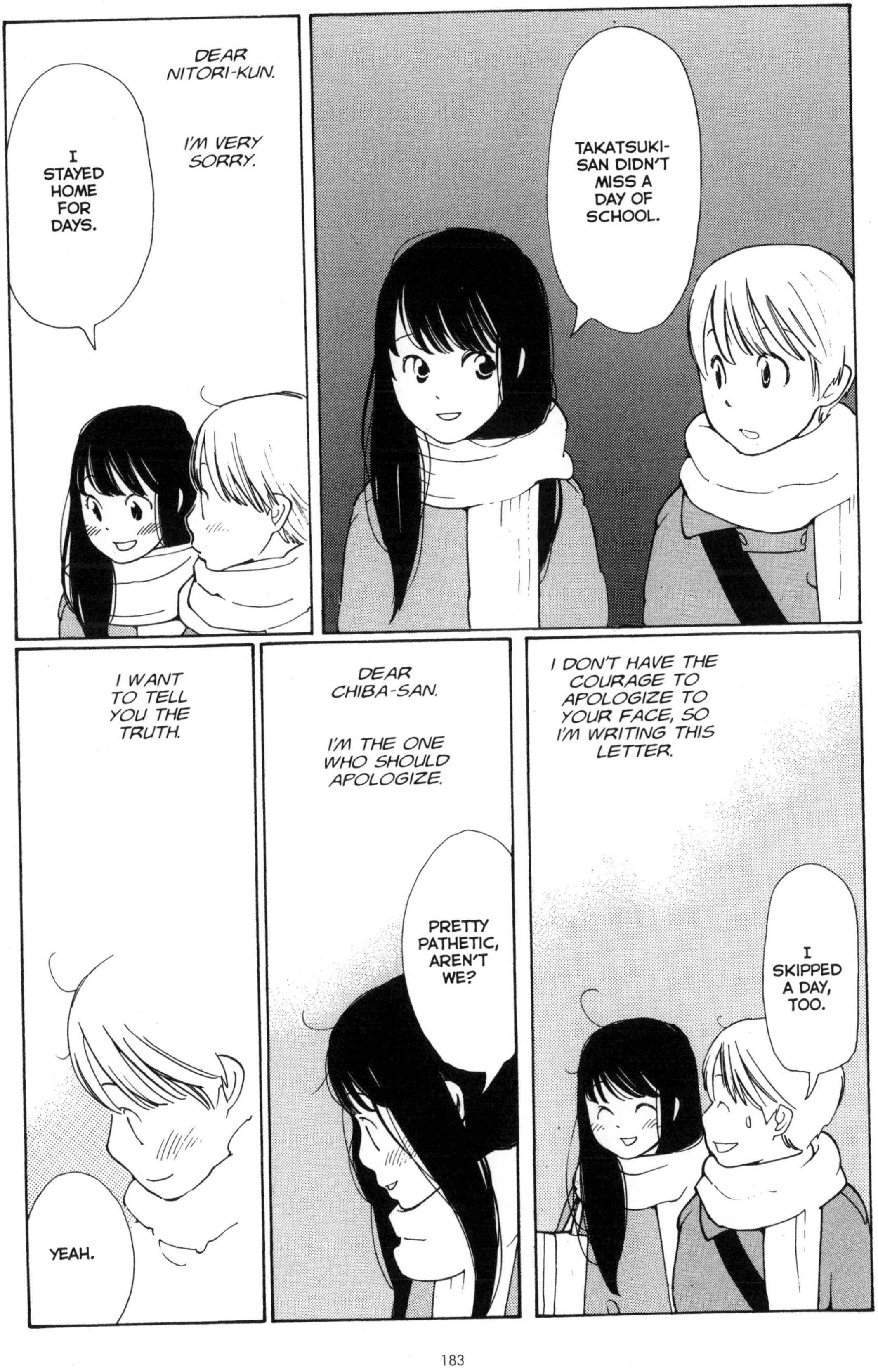
TAKATSUKI-SAN DIDN'T MISS A DAY OF SCHOOL.
DEAR NITORI-KUN.
I'M VERY SORRY.
I STAYED HOME FOR DAYS.
I DON'T HAVE THE COURAGE TO APOLOGIZE TO YOUR FACE, SO I'M WRITING THIS LETTER.
I SKIPPED A DAY, TOO.
DEAR CHIBA-SAN.
I'M THE ONE WHO SHOULD APOLOGIZE.
PRETTY PATHETIC, AREN'T WE?
I WANT TO TELL YOU THE TRUTH.
YEAH.

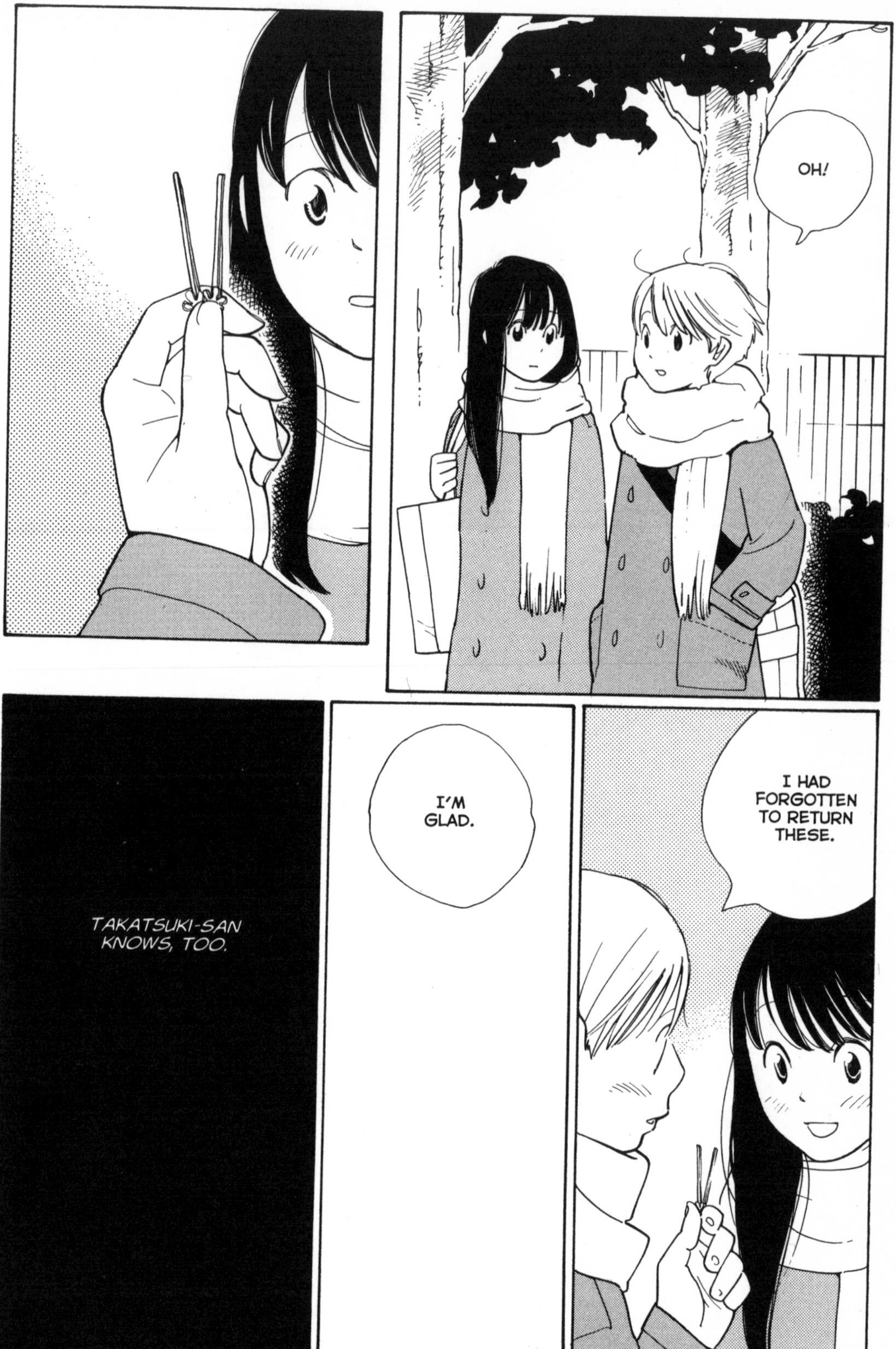
OH!
I HAD FORGOTTEN TO RETURN THESE.
I'M GLAD.
TAKATSUKI-SAN KNOWS, TOO.

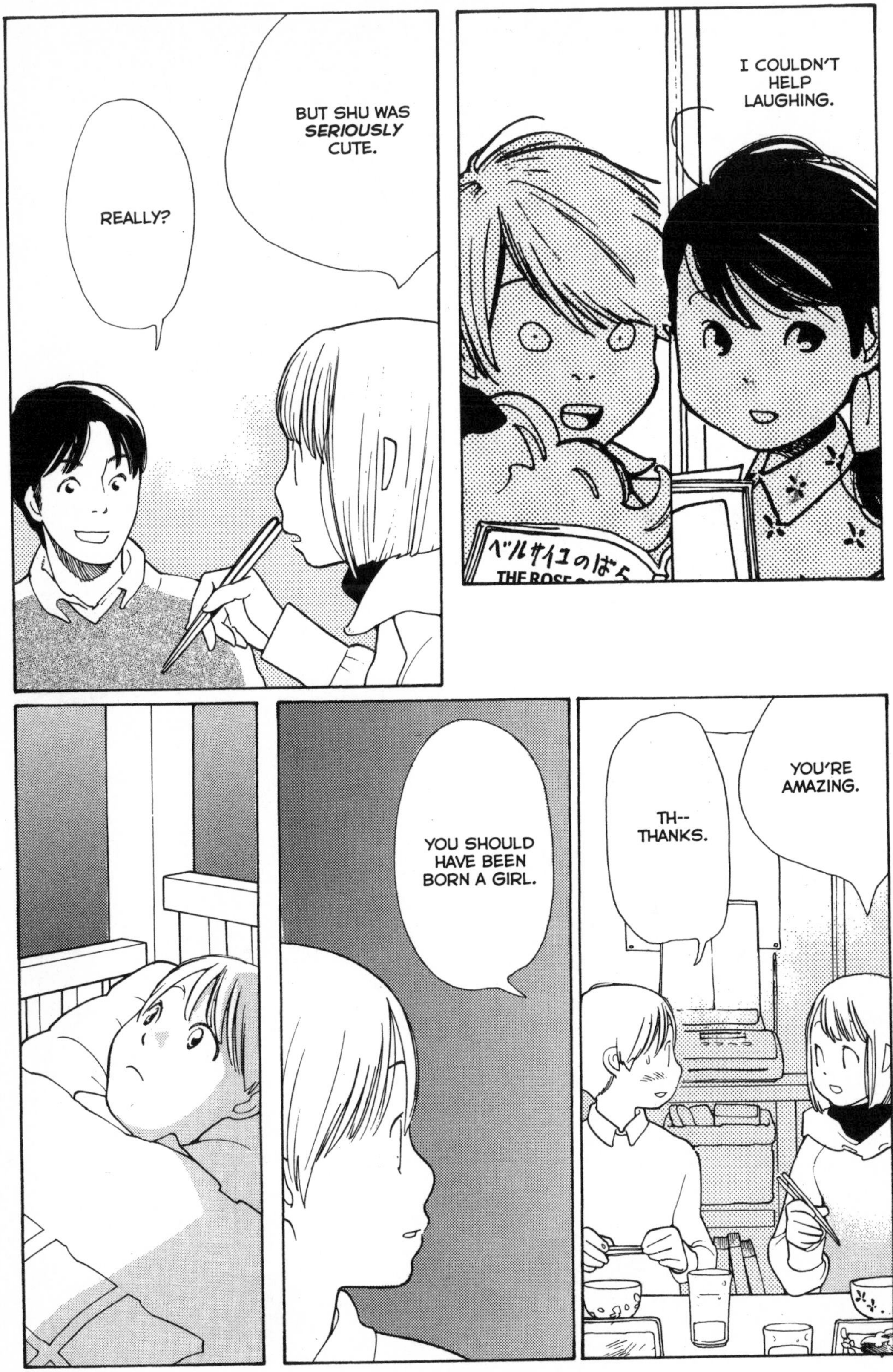
I COULDN'T HELP LAUGHING.
ベルサイユのばら
BUT SHU WAS *SERIOUSLY* CUTE.
REALLY?
YOU'RE AMAZING.
TH-- THANKS.
YOU SHOULD HAVE BEEN BORN A GIRL.

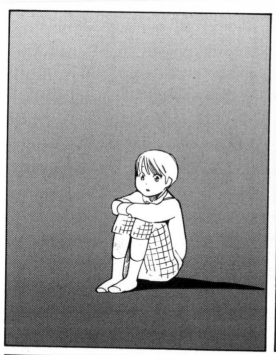

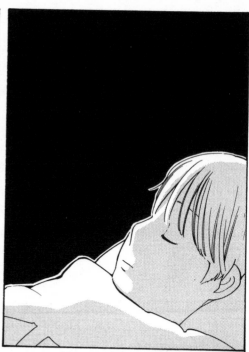

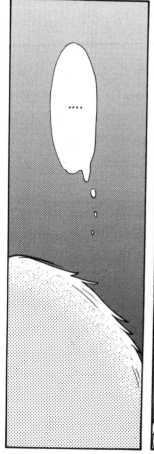

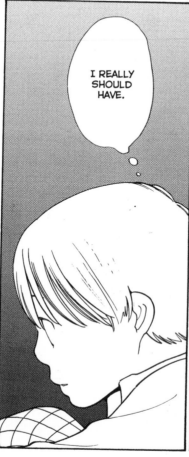

YOU SHOULD HAVE BEEN BORN A GIRL.
YEAH.
I REALLY SHOULD HAVE.
....

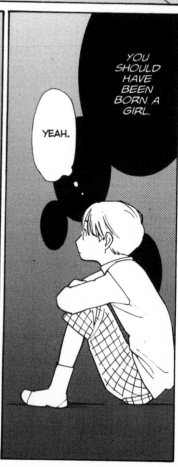

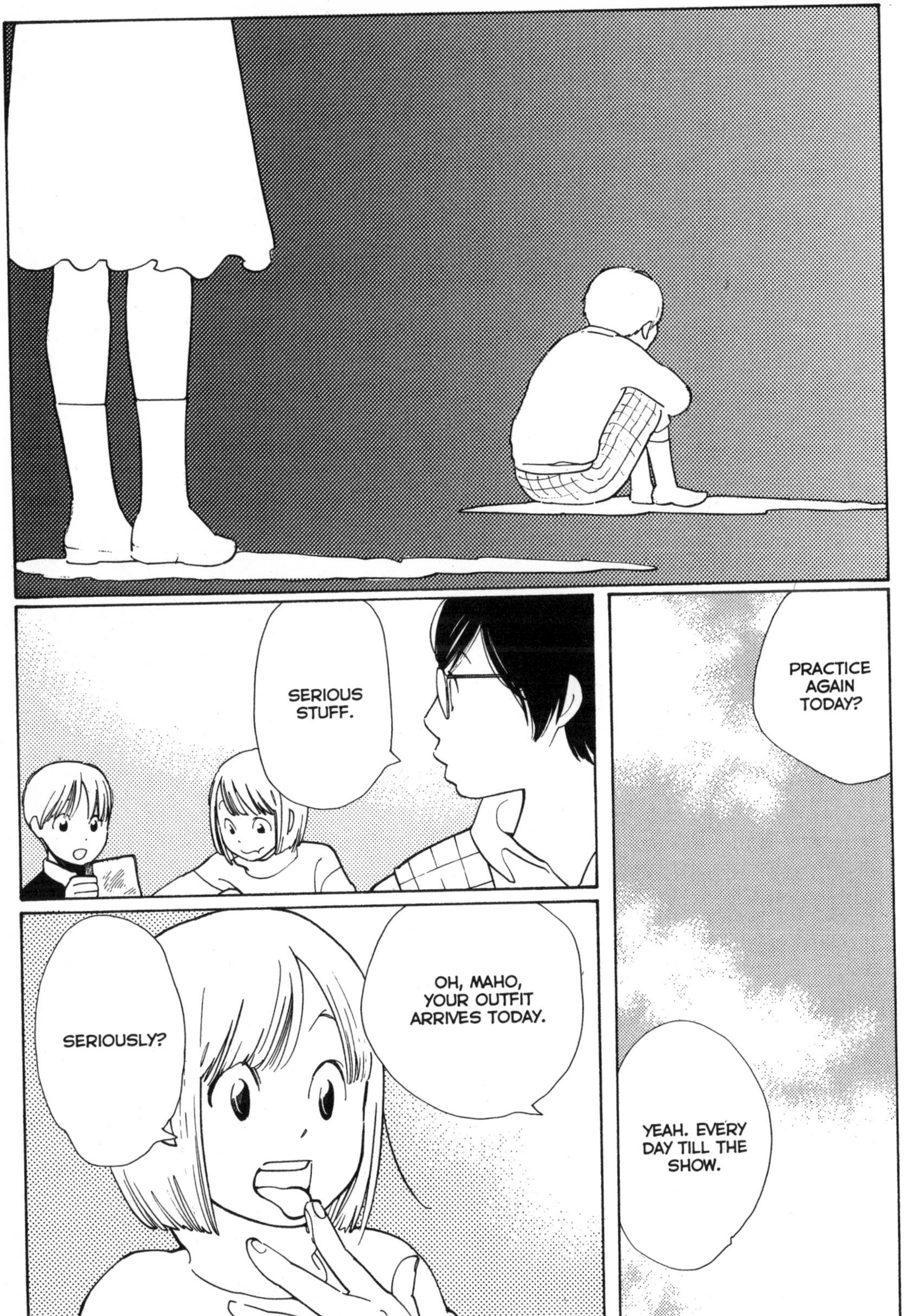
PRACTICE AGAIN TODAY?
YEAH. EVERY DAY TILL THE SHOW.
SERIOUS STUFF.
OH, MAHO, YOUR OUTFIT ARRIVES TODAY.
SERIOUSLY?

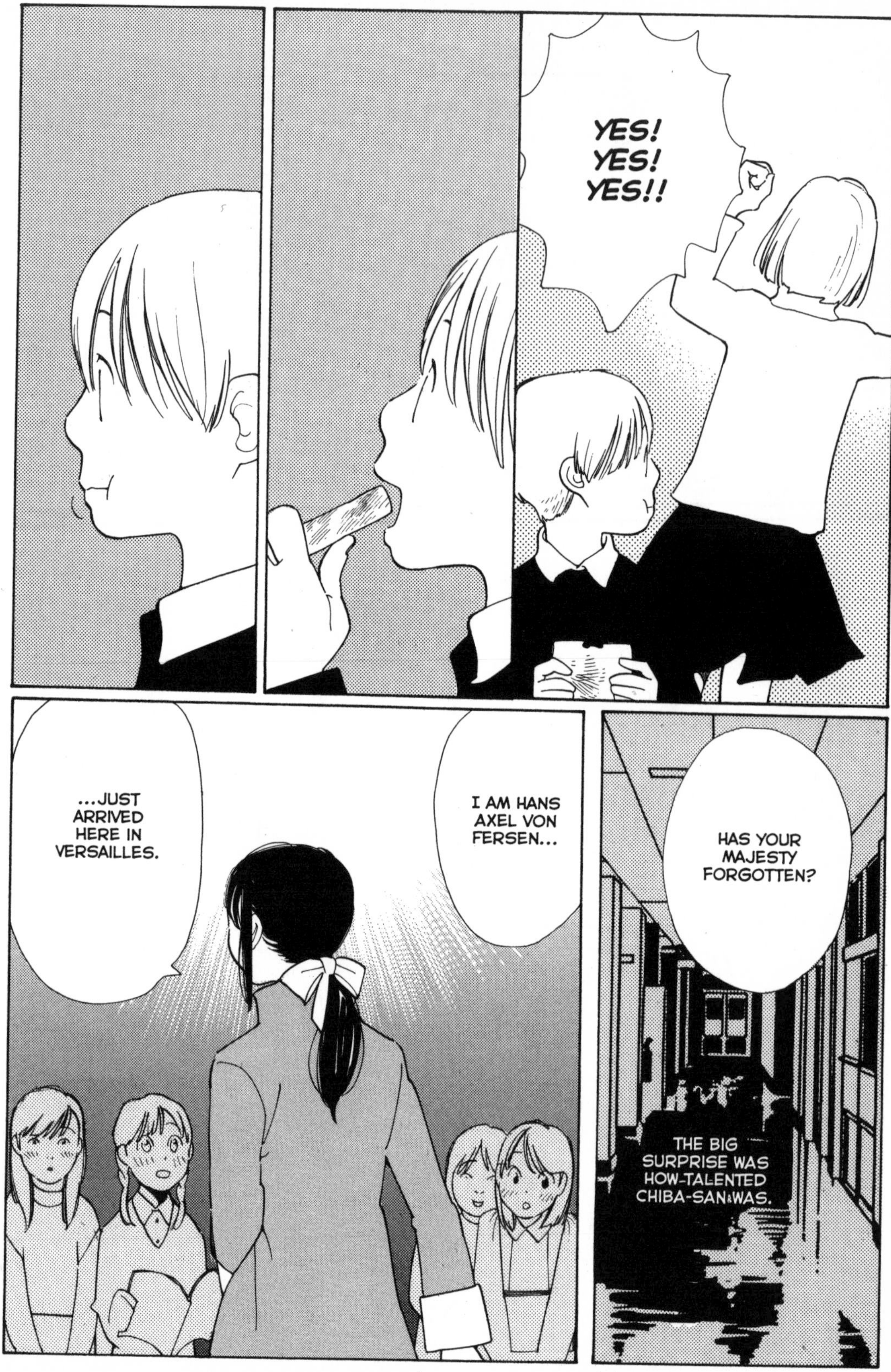
YES! YES! YES!!
HAS YOUR MAJESTY FORGOTTEN?
THE BIG SURPRISE WAS HOW TALENTED CHIBA-SAN WAS.
I AM HANS AXEL VON FERSEN...
...JUST ARRIVED HERE IN VERSAILLES.

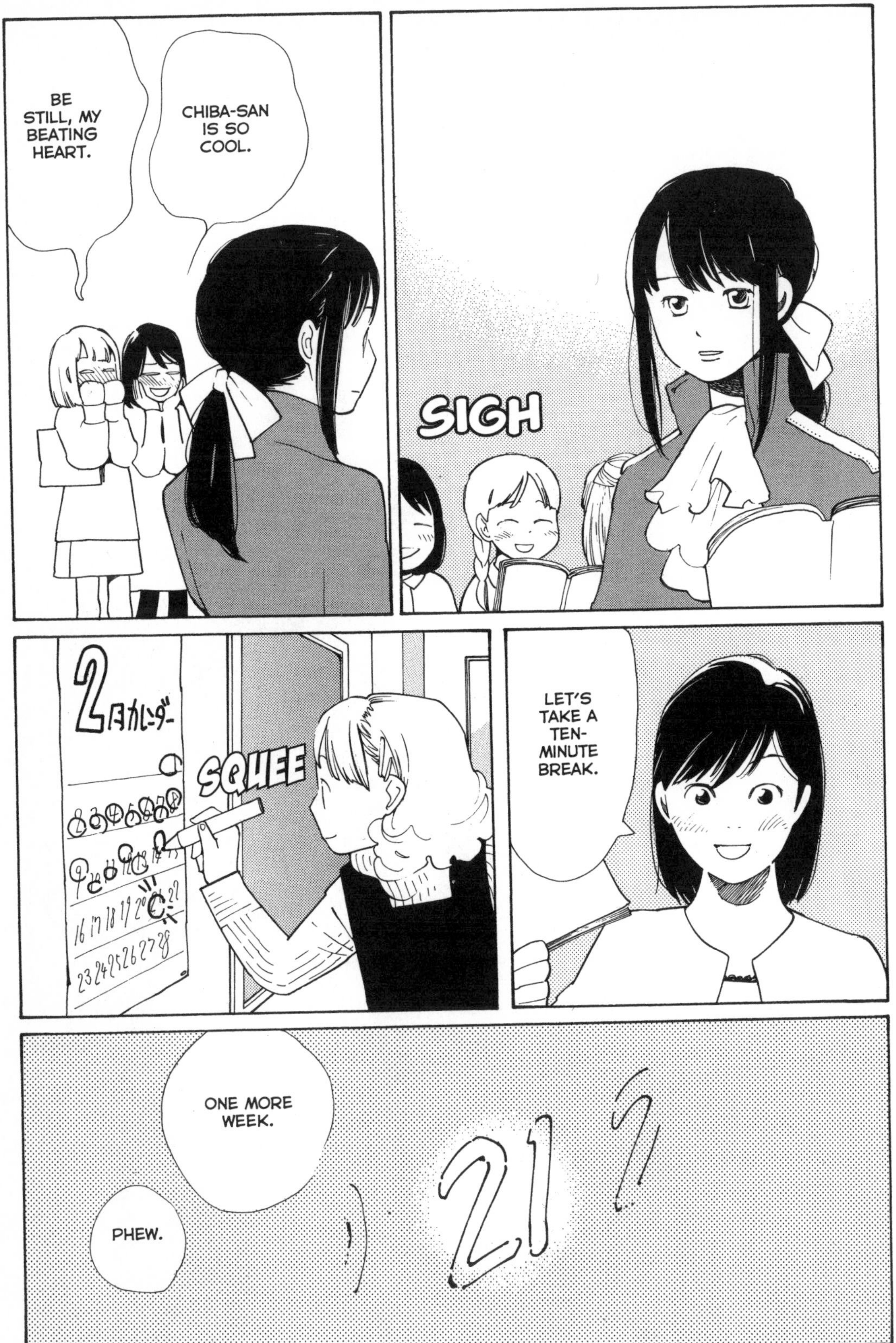
SIGH
CHIBA-SAN IS SO COOL.
BE STILL, MY BEATING HEART.
LET'S TAKE A TEN-MINUTE BREAK.
SQUEE
2月カレンダー
ONE MORE WEEK.
PHEW.
21

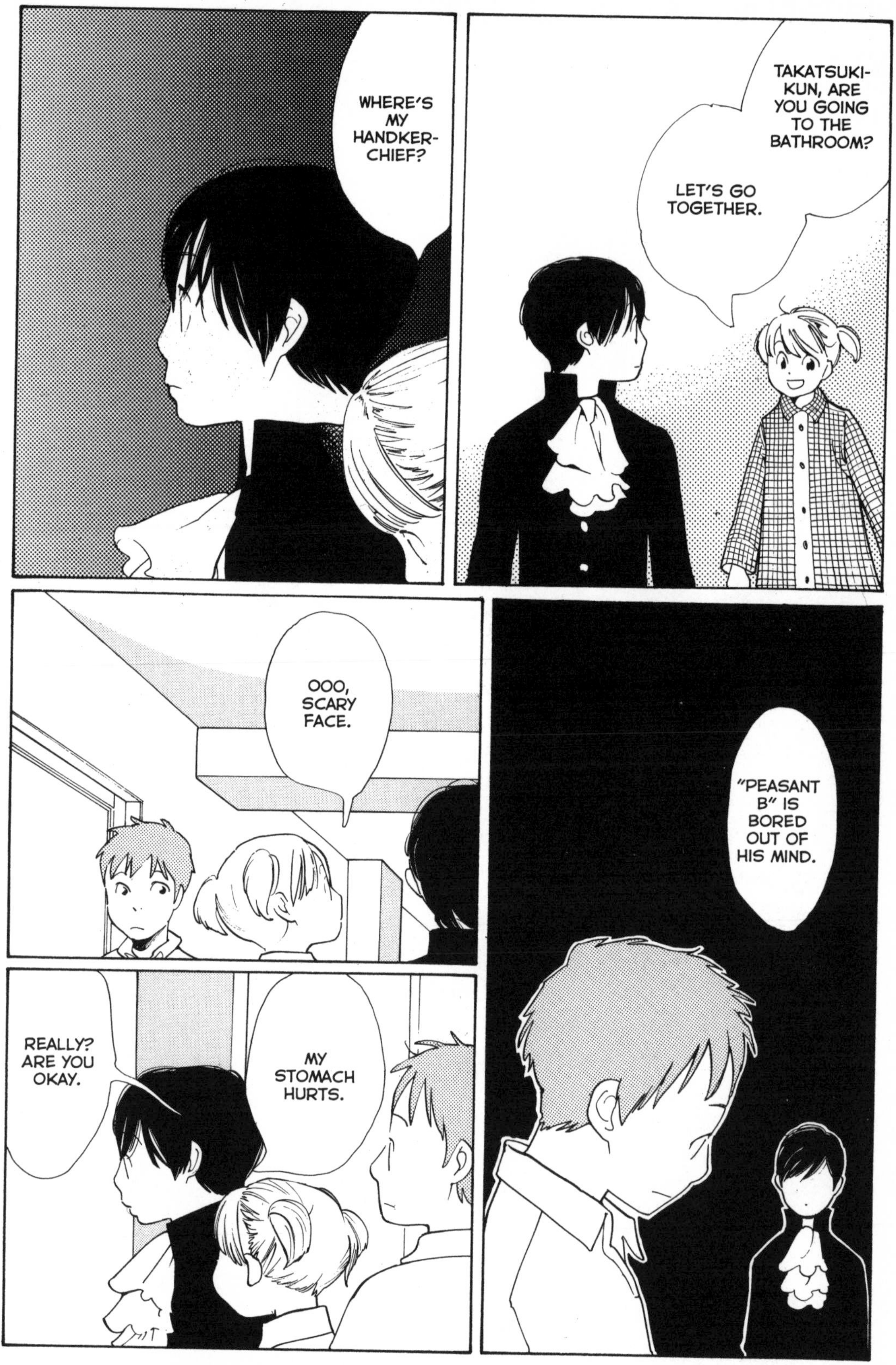
TAKATSUKI-KUN, ARE YOU GOING TO THE BATHROOM?
LET'S GO TOGETHER.
WHERE'S MY HANDKER-CHIEF?
"PEASANT B" IS BORED OUT OF HIS MIND.
OOO, SCARY FACE.
MY STOMACH HURTS.
REALLY? ARE YOU OKAY.

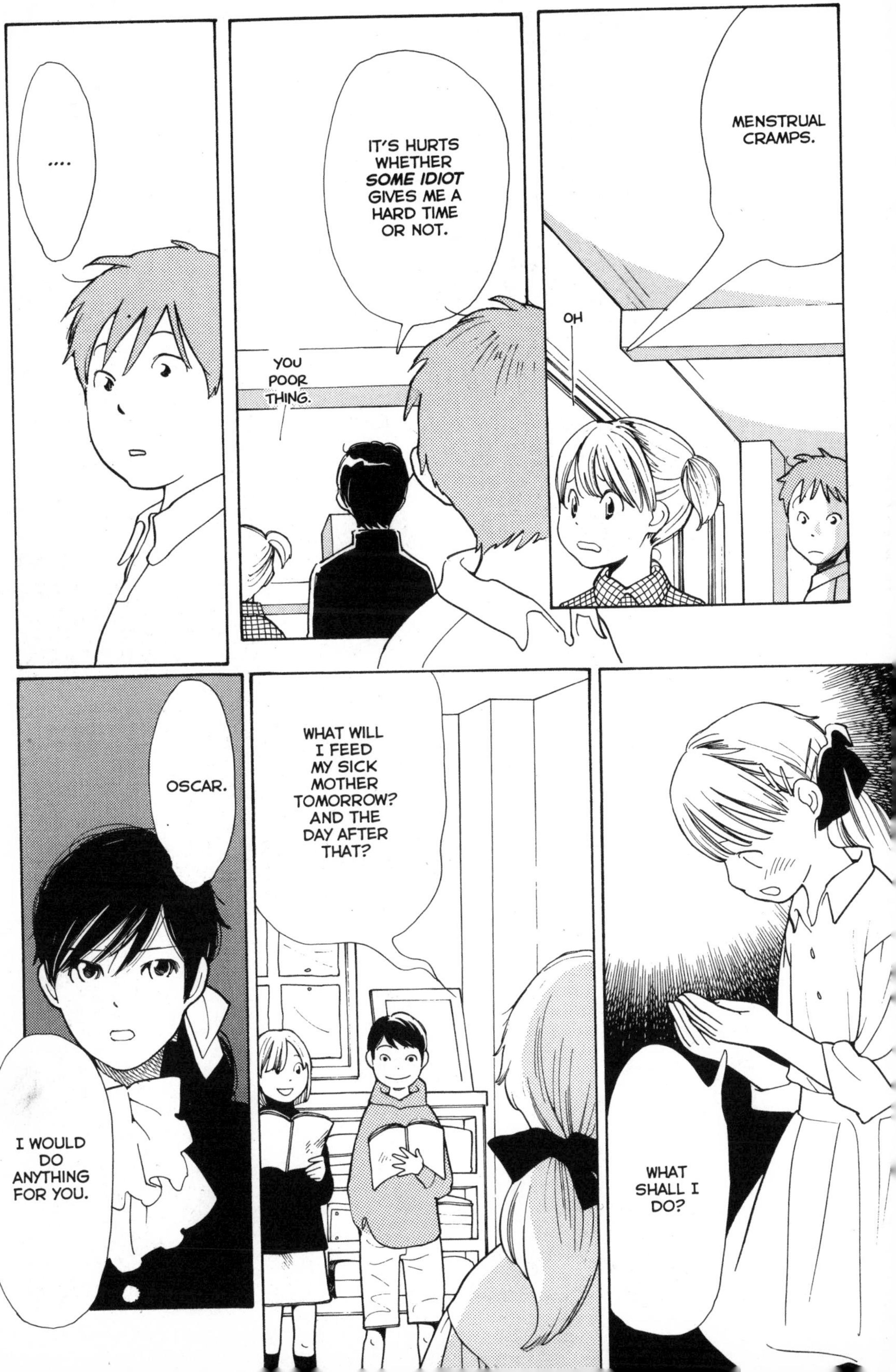
MENSTRUAL CRAMPS.
OH
IT'S HURTS WHETHER ***SOME IDIOT*** GIVES ME A HARD TIME OR NOT.
YOU POOR THING.
....
WHAT SHALL I DO?
WHAT WILL I FEED MY SICK MOTHER TOMORROW? AND THE DAY AFTER THAT?
OSCAR.
I WOULD DO ANYTHING FOR YOU.

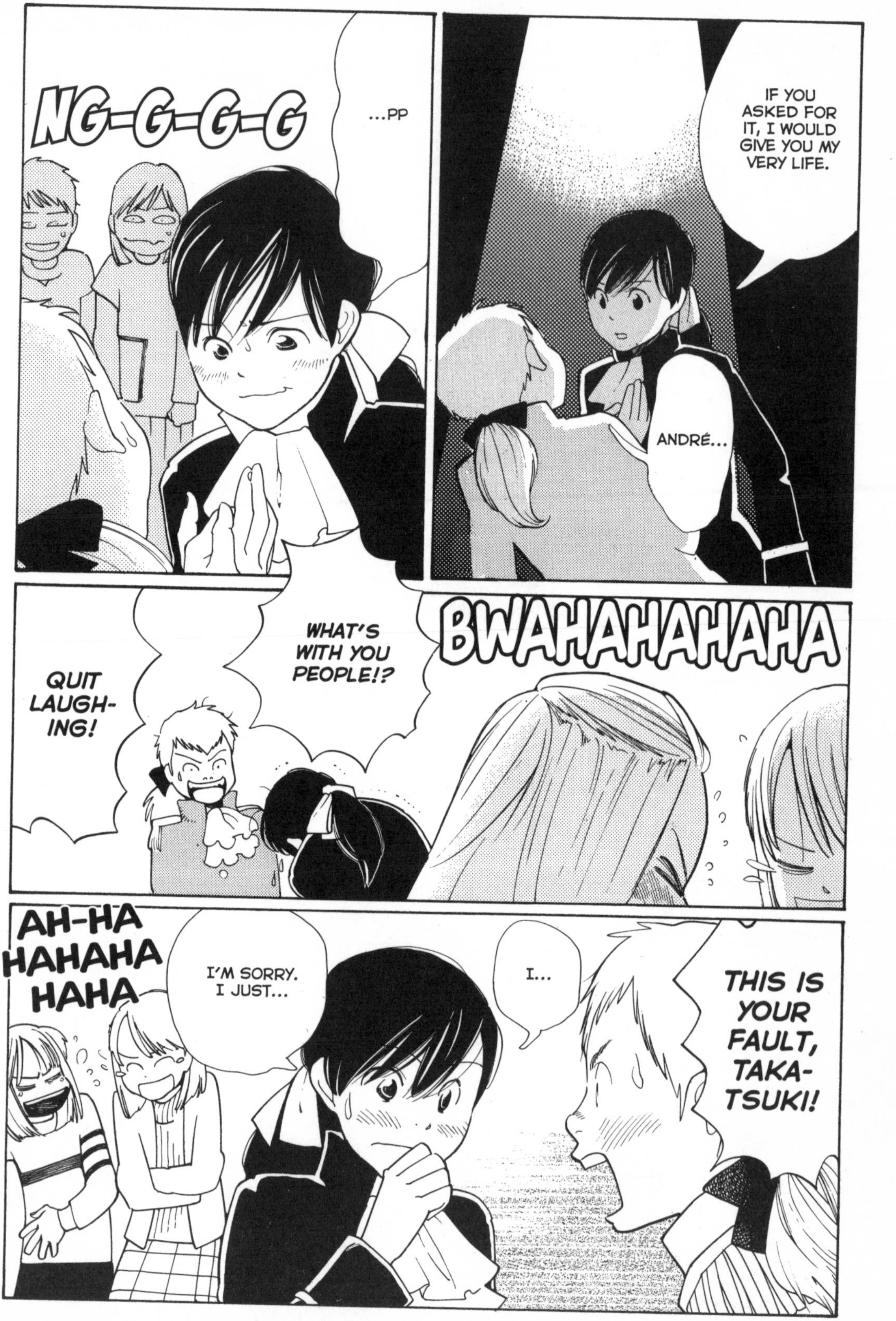
IF YOU ASKED FOR IT, I WOULD GIVE YOU MY VERY LIFE.
ANDRÉ...
...PP
NG-G-G-G
BWAHAHAHAHAHA
WHAT'S WITH YOU PEOPLE!?
QUIT LAUGH-ING!
THIS IS YOUR FAULT, TAKA-TSUKI!
I...
I'M SORRY. I JUST...
AH-HA HAHAHA HAHA

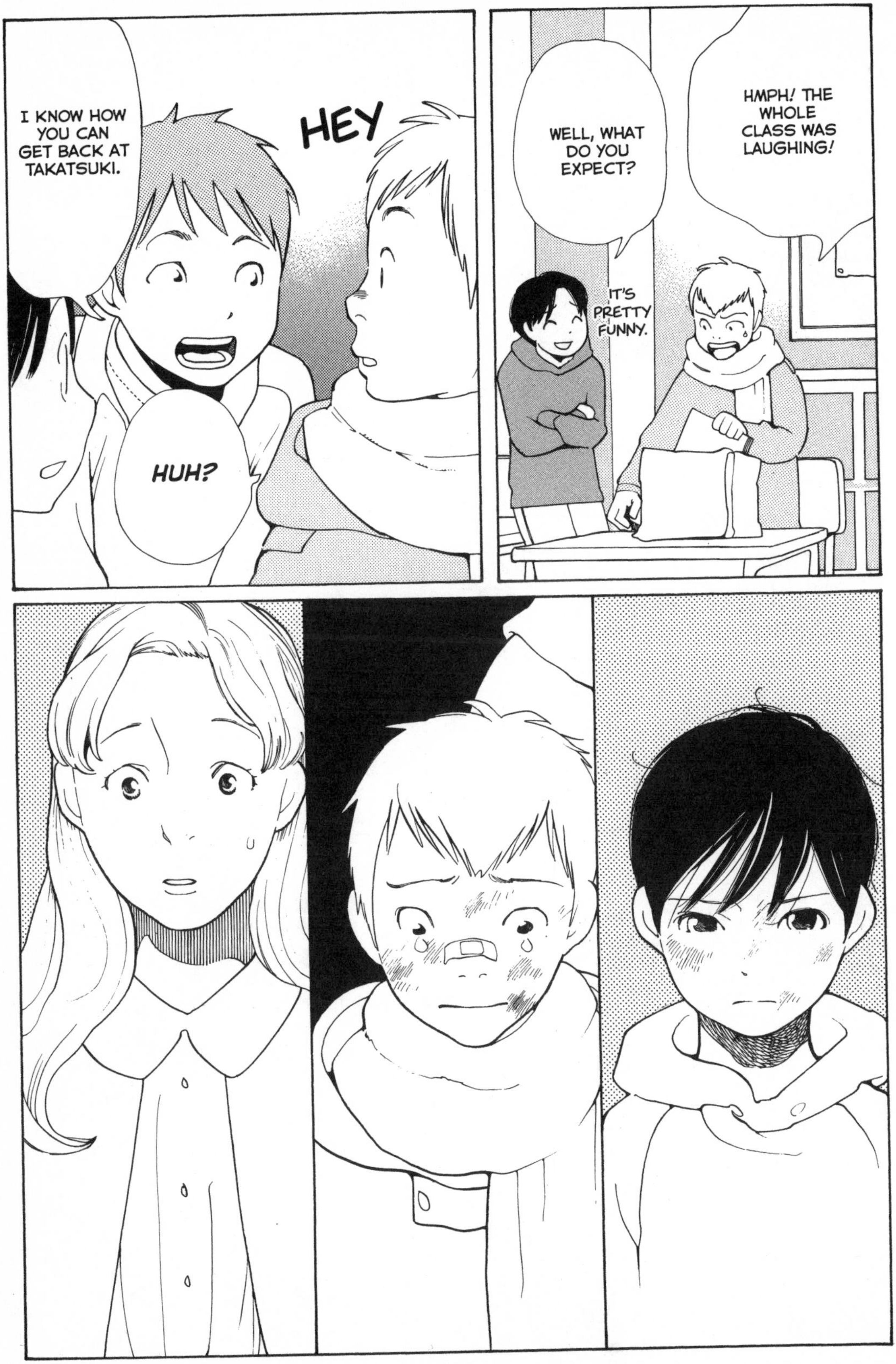
HMPH! THE WHOLE CLASS WAS LAUGHING!
WELL, WHAT DO YOU EXPECT?
IT'S PRETTY FUNNY.
HEY
I KNOW HOW YOU CAN GET BACK AT TAKATSUKI.
HUH?

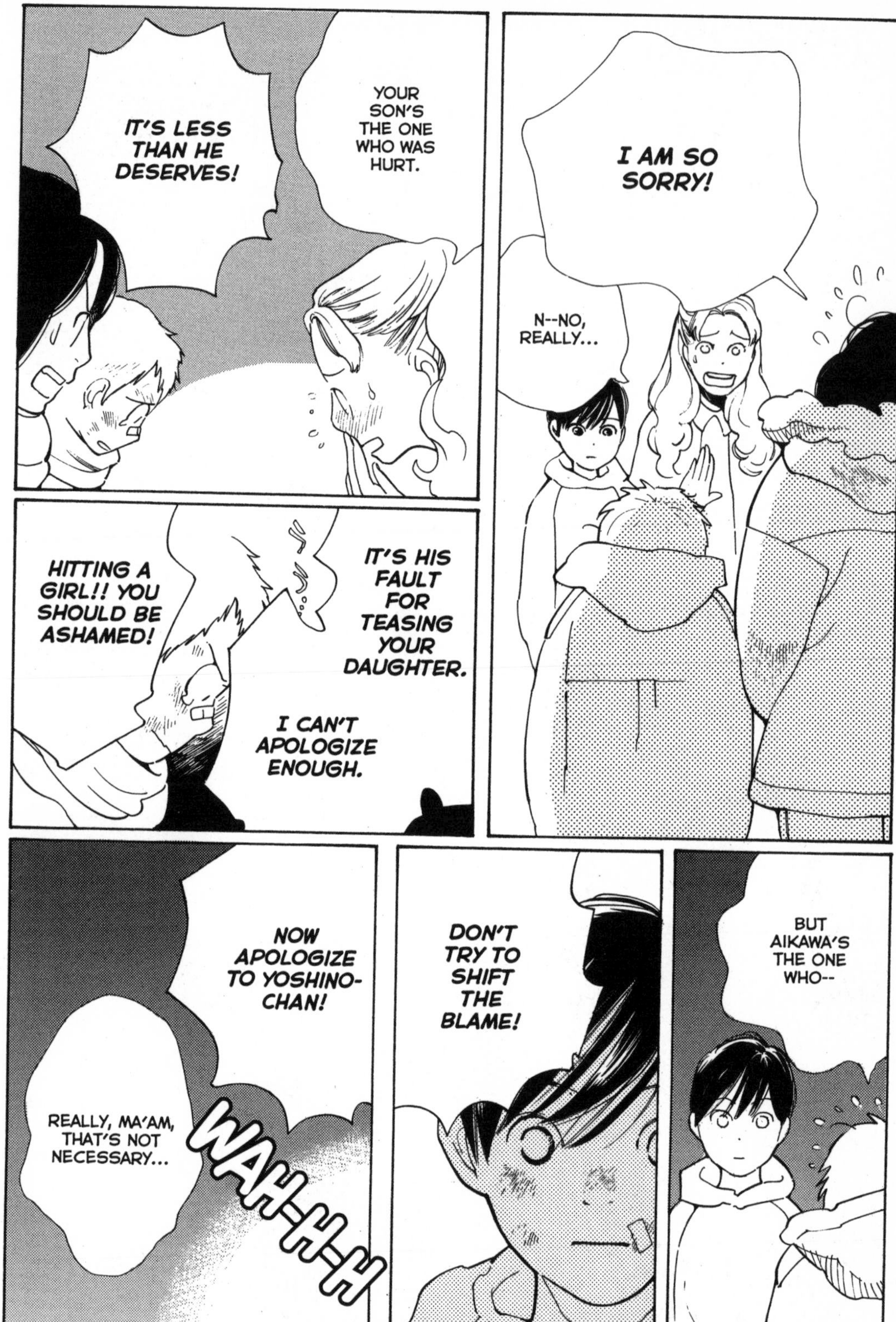
I AM SO SORRY!
N--NO, REALLY...
YOUR SON'S THE ONE WHO WAS HURT.
IT'S LESS THAN HE DESERVES!
IT'S HIS FAULT FOR TEASING YOUR DAUGHTER.
I CAN'T APOLOGIZE ENOUGH.
HITTING A GIRL!! YOU SHOULD BE ASHAMED!
BUT AIKAWA'S THE ONE WHO--
DON'T TRY TO SHIFT THE BLAME!
NOW APOLOGIZE TO YOSHINO-CHAN!
WAH-H-H-H
REALLY, MA'AM, THAT'S NOT NECESSARY...

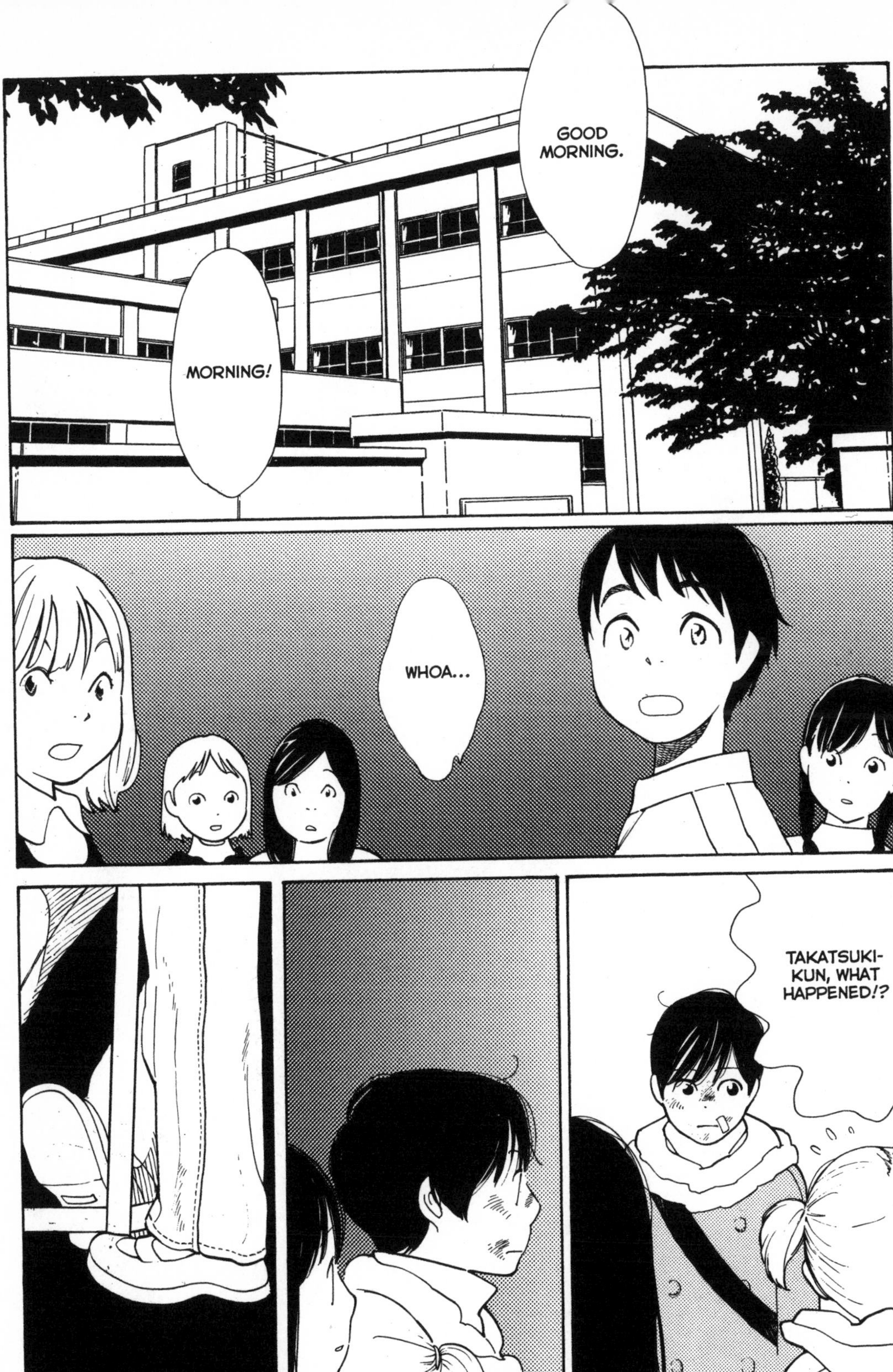
GOOD MORNING.
MORNING!
WHOA...
TAKATSUKI-KUN, WHAT HAPPENED!?

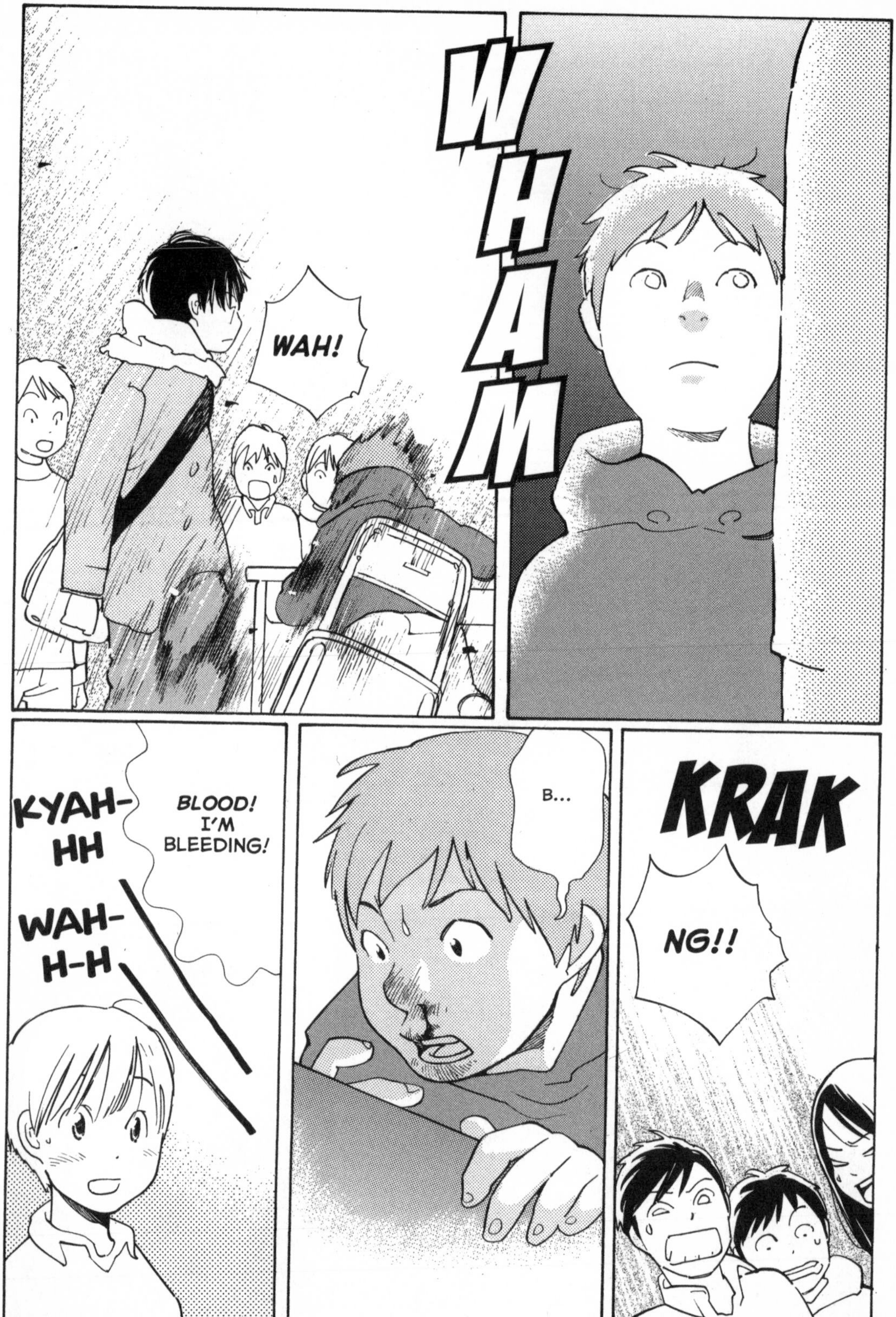
WHAM
WAH!
KRAK
NG!!
B...
BLOOD! I'M BLEEDING!
KYAH-HH
WAH-H-H

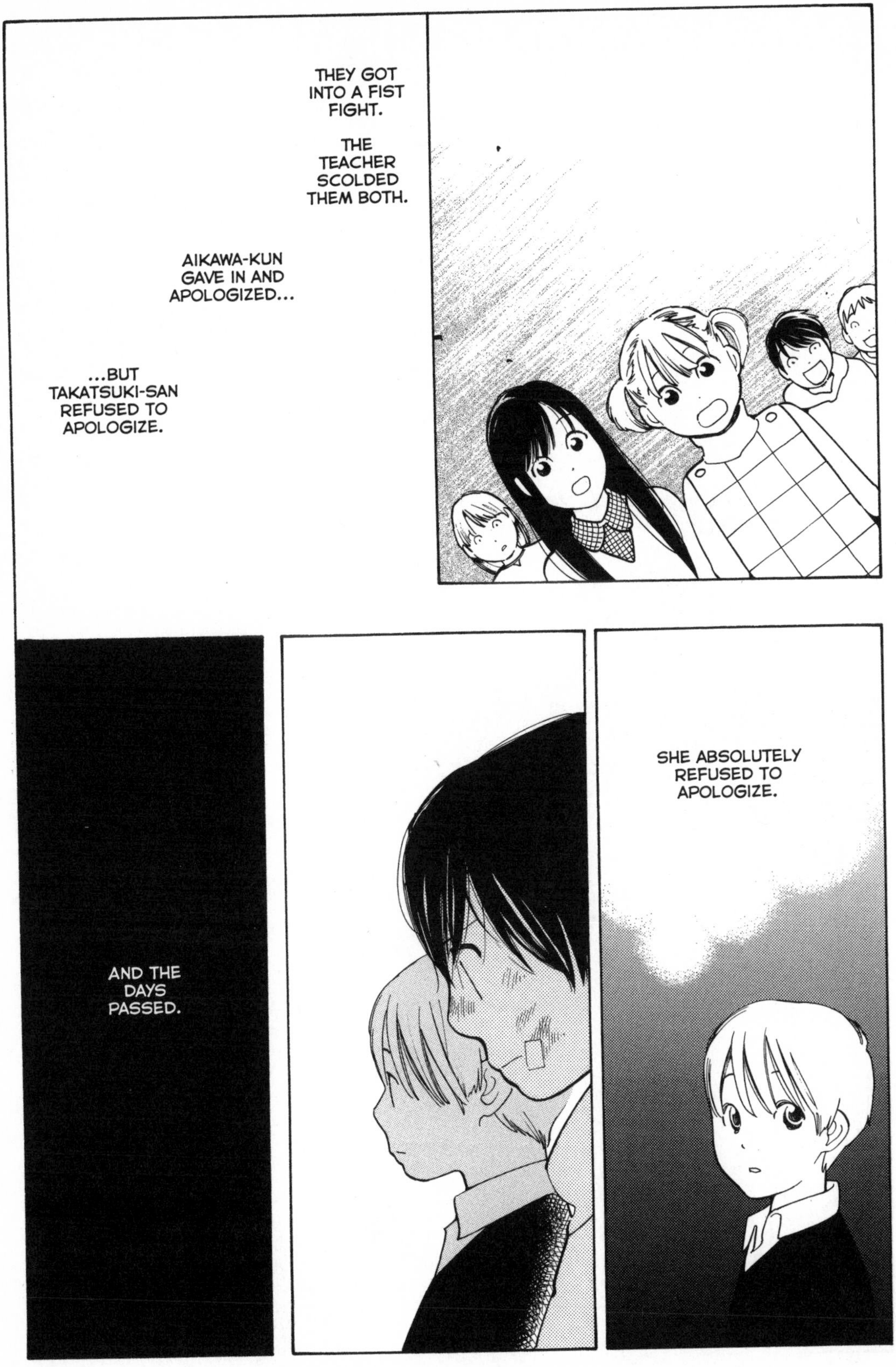
THEY GOT INTO A FIST FIGHT.
THE TEACHER SCOLDED THEM BOTH.
AIKAWA-KUN GAVE IN AND APOLOGIZED...
...BUT TAKATSUKI-SAN REFUSED TO APOLOGIZE.
SHE ABSOLUTELY REFUSED TO APOLOGIZE.
AND THE DAYS PASSED.

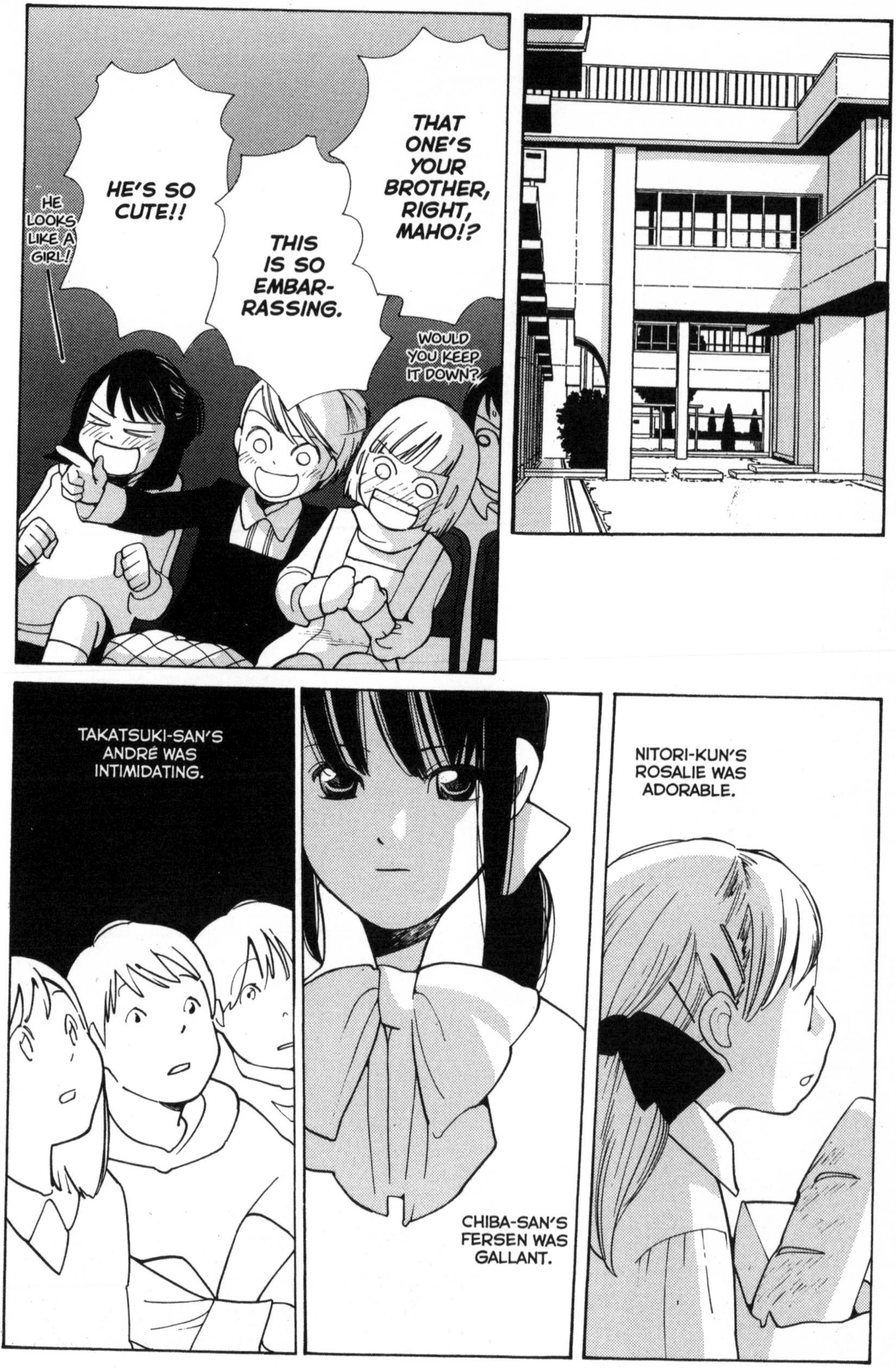
THAT ONE'S YOUR BROTHER, RIGHT, MAHO!?
THIS IS SO EMBARRASSING.
HE'S SO CUTE!!
HE LOOKS LIKE A GIRL!
WOULD YOU KEEP IT DOWN?
NITORI-KUN'S ROSALIE WAS ADORABLE.
CHIBA-SAN'S FERSEN WAS GALLANT.
TAKATSUKI-SAN'S ANDRÉ WAS INTIMIDATING.

AND THE SIXTH GRADERS' FAREWELL ASSEMBLY WAS A SUCCESS.

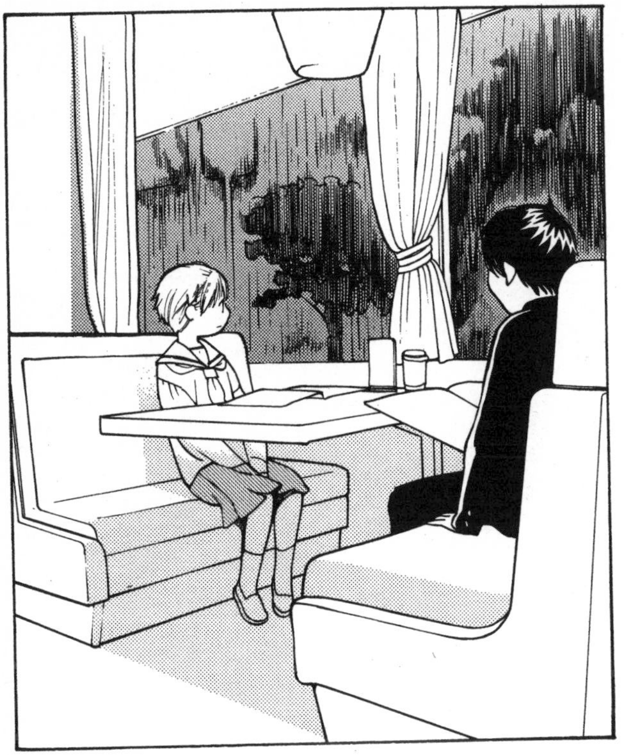

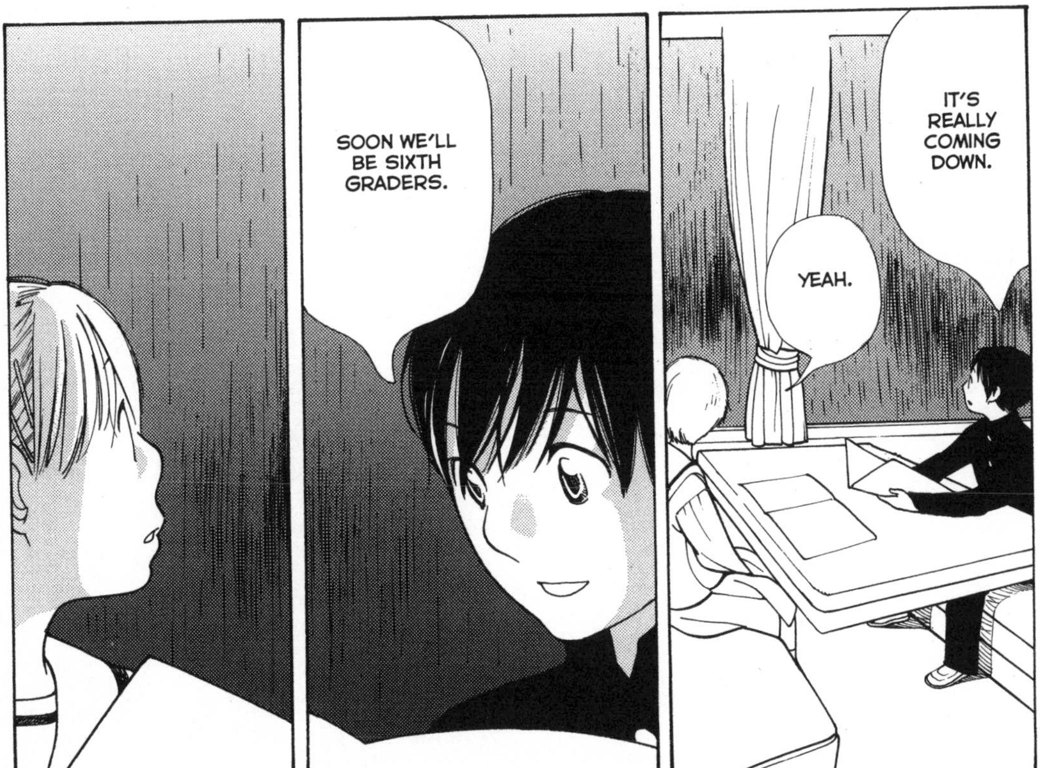
IT'S REALLY COMING DOWN.
YEAH.
SOON WE'LL BE SIXTH GRADERS.

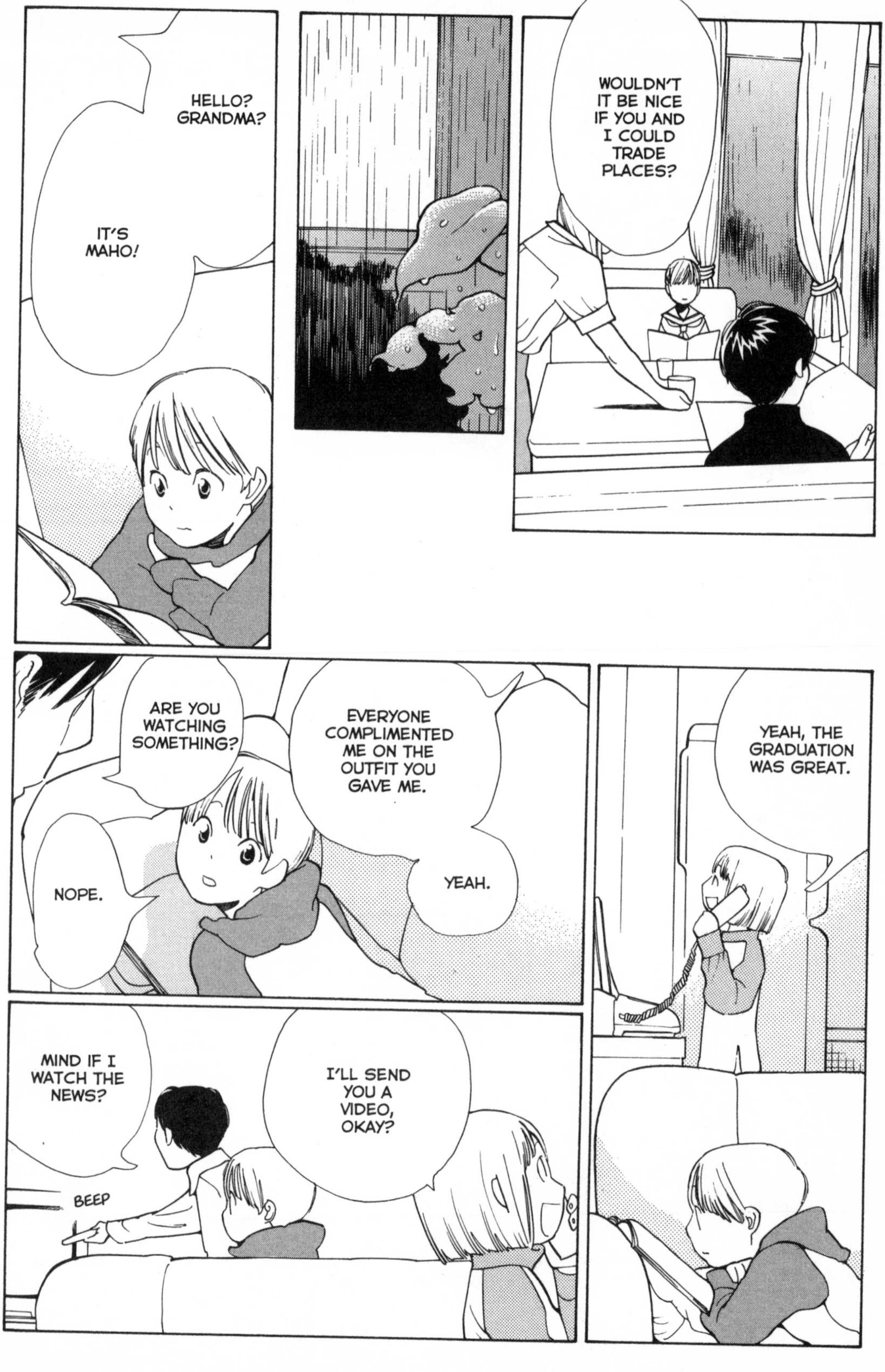
WOULDN'T IT BE NICE IF YOU AND I COULD TRADE PLACES?
HELLO? GRANDMA?
IT'S MAHO!
YEAH, THE GRADUATION WAS GREAT.
EVERYONE COMPLIMENTED ME ON THE OUTFIT YOU GAVE ME.
ARE YOU WATCHING SOMETHING?
YEAH.
NOPE.
I'LL SEND YOU A VIDEO, OKAY?
MIND IF I WATCH THE NEWS?
BEEP

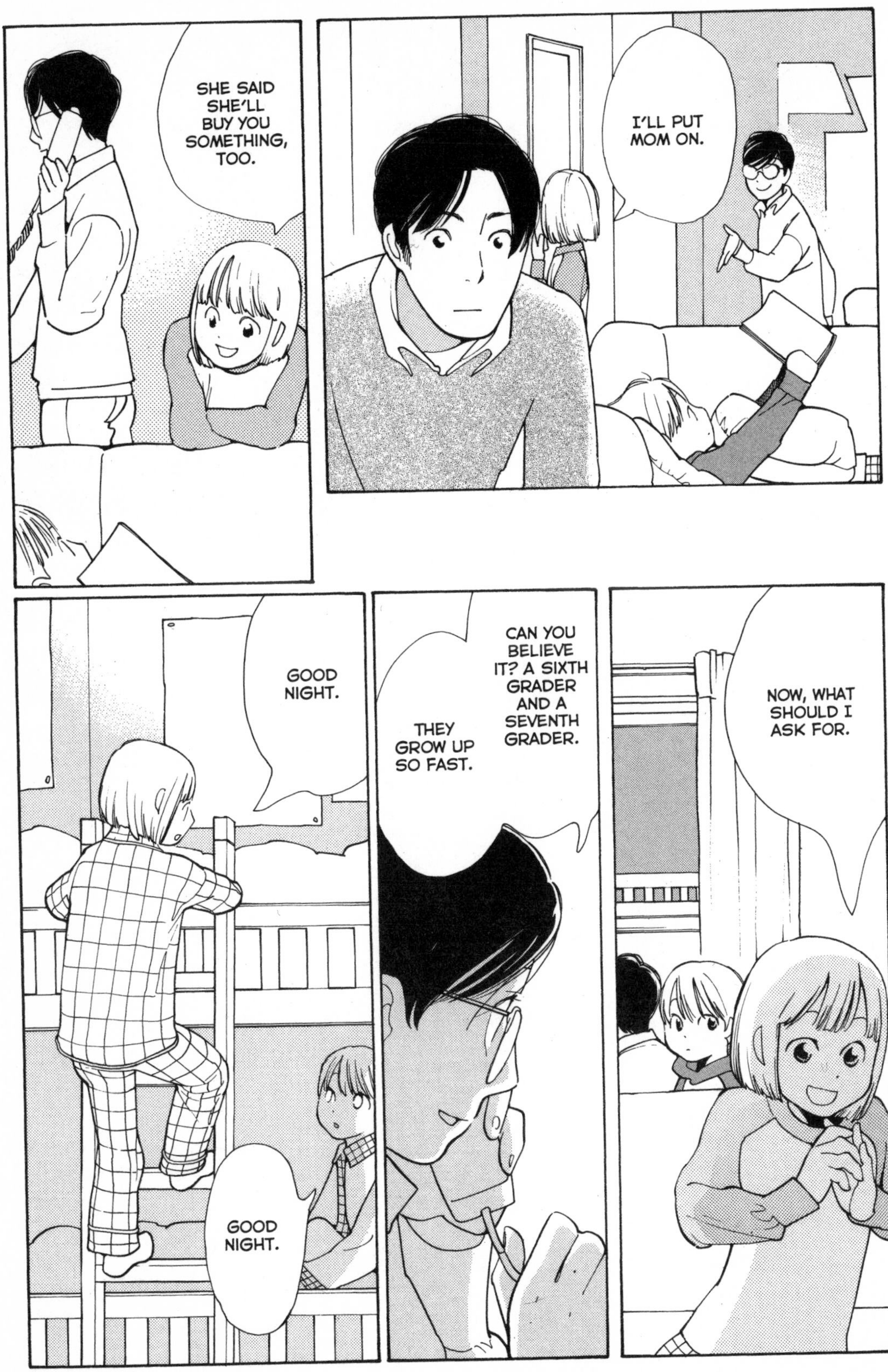
I'LL PUT MOM ON.
SHE SAID SHE'LL BUY YOU SOMETHING, TOO.
NOW, WHAT SHOULD I ASK FOR.
CAN YOU BELIEVE IT? A SIXTH GRADER AND A SEVENTH GRADER.
THEY GROW UP SO FAST.
GOOD NIGHT.
GOOD NIGHT.

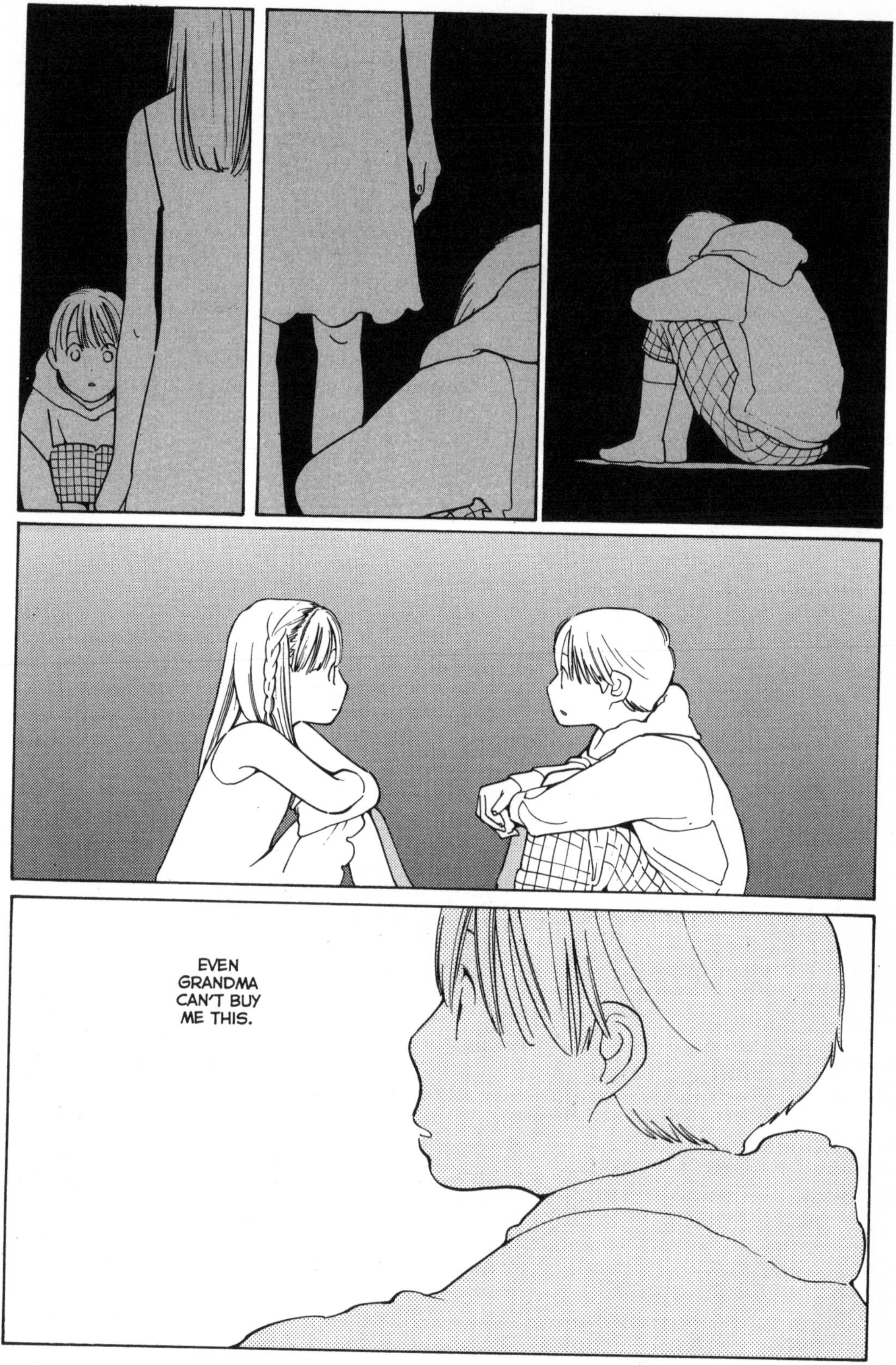
EVEN GRANDMA CAN'T BUY ME THIS.

JUST BEFORE TRANSFERRING ⟵ **BONUS MANGA**

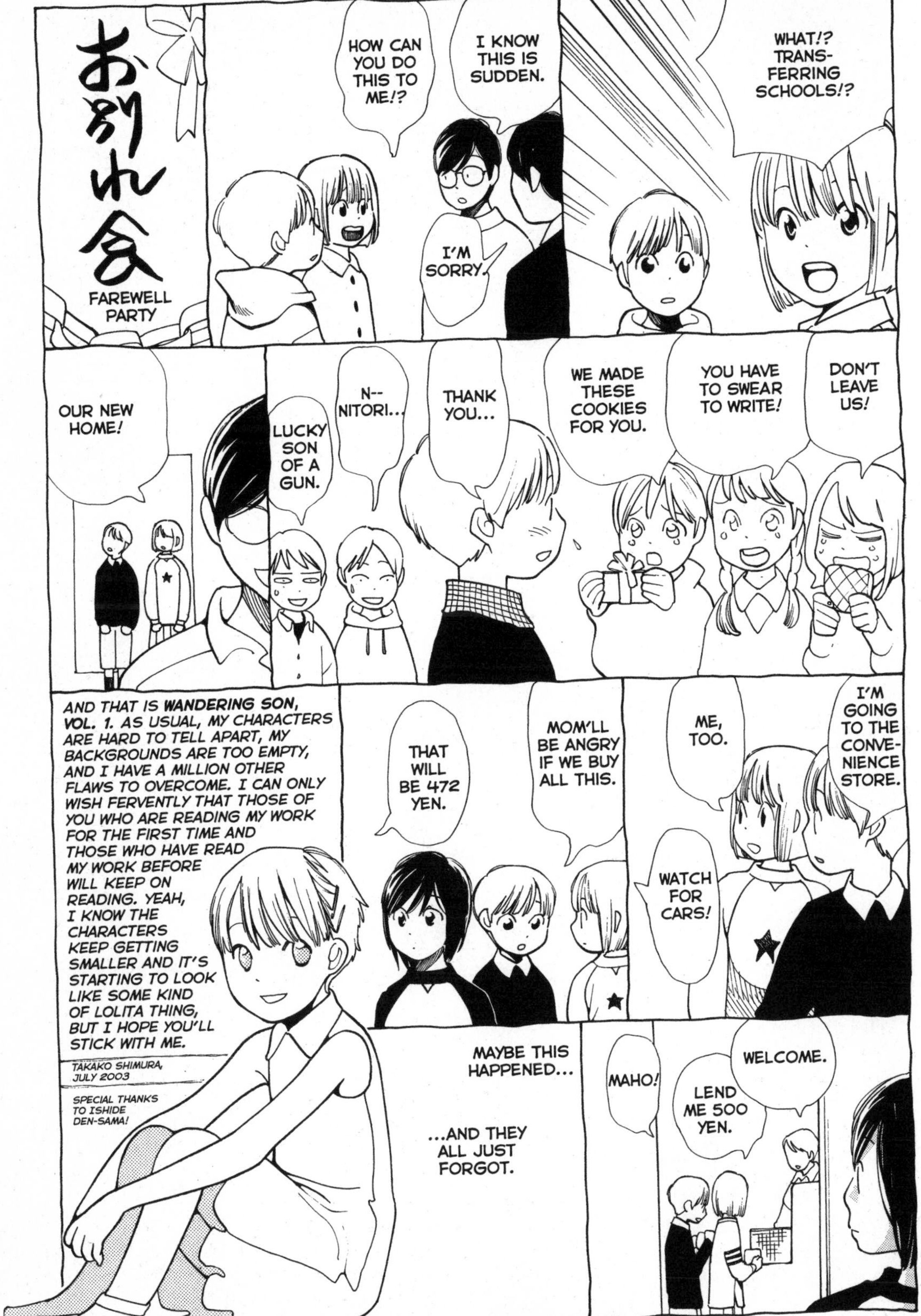

WHAT!? TRANS-FERRING SCHOOLS!?
I KNOW THIS IS SUDDEN.
HOW CAN YOU DO THIS TO ME!?
I'M SORRY.
お別れ会
FAREWELL PARTY
DON'T LEAVE US!
YOU HAVE TO SWEAR TO WRITE!
WE MADE THESE COOKIES FOR YOU.
THANK YOU...
N-- NITORI...
LUCKY SON OF A GUN.
OUR NEW HOME!
I'M GOING TO THE CONVE-NIENCE STORE.
ME, TOO.
WATCH FOR CARS!
MOM'LL BE ANGRY IF WE BUY ALL THIS.
THAT WILL BE 472 YEN.
WELCOME.
LEND ME 500 YEN.
MAHO!
MAYBE THIS HAPPENED...
...AND THEY ALL JUST FORGOT.
AND THAT IS WANDERING SON, VOL. 1. AS USUAL, MY CHARACTERS ARE HARD TO TELL APART, MY BACKGROUNDS ARE TOO EMPTY, AND I HAVE A MILLION OTHER FLAWS TO OVERCOME. I CAN ONLY WISH FERVENTLY THAT THOSE OF YOU WHO ARE READING MY WORK FOR THE FIRST TIME AND THOSE WHO HAVE READ MY WORK BEFORE WILL KEEP ON READING. YEAH, I KNOW THE CHARACTERS KEEP GETTING SMALLER AND IT'S STARTING TO LOOK LIKE SOME KIND OF LOLITA THING, BUT I HOPE YOU'LL STICK WITH ME.
TAKAKO SHIMURA, JULY 2003
SPECIAL THANKS TO ISHIDE DEN-SAMA!

THE END

STOP!

THE MANGA IN THIS BOOK IS "UNFLIPPED." MEANING PAGES RUN BACK-TO-FRONT AND PANELS START AT THE TOP-RIGHT AND END IN THE BOTTOM-LEFT. TURN THIS PAGE AND YOU'LL BE AT THE END OF THE STORY. FLIP THE BOOK AROUND FOR A MUCH MORE SATISFYING READING EXPERIENCE.

person is "junior" to the speaker within the school or workplace. School teachers are generally expected to address girls as -san and boys as -kun, though some male teachers will gruffly call a pupil by his or her surname, with no honorific.

-chan: An affectionate, diminutive form of -san. It is commonly used among family members for both sexes, and for girls among close friends. When it is used in speaking to or of a boy or man among friends, it is usually because it has become part of a nickname. Despite all the rules of who should address whom in what manner, when it comes to nicknames (which are very common in Japan), anything goes.

sensei: This is both a title and an honorific, used to address a teacher or any accomplished scholar, writer, or artist. It can be applied with equal validity to your aerobics teacher and a Nobel Prize Laureate.

These are the honorifics I will be retaining in this translation. There are other common forms of address that I will (for the most part) not retain. For example, it is standard practice for someone to call an older sibling oniisan/oniichan, "older brother") or oneesan/oneechan, "older sister") rather than by the sibling's given name. The same titles are commonly used when addressing or speaking of a young woman or man whose name is unknown. Similarly, a mature woman unknown to the speaker can be addressed as obasan ("aunt") and a man as ojisan ("uncle"), an elderly woman as obaasan ("grandmother") and an elderly man as ojiisan ("grandfather"). I will retain these usages only when it is crucial to understanding the story.

Two more points.

First, given names are generally used only by family members or fairly close acquaintances or friends. For the most part, Japanese call each other by their surnames. In particular, boys in the same grade are likely to call each other by surnames, without any honorific, or by nicknames. Girls are more likely to err on the side of politeness. Calling someone with whom you are not intimate by his or her given name is considered presumptuous and can be seen as rude. In any other translation, I would adopt the English style of mostly using given names, but not in *Wandering Son*. In keeping with the use of honorifics, I am also preserving the Japanese name order where full names are used: surname first, given name second.

Second, the honorifics I've introduced should not be taken at face value in every case. Japanese will sometimes use them in inappropriate situations, either consciously (with irony or malice) or unconsciously (because they have misread the nature of a relationship). Honorifics can also be omitted as a show of contempt. (Addressing someone older than yourself without using an honorific is akin to a slap in the face.)

This may sound like a lot to chew on, but I'm hoping you'll find it worth the effort.

Matt Thorn
KYOTO

gender, but in Japanese it is possible to converse in the most natural way about, for example, "Chiaki" (a name, like "Pat", which can be given to boys as well as girls) for a full thirty minutes without once indicating Chiaki's gender. It is much more common to refer to the person by name or as *ano hito* ("that person"). (For that matter, it is much more common to address someone by name or title than using a second-person pronoun, which, depending on the context, can seem either rude or aloof.)

Relative age complicates things further. When people of roughly the same age meet each other in Japan, they will try to pinpoint their relative ages--down to the month or even day, if necessary--either directly ("I don't mean to be rude, but how old are you? Oh, really? Me too! What month were you born?") or indirectly ("So you're a college student?"), in order to figure out the appropriate way of speaking to each other. The closer they are in age, the less likely they are to be formal, but in some cases even a day--or a few minutes--can define the relationship. There are no "brothers" or "sisters" in Japan: only "older brothers," "younger brothers," "older sisters," and "younger sisters." Even in the case of twins, one is arbitrarily defined as the "elder." (Traditionally, the second to come out of the womb was defined as the elder, based on the notion of "first in, last out"; today it is common to define the first out as the elder.)

Particularly among school children and students, it is expected that one address someone in a higher grade as *senpai*, which can be awkwardly translated as "senior colleague." (The antonym, *kōhai*, "junior colleague," is used as a descriptor, but not as a form of address.) This form is also used in many workplaces. And while there is usually a direct correlation between "seniority" and age, beyond high school it is not uncommon for a younger person to be "senior" to an older person. In such cases, the older *kōhai* will address the younger person as senpai, but the senpai will still be expected to use polite forms of speech, demonstrating respect for the kōhai's age.

Have I lost you yet?

Sociologically, this is fascinating stuff. But for those of us in the business of translating Japanese into English, it represents an all but insurmountable obstacle: there is simply no elegant way to convey in English the nuances--the inherent relativity and conditionality--of all those Japanese personal pronouns (or rather, what pass for personal pronouns). In most cases, it is

hardly important. In *Wandering Son*, which is essentially all about gender, it is too important to gloss over. But since I can't just make up new English pronouns, or expect you to memorize Japanese pronouns, I am forced to deal with the problem indirectly, by trying to give each character a distinctive yet natural voice that conveys, as best as possible, his or her sense of self and his or her position vis-à-vis others.

However, there is another aspect of the Japanese language, similarly infused with gender implications, that can be dealt with more directly, and that is the use of honorifics (the best-known example being the "-san" commonly appended to a person's name). People who have heard me pontificate on translation before might know that I think the retention of honorifics that has become so common in manga translations is generally an unnecessary and even wrong-headed practice. In fact, after twenty years of professionally translating manga, I am hard pressed to recall a case in which I retained honorifics (without an editor holding a gun to my head). Retention of Japanese honorifics without good reason seems to me to be an affectation intended to make self-described *otaku* feel part of an exclusive club that understands, for example, what the honorific "-chan" means.

In the case of *Wandering Son*, though, skipping over honorifics would not only make my job more difficult, but also completely close off to the reader an aspect of the work that is both important and intrinsically interesting. But if I'm going to retain the honorifics, I'm going to do it right. So bear with me while I offer a glossary that is, I hope, more thorough and nuanced than the kind you'll find in most manga translations.

-san: The best-known and most common honorific, it is, in most cases, neutrally polite and applicable to both sexes and between people of differing ages. Some women or girls can be very intimate, yet never stop addressing each other as -san. In school or in the workplace, -san is more commonly used in addressing girls and women. When in doubt, surname + san will get you through most situations.

-kun: A form of address used most commonly in speaking to younger boys or men, but which can also be used in speaking to younger girls or women. Some bosses will address all their subordinates as -kun, regardless of the subordinate's gender. As a rule, it is never used to address someone older, even if that

SNIPS AND SNAILS, SUGAR AND SPICE

A GUIDE TO
JAPANESE HONORIFICS
AS USED IN *WANDERING SON*
BY MATT THORN

GENDER AND LANGUAGE are inextricably linked. English has its own gender quirks, such as the difficulty of speaking of a person (particularly a hypothetical one) without specifying his or her gender (as this sentence demonstrates). And as any first-year student of Japanese will tell you, Japanese has gender quirks aplenty. The most obvious is the personal pronoun, or rather, as the anthropologist Robert J. Smith put it, "the absence in Japanese of anything remotely resembling a personal pronoun."

What Smith meant (and he is not the only scholar who ever made the claim) is that the relative social positions of speakers are so fundamental in Japanese communication that there is no way to "fix" any player's position--be it first-, second-, or third-person--with a single, one-size-fits-all pronoun. The twenty-five year-old man who refers to himself as *oré* among schoolmates would be considered arrogant, uneducated, or childish if he were to use the same term, instead of the more polite *watashi*, or at least the more humble *boku*, in speaking at a business meeting that included people older than or superior to himself (let alone, heaven forbid, a client). For a twenty-five year-old woman, the

choices would differ. Let's not even get into "you." An attentive first-year student of Japanese might be able to tell you a half a dozen different words for "I/me" and another half dozen for "you." I could offer up to two or three times as many off the top of my head, and a scholar of pre-modern Japanese could no doubt list ten times the number I could come up with. Many first-person pronouns originally intended to be humble, including *oré*, are today seen as haughty, while some second-persons pronouns that once conveyed respect, such as *kisama*, now convey contempt.

If all that still sounds like a variation on the kinds of pronouns found in English or Romance languages, consider this: Many, if not most, Japanese pronouns have switched from second- to first-person (or, less commonly, vice versa), over the centuries, and even today there are pronouns, such as *jibun* or *boku*, that can be used in both first and second person.

What may seem even more odd to the English speaker is the scant use of the gendered third-person pronouns *karé* ("he/him") and *kanojo* ("she/her"). In English, it is all but impossible to talk about someone in the third person without indicating the person's

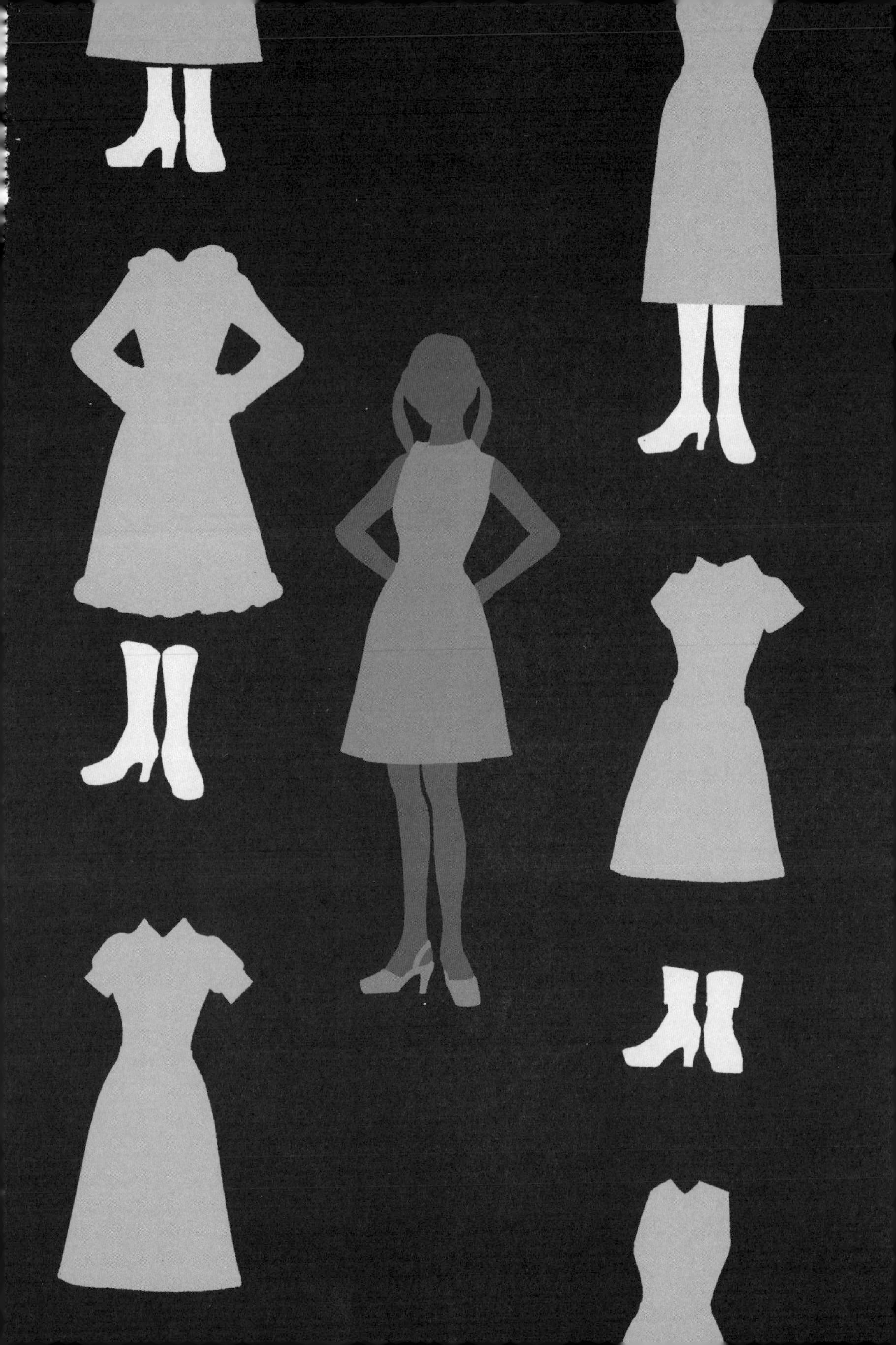